The Graduate School Mess

LEONARD CASSUTO

The

Graduate

School

Mess

What Caused It
and How We Can Fix It

||| Harvard University Press   *Cambridge, Massachusetts, and London, England*
2015

First printing

Library of Congress Cataloging-in-Publication Data

Cassuto, Leonard, 1960–

The graduate school mess : what caused it and how we can fix it / Leonard Cassuto.

    pages   cm

  Includes bibliographical references and index.

  ISBN 978-0-674-72898-1 (cloth: alk. paper)

  1. Universities and colleges—United States—Graduate work. 2. Education, Higher—Study and teaching (Graduate)—United States. 3. Educational change—United States. I. Title.

LB2371.4.C27 2015

378.1'550973—dc23   2015011241

To KC Osofsky,
whose choices lie before her,
this book, with love

Contents

Introduction: In Search of a Usable Future   1

1   Admissions   17

2   Classwork: The Graduate Seminar and Beyond   57

3   The Comprehensive Exam: Capstone or Cornerstone?   82

4   Advising   91

5   Degrees   130

6   Professionalization   162

7   The Job Market Reconceived   183

Conclusion: In Search of an Ethic   209

Notes   *241*

Acknowledgments   *295*

Index   *299*

The Graduate School Mess

In Search of a Usable Future

IS GRADUATE SCHOOL "broken"? I ask this advisedly, for talk about "broken" institutions has become a tired cliché. But it's a tricky question in this case, because you can declare something broken only if you know how it's supposed to work in the first place.

Most academics, from graduate students to faculty and administrators, harbor their own assumptions about what graduate school is supposed to do and their places within it. Such assumptions can be hard to discern, partly because they're closely interwoven with how we were socialized into academic society after we chose graduate study ourselves. Academia is strapped for resources in the twenty-first century, and the enterprise is under high—and frequently harsh—social scrutiny.[1] We need to examine those assumptions now, during these challenging times. And when we do, we will need to overturn some of them.

One of the most prevalent of those assumptions is that graduate school is supposed to prepare graduate students to become professors, especially the kind who do lots of scholarly research. If that were the only measure of what graduate school—and graduate students—are supposed to do, then graduate school really is broken. Thousands of professors are currently in the business of preparing thousands of graduate students for jobs that don't exist—or more precisely, those graduate students are being taught to want academic jobs that only a few will get, and in the process, they are learning to foreclose the prospects that actually exist for them.

The notion that graduate school is a specialized training ground for future professors has been untenable for more than two generations, but the antiquated structure of graduate education marks our collective longing for a brief postwar golden age when a job as a professor was waiting for anyone with a doctorate. This old-fashioned training leads graduate students to a narrowly specialized course of study that is at best impractical and at worst destructive. It teaches them to want and expect the wrong things. It conveys assumptions worth examining—and changing.

Public conversations about graduate education were thin on the ground for many years, but they're becoming more common these days. That's because discontent with graduate school is rising fast, as graduate students spend longer and longer on degrees that lead fewer and fewer of them to the jobs they desire. I was invited not long ago to have one of those public conversations, focused on the future of the doctoral dissertation.[2] My copanelist and I anticipated a conversation about the nature of dissertations in different fields, how professors direct them, and how digital technology might change them. But the exchange ranged far wider than that. It encompassed the overall conservatism of graduate education, the stricken academic job market, graduate student funding (and with it the deplorable use of contingent labor in the American university), the increasing time to degree, and the role of collaboration in the individualistic graduate school culture that prevails in the humanities and humanistic social sciences. In retrospect, the proliferation of topics—which flowed quickly from one to another—should have been obvious. The problems facing graduate study today are braided so tightly together with each other, and with larger institutional problems in higher education, that they cannot easily be separated.[3]

So if graduate school is broken, it's fractured all through. For this reason, discussions about reforming graduate education in general—and in the humanities in particular—have to be conducted holistically. It won't do to single out the doctoral dissertation for blame; there are a host of other factors that have undermined the harmonious and productive operation of graduate education and, worse, made it increasingly unlikely that the education that students receive actually prepares them for jobs they will find.

Let me say a quick word about my focus on the humanities in this book. Many (if not most) of my arguments apply to other fields as well, and I often step back to encompass the larger range of the arts and sciences. But I am concentrating on the humanities fields because they're the proverbial canary in the coal mine. Utility-driven arguments about the usefulness of fields of study reach the humanities first—they are the front line for debate about the value of advanced study, and they are the chin that takes the first blows aimed at the entire academic enterprise. Humanists also make up the largest part of the group of discontented graduate students and recent Ph.D.'s who feed the adjunct-teaching machine now fueling most research universities. As important, though, the humanities are also the site of some of the most creative thinking and innovation about what to do differently. Thoughtful people inside and outside professional organizations like the American Historical Association (AHA) and the Modern Language Association (MLA), among other groups, have moved beyond denial and are trying to point a way forward. For all of these reasons, the humanities are a good site to examine both problems and possible solutions.

The range of difficulties facing graduate education in the humanities has to be identified then, and we need to take a broad and systematic approach to solving them. Change will come only when we recognize how each problem is tied to and, indeed, exacerbates the others. It's time for graduate educators to start leading an examined life, even as we acknowledge that the job ahead will be comprehensive and challenging, because we've been living an *un*examined—even blinkered—life for a long time.

Many of the difficulties have been clear for a while. Virtually all graduate students receive their Ph.D.'s from research universities. They get their first teaching experience there, and their dissertations are mainly guided by professors whose research occupies a prominent place in their professional lives. We should hardly be surprised that dissertation advisers typically become the first role models for graduate students. But most academic jobs aren't at research universities, and those other jobs look jarringly different to graduate students than the ones that their role models have.[4] The identities of "professor" and "researcher" have increasingly converged over the past fifty years, and that fact drives the training of graduate students. Teaching gets elided— even though most professorships are at teaching-intensive colleges and universities. This disjunction ought to be blindingly obvious (and some commentators have noticed it), but I was years out of graduate school before its import registered on me. It amounts to this: graduate school is professional school, but most Ph.D. programs neglect graduate students' professional development. We spend years of their training like that, and then, only at the last moment when students are about to hit the job market, do we attend to their immediate professional needs. By neglecting graduate students' career goals until then, we allow their desires to coalesce from their immediate surroundings—the research university—and then harden over time. Thus do we teach graduate students to want the kinds of jobs that are most scarce and that most of them won't ever get.

The doctoral dissertation that graduate students are taught to write is a rigid requirement likewise designed as preparation for work at a research university. As students advance on the road toward that dissertation, too many fall off. Attrition from doctoral programs stands at about 50 percent, and an alarming number of those departures occur not after a quick diagnosis ("I tried this and it isn't for me") but rather after years of graduate school. For those who make it to the end, time to degree in the humanities stands at about nine years, an ethical atrocity that deprives young people of earning years while they accumulate an average of $29,000 in grad student debt.[5]

This is institutional disorder on a grand scale, and it bears out longtime Harvard president Derek Bok's estimation that "graduate schools are among the most poorly administered and badly designed of all the advanced degree programs in the university."[6] But let us not take our eyes from the ground too quickly: it's also bad teaching, plain and simple. Yet bad teaching doesn't usually come up in the discussions of what's wrong with graduate school. It's almost as though we take bad graduate teaching for granted.

The Graduate School Mess explores the problems of graduate school, and some possible solutions to them, in terms of teaching. Over the course of this book, I'll show why graduate teaching matters outside as well as inside the classroom and how teaching, broadly construed, should be part of the debates over the mission and future of the American university and its relations with society at large. "No university is a private institution," observed Rutgers president Robert C. Clothier in 1932.[7] We need to act in accordance with that sentiment.

The central argument of *The Graduate School Mess* is that effective graduate teaching in these times must acknowledge the professional system in which it's taking place. That means professors, administrators, and students, too, must recognize that:

- the job market is such that most Ph.D. candidates will never have the kinds of jobs that their professors have;
- professors who now teach in graduate programs need to make this reality clear at the outset to prospective and admitted students by (among other things) both publishing and disseminating the cold, hard placement numbers, even if they discourage some students from attending; and
- for those who do attend, graduate programs in all fields need to find a raison d'être other than asking young people to spend years of their lives training to enter a low-paying, disrespected, migratory, contingent workforce.

To this end,

- graduate programs need to revamp their curricula, structures, and standards in a way that prepares today's graduate students for a wider range of employment, not just academia; and
- students should be able to acquire this preparation (and the credential that accompanies it) in a reasonable period of time.

In short, professors and their universities need to take better care of their graduate students—and we need to make these changes loudly and openly. The concluding chapter of this book, "In Search of an Ethic," brings the ideas of teaching and public service together into a call to re-create a shared equilibrium between university research and education—that is, between the production of knowledge and the production of students—and between the university and society at large. Good teaching and good advising matter, but never more than now. Graduate students in the arts and sciences face greater employment difficulties now than at any time in the history of American higher education, and their professors aren't doing enough about it. Nor are we doing enough to train them for the kinds of jobs—not just academic ones—that they might fill.

Why, one may reasonably ask, should graduate school prepare people for other professions? Would-be lawyers go to law school, prospective doctors to medical school. Why shouldn't graduate school be reserved for people who want to be professors?

First, just because one goes to graduate school in search of an academic job does not mean that one's goals remain the same throughout—or that they can't expand. Ian Niles, who holds a Ph.D. in philosophy from the University of California, Irvine, said, "After I finished my doctorate, I wasn't much interested in teaching." Now he works on computer search engines. Eric Kaplan, a Berkeley philosophy Ph.D., said that he "decided to work in the private sector in 1996," after his oral exam. "I was worried about the tightness of the job market," he said, "and also thought it would be fun to try writing for a bigger audience," so now he works in television.[8] Such examples—of both the ordinary and the glamorous varieties—are not hard to find. Graduate school takes a long time and demands a lot. It's only natural that many graduate students change their minds about academia after they've been in it awhile.

Not all lawyers practice law, and not all doctors care for patients, though most use their training in some way. Graduate students may start doctoral programs because they're inspired to be professors, but as they learn more, some decide against that profession. Nor is this a recent demographic development, either. The authors of *The Education of Historians for the Twenty-First Century*, an AHA-sponsored study, say that it is "quite false" to assume that all Ph.D.'s have sought careers in academia. Such notions, they say, are remnants of the so-called Golden Age when there were professorships aplenty—and they result in graduate education that is "striking for its narrowness."[9] That graduate students would get their degrees and then decide to do something else—or make the same decision before receiving the degree—should be expected. And if we expect it, we should teach with that fact in mind.

Another problem with admitting only enough graduate students to replace the small number of retiring professors each year is that if we shrink graduate programs to a nub, we will trim the diversity—intellectual as well as socioeconomic, racial, and ethnic—right out of them. Graduate programs in the arts and sciences should be small, certainly, small enough to deliver individualized training, including career guidance. But they should not be so small as to direct all Ph.D.'s to universities. "Students who want to study the humanities," says the MLA's 2014 task force report on doctoral study, "will make contributions to academic and public life in their work."[10] This Jeffersonian argument claims an inherent value in having more Ph.D.'s in public life, not just academia, because an educated population leads to a healthier democracy.

Nor need Ph.D.'s abandon the intellectual life if they leave the university. Katina Rogers, a leading thinker about alternative academic (alt-ac) careers who has fashioned one for herself, describes "alt-academic" as

> not so much a specific job, career, or field, but rather an approach: a way of seeing one's work through the lens of academic training, and of incorporating scholarly methods into the way that work is done. It means engaging in work with the same intellectual curiosity that fueled the desire to go to graduate school in the first place, and applying the same kinds of skills—be they close reading, historical inquiry, written argumentation, or whatever else—to the tasks at hand.[11]

This kind of extramural scholarly engagement is easier to talk about than to do—and there are many Ph.D.'s embittered by what they see as "false promises."[12] Such discontented graduates are our responsibility as teachers. The very existence of these unhappy former students points to the need for graduate programs to be very clear about what they offer and about the need to expose their students to a range of their possible outcomes, not just the academic ones.

Of course, most people who enter doctoral programs in the humanities are at least considering an academic career. (Some master's degree candidates have similar goals, but not all of them.) But the question is, how may we reduce their gamble and make the training appropriate for other things? Graduate programs need to seek the best fits for their students. For some, that will be academia. But the idea is to find other fits, too—and for some students, the alt-ac possibilities will be best. Others will leave the academic orbit entirely.

The good news is that if they do, they need not feel lost. Ph.D.'s aren't just overtalented bookworms. They do certain things better than any other professional you can hire at out of school. Richard Wolff, an executive in corporate communications for many years, started hiring Ph.D.'s when he ran his own firm, Golin Harris, in the late 1990s and early 2000s. "Some of my senior partners were skeptical when I started recruiting Ph.D.'s," he recalled. "But they went along with it, "and it worked." He estimates that at one point almost a fifth of his seventy-person staff had doctorates.[13]

"Ph.D.'s," said Wolff, are an underexploited professional resource in purely economic terms. "They have a highly developed skill set that someone else paid for, so you can get them at excellent entry-level salaries" that are higher than what they would make as teachers. "I would hire Ph.D.'s at midlevel positions," Wolff said, "because within a short time they were functioning at that level. They would go up the learning curve in dramatic fashion compared to B.A.'s with more specialized training."

The skill set that Wolff refers to is broad and useful. Ph.D.'s typically have an exceptional ability to organize and analyze large amounts of information. They understand the need to read and learn widely and deeply in order to understand something (including looking beyond the immediate subject area), and they can carry out that task with minimal supervision. They can manage long projects and work on their own—and of course their dissertations demonstrate their ability to finish these projects.

But the bad news is that graduate education as it is now constituted does not prepare graduate students mentally—let alone practically—to seek the jobs that would allow them to use these skills. In fact, we teach them to *not* want such work and that to accept it amounts to a poor second choice at best and a disappointment to their teachers. And of course we offer no guidance in how to seek it, with the result that too many Ph.D.'s are underemployed and unhappy.

The failure to place graduate students in viable jobs has vast implications, but it is itself a consequence of the failure to teach and advise graduate students properly. As such, it illuminates the larger crises roiling academia in the United States: the funding problems faced by both the humanities and the sciences, the rise of the for-profit university, and the attacks on tenure, to name a few. Various commentators have persuasively argued that the graduate school system is grievously malfunctioning on a human level—and that we must not divert our attention from the exploitation of students and adjuncts by universities. There's considerable truth to that, and the calls for reform in this vein by Marc Bousquet, Christopher Newfield, and others deserve our attention.[14]

Some people may think that problems with graduate school pale alongside these more fundamental critiques of academia as a whole. One might consequently argue that my agenda amounts to a fruitless pursuit: redecorating while one's house is on fire. Not so. First of all, reform of the system depends on respect for its mission. Teaching students—including graduate students—lies at the heart of what professors do. Moreover, who on the outside will support the repair of a system whose owners refuse to examine it, let alone admit its flaws and try to correct them? As long as those who administer and impart graduate education look away from the facts of the present day, they show no respect for their own enterprise. Such disrespect discourages efforts at changing those facts, whether globally or locally. Trying to fix these problems will help to save our profession—and they don't preclude other efforts at reform, either. Second and more important, if universities don't respect the students who sacrifice to gain graduate degrees, why should they deserve the respect or sympathy of those who would implement more faculty- or education-friendly policies? Educators and administrators are overwhelmed by the mess around them—and the first step toward cleaning it up is for us to start with what is close at hand: our own workplace.

That work begins with teaching. The current practice of graduate teaching essentially retails expired passports. The future of the American scholarly enterprise requires that we both do our job better now and also formulate a new caretaking ethic for higher education in the twenty-first century. The next ten years may be harder than the last thirty, because instead of going to sleep and hoping it'll be all right in the morning, we're now wide awake with a job before us.

American graduate education has a lot of high-profile ills. The highest-profile of them is the academic job market, which has gone from bad (during the 1970s) to worse (during the 1980s) to even worse (in the 1990s and 2000s) to downright abysmal (following the recession in 2008). Recent problems with the nonacademic job market—consonant with the Great Recession—have made the employment situation for recent Ph.D.'s even more dire. Yet time to degree has risen steadily over the decades across the disciplines, and graduate programs continue to launch their students into empty scholarly space, equipped with skill sets so specialized and desires so narrow that they can only imagine themselves doing one thing.

The old axiom of "publish or perish" meanwhile remains largely unexamined. Yet libraries buy fewer books, and publishers are changing their strategies in response to these pressures, while the market share for e-books, whose credibility a conservative academy remains reluctant to accept, creeps inexorably upward. The traditional dissertation-based format of American higher education has not been adapted to the new world of digital information. New collaborative forms of research are appearing every day, along with new electronic forms of dissemination. The culture of evaluation within the university has been painfully slow to acknowledge, let alone privilege, these innovations—but even without new forms and new technologies, the dissertation is often poorly calibrated to the kinds of work that doctoral students actually perform once they leave graduate school.

Before I go further, let me say a few more words about technology. Some professors and administrators think that some panacea, whether technological or otherwise, will step in and rescue us, but this amounts to kicking the can down the road. Neither new technologies of dissemination, new theoretical pursuits, nor the emergence of new fields will change academia's current trajectory. In fact, some of these changes (such as the use of massive open online courses, or MOOCs, to cut costs) may accelerate the problems that we currently face.

The digital humanities are all the rage at this writing, and they are something more than a fad. They present new ways to approach the work of humanities scholarship, and they have already delivered not just new results but new kinds of results. So there's every reason to be excited about the possibilities that computers offer the humanities. I'm aboard this train and am eager to see where it heads.

But this is a book about graduate school, and I don't think that the new computer technology changes the graduate school playing field very much in the long run. It certainly doesn't affect the main problem that faces graduate school in the United States right now, namely, that it points students toward nonexistent professorial jobs and teaches students to want those jobs at the expense of others. That's why I have little to say in this book about the digital revolution in the humanities.[15] The main problems with graduate programs lie elsewhere: in the classroom, broadly conceived.

We've been facing those problems for a long time. According to Walter Jessup, the president of the Carnegie Foundation for the Advancement of Teaching, "American graduate education appears confused as to purpose—without clearly recognized aims."[16] Education scholar James Baxter complains that "overproduction of members of the teaching profession is no new phenomenon," and he suggests limiting the number of graduate students to prevent "the development of a proletariat of scholars" (such as a class of adjuncts working for low wages).[17] "Can the time for the dissertation be shortened without cutting standards?" asks education scholar Bernard Berelson.[18] These complaints sound like they could have been made yesterday, but Jessup was writing in 1944 and Baxter in 1933. Berelson was much later: his concerns about time to degree date from 1960.

One reason for the consistency of our problems across time is that resources were abundant and misery relatively lower. Adjuncts were much less numerous, for example, and the times to degree that Berelson was complaining about rarely exceeded four or five years. But another reason that our problems remain is that we haven't been doing enough to fix them. Why have they proved so persistent? Because the culture itself is persistent.

American graduate culture coalesced around research first of all. American university culture in general (that is, not just graduate schools) has proved pluralistic—and fractious—but the values of research culture nevertheless rule our academic land: you can tell how powerful and pervasive these values are from the research-based standards that professors use to assess each other's work at all levels of the academic food chain. Teaching has always mattered in American higher education but not as much as research, at least not since the arrival of research universities in the late nineteenth century.[19] I'll have much more to say about how these values affect graduate education over the course of this book. Academia is conservative with a small *c* (in the sense that it's resistant to change), but graduate education is conservative even by academic standards. It has long placed research above all other goals, and that has made talking about those other goals—including teaching—more difficult.

Broadly speaking, graduate education needs to be more effectively tailored to fit the graduate student. We aren't admitting armies of Ph.D. students anymore, so it's eminently possible to contour humanities doctoral education to the individual—and evolving—goals of those who seek it. Put simply, we have to teach graduate students in a more useful way.

Our bias toward manufacturing "mini-me's" in the research university mold makes us embarrassed to talk about the practical usefulness of a humanities Ph.D. There are two main reasons why. First, there's the concrete and practical one: to do so would involve acknowledging that most humanities Ph.D.'s do not in fact move into tenure-track positions at research universities. As long as we continue under the illusion that these are the jobs we're training our students for, we'll continue to adhere to a counterproductive approach. In doing so, we'll keep overtraining the majority of our students in one way and undertraining them in others, thus losing the kind of flexibility we need to prepare them for positions outside—as well as inside—higher education.

Second, there's a historical reason why we don't talk about usefulness: it has always been a vexed subject in the annals of American higher education. The German ideal of pure, disinterested research that underwrote the earliest American research universities evoked a lot of lofty rhetoric from the first presidents of those universities, but that mission has never been a perfect fit in the United States. For one thing, the American research university arose in tandem with the rise of middle-class professionalization in the postbellum era, and universities happily assumed an important—and explicitly practical—credentialing role in that social shift.[20] As well, the advent of the research university in the United States roughly coincided with the enactment of the Morrill Act, which established the land-grant universities. The language of that law, which President Abraham Lincoln signed in 1862, binds together "liberal and practical education," privileging both. In other words, the job of these public universities was, from the beginning, to advance all kinds of professions in utilitarian as well as theoretical ways. We should therefore not be surprised that "U.S. research universities, almost without fail, developed as individual variations of a national mold based on industrial research." Nor should we be surprised that lawmakers would fund the university because they saw it as an instrumental good, "to help the nation compete."[21] Nor should we be surprised by Johns Hopkins president Isaiah Bowman's 1939 statement—made in a report to the federal government—that "the use that is made of one's education matters or education does not matter."[22] Utility has always been a part of the conversation about the purpose of higher education in the United States, and we ignore that fact at our peril.

"Shall the University Become a Business Corporation?" Professor Henry W. Pritchett was led to wonder. That's another familiar question, but Pritchett asked it in 1905.[23] Clearly, the ideological blueprint for the huge American higher-education sector—including the opposition between liberal and technical education, between the pursuit of knowledge and the pursuit of the dollar—was in place long before the GI Bill and Sputnik provided funds to build higher education to its present large dimensions during the postwar golden age of academic plenty. Not for nothing did Clark Kerr name his classic 1963 treatise *The Uses of the University*.[24] As long as that blueprint still describes what we do, we must recognize its distinctiveness and demands.

The kinds of changes I suggest in this book will not be easy to make unless we change some of our entrenched attitudes toward graduate education and surmount a number of institutional hurdles. We can no longer afford to proudly proclaim the uselessness of the humanities, for instance. It's certainly true that the humanities (and the social sciences, and the sciences) are in part dedicated to knowledge for its own sake. But it's also true that the humanities represent a space for thinking critically about American society's near-obsession with the practical and the pragmatic. It simply does not make sense to stake our claim for the value of the humanities on its uselessness beyond training young scholars to teach college and university humanities courses. Any realistic twenty-first-century approach to graduate education in the humanities needs to recognize that such an education involves the teaching of practical, transferable skills that can prepare graduates for a wide range of jobs outside higher education. As long as we take refuge in the seemingly high-minded idea that the humanities are valuable for their own sake or because they lack or resist utility, the harder it will be to address the whole issue of vocational training for graduate students—which is a problem that will *not* simply take care of itself.

Graduate teaching is our purest humanistic pursuit for the simple reason that it involves caring for humans. That's the part of the enterprise that I see most often overlooked—because American graduate education is teacher-centered rather than student-centered. As I will elaborate, it is structured according to the needs of the teachers and the institution rather than to those of the students who make it possible. That's a vexing design problem that needs to be solved both locally and globally. Research will always go on, as it should, but the enterprise has to center on students too. In local terms, this book details concrete ways to work from the students' needs, beginning in the classroom and proceeding through dissertation advising and the all-important job market. I'll reframe the job search in terms that are broader and more appropriate for the future of students—who typically know full well that most of them won't become professors.

The widespread neglect of the art and craft of graduate teaching and advisement is jarring from a pedagogical point of view, but much more than pedagogy is at stake. Graduate schools—and with them universities—must accept responsibility for the professional lives of the apprentices they admit to their midst. For those apprentices, the care they receive can mark the difference between professional survival and extinction. Moreover, what goes on in graduate classrooms—and in graduate education generally—can't be separated from the larger problems facing higher education in the United States. So I'm not going to try to separate them. Instead, I am going to use graduate education, especially graduate teaching, as a porthole through which to focus on the concerns of American academia today. The graduate school mess leads to all of the other messes.

The Graduate School Mess therefore combines "what's wrong and why" with "how to do things better." Consider the example of graduate students who are stuck in dissertations that they're clearly not going to finish. All professors recognize such students from their own teaching or from their own graduate school years. The struggles of these unfortunates are pitiable, and their agonies can go on for years. In this book, I offer pedagogical strategies designed for professors to help such students get on with their lives, but I also go to the root of the problem and uncover its history and wider significance. The very existence of hopelessly mired dissertation students results from the reluctance of many dissertation directors to understand that time to degree is a problem (and that problem goes further back than is generally assumed). It also shows a failure to see withdrawal from graduate school as a viable career choice rather than a failure. Part of the reason that stalled graduate students torture themselves year after year is that they think they will disappoint their professors if they leave school. Their education therefore needs to encompass a more realistic sense of their own alternatives—and advisers need to take responsibility not only for their star graduate students but also for those who would be better off doing something else. That's because *graduate students trust their professional lives to their professors,* especially their dissertation advisers. We need to take that responsibility more seriously than we do.

Why, then, do we not instruct professors in how to teach or advise graduate students? The careless and shortsighted instruction of graduate students receives little attention amid the much-trumpeted woes besetting the academic enterprise. Rather than the classical pedagogical image of an artist molding clay, it's as though graduate students are assumed to be hardy and self-sustaining plants that require only a little pruning now and then—how else to explain that for all of the books and articles on undergraduate teaching that appear each year, there has never been a book on how to teach graduate students? Educators spend a lot of time discussing undergraduate teaching and learning, and I'm fully supportive of those efforts. But the bottom line is that professors (including administrators) don't spend much time understanding how graduate students learn and then helping them do it. Nor do we spend much time thinking about what graduate students want to learn and what they ought to learn. (Those two areas sometimes overlap but not always.) This is not a "gap in the literature." It's a Grand Canyon.[25]

The first innovation of *The Graduate School Mess* therefore is its focus on the instruction of graduate students. A closely connected second is the primary audience it claims: teachers of graduate students. I've tried to write this book for many audiences, but I've addressed it foremost to teachers of graduate school. There are many books out there addressed to graduate students, including a shelf of different volumes offering dissertation coaching—the existence of which suggests that graduate students aren't receiving enough of that from their advisers. Graduate students also write books and articles to each other, including many vituperative and discontented blogs. But graduate students are taught by professors. That audience needs to cohere into a community that talks together about what we all do.

But this book's audience does not end with graduate professors by any means. I use the word "we" a lot in this book and readily admit to at least two different meanings by it: (1) professors and (2) all of us, in the humanities and often other fields as well. I'm on the students' side first of all; but for their situation to improve, their education has to change, and students can't do that by themselves. I write a regular column for the *Chronicle of Higher Education* called "The Graduate Adviser" that is usually addressed to graduate teachers, but my readership not surprisingly includes thousands of graduate students. It also includes large numbers of professors who don't teach at the graduate level themselves, administrators, and quite a few nonacademics who are interested in the workings of the university. Together, these groups make up the larger audience for the book.

That larger audience makes up the collective membership in an academy that is reprehensibly complacent about the preparation of its apprentices and reprehensibly casual about the economic currents that are shipwrecking the professional lives of so many of them. We may not be able to make all of our graduate students into professors. Indeed, many of them *shouldn't* be professors. But their welfare is our responsibility—and once we admit them to our programs, we've accepted that responsibility. That means we need to be more creative about looking after graduate students, outside the academy as well as within it.

One reason to look more closely at our student care is that the students themselves are mad as hell about how they've been treated. They feel that they deserve better, and it's hard to disagree. Graduate teaching offers a window onto this crucial conflict. The failure to promote graduate teaching highlights the neglected caretaking of the university's next generation of researchers. The employment crisis for Ph.D.'s underscores this neglect on the administrative as well as the departmental level. It also highlights the university's loss of public support and funding. The politicized scorn for professors makes good copy for a public eager to read about academic foibles and folies, and the desperate economic straits of so many recent Ph.D.'s offer further prurient interest. When we look at graduate teaching, in other words, we can see a version of almost everything that has gone wrong in American academia that doesn't involve athletics.

The Graduate School Mess is divided into the different phases of graduate education. It follows the life cycle of a graduate student, from admission through coursework, advising, the degree, and the job search. As important, the book uses graduate teaching and advisement as the point of entry to outline an agenda of recommitment for professors—a set of guidelines and suggestions—so that we may take responsibility for the crumbling academic edifice. I end by suggesting where this recommitment might start. Specifically, I propose a new ethic for higher education that is based on the most successful progressive model of the past century: the environmental movement. Even those who search for oil speak the language of environmental stewardship. If American higher education is to save itself, it must take control of the discussion similarly, and the way to do that is for the university to adapt its own caretaking ideal to the demands of these times.

The answers to our problems may not all lie in the graduate classroom, but the classroom has to be central to any strategy to face them. Our graduate students need our help. By committing ourselves to teaching them better, we can understand what has gone wrong with American higher education and begin to fix it.

CHAPTER ONE

Admissions

FOR PROSPECTIVE STUDENTS, getting into graduate school can feel like a full-time job. They dedicate months to studying for the GRE (that is, the Graduate Record Exam); they agonize over every word of their personal statements; and they pray that their letters of recommendation will distinguish them from the pack. During this rite of passage, students try to fashion themselves into acceptable proto-graduate students. The admissions process essentially teaches applicants to present themselves as potential scholars—and so, as the first major "qualifying exam" in a young student's graduate career, this ordeal has a certain pedagogical function. At the same time, the admissions gauntlet, because it deals in the currency of exclusivity, plays a substantial role in maintaining an academic culture that loves prestige rather too well. It fills students with anxiety, not to say fear and loathing, and prepares them to take a subordinate position at the bottom of the academic food chain. Graduate admissions practices thus begin by persuading accepted students to feel lucky that they're now at the bottom of the academic hierarchy.[1] The admissions system teaches through the exertion of the power of that hierarchy. When brought to bear on individuals, it shapes their institutional identities.

It also shapes the identities of the institutions the students are trying to get into. The process ennobles universities as selective and therefore exceptional—which it does by dignifying them with prestige. The mechanisms that determine who gets into graduate school, and why they get in, are central to the enterprise itself and by extension to the academy's prestige culture. Gatekeeping centers in equal parts on who's allowed inside and who's being kept out. The decisions about who gets into graduate school and why are therefore integral to the mission and function of the enterprise itself. Admissions provide the first glimpse of who we are and how we train others to be like us.

Remarkably, no one has yet written a history of graduate admissions. Much valuable—and sometimes prurient—attention has been paid to the subject of undergraduate admissions, but the story of graduate admissions has never been unearthed, let alone told. No one has even gathered the data.[2] Having never been explored, the relation of graduate admissions to today's graduate school is right now a cipher. It absolutely should not be. Many scholars have written about the history of graduate schools generally, and much ink has been spilled by researchers, professional societies, and think tanks about the many so-called crises that have long plagued doctoral education.[3] In order to put those crises into historical perspective, admissions, as a key component of American graduate school, needs attention, if only because the selection of graduate students is controlled by the economic issues and the cultural values that are at issue in the wider discussions about the utility and purpose of American higher education.

In fact, when we look closely at the history of graduate admissions, we can limn the whole history of graduate school—how graduate schools evolved and how they operate. We can see the history of the research university in broad outline there, because the development of the admissions process is so crucially involved in negotiating the university's identity. This story has been too long untold, and this first pass at it makes this the most historical chapter in this book. What follows is a pointed history of admissions— pointed, that is, toward using the past as a way to account for and explain today's practices. To explain those practices is not, as will become clear, to defend them. The largest emphasis in this chapter falls on the early years of the research university, because we see all of the familiar patterns developing then. Such is the conservatism of graduate school that the values that evolved more than a century ago remain the basis for today's practice.

The archives of Harvard and Michigan and, to a lesser extent, Yale, Berkeley, and Johns Hopkins inform this story at ground level. They're a representative selection, a small group of institutions that span public and private, but they are not a random group: I'm seeking to spotlight schools that have been highly influential in the development of American graduate education. Applications are, of course, unavailable to examine. For a long time in the history of graduate school, applications did not exist, so figures like admittance rates don't exist either. Instead, we have to view the process from a remove, through the annual and biennial reports authored by the presidents of universities and by the deans of their graduate institutions. I've divided the story into three parts, beginning with the early days of the American graduate school (from the late nineteenth century to 1900), when the admissions process largely crystallized, and then moving to important developments in two subsequent periods, the middle years (from 1900 to 1945) and the postwar expansion (after 1945).

These partitions roughly reflect major changes in the history of the graduate admissions process. But American graduate schools did not march in lockstep; their admissions policies grew at different rates and in different ways. These differences in development mean that there is no single history of American graduate admissions that can be neatly organized into pat stages, a fact illustrated by an anecdote shared by historian Stanley N. Katz:

> When I applied to graduate school in 1955 there was already a graduate admissions office, but I am sure that individual profs had much more influence. But when I moved to Wisconsin in 1965 they did not use a graduate admissions office—instead, students could apply to up to three seminars offered by individual professors, and each professor admitted his own grad students.[4]

Katz's story reveals, first of all, that today's bureaucratic graduate application process has not always been the norm. Rather, admissions was once a much more informal affair, and it was often largely under the purview of individual professors. Second, Katz's experience demonstrates how the formalization and standardization of graduate admissions evolved differently at different locations. There was an admissions office when Katz applied to Harvard in 1955, but as late as 1965, the University of Wisconsin had none.

Today, Wisconsin has a graduate admissions office with a director and staff of four, and it has instituted admissions technologies pioneered at the universities at the center of this story.[5]

In general, the most prestigious universities have set the trends in admissions processes, which are then adopted by other institutions. Like Wisconsin, the Graduate Center of the City University of New York (CUNY) has not always kept pace with other universities in its graduate admissions practices, but in 2013, CUNY announced a plan to restructure its policies. CUNY reduced its graduate admissions and raised fellowships for those who are admitted. This move toward a leaner, full-time model was designed to bring the public university into line with more elite institutions. The initiative, lauded by some observers, also prompted criticism that its aim was inconsistent with CUNY's mission to serve New York's citizens more broadly.[6]

CUNY's move to emulate the elites has considerable precedent in the history of graduate admissions. The archives show a tendency toward conformity of practice, typically motivated by the quest for prestige. The prestige race dominates much graduate school practice, and it creates a landscape I examine from different angles throughout this book. Admissions opens a clear window onto some of the ways that universities have protected and nourished their research cultures and defended their cherished research mission over the years—often in the face of different imperatives urged onto them by their critics, both intramural and extramural.

Even though academic institutions develop at different rates, they compete with one another in the same drive for institutional credibility. This contest for academic honor, as the higher-education scholar J. Douglas Toma points out, often takes generic approaches. The attempt to attain a higher place on the academic prestige ladder inevitably leads, Toma shows, to a stagnating conformity in which "everything that rises must converge." Unlike those firms in more dynamic markets that seek to distinguish themselves through differentiation (so that one footwear company may make shoes, another sneakers), American universities often end up mimicking one another.[7] The history of graduate school admissions is a particular case that proves Toma's general point: graduate schools, playing the prestige game, have installed similar admissions policies until, over time, there has been an almost complete standardization of the process. The standard is set at the top of the food chain, where the fewest graduate students live and where their experience is least typical. Public universities, formed under different mandates, consistently seek to emulate their smaller, usually wealthier, counterparts even when their mission statements suggest that they should pursue more accessible goals.

Rankings provide the main arena for the prestige competition among universities, and the fight for position on that ladder permeates much graduate school practice. (In Chapter 7, for example, I discuss how it shapes our conception of the job market.) While the fight for rankings causes a convergence of practice, it also produces a kind of monoculture in the graduate student body. With so many graduate programs subscribing to the same values and aspiring to the same status, they institute similar policies that are all designed to promote the recruitment of more prestigious students. Graduate admissions thus elevates those students who endow universities with the most respect: the specialist scholar-researchers in training.

Admissions processes have developed over time precisely in order to woo these particular student-assets. Research has its benefits, of course, and it cannot be conducted without researchers. But the single-minded pursuit of a certain kind of graduate student has meant that universities often neglect their other responsibilities, namely to train teachers and liberally educated, public intellectuals. Many graduate programs have explicitly designed their admissions processes to marginalize and to exclude those students who do not fit the specialist scholar-researcher mold, despite the fact that administrators have recognized that they are responsible for the promotion of democratic values and for the education of a diverse range of types of student. As I suggest at the end of this chapter, this strong bias toward potential "knowledge producers" extends to the present, when we find it at every stratum of the rankings hierarchy.

This brief discussion shows how admissions renders the conflicts within graduate school, and the research university generally, in embryonic form. We'll see how admissions reflects the marginalization of the master's degree to the point where it lacks a clear identity or purpose, and how fear of the dilution of Ph.D. research led graduate programs to draw sharp divisions between their student populations and in some cases even to segregate them on other campuses. Driving the history of graduate admissions is an overarching quest for selectivity. Like undergraduate institutions, which are today engaged in an absurd arms race to see who can reject the most applicants, graduate schools have long sought to demonstrate their prestige through spectacularly parsimonious admissions practices. It is a goal that graduate schools achieved only relatively recently—and only as a result of the bad economic times that have squeezed universities and resulted in books like this one.

To see how it all started, let's go back to the early days of the research university, in the decades surrounding the turn of the twentieth century.

ADMISSIONS IN THE EARLY DAYS OF RESEARCH UNIVERSITIES

Today graduate schools are adrift, unsure how to reconcile the need to encourage research with the need to cultivate teachers. These tensions were on display from the beginning—and we see them in admissions practices. Graduate programs developed rapidly at the new research universities, both public and private, and at existing colleges, many of which became universities when they added graduate schools. These new graduate schools were tiny by today's standards, with graduate study mainly concentrated in humanities fields (the days of big science having not yet arrived), and they lacked familiar bureaucratic elements of today, such as admissions offices.[8] In the growth of these programs, we see the early contours of today's landscape.

Admissions practices were, even at first, largely governed by economic necessities. The first attempts in the 1890s to create a selective admissions process were motivated more by a lack of resources than by any sense of what we today call "competitiveness." In those early days of the research university, graduate schools in the United States were highly provincial affairs. Universities were not involved in any national network but were localized, serving their immediate communities, and so they did not necessarily see one another as direct competitors for students. Being small and provincial, graduate schools had no need for today's bureaucratic application process. Applicants often were known personally and could easily be assessed by graduate faculty. A student of the 1890s might be admitted for graduate study simply by showing up and having an informal chat with a professor in his field of interest. (I use the male pronoun advisedly here.) Often, the student was simply staying on at the same institution where he had done undergraduate work. Sometimes his prolonged stay wasn't even directed toward an advanced degree, and occasionally he hadn't even finished a bachelor's degree, which might be awarded later, in course. It wasn't until the first decade of the twentieth century when administrators even put into writing their most basic requirements for applicants for graduate study, a formalization of procedure that evolved as universities associated themselves within a national graduate education system. At that point, degree systems became standardized, fellowships came under the purview of specialists, and graduate schools used admissions to more fully articulate themselves as research institutions.

But we're getting ahead of ourselves when we talk about graduate school admissions as growing out of an informal process, because, strictly speaking, the graduate school as we know it did not yet exist until around the time that its admissions systems became formalized: the codification of the admissions process helped to crystallize the graduate school as an institution (not just vice versa). Early American graduate study often took place in "graduate departments" and "graduate divisions," before these were gathered into proper schools with their own institutional identities.

During the late nineteenth century, nascent graduate schools were riven by something like an identity crisis. They had poorly defined boundaries and contradictory aims. In already existing colleges, like Harvard and Yale, which built graduate enterprises on top of their venerable undergraduate schools, graduate programs extended out from these colleges, and so they were forced to create their institutional identities in a touchy relationship with the humanistic liberal arts curriculum, which they would supersede, when they later gained hierarchical superiority over the colleges that they grew out of. At other places, like Johns Hopkins (founded in 1876), graduate schools were created from whole cloth. Not having to contend with established collegial traditions, they could institute from the start some of the admissions policies that later became the custom of the country. Meanwhile, public universities like California and Michigan looked to these eastern private schools as models for creating graduate programs, often seeing their own democratic obligations to the citizenry as an obstacle to implementing the kinds of admissions policies that might help them create competitive graduate schools that would train elite scholars.

For most administrators during this period, the graduate school existed as an ideal before it existed as a reality. East Coast private schools looked to European universities as their models. (Though it should be noted that American universities, being of their own place and time, did not so much reflect their European inspirations as refract them.)[9] Public schools looked to Europe as well, but also to their East Coast rivals. Administrators mostly dreamed of the graduate school as research driven, and they assumed that its aims were quite distinct from the liberal arts curriculum of the undergraduate college. But graduate schools were not uniformly identified with research in the early days, nor were they so focused on granting the Ph.D., the degree that came to symbolize research culture. Graduate study was going on before graduate schools proper were even created, and universities were offering a much greater diversity of higher degrees.[10]

Without clear institutional structures, and with the degree system still in flux, the identity of the graduate student was not clearly circumscribed. By developing graduate admissions policies, schools encouraged the recruitment of certain kinds of students and discouraged the pursuit of others—and hence were able to give shape and character to the graduate school itself as a prestigious place for research.

Harvard, for example, experienced a good deal of confusion about how its college and its graduate school were related. Surprisingly, the Harvard Graduate School, established as a department in 1872 and as a school in 1890, often granted the bachelor's degree to many of its early "graduate" students, a practice that continued into the early twentieth century. It was understandably hard to distinguish between the graduate school and the college when both were awarding bachelor's degrees. The Harvard Graduate School dean, John Henry Wright, worried that the practice "blurs the definition of the Harvard A.B."[11] Admissions standards were instituted in order to define the graduate school against the undergraduate college. This was an important way that admissions practices helped shaped the institution at a formative stage.

A similar degree problem perplexed the administrators at Yale, where the college, not the graduate school, administered the master of arts degree. Yale's undergraduate schools meanwhile operated "graduate extensions" side by side with the graduate school. It wasn't until 1912 that the Yale college faculty "surrendered its rights in the M.A. degree" to the graduate school. This organizational snarl shows how the meaning of the master's degree in particular proved vexed early on. The problem at Yale signaled the beginning of a perennial tension that runs through the history of American higher education: graduate schools want to grant master's degrees, but there is no agreement between them—or anyone else—about the meaning of that degree.[12]

As graduate schools grew, the most prestigious degree associated with the graduate school, the Ph.D., was given primacy over other degrees. More important, what the Ph.D. represented—the identity and practice of the researcher—took precedence over teaching and application, values that were associated with the M.A. The M.A. has, even for centuries, had a hard time finding a meaning. Administrators at all of the schools in I examine here complained, at some point or another, that the purpose of the master's degree isn't obvious. Sometimes it entails preparation for a doctorate; sometimes it stands as a teaching credential; and sometimes it's a consolation prize to failed Ph.D. students. Its nebulous meaning made it, during these early days, hard for administrators to place and easy for them to scapegoat. Admitting M.A. students was a consistent cause for concern, because they took away valuable resources from the more prestigious doctoral students. At the same time, the numbers of master's students, and their tuition support, enabled the work of doctoral students and their professors. Such disrespect for the master's degree laid the foundation for its low status more than a century later, in today's university.

During the early period, "all persons who hold a respectable Bachelor's degree" were welcome to undertake graduate study at Berkeley, a precondition for admission that, at the time, was stricter than the standards at Harvard.[13] The degree issue had not been worked out yet at Berkeley either, and it prompted a concern that quickly became familiar: that the university was admitting students for whom "graduate work is not the most serious and continuous sort"—that is, master's degree students. These students, worried president Benjamin Wheeler, would corrupt the atmosphere cultivated for doctoral candidates. Berkeley's populism—its lack of tuition and its broad acceptance of students—caused administrators to ask if they were really operating a graduate school. Freeloading students were "attaching" themselves like parasites, perhaps because they had no other "opportunity for occupation." The small number of students actually earning degrees exacerbated these concerns and led administrators to the need to more clearly delineate between Berkeley's graduate and undergraduate schools.[14]

These confusions and concerns about "genuine" graduate study bothered administrators at Michigan a great deal. President James B. Angell considered the granting of the master's degree one of the school's most important social obligations but also one of the greatest detriments to creating a strong research culture. Angell's concern was that the Michigan graduate school was in the business of preparing mere teachers. Moreover, the school was filling up with students "without any special effort on [the university's] part to build up a graduate school."[15] The demand for graduate education was coming almost entirely from the citizenry of Michigan, who by and large weren't interested in research. Angell argued that fostering research was necessary in order to improve Michigan's reputation. Doctoral study, he admitted, was extremely costly, but he proposed in 1891 that the faculty should organize advanced graduate student research.[16] Michigan introduced the German seminar model for graduate classes, because "its advantages in promoting habits of research and independent study are very great." But Angell was also aware that Michigan had a "duty" to train high school teachers because of the university's "relation to the public school system of the State." At that time, the graduate school served the state by credentialing teachers with master's degrees. While Michigan's graduate population swelled, it was only the rare student who actually pursued the Ph.D. Most of students were in M.A. programs, and they graduated to become "chairs or instructors in schools, seminaries, colleges, and universities."[17]

While administrators at Michigan believed that graduate study would serve the state in the long term, they knew it was expensive and hard to reconcile with the university's immediate and primary responsibility to educate undergraduates and train teachers. Angell in 1896 described how a graduate school might appear a distraction from the university's mission, but he argued that in fact it would directly benefit the state because "the presence of such a body of mature and aspiring students is uplifting and inspiring in its influence on the undergraduates." Angell's great hope was for a university that would give its "exclusive attention to graduates." He seems to have regretted the less prestigious "collegiate work" that paid the bills and fulfilled the university's original purpose. Thus, Michigan took on double duty for itself, fulfilling its immediate obligations to train the masses while also looking for the resources to build up a research culture, "else the sons and daughters of Michigan must needs go elsewhere to find it."[18] In 1892, the Michigan faculty inaugurated the graduate school.[19] In the following year, the university tightened its Ph.D. degree requirements and increased residency requirements; and it put more emphasis on the dissertation, "in harmony with the better American Universities."[20] The development of Michigan's graduate program in those early years was in large part a response to the "better Universities" in the East.

The history of Michigan's graduate school shows a continued preoccupation with keeping up with those Joneses of the East.[21] Angell declared in

1896 that having a graduate school helped Michigan compete against graduate schools in other states. He argued that the Midwest needed public universities that could go head to head with private, eastern universities. Those more venerable institutions provided him with a model for graduate education: they're the more mature schools against which Michigan appeared to be trapped in a state that Angell himself described as arrested development.[22]

Angell frequently discussed the high costs of graduate school, and he begged benefactors to create fellowships for graduate students.[23] In this area too, he viewed his Ivy League competitors with envy and openly wished to establish the kinds of scholarships and fellowships that make it possible to train researchers: "By the aid of such fellowships Harvard, Cornell and Chicago are constantly drawing some of our most promising students to their halls."[24] Such fellowships and scholarships for "genuine" graduate study came rather late to Michigan; as Angell knew, graduate funding had already been established at eastern private schools. Angell clearly saw Michigan's graduate school as second-rate due to its "collegial" obligation, and he worried about other schools poaching the "most promising students" while Michigan did the unglamorous work of preparing teachers. Belatedly following Angell's advice that Michigan learn to mimic other schools, the regents finally created funds for research in 1922.[25]

But contrary to what Angell may have imagined, universities like Harvard and Yale had no easy time financing graduate education and administering their fellowship funds. Graduate scholarships at those institutions were as convoluted as their half-baked degree systems. At Yale, fellowships for the Ph.D. had been established in the nineteenth century, before the Yale Graduate School existed as such, and therefore fellowships were placed under the control of the faculty of Yale College.[26] This gave the college quite a lot of control over the graduate school, and the college's historical precedence shaped the way fellowships were doled out. In practice, this meant that fellowships for graduate study were for the most part granted only to graduates of Yale College. Similarly at Harvard, students were admitted and fellowships were awarded according to a not-yet-professionalized system. Private foundations often gave fellowships directly to graduate students for them to attend Harvard, and in many cases, these foundations themselves decided which students received their fellowships.[27] At the same time, the graduate school dean, James Mills Peirce, complained that many of the applicants for fellowships were "personally unknown to any of the instructors at this University."[28] As at Yale, where the college controlled the fellowships and gave them to Yalies, Harvard's graduate funds went to Harvard men. Harvard's graduate school became gradually more professionalized, bureaucratized, and linked into a larger national network—enough that the school got a big pool of applicants—but it relied on local relationships to make fellowship decisions. Graduate admissions were by this time determined not by departments but by a committee of faculty from different areas, headed by the dean.[29] Appointments to intramural graduate fellowships were likewise centralized under the aegis of the faculty in 1892, after having been made in a confused fashion, with some under the purview of the faculty and some controlled by the graduate school's Academic Council. Vetting fellowship applications through departments meant that students were judged in terms of their areas of specialization, which looked ahead to modern practice.

This preference for funding homegrown products had to do with the informal and liberal manner in which funds were administered at Harvard and Yale. But quite different was the system in place at Johns Hopkins, where the modern graduate funding package was essentially pioneered. Founded with graduate education as its stated goal, Hopkins emerged as the industry leader during the formative early decades of graduate study in the United States. The university created fellowships that would support researchers-in-training over the course of their studies, and it instituted them in a more bureaucratic, less provincial, more impersonal way than at the older colleges. Johns Hopkins himself in his will called for the establishment of scholarships to be distributed according to "character and intellectual promise."[30] He also bequeathed money for the creation of undergraduate scholarships ("Hopkins Scholarships") for students from Maryland, Virginia, and North Carolina. With this gesture, Hopkins was building a regional university, rather than a local or a state one.[31] The school's commitment to becoming a national research institution (though one with strong regional roots) was thereby built into its graduate admissions structure from the very beginning. So was the university's commitment to academic research over liberal humanism. The first scholarships at Johns Hopkins were awarded by exam; and so they were administered more impartially than were the funds at Yale and Harvard.[32] The funding package—awarded by examination, disbursed over four years rather than annually, and allotted to advanced students—displayed a commitment to nurturing researchers-in-training over the whole course of their advanced studies.

Fellowships at Johns Hopkins (as opposed to scholarships) were funded annually and were similar to what we would call a postdoctoral fellowship today. They were aimed at specialist students "engaged in study" who intended "to prosecute higher studies."[33] Between the fellowships and scholarships at Johns Hopkins, a funding-award system had been implemented to recruit specialized researchers-in-training. When the university opened, its student body clearly reflected how its admissions procedures had built up a body of students recognizable as graduate-level researchers. Of the first class of eighty-nine students, fifty-four of them (60 percent) already had degrees.[34] These demographics immediately helped to realize the dream of Johns Hopkins as a national, research-centered university.

While Hopkins established itself as a national research institution and implemented admissions protocols that encouraged research culture, more liberal universities like Harvard and Yale and more populist universities like Michigan and Berkeley sought to keep pace. As these schools competed to prove that they were engaging in "genuine graduate study," they sought ways to recruit what Angell called the "most promising students," and they discredited students who were not necessarily engaged in research. These practices laid the ground for the researcher bias that endures today—with teachers barely allowed on the island and then only because their tuition supports researchers. And most important, teaching is explicitly disrespected as a constituent part of the research enterprise.

A tale of intramural conflict at Harvard vividly illustrates this emergent value system. During the 1890s, Harvard's funding structure recognized teaching and research as two distinct ways of being a graduate student. Not until 1947, when the university "liberalized" funding sources for graduate students, could an individual graduate student hold both a research scholarship and a teaching fellowship simultaneously.[35] In the early days, Harvard teaching fellowships were not part of a student's acceptance package and were unconnected to his work toward a degree. Instead, they were contingent forms of *employment,* raising the question of whether fellows should be seen as teachers or as researchers-in-training.[36] The Harvard Corporation Board defined the fellowship position in terms of teaching rather than research but conceded faculty authority to recommend (but not to grant) appointments.[37] In this debate about whether the teaching fellowship is an "aid" to a student or a "salary" for a teacher, the faculty argued, in essence, that funding structures should be designed as investments in research culture, while the Harvard Corporation sought to use funds for the sake of the undergraduate curriculum (i.e., to support teaching). The policies that regulated admissions and fellowships thus turned into the site of struggle for determining the university's priorities. Some people fought to keep liberal culture at the center of the curriculum. But those with an eye on prestige sought policies to promote research culture. In the end, the latter group won the day—and their ideas continue to guide graduate admissions in the United States.

THE UNIVERSITY GROWS: 1900 TO 1945

During the first half of the twentieth century, the relatively young American graduate schools weathered three national emergencies: a depression sandwiched between two world wars. Graduate study throughout this period was nevertheless ascendant, with student populations rising faster than schools could handle. Private foundation support aided the growth of research universities starting in the 1920s. Foundations had previously distributed their support between colleges and universities, but after World War I, foundation officials concluded that "to aid fruitful research is, in the estimation of a great body of intelligent people, perhaps the best use of trust funds."[38] This move further signaled the growing dominance of research culture.

The university grew in spurts. Student populations, including both graduate and undergraduate students, grew by 40 percent in the 1890s and by 60 percent in the first decade of the twentieth century.[39] During the next decade, student populations grew much faster, by 75 percent between 1909 and 1920; the number of graduate students was approximately 4,700. (World War I brought only a brief dip.)[40] Enrollment doubled throughout the 1920s, and the number of graduate students in the United States increased to about 6,200. This figure doubled by 1929 and was around 18,000 in 1939.[41] This increase led to a more variably prepared applicant pool and led graduate schools to institute admissions policies that were more formalized—and more selective.[42] Under these new admissions systems, the student body became less eclectic, with admissions processes favoring the acceptance of researchers-in-training. Administrators had to meet their democratic responsibility to educate the masses, but they also had to balance budgets increasingly strained by growing numbers of graduate students. During this period, increasing size led to increasing selectivity in the graduate admissions process. Selectivity started as incidental—universities sought prestige in other ways—but increasing population caused selectivity to take hold as a determinant of prestige.

The growth of graduate schools between 1900 and 1918 was modest compared with the decades immediately following; but schools became more closely linked to each other during this time, and they evaluated their needs not only separately but also in consultation with one another.[43] As American universities involved themselves with each other nationally, these new ties necessitated a standardized system for the exchange of faculty, students, and credentials across institutions. As universities entered into a national network, the Association of American Universities (AAU), established in 1900, resulted in, among other things, nationalized norms for graduate admissions. Such professional organizations, especially the AAU, knit universities together.

The AAU was dedicated to advancing the national standing of U.S. research universities, and the ties it created among schools enabled the standardization of American universities as part of a "deliberate, concerted action." As its first priorities, the AAU set out to establish greater uniformity in Ph.D. requirements to achieve foreign recognition of the American doctorate, and to bolster standards of the weaker U.S. universities. Together, these guaranteed the value of the American Ph.D. product and guarded it against cheap imports. Initially the AAU regulated only its own members, but gradually it gained sway over other schools. That is, although the AAU itself contained only elite universities, it functioned as a kind of governing body for all of them. It took up questions of publishing dissertations and also of classifying bachelor's degrees to create shared and transferable standards.[44] The difficulty of this task had to do with the fact that bachelor's degrees across the country were not standardized, but in 1911, the AAU released its preliminary "Classification of Universities and Colleges with Reference to Bachelor's Degrees," and this list helped to "reduce to some sort of order the chaos of American college degrees."[45] For administrators at Harvard, the AAU's list aided the effort to make the graduate school into a training ground for professors and investigators.

Calls for reform led also to a form of accreditation abroad. During the first decade of the twentieth century, the U.S. Bureau of Education (now the Office of Education) classified schools for graduate work.[46] The AAU became an accrediting agency in 1913 at the request of the University of Berlin, which asked for a list of American colleges whose graduates could be assumed to be ready for graduate work.[47] Thus, the AAU became established in its leadership role, especially as its list of accredited colleges became a tool for administrators to compare different bachelor's degrees.[48] The AAU also played an important role in standardizing graduate admissions when it first created a national calendar for admissions decisions. The organization intervened similarly to regularize financial support of students. In December 1906, the AAU suggested that its members "should agree upon a uniform practice in the assignment of fellowships and scholarships for Graduate students."[49]

At the turn of the century, universities wrote down, and hence formalized, their graduate admissions practices. Admissions to Princeton's graduate school became more rigorous in 1903–1904, for example, when it was decided that "only graduates of Princeton and of other universities maintaining a similar standard for the bachelor's degree may be enrolled on their diplomas as graduate students. Graduates of other universities and colleges may be admitted as graduate students only upon examination."[50] Such policies made clearer that the graduate school ranked above the undergraduate college. Universities were simply making official what had already become the standard: graduate schools tended to favor students who had earned the B.A., especially from their own institutions.

These new, formal admissions procedures meant that graduate schools became less diverse, with less variety of different kinds of students. Harvard, for example, passed regulations aimed at limiting part-time students, who had amounted to about a quarter of its enrollment.[51] These reforms institutionalized the divide between one kind of student (the teacher) and another (the researcher)—and they anticipate twenty-first-century moves by graduate schools to eliminate part-timers to serve the same goal of promoting research.[52]

The stigmatization of certain kinds of graduate students is evident in Harvard's graduate school annual report of 1909–1910, in which Dean Charles H. Haskins argued that stricter admissions standards were required in order to recruit more researchers-in-training: apparently, second-rate students who were "limited in outlook" and not passionate about "the academic career" were managing to infiltrate the graduate school. These students with extra-academic obligations, working outside the university, enrolled only part-time, and studying to be teachers rather than researchers, were considered unsuited to be the "professor and investigator of tomorrow."[53]

The professionalization of graduate study at Harvard, enabled in part by the AAU, paralleled developments at Berkeley. There, administrators remarked proudly that the graduate population was becoming increasingly male and, concomitantly, increasingly research driven. Women made up the majority at Berkeley's graduate school until 1912, when most students there were pursuing teachers' certificates.[54] More men meant more research and more Ph.D. students, and it meant fewer women and fewer secondary-education students. The Berkeley administration remarked approvingly that "the Graduate School is taking on more definiteness and firmness of organi-zation."[55] Such research-driven "firmness" was solidified by a more rigorous admissions practice, advanced through the AAU's national credential system and enacted in 1915.[56]

Graduate schools continued to grow nationally, and administrators needed to limit enrollments to apportion resources properly. By the early 1920s, Roger Geiger writes, "it had become apparent to most research universities that they would have to limit their enrollments for reasons inherent in their fiscal structure and physical facilities. Once they decided on this step, how-ever, they faced a second and more controversial decision about determine whom to admit."[57] They relied on attrition to limit their numbers—a kind of selectivity imposed after the formal admissions process that essentially in-volves taking tuition money from the students while the institution decides whether to admit them. With the onset of the Depression, universities sought to weed out students who were not sufficiently specialized and professional, and it was possible to do this because the graduate schools had been moving in that direction for decades. Harvard's graduate school dean, Charles H. Haskins, reported that "in increasing degree the Graduate School has come to stand for research."[58] Current attrition from doctoral programs in the United States stands at 50 percent. One reason we tolerate it is that it rou-tinely used to be much higher.[59]

When the Harvard Graduate School's growth became "an insistent problem," the proposed solutions were two: enlarging the teaching staff and/or instituting "a more rigorous sifting process."[60] Yale faced a similar problem. Due to a lack of resources, Yale in 1927 undertook what president James Rowland Angell (not to be confused with Michigan president James

Burrill Angell from the previous generation) called "a venture never before taken": the restriction of entry to the university on the basis of academic credentials (at both the undergraduate and graduate levels). Angell lamented that "there is no social justification for refusing opportunity to those endowed with the necessary gifts."[61]

In 1929, a committee at Harvard was advised that the admissions board should change its admissions policy to favor students who had exceptional records, such as graduation with honors or distinguished work in a special field. Following this change in policy, in 1931, "the academic records of applicants for admission to the School were closely scrutinized," and selectivity increased (though the school was still admitting 75 percent of its applicants). At the same time, Harvard created a more formal procedure for dismissing wayward students. The university's new selectivity was celebrated in an article in the *Journal of the AAU* by James Baxter, who suggested that other schools take up such measures.[62]

Michigan was one that did so. In 1924, the graduate school dean, Alfred H. Lloyd, described M.A. students as inferior to doctoral students. He understood their prevalence at Michigan as a dilution of the university's prestige. "Where ten seek the doctorate," Lloyd wrote, "hundreds would be masters." For Lloyd, educating master's degree students was "real service," but he suggested as well that such charity work also made the graduate school "superficial."[63] Lloyd wanted to push back against the public's demand for the master's and to create a graduate program focused on granting the Ph.D., the degree that symbolized research culture. Michigan's institution of funding packages and stricter admissions standards followed Lloyd's agenda to create a graduate school devoted to training researchers.

With Michigan's investment in research, the university began to question how to regulate the admissions process, noting especially the fact that many students come from small colleges.[64] When admissions become stricter in 1925, the university admitted fewer such students. The new funding and the new standards meant that Michigan was, in its own view, "now standing with other universities, Harvard, California and others."[65] Again, there was a sense of inferiority and of competitiveness, of wanting to institute stricter admissions standards in order to create a research culture.

In 1929, the administration at Michigan considered how to limit graduate enrollment further. Michigan graduate school dean G. Carl Huber repeated what was already becoming an old saw—there are different types of graduate student, some less desirable than others. Like deans before him, Huber divided the graduate student population into researchers and advanced teachers pursuing graduate degrees. The former he called the "desirable students"; the others he called an "asset." Like his colleagues at Berkeley and Harvard, Huber made clear which kind of student he preferred.[66] Meanwhile, the student population at Michigan was soaring: "The growth in the number of students registering for graduate work has been so rapid that it has taxed the facilities for graduate work and particularly so in certain fields." In response, administrators decided to tightly regulate admissions to M.A. programs.[67]

Maintaining an open and democratic graduate program was expensive and not very prestigious, so during times of resource scarcity, it was obvious which kinds of students should get the boot. At the same time that Michigan was trying to get its "obligations" off the books, Huber asked that the university provide more fellowships, precisely in order to recruit the more desirable students. Huber called such funds "a means of bringing the gifted students, otherwise often unable to continue further study and research, to the Graduate School."[68] Thus, scholarships and fellowships were aimed at creating a population of researcher-students. But even as the university was promoting research with these fellowships, it continued to try to fulfill its obligation to train teachers.[69] Had Michigan not suffered from limited resources, it might have found a way to serve all of its applicants. But as at Harvard and Yale, budgetary needs became a rationale for narrower admissions policies that favored the researcher-student. The resource crunch during the 1930s led, then, to a tightening of standards in the curriculum and in admissions at Michigan, emphasizing research specialization over liberality and accessibility.

Yale's enrollment cap was innovative and anticipated today's practice. Graduate admission was limited, based on the capacity of each individual department. In this manner, applicants were more tightly bound to their departments, whose capacity determined how many students could enter. At the same time, Yale especially privileged autonomous researchers, with "the emphasis placed upon genuinely individualistic work."[70] The acceptable applicant, then, was one who fit into a particular discipline and was prepared to become a self-driven researcher. Still, Yale's graduate school had not quite thrown off its collegiate feel. The culture at Yale was a diverse one: "like other graduate schools, our own is set to serve several definite functions not entirely consistent with one another."[71] Trying to maintain this diversity, Yale attempted the "extremely difficult" task of limiting enrollments "only due to material constraints."[72]

"Short of some economic calamity," Yale president James Rowland Angell prophesied in 1928, "we are far from the mythical 'peak' of student attendance in this country." Of course, a great economic calamity *did* shortly ensue, and America's graduate schools were staggered.[73] Admissions officers at Yale were suddenly besieged by applications in numbers far in excess of former years, as college graduates, thrown out of work by the Depression, sought refuge in graduate school. "We cannot jeopardize our hard-won standards of excellence," wrote Angell in response to this surge in applications.[74] In other words, the selective admissions protocols, though put in place with a good deal of regret at Yale in particular, were cherished once they were enacted.

At Harvard, applications for fellowships and scholarships increased drastically, but admissions themselves dropped due to economic conditions in 1932 and then again in 1933. Applications also went up at Berkeley, and graduate work continued during the Depression with "normal efficiency in subnormal years."[75] Meanwhile, in a scenario painfully familiar to twenty-first-century observers of U.S. higher education, American educational institutions reacted to the Depression by cutting their teaching staffs, so that it became increasingly difficult for universities to find jobs for their recently minted Ph.D. students. This situation caused the administrators at Yale to "search their hearts" and to ask hard questions about whether the school was educating too many students. According to the logic of the market, Yale was overproducing Ph.D. students and therefore should cut enrollments. Yale's administration wished to increase fellowship sizes by decreasing the number of appointments. Democratic spirit abhorred this sort of elitist discrimination, however, and Yale responded to the crisis with some sense of conflict. Administrators were particularly eager to cut enrollments, while faculty wished to accept as many students as possible.[76] In rhetoric all too familiar to a twenty-first-century observer, Angell blamed the "tender-heartedness of teachers" for letting mediocre graduate students stay on. In response to the crisis, the university decided to reduce admissions. The Depression also meant that Harvard could find jobs for fewer graduates, and hence the administration welcomed the decrease in its graduate student population.

Circumstances thus encouraged universities to become more selective, but selectivity also expressed prestige. Putting limits on enrollments created logistical problems and also raised salient questions about the meaning of higher education in a democracy. But administrators soon found a silver lining: more stringent criteria raised the intellectual caliber of the student body.[77]

As far back as 1939, it was clear that developing consistent admissions procedures had become a persistent problem for graduate schools. Of eighty-eight schools surveyed by William J. Brink in 1939, nineteen determined admission by a central admissions office for the entire university; fourteen determined admission by the dean of the graduate school; and thirteen determined admission by a graduate school committee. Very few decided on the basis of decisions by a departmental committee.[78] Around the same time, administrators complained that faculty were gaining too much input in the admissions process, a harbinger of greater administrative control later on.[79] Admissions offices were establishing a strong foothold, and formal letters of recommendation got their foot in the door as they became part of the application process for fellowship applicants.

During the prewar years, admissions now focused on the undergraduate record and the institution from which the student received the B.A. Personal interviews were also frequently conducted (though recommendation letters were rarely given much consideration as yet). In an argument that might have been formulated yesterday, Brink asserted in 1939 that schools should decide as definitely as possible what their objectives are; analyze these objectives in terms of the prerequisites that prospective students should possess; select or develop techniques appropriate for the study of each applicant for admission; and encourage to pursue graduate work only those for whom there is reasonable probability of success. In other words, schools should seek to admit graduate students with a sense of commitment and a likelihood that they will do well at the kind of study that would be required of them.[80] That wasn't exactly what happened.

The need to assess students was a challenge that one university could not meet alone. The U.S. academic community began to recognize a need for national graduate student standards starting in the 1930s, as the academic industry grew to such a point that the evaluation of prospective students through letters of recommendation and transcripts became more difficult. Inspired by requests from the graduate deans of Columbia, Harvard, Princeton, and Yale, the Carnegie Foundation for the Advancement of Teaching began to support a series of examinations for entering graduate students that were somewhat similar to the examinations given by the College

Entrance Examination Board. This development proved highly important, but not right away. In these first gropings toward standardized testing, scholars nominated by graduate school deans began to prepare the exam questions, and the test took shape through a process of trial and error. Schools initially administered the tests to students *after* they had been accepted, in order to measure the test's effectiveness. In the late 1930s, the Carnegie Foundation supported new standardized examinations and coordinated a group effort by the graduate school deans of Harvard, Princeton, Yale, and Columbia. The resulting exams were the direct ancestor of today's GRE.[81] American graduate schools had reached the tipping point toward the bureaucratic standardization of admissions.

These efforts temporarily lost their usefulness when graduate school registration fell sharply with the U.S. entry into World War II.[82] Admissions levels at Harvard stayed low throughout the war years, so that admissions practices needed no reorganization. At Michigan, "the number of graduate students reduced to a minimum." Michigan likewise had trouble filling its quota of fellowships and scholarships with promising students during the war. As Dean Clarence S. Yoakum reported, students sought better stipends elsewhere, or more likely served in the war effort. Staff was also thinning out, with better-known faculty requisitioned by the government, a phenomenon that "reduces the value of a department," said Yoakum, and "is quickly recognized by the prospective graduate student." The dean's language of prestige deserves particular notice here: even in the midst of World War II, Yoakum was concerned about competing for graduate students with more elite schools, and about the "value" of the department as conferred by celebrity scholars. Maintaining a research culture clearly remained a high priority even in wartime: "for research and research itself have proven themselves important most clearly in the emergencies created by war."[83]

A BRIEF POSTWAR GOLDEN AGE, THEN A LONG DEPRESSION

Even after the end of hostilities, enrollment remained below its peacetime maximum for some time, and administrators welcomed the gradual return of graduate students.[84] This gradual increase quickly built to a flood when the G.I. Bill of 1944 sent more and more students to school. The great swell of incoming students was initially difficult for universities to handle and radically changed the structure of higher education nationwide. During the postwar period, the selectivity story that runs through the history of graduate admissions climaxes. Graduate schools finally instituted selective, research-driven cultures—but they succeeded in doing so only as the support for those cultures began a long process of erosion. In a parallel important development, a focus on diversity, today deeply entrenched, emerged during this period. Affirmative action came on the scene, followed closely by its discontents.

Graduate schools were faced with more applicants than ever before immediately following the war. "The number of students in the regular session" at Michigan "exceeded that of any previous session," reported Assistant Dean Peter Okkelberg. "This, of course, was due to the return of veterans." Harvard was likewise "flooded with applications," and Yale responded to its own admissions glut by maintaining its stringent, standardized methods of selection. The formerly "placid atmosphere" at New Haven was transformed into "the crowded, active, and mechanized headquarters of the Hall of Graduate Studies."[85]

Faced with an overwhelming number of applicants, graduate schools needed to reappraise their admission practices. At Harvard, for example, a "record of distinction" had previously been the primary criterion; but now Harvard began looking to the GREs, and the deans set up a committee to seek departmental advice on admissions. By the end of the 1940s, the graduate admissions process had developed into the form that we recognize today. That process has simply continued on, through a universe of changing circumstances. One of those circumstances was the space race that followed the Soviet Union's launch of the satellite Sputnik, a fevered competition that not only increased government interest in higher education but also increased demand for graduate school among undergraduates.[86] Still, while college students were highly interested in graduate study, few actually went on to do graduate work.[87] Jewish Americans were far more likely to attend graduate programs during the 1950s, prompting a certain anti-Semitic backlash.[88]

The backdrop to this imposed bureaucratic standardization of admissions was the greatest boom in the history of American higher education. That boom proceeded in two main phases. First, the G.I. Bill made higher education available to a larger segment of the U.S. population than ever before. College enrollments swelled with the former soldiers—and of course professors were needed to teach these new students, which created a demand for graduate school to produce those teachers. Moreover, many of these new college students went on to graduate school themselves. Then, in the late 1950s, especially after Sputnik, the federal government invested heavily in higher education, in a concerted attempt to forge ahead not only in the arms race but also in global technology and useful knowledge generally.[89] This unprecedented level of financial investment was closely followed by the in-flux of the first baby boomers, born after World War II, into colleges and universities whose facilities had already been enlarged to receive them.

The exponential growth of research in our time was essentially a Cold War bargain, and it further overlapped the identities of "professor" and "researcher." The university essentially became the research-and-development lab for the Defense Department and, indeed, for the whole country. The government started funding all kinds of academic research, with special emphasis on the STEM disciplines (science, technology, engineering, and mathematics). Pro-fessors in those fields were given extra money to do research, and in order to accomplish this work, they were allowed to teach less. To prevent intramural rivalries and tensions—and also because research culture had always encom-passed all fields—other disciplines were given the same deal: teach less and publish more. So teaching loads dropped, and research universities showcased the professor as a knowledge producer who also taught, an influential role model that now stood before every graduate student.[90]

Federal support for higher education grew at 15 percent a year on average during the 1960s, a staggering rate. But the number declined drastically starting in 1969, the first year of the Nixon administration.[91] The number of graduate students supported by federal fellowships and traineeships, reports the economist David W. Breneman, reached its high point of 51,000 in 1968 and fell nearly 20 percent to 42,500 in 1969, the first year of what proved to be a decades-long decline. By 1974, the number was down to about 6,600.[92]

Stricter admissions policies helped to deal with the postwar boom. To handle the glut of applicants at Michigan, for example, "many students had to be denied," because resource scarcity required "that the best qualified students would be given first opportunity for higher study." But stricter admissions standards also came with benefits, since "these higher standards of selection may be maintained after the pressure of numbers is over," and these standards would "help in excluding or eliminating students who are not qualified for graduate work."[93] Michigan thus faced the old question of how to reconcile its populist mission with its elite ambitions. Admissions policies took the form of a compromise between these competing agendas. Michigan instituted stricter admissions requirements (it would now accept only applicants "with outstanding records"), but those standards applied only to nonresidents and to students applying for fellowships and assistant-ships. With this move, Michigan partially conformed to the admissions standards already established at other institutions, but it still left plenty of room for serving the masses. Administrators meanwhile hoped that the proportion of residents to nonresidents could be kept within "reasonable limits, say 35 to 40 percent."[94]

Harvard's graduate school received a huge number of applicants after World War II and began to work closely with department chairs in order to establish its own admissions limits.[95] Now students were asked to file three letters of recommendation, with transcripts, and departments were consulted in the case of each applicant.[96] The new system generated many rejections, but "no statistics pertaining to race, color or religion" were kept.[97]

Harvard's administration told this story again decades later in *The President's Report, 1993–1995: Diversity and Learning* (1995). For Harvard administrators looking back after nearly fifty years, the postwar period became a watershed moment in the university's admissions practices when, responding to a glut of applicants at the undergraduate and graduate levels, Harvard came to rely on "objective" criteria such as aptitude tests, grade point averages, and class ranks. But "while Harvard placed a very high value on academic standards throughout this period, . . . the university continued to strike a balance between numerical measures and more complex forms of assessment in admissions."[98] Letters of recommendation were now required of all candidates, not just fellowship applicants, and "every possible bit of evidence was scrutinized before admission was granted."[99] Personal interviews remained desirable, but they were no longer feasible.[100] Administrators lamented the change in the admissions process at the time. In those prewar days, admissions had been a simple process; an applicant with a record of B's was granted entry by the administrative officer in charge of the school. Now students were asked to file transcripts and three letters of recommendation, and the departments concerned were consulted in each case.[101]

Just after the war, the GRE was found to be unsatisfactory as an admissions criterion because it demanded unfamiliar knowledge of recent veterans. But the administration at Harvard was attracted by the bureaucratic efficiency of standardized tests and entered into discussions with GRE representatives that eventually led to the adoption of the test into the application process during the 1945–1946 academic year. In the short run, though, Harvard began developing its own admissions test.[102] At an admissions office now "flooded with applications," the newly adopted admissions procedure at Harvard featured an initial evaluation by the dean and then a referral of applications that the dean saw as worthy of consideration. Recommendations from each department were next forwarded to the school, where the applications were reviewed once again; and then final disposition was made by the dean.[103] Though department recommendations were followed in most instances, the growing power of the administration in the admissions process was notable.

As the enrollment boom began in the 1940s, the swelling undergraduate colleges needed more teachers. Since the early days, graduate students had formed a labor pool that could help to meet that need. That relation has grown toxic today, with graduate students impressed into armies of contingent laborers whose work maintains the undergraduate curriculum, but it was relatively harmonious in the postwar decades.[104] Indeed, universities showed a humane concern about the problem of graduate student placement. That concern may appear strange, given that a time of unprecedented prosperity had begun, but there was no telling how long it would last. At Harvard, deans worried that when the G.I. Bill expired, there would be no money to keep graduate programs running: "Though the number of openings for our graduates has been large in all areas" since the war, they believed that "this situation cannot be expected to last indefinitely." In fact, they foresaw "a dwindling market" into which they would be sending "huge crops of graduates."[105] Of course, the post-Sputnik deluge of federal investment put off this reckoning for several decades, but we might say that today's withered academic job market was predicted over half a century ago.

The end of government assistance, administrators thought, would mean that many students would not be able to go on to graduate school.[106] Though this proved a misjudgment, it shows the dependent financial relation that was growing between the university and the government. Harvard was in every way typical in this regard; the development of these close financial ties presaged the difficulties that ensued when federal support began to drop later on.

Scholarships and fellowships were consolidated at Harvard after the war, so that one student could hold both kinds of appointment, and the school set up a Graduate Loan Fund.[107] In a sense, this "liberalization" of funding brought together the roles of teacher-in-training with researcher-in-training and helped to create the vexed and confusing—and overloaded—identity of the modern graduate student, who is expected to become both a teacher and a researcher. Admissions standards, now depersonalized and professionalized, helped to bring such an identity into being, and the paucity of professors' jobs has made it into a harsh crucible.

Even in the postwar era, graduate student wasn't an easy identity to take on. Graduate schools nationally came under fire for not adequately training teachers, most notably in the 1947 report of the U.S. President's Commission on Higher Education (the Truman Commission).[108] The commission charged that programs were too specialized. (Its report, the first of its kind dealing with higher education, also demanded greater commitment to racial and economic diversity and called for the creation of community colleges. It gained no legislative traction during the term of Harry S. Truman, the president who commissioned it, or that of his successor, Dwight D. Eisenhower, but it later provided the blueprint for much higher-education reform during the Kennedy and Johnson presidencies in the 1960s.)[109] Harvard declined to divide its graduate school into a teaching division and a research program as the Truman Commission suggested, nor did it create classes to train its graduate students in pedagogy. Instead, departments and faculty were asked to informally advise students about how to teach.[110] It seems to have been resource scarcity that inspired Harvard to liberalize its funding packages for graduate students, making them researchers and teachers simultaneously. While conceding the need to train students as teachers, the university didn't create formal structures for pedagogical instruction—suggesting that teaching did not need to be taught. This minimal treatment of the commission's recommendations implicitly contradicted the mission of the hundreds of master's programs in teaching that had sprung up around the country (including at Harvard) during the previous generation, but no one acknowledged the inconsistency.

At Michigan, a glut of applicants required a stricter admissions policy, but administrators saw this as an opportunity to create a more prestigious graduate school. Using the GRE became a "considerable aid" to "the selection of students for advanced study."[111] As will presently become clear, this kind of reliance on the GRE continues to this day.

There was also a further segregation of degrees, with the M.A. reaching a new low in status. At Harvard, the M.A. now counted as little more than a B.A., and it turned into a cheap parting gift handed to failed doctoral students on their way out. This devaluation of the M.A. clearly follows from generations of lack of concern for the degree. Its middling status meant that it never had a clear meaning, and that lack of purchase now meant it was being pushed off the table. Harvard acknowledged this "perennial problem of the Master's degree," and the dean admitted that "there is no consensus among those dealing with graduate students as to what this degree should signify in the way of achievement."[112] Similarly, at Michigan, Assistant Dean Peter Okkelberg regretted the "large" number of "special or professional master's degrees now given" and noted "the whole problem of the meaning and purpose of the master's degree and of the differentiation in titles and requirements."[113] The stigmatization of the M.A. increased as schools tightened standards. Trivializing the M.A. had to do with a sustained effort to keep graduate schools exclusive.

Michigan faced a different version of the same problem of how to be exclusive. There the segregation of degrees was literal, as the university's Rackham Graduate School increasingly relegated the instruction of teachers to physically separate programs throughout the 1940s and 1950s . In 1937, the university began a cooperative plan with state colleges of education that outsourced much of the training of teachers to satellite campuses over the next fifteen years.[114] These "Graduate Study centers"—at outposts like Battle Creek, Grand Rapids, and Saginaw—enrolled about 1,200 students each term, "mainly teachers in the public school systems of the state, who in this way are able to take part-time, in-service training during the school year." The graduate school was responsible for developing some of the curricula at these teaching colleges, but it's suggestive that by 1953, two colleges had withdrawn from the cooperative plan and were granting the M.A. autonomously.[115] The graduate school had managed to contract out its troublesome master's students in education.

With teachers-in-training exiled to separate homelands, research was the unchallenged norm at the University of Michigan's graduate school by the 1960s. The spiking number of doctoral degrees granted in 1961 was described as a "major breakthrough," especially "due to the much larger fellowship and research support received in the last few years through aid from the National Science Foundation, The National Institutes of Health, and other agencies of the federal government."[116] Federal money was helping to create the golden age of research culture.

Bernard R. Berelson's 1960 survey *Graduate School in the United States*, commissioned by the Carnegie Corporation, made a lasting contribution that was cited as authoritative for a more than a decade. Berelson's study of admissions from the late 1950s yielded the conclusions that nearly all students who applied to graduate schools were accepted, that admissions processes were far too lax, and that most graduate deans believed that their schools were doing a poor job of selecting good students. Faculty tended to corroborate this dissatisfaction. At the time, however, there were too few doctoral candidates, in Berelson's view, so raising admissions standards was not an option. Berelson proposed that graduate schools recruit more applicants in order to have a stronger admissions pool—that is, in order to reject more of them, much the way that selective undergraduate colleges do today.[117]

It's worth lingering on these observations for a moment: Berelson portrays the so-called golden age of abundance from the faculty's point of view. This is a perspective rarely glimpsed amid the long-felt and understandable nostalgia for a job market that afforded academic placement to essentially all doctorates who wanted it. Faculty and administrators at the time did not perceive an age of plenty for graduates; instead, they focused on admissions and what they saw was a slippage into looseness.

As late as 1972, the education policy specialists Lewis B. Mayhew and Patrick J. Ford agreed with Berelson's characterization that there were too few graduate applicants. The better-known universities frequently accepted more students than they expected to graduate, engendering a low retention rate.[118] Though reformers argued that this process actually weeded out the most creative and interesting students, attrition remained a tool to reduce class size after the fact.[119] Intramural discontent with graduate admissions—which now appeared haphazard and capricious—became increasingly apparent throughout the 1960s.[120] Certain studies suggested that college grades were poor predictors of real-life success, leading many universities to minimize grade point averages and other accepted evidence of "intelligence," though other studies from this period recommended increased selectivity.[121] But few concrete recommendations for change appeared.

The only truly innovative change, according to Mayhew and Ford, was that some graduate schools attempted to recruit minority-group members who did not meet the formal admissions criteria. Historically, administrators have tended to require superior qualifications from minorities, but these universities "gave the benefit of the doubt" to black, Mexican American, and Native American students, raising many questions about the selection process.[122] Thus did affirmative action gain traction in graduate admissions, where it exemplified a larger commitment to diversity and "the politics of personal identity" that was transforming higher education.[123] On the level of graduate admissions, that commitment remains fraught. Not only do high entrance requirements bar the door to many minority applicants, but the question of recruitment of disadvantaged students remains unsettled.

The "new depression" in higher education arrived without warning and had fully set in by the mid-1970s. Its most obvious symptom was the sudden shift in the labor market for Ph.D.'s from conditions of excessive demand to excessive supply.[124] Generated by both a less rosy economic outlook and a decrease in government investment in higher education, these changes in the landscape affected the number of graduate students enrolled in American universities. Thus did graduate school finally get its paradise of selectivity, but the worm was already in the apple. The buyer's market for graduate schools became a fertile site for economic exploitation of graduate students in a system that valued them in one way for their research and in another for the cheap labor that they could provide in undergraduate classrooms.

Michigan's enrollment declined by about two hundred students per year over the course of six years beginning in 1976. Reasons for the drop included rising tuition rates, the lack of funding for research assistants and graduate fellowships, and the lure of high-paying jobs that didn't require a doctoral degree. By the 1990s, "the poor economy and rapidly dwindling state support for higher education through the prior two decades took a toll," but the graduate school worked to make up the shortfall and secured additional student funding from private foundations, the largest of which have been propping up the humanities enterprise in different ways for many years since.[125]

Even though federal support for graduate students rapidly decreased, graduate programs continued to expand throughout years of scarcity.[126] This pattern of wishful administrative thinking ("if we build it, they will come") continued through succeeding decades as government support for higher education dropped steadily. The combination of decreasing government support for higher education and institutional expectations that such support would return pressured graduate admissions from two sides. On one side, less government money meant less financial support for graduate students.

But on the other, residual optimism and a longing for the golden age led universities to keep admitting students in numbers that have not always proved sustainable.

Those debates have been inflected by unreasonable projections. Well-intentioned academics produced demographic reports during the 1980s and 1990s declaring that old-time abundance lay just beyond the next corner. We know what happened: the retirement of faculty hired during the boom generation did not result in their replacement by full-time, tenure-track professors.[127] The nation's graduate programs gradually cut back from their peak admissions levels that they reached during the 1960s, but debates persist over what ought to be the "right size." Only recently has the realization begun to take hold that we now inbuilt a "new normal" and that policies must change to accommodate it.

WHAT NOW? LOOKING AHEAD

When we look at the story of graduate admissions, we see many of the issues that higher education faces today in embryonic form. The formation of a prestige-driven research culture in the new American universities in the nineteenth century shaped the entire history of those universities—and we see that in graduate admissions at every stage. The pressures toward selectivity that characterize the development of graduate admissions have always been directed toward the promotion of a class of researchers, usually at the expense of training teachers. The devaluation of the master's degree is an inseparable symptom of these intramural class struggles. Through it all, the production of doctorates has served the goals of the researchers who trained them over the needs of the students themselves. There have been benefits, to be sure: the United States established the world's best university system during the period I've been looking at. But the personal costs have been considerable too. Huge attrition rates—which persisted even during the so-called golden age and continue to the present day—served the reputational needs of faculty, who could discard all but the most promising researchers-in-training, whose later placement "into other strong departments conferred prestige upon their mentors."[128]

I noted at the beginning of this chapter that research into the history of graduate admissions practices has remained sparse. But an illuminating new study by Julie R. Posselt throws a likewise-needed spotlight on present practice. Posselt witnessed the graduate admissions process in a number of departments at three different graduate schools. Her observations became the basis for *Faculty Gatekeeping in Graduate Admissions,* a compelling analysis of the way that faculty admit graduate students today.[129]

Posselt's findings ought to disturb us. Her main conclusion is that faculty admissions committees push relentlessly toward normativity, where the norm is themselves. In Posselt's terms, members of admissions committees engage in a complicated form of "homophily" (or love of same—that is, admitting people like ourselves). We don't look for younger versions of ourselves, exactly ("participants are cognizant that personal similarities shape professional judgment"), though "individual tastes" matter a great deal. Instead, "disciplinary values"—the ones that socialize us into the academic profession—serve to mediate homophily: instead of searching openly for our younger selves, we search for people who have values and attainments like ours. Disciplinary values smoothe out disagreements among committee members and build toward the very important goal of consensus (which makes everyone collectively responsible for decisions).

One of the keywords often used to describe the admissions process is "fit." Faculty say that they're looking for potential graduate students who will fit into the department's culture and mission. That aim looks benign enough—and indeed, the same idea of fit comes up a lot in discussions of faculty hiring. But hiring one new department member is not the same thing as filling a cohort of apprentices. On the graduate student level, "fit" assumes that it's the student's job to fit the department and not the other way around. As an admissions heuristic, it's deeply conservative. Faculty would defend "their judgments and rationales," says Posselt, "using long lists of adjectives that captured the personality of the reviewer as much as the qualities of the applicant." She observed "how laden these lists were with the tastes of those who compiled them, and how these impressions were often admitted into deliberations with as much weight as universal criteria."

Bureaucratic practice, writes Posselt, also conceals political differences and creates a veneer of objectivity that allows the complex process of homophily to proceed. The machinations of bureaucracy use "a logic of formal rationality" that serves to "minimize ambiguity by applying quantifiable standards to large numbers of applicants." Numbers, in other words, conceal subjectivity from those who exercise it. These quantitative measures "suppress the complicating role of individual values and ensure that outcomes are predictable and consistent." The result is a selective pressure toward applicants who distinguish themselves in specific and prescribed ways: a certain kind of graduate student. That pressure produces a more uniform graduate student body, which will in turn provide the pool for the selection of future faculty. Admissions fuels the reproductive process, which proceeds inexorably.

The most important of these quantitative measures turns out to be the GRE. Faculty members don't exactly believe in the GRE, says Posselt, but they use it anyway, as a kind of magic bullet—or a magic meat axe—to cut down the applicant pool. This use of the GRE offers a specific instance of what is generally true throughout the admissions process, namely that bureaucracy depersonalizes. Bureaucratic practices thus increase the likelihood that researchers will choose people who display the desire and potential to be researchers like themselves, and so they perpetuate a culture that values those practices. Posselt found that "doctoral education in the programs [she] studied was chiefly a matter of producing knowledge producers. Each year, these programs took steps to refashion themselves through the students they admitted and scholars they hired." This finding is perhaps not surprising, but it's remarkable how closely it aligns with the formation of research culture in the early days of the university. Homophilic admissions practices enshrine old values in a static structure. So nothing changes.

Graduate admissions therefore emerges as the front line of academia's push toward conservatism of its own culture. This conservatism obviously makes reform more difficult, but the problems go deeper and further than that. Homophily, Posselt observes, leads to "broader patterns of inequality" because it keeps those who are not like us out of the charmed circle. As Posselt puts it, "When those with privilege look at others with privilege and instinctively see them as 'the fairest in the land,' it becomes difficult for those from more modest personal backgrounds." Given the widespread commitment to diversity throughout higher education, it is of more than passing interest that graduate admissions practice has historically pushed in the opposite direction.

Here I shift from the historical to the prospective mode. I've described a system whose values were established with the institution of universities themselves and how those values have been consistently enabled by admissions practices—and vice versa—right up to the present day. So what policy recommendations might improve this system, if only by making it more self-aware? How should we admit graduate students anyway?

Let me begin my answer with a case study of a student of my own. Nora (a pseudonym) was admitted to my department's Ph.D. program during one of my two stints as its graduate director. Because she was in my subfield, she was admitted largely on my say-so. Nora's upward mobility figured into my endorsement of her: she had started at a community college, transferred to an undistinguished local university for her B.A., and then got a master's degree in the CUNY system. I liked the determination that Nora showed. (And I now see that it reflected a certain homophilic tendency: I saw values in Nora that I respected and that—on my good days, at least—I think I have myself.)

Nora took a couple of classes with me and did well, and then she asked me to direct her dissertation. As that dissertation neared completion, we sat down over lunch and discussed her future prospects. That was when she told me of her intention to go on the academic job market that coming fall—a year sooner than I expected her to—and also of her long-held plan to seek a professorship at a community college like the school where she had started her own higher education.

Nora attained her goal, clearly aided by the credibility of her own community college degree. She received two job offers, chose one with difficulty, and then raced to finish her dissertation a few weeks before she began her new assistant professorship. Today she is happily ensconced in the job she always wanted. I consider Nora an A+ job placement, and I get a great feeling of satisfaction whenever I think of her.

Nora didn't tell me that she wanted to teach at a community college until she was finishing her Ph.D. What if she had declared her career goal in her original application to doctoral programs? It almost certainly would not have done her any good and probably would have hurt her. For evidence, I need look no further than myself. If Nora had been more forthright, I have to admit that even I—who was inclined in her favor—might have been skeptical of her application. I too have been socialized into research culture, and even though I try to stay alert to my own biases, I don't always see them in the moment. And as much as Nora's ambition shows her focus and integrity, her desire to teach at a two-year college ranks low in the hierarchy of our research culture. Even though most professors respect teaching, we don't respect applicants who tell us that teaching is most important to them. Early members of research culture ourselves, we are taught the values of that culture—so we look for research first.

We can see, then, that graduate teaching—and graduate learning—begin during admissions. The application commences the process of professionalization through which students reshape themselves to conform to the research culture that beckons. The personal statements that applicants write encourage these would-be apprentices to impersonate researchers with fully developed agendas. They know that they gain credibility only through such incredible posturing.[130] The conservatism of the application process likewise teaches them that they must excise the parts of their profile that don't fit this restrictive model. Thus are prospective graduate students given research biases before they are even admitted to research culture.

I obviously have not hesitated to editorialize during my recounting of this brief history of graduate admissions. The story does not exactly highlight the virtues of graduate study, but it does point the way ahead. Throughout this book, I argue that the systematic disrespect of the teaching ranks—and of teaching generally—by graduate schools is not just mendacious but also counterproductive. We must embrace the teaching mission of graduate study as well as the research mission. I elaborate that argument throughout this book, beginning in the graduate classroom. We need to build an admissions process that can honor the career goals of a graduate student like Nora, whose research is as likely to grow out of her teaching as the other way around, and whose scholarship—broadly conceived—will center on her teaching.

Let me be clear: I am not suggesting that we aim to admit students who have no interest in research. Professors who don't keep expanding their intellectual footprints ill serve their students. But we need to conceive of scholarship more broadly than simply as the stuff you publish. Both professors and universities are typically measured according to what is sometimes called "knowledge creation." It's also called "productivity." And it's always called "publication." The system is pretty publication heavy now, and its lack of proportion warps a lot of lives, starting with those of graduate students. John Guillory, an English professor who studies the workings of the university, has observed that professors are so busy writing books now that they literally don't have the time to read them.[131]

It's even worse for graduate students. They have that problem, certainly, and another one that's worse: the buyer's market for professorships allows employers to demand skills in both research and teaching. So graduate students have to train to be scholars to please their departments, and they train to be teachers to please their potential employers. In other words, graduate students have to be everything to everybody. It's no wonder time to degree is so high.

Most of the academic jobs out there emphasize teaching (and teaching skills are of obvious value in many of the alt- and non-academic ones), so why should we disrespect students who privilege it when they apply to graduate school? It should also follow that graduate programs should stop selling the dream of a professorship to prospective graduate students in its older packaging. It has taken nearly two generations for that argument to assert itself. But the best way to promote a course of graduate study that prepares students for the reality of diverse outcomes is far from clear. We need to broaden the profile of the graduate student we seek.

We also need to think about the numbers in which we seek them—that is, the size of incoming classes. Whenever a discussion opens about nonacademic employment for Ph.D.'s, it isn't long before someone suggests reducing graduate school admissions. "The market for full-time scholars has fallen off a cliff," this argument goes, "so why not just train fewer of them?" The strategy to reduce the number of Ph.D. students recurs in those conversations because it's sensible. When there's insufficient demand for professors in the marketplace, the simplest response is to decrease supply.

But that's not the only response, and I don't think it's the best one, either. Before I go on, let me say first that many graduate programs do need to shrink, because they're too big to educate their students with the attentiveness that these straitened times demand. Diverse career prospects require more personalized training, and that kind of teaching and advising cannot be wholesaled to large numbers of students. Second, graduate enrollments *are* shrinking after years of irrational expansion, partly for that very reason.[132] Doctoral programs are admitting fewer students overall, with the most notable declines occurring in the biggest programs and in the arts and humanities fields. It's too early to track the effects of those cuts, but they will certainly continue as programs seek to "right size," as a University of Maryland graduate dean put it.[133]

But what exactly is the "right" size? If the goal of graduate programs is to produce only enough Ph.D.'s to fill the hiring needs of colleges and universities, then that number is bound to be pretty small. Marc Bousquet and others have argued that if universities (especially large state universities) stopped using graduate students as low-cost laborers and reserved their courses for full-time faculty, the number of professors' jobs would increase. This is a desirable goal, certainly, but in today's present, it is also utopian—for the cost of this shift would explode the budgets of many public universities. It's reprehensible that administrators and faculty have come to rely on graduate students to do their low-caste teaching (yes, faculty too—for these decisions are not just economic and administrative but also curricular); but it is certainly a fact, and part of my strategy in this book is to confront the facts on the ground.

So if graduate programs aim only to train future faculty, their numbers are going to be so small that it will cause drastic changes in the structure of graduate education. Consider the recent decision by the art history department at Maryland to admit a class of just two doctoral students. It doesn't take a Ph.D. in math to see that classes of two can't be supported by the traditional seminar method of teaching. Departments with just a handful of graduate students at the coursework stage would need to devise another method of delivering course credits. A change like that needn't be a bad thing. It might even be salutary, in that it would force professors to reflect on their graduate pedagogical goals—something we don't do often enough.

But the real bottom line here is not a tiny class of entering doctoral students. If professors decided to confer only enough Ph.D.'s to fill vacant professorial positions, the more credible outcome is that lots of doctoral programs would go under. Some observers urge faculty members to take the initiative and start closing Ph.D. programs because of the dismal job market. Let's keep following this hypothetical scenario. What would happen if most Ph.D. programs in the United States did close?

To begin with, it's clear which ones would remain standing: the established, rich, elite ones. Others would also survive the cut too, of course, but a sharp reduction in the number of graduate programs would increase the power and influence of the wealthy elites. That small group of venerable institutions would gain disproportionate influence in supplying the rest of the country with Ph.D.'s. Of course, those institutions would be selective—we would expect them to be, given that they would be screening a lot of candidates for a small number of desirable jobs waiting in the future. But selective in what way? In the conventional, establishment-oriented way that would befit their institutional histories.

We might then expect the problems of inbreeding associated with dynasties. Rare would be the opportunity to take a risk on an "interesting" applicant, because doing so would deprive a more sophisticated student who did all the right things and hit all of his—or her, but more likely his—marks with precision.

Such a straitened admissions system would confer great advantage to the wealthy and the privileged, naturally. Those who have the time to work directly with professors (rather than, say, at wage-paying jobs to make ends meet), to acquire languages, even to publish (yes, a small number of undergraduates do publish) would benefit not only from their own talent and commendable ambition but also from their head start in the game. And let's face it: many of those high achievers would hold undergraduate degrees from the same institutions whose Ph.D. programs survived this hypothetical cutback.

The whole scenario recalls the old days at the beginning of this story, when American graduate education operated on just such a small, elite scale. Getting in depended not on formal application but rather on the opportunity to be noticed by a well-connected senior professor, who might then reach out to a colleague at another university and arrange for a promising student to be admitted for advanced study. It was easier to be noticed if you schooled in Princeton than in Podunk.[134] It also helped to be white and male.

We already know that increased graduate enrollments were what made it harder to maintain inbred populations of students and professors. But how could that same outcome be avoided if graduate education boils itself down to a few elite universities that cull a small number of elite students from the applicant pool to keep the Ph.D. alive? Academia escaped elitism once already when colleges and universities opened their gates wide after World War II. Higher education has lost some of the democratic access we gained in those years, but it hardly befits us to march toward exclusiveness. That possible future bears a disturbing resemblance to American graduate education's overbearing past.

But that's not our only possible future. Recall the assumption guiding our speculation here, namely, that the purpose of graduate programs is to manufacture professors. Graduate programs already operate under that assumption in all kinds of ways, such as the still-widespread and stubborn insistence on defining a "successful" job placement as a tenure-track professorship, preferably at an institution with its own Ph.D. program. That assumption, as the historian Thomas Bender has pointed out, blotted out the long-standing fact that, for many decades, Ph.D.'s graduated to all kinds of work. Only after World War II did the Ph.D.-to-professor career path become the default, when the country needed professors to staff its rapidly expanding higher-education sector that had to accommodate an influx of former G.I.'s and then a generation of baby boomers.[135] The oversupply lasted about a generation, and its beneficiaries are now in their seventies. It seems high time that we changed our baseline assumptions to reflect the realities of our students and not their grandparents.

The effort to reconceive the guiding assumption that Ph.D.'s are supposed to become professors needs to be collective, and it needs to start with admissions. If we are to alter students' training to prepare them for the full range of jobs they will be able to get—a subject I develop in the chapters that follow—then we should alter the standards and presumptions under which we admit them. I'm speaking about diversity in a larger sense. (And in the traditional sense too: graduate schools do a poor job of attracting students from underrepresented groups and disadvantaged backgrounds. Part of that problem goes back to secondary school and college preparation, for the pool of potential candidates from these groups is small. If we want to enroll them, though, we have to seek them out and recruit them, not wait for them to come to us—and I see too little of that.)[136]

Graduate school diversity must go beyond identity politics. We need to promote diversity of students' goals. Reforming graduate admissions has to be part of a larger movement to professionalize students differently, to allow them more range. For now, it must suffice to say that the problem with admissions is part of a larger one of rigid values. There's nothing wrong with a system that privileges research—unless that system reproduces values that undermine the support of everything else.

The ideal of the graduate student structures the admissions process, and the values of the system structure that ideal. We need to make those values more flexible. Let us start with what graduate school is for: to train not only researchers but also teachers—and work backward from that. That's part of what this book does: I want to peel back the assumptions we so rarely examine so that we can look at just what it is that we're doing when we populate and run a graduate school.

If we do those things, then we can "right size" Ph.D. programs at a level that is both viable and responsible. That level will be smaller than it has been but not so small as to return us to the practices of our aloof and arrogant past. And those smaller cohorts will contain not just the mini-me's that result from homophily but a group of intellectuals with a spectrum of aims. And the country—not just the professoriate—will benefit.

CHAPTER TWO

Classwork: The Graduate Seminar and Beyond

JUST ABOUT EVERY professor wants to teach graduate school. Lots of them regard it practically as their birthright, in fact—which isn't so unusual when you consider that the experience invokes their own birth as professional intellectuals. Just as the child claims in advance the right to be a grown-up, the experience of being taught in graduate school germinates the desire to become the professor and teach one's own graduate students in turn.

That desire encoded itself in the institutional DNA beginning in the 1920s and 1930s. Seminars made their appearance in American graduate school early on. Pioneered by the likes of Henry Adams, they had become widespread by the 1880s, when graduate school was still nascent in the United States.[1] The changes in scale that began in the 1920s made graduate school itself more of a presence in the American university. According to historian Roger Geiger, the growth of the research university during that period, including the admission of many more graduate students, allowed for more seminars to be offered. "Productive scholars," he writes, "could be favored with graduate instruction, while more-plodding colleagues handled large undergraduate lectures."[2] With such incentives, the teaching hierarchy took hold, with graduate teaching perched at its summit.

I inherited my own awareness of that hierarchy. At the beginning of my career, graduate teaching looked like the pinnacle of professional existence. Perhaps because I had to wait more than five years to teach a graduate seminar, I felt lucky rather than entitled when the opportunity came. I still do.

Looking back at that time, I realize that I was chasing something I knew little about. Although I wanted very much to teach graduate students, I had no particular ideas about how to do it, nothing special I wanted to try. (I did have more than a few negative examples from my own life as a graduate student, so I knew a lot of ways *not* to teach graduate school.) Even though graduate teaching was one of my major professional desires, I had no graduate pedagogical vision. I just wanted to be a grad school professor. In that respect, I believe I was fairly typical.

If almost everyone wants to teach graduate students, then why do so few professors think hard about how to do it? One reason is the inherent conservatism of academia. Senior professors don't want to change their ways, observed Derek Bok recently. "After all, that is how *they* learned to teach."[3] But another reason is surely that one can teach a graduate seminar without doing much work. Most graduate students are heavy lifters, and they will usually carry the load for you if you don't step forward to do it. True, their performance is uneven—they're not experienced pros—but whether or not they're on their game, the professor doesn't have to do much if he or she doesn't want to.

I had teachers in graduate school who certainly didn't want to do much. Many of my seminars as a graduate student ran by what I call the beach ball method: just as a crowd at an arena bounces a beach ball at random from one person to another, the professor depends on the students to just talk— which they do, bouncing from topic to topic without design.[4] Or it can be worse. Historian David Gerber recalls one of his own graduate seminars that had no assigned readings at all:

> The professor . . . largely improvised the course as he went along. There was no syllabus, printed or otherwise; nor was there a schedule of goals for our individual meetings. He suggested—forcefully enough that one may rightly say "assigned"—each of the six or seven of us a topic closely related to his work. Occasionally and randomly, without apparent method, we were to re-

port on "what we were finding." Otherwise the seminar sessions were spent in listening as he read, here and there as it was evolving, from his own work-in-progress.[5]

This professor's lazy narcissism would be breathtaking if its outlines weren't so familiar, even a couple of generations after the fact. Gerber and his cohort got no help with their own research because their scholarship wasn't the real focus of the course.

Such professors aren't just leaving the work to the students—they're abdicating their responsibility to design and shape the course around the students' own educational requirements. A performance like that in an undergraduate classroom would be considered insane and would usually be called to account if it took place on that level. But in graduate seminars, it's allowed to pass, with the only complaints coming at the student watercooler. How do such professors get away with it? The answer is simple when you think about it: they take advantage of a remarkable baseline assumption about graduate seminars, namely, that while the students are expected to learn, the professor isn't actually expected to teach anything.

Laziness alone can't account for all of the collective desire to teach on the graduate level, though. Stereotypes to the contrary, most of the professors I know work pretty hard—and hard workers want to teach graduate school too. Another lure of graduate teaching is surely the high level of mutual learning that takes place in graduate classes. The discussions can be stimulating, and the best graduate students teach their teachers.

But that's not all there is to it, either. Much motivation to teach graduate students has to do with what social theorists call cultural capital or, in this context, prestige. Teaching graduate school confers a lot of it because graduate teaching is the highest spot on the pedagogical food chain. There's nothing inherently sinful about wanting to occupy a position of respect in one's workplace, so no one should be pilloried for the desire, secretly harbored or openly expressed, to have a fancy job that includes teaching in a graduate program. But that privilege comes with responsibilities that have never been greater.

Graduate professors are entrusted with providing the final training before a student takes a job. We provide the last arena for students to practice, when their skills are already considerably well honed, and it's our job to help them become the kind of professionals that they want to be. That requires thinking about graduate students *as learners*. There is a large body of scholarship dedicated to how undergraduates learn and how to teach them accordingly. I'm not suggesting that we apply those findings to graduate school wholesale; graduate students are different from undergraduates. Instead, we have to ask the same question about graduate students: how do they learn?

As I do throughout this book, I'm suggesting that professors should not take the design and execution of graduate teaching for granted. In fact, we should assume as little as possible and learn and test as much as we can. We need to think about the needs of graduate students as learners—just as we do with undergraduates—and as future professionals and then position ourselves to meet those needs as well as possible.

Another reason to examine our baseline assumptions is that graduate education is starting to change. One driver of that change is program size. Graduate programs rely on built-in economies of scale that we mostly take for granted, but the size of graduate programs is in flux. Enrollment in many M.A. programs is dropping, and many graduate schools are reducing the enrollments in Ph.D. programs. "At the same time," observes Frank J. Donoghue, humanists naturally continue to "hire new faculty members to keep pace with emerging fields." In Donoghue's own discipline of English, such "emerging fields" include "Latino/a studies, sexuality studies, Native American studies, digital media, and so on." But that creates a numbers problem: "Year after year, we simply don't have enough graduate students to go around, and as a result graduate seminars are canceled due to underenrollment."[6]

Shrinking graduate programs will have myriad practical implications for what graduate study will look like in the future. The "soft" fields—the humanities and certain social sciences—may have an easier time creating a smaller model of graduate education than the sciences will. That's because the educational infrastructure in the humanities fields is mostly made up of people, not technology.

The humanities model is based on personal exchange: education happens when people communicate with each other. Right now the model for that conversation centers on the seminar (for master's and doctoral students), with Ph.D. students proceeding to an apprenticeship under a dissertation adviser, who is flanked by committee members.

We haven't questioned that format for generations, but that doesn't mean it can't be revised relatively quickly. A move from seminars to a tutorial system, in which graduate education is delivered in groups of one, two, or three people plus the teacher, wouldn't require any buildings to be razed and rebuilt. Some countries (such as Britain) already deliver graduate education that way.

Not that such a shift would be easy. For one thing, many professors would resist, for we love our graduate seminars rather too well, if not always wisely. But the curricular implications of a tutorial-based system matter more—and are more vexing—than any personal objections. Without periodic offerings on the annual seminar menu, scholars in more esoteric subfields would encounter fewer graduate students, and departments and programs would have to figure out how (or perhaps whether) to sustain those areas.

The possibility of subfields having to compete for graduate students in a program will raise significant questions of purpose. For example, the endangered fields could include newer ones (including those based on minority discourses and points of view) that challenge long-established canons. Taking those subfields out of seminar circulation—which is where they often attract new adherents—could stifle them and effectively serve to enshrine the intellectual status quo.

Such are the problems of the future. We're not there yet, but no one should deny that graduate education needs critical scrutiny before then. Any serious effort to reform it has to start in the graduate classroom (broadly construed), and graduate teachers run that domain, not administrators. The urgency of the concerns facing graduate programs in these straitened times—and the changes that those trends are already forcing in programs—have made clear that we can't separate what happens in graduate classrooms from what's happening to graduate programs around the country. And as the troubled job market for new Ph.D.'s illustrates, we can't separate what's happening in graduate programs from the troubles faced right now by universities generally.

These problems will demand creative solutions—and I'll survey both problems and some possible solutions in this chapter. Graduate seminars aren't going anywhere just yet, but they'll have to adapt if they are to remain a viable part of the future of graduate study in the humanities. Regardless of how we wind up doing it, we have to approach the job of teaching openly and creatively. Graduate teaching, while important in itself, also connects to everything else in higher education. Each graduate teacher who tries to do his or her job better is helping to pull graduate school out of the morass it's in—but we'll pull harder if we pull together.

OFFERINGS VERSUS CURRICULUM

We can start by thinking of graduate teaching as collaborative in a departmental sense. It's the job of a department to offer its graduate students the courses they need to take in order for them to do their best work. That sounds simple—and it ought to be. But it's proved devilishly difficult in practice. The specialization of professorial research, along with the priority placed on that research at the research universities where most graduate teaching takes place, leads naturally to narrow specialization in graduate course offerings.

To get a sense of the problem, imagine a distant grocery store that advertises that it can meet all of your cooking and eating needs. You make the trip, and when you get there, you discover that you can buy only lemongrass, pomelos, and Sriracha sauce. You ask about the limited selection, and the manager tells you to wait till next week, when they'll be selling pimentos, artichoke hearts, and brandied cherries.

That's what it's like to pick your courses when you're a beginning graduate student in the humanities. Term by term, year by year, the graduate course offerings in humanities departments don't make sense together. They're a hodgepodge of specialized inquiries: snapshots of books and articles in progress by professors who know what they're determined to teach, but not what their students need most to learn. Nor do most professors know what their colleagues are teaching alongside them.

It would be both too easy and misleading to single out this course or that one—and if I did, my complaint would look too much like a snarky political attack on the "irrelevant" humanities that have lost their way. Moreover, the problem does not lie in single courses. Instead, I want to emphasize the overall effect of the whole practice.

Let's look first from the student's point of view. Humanities graduate students pick through the eccentric course offerings on the buffet table and try to make a balanced meal out of them. They know that they have to grow and get stronger for the comprehensive exam that's ahead of them. But how do you gather together a bunch of specialized inquiries into preparation for a general and comprehensive one? That's the problem that faces most graduate students in the humanities. Most of them solve it—that is, they pass their comprehensives—but it takes time, and graduate school is already too long.

Now let's look at that problem from professors' point of view. Most teachers of graduate students share a concern with creating learning communities, from lively seminars to collaborative lab work, from grad student teaching workshops to even something basic like common department space, as humble as the proverbial mailroom, where graduate students (and faculty) can gather for collegial exchange with each other.

But when do professors talk to each other about what we're doing when we teach graduate school? Members of a department teach the same graduate students, so it ill befits us to be working at cross purposes, even accidentally. Yet we rarely check with each other to see just what our purposes are. What courses do we want to offer students, and why? I don't mean to suggest that this kind of discussion never happens, but I more often see faculty members of liberal arts colleges (where teaching is woven more tightly into the institutional culture) exchanging ideas about their common undergraduate teaching goals than professors in graduate programs talking together about what they want their graduate students to learn. Nor do I mean to imply that these conversations are easy, especially in light of still-expanding humanities canons. Philosophically speaking, they can't be avoided. But in practice, we avoid them constantly.

Gerald Graff, during his 2009 term as president of the Modern Language Association (MLA), warned against "courseocentrism"—the problem that "teaching in isolated classrooms leaves us knowing little about one another's courses" and how this bewilders undergraduate students because it makes our work "opaque" to them. That isolation problem—the belief that teaching is a "solo act"—has different but equally disastrous effects on the graduate level. Joseph Tussman observed in 1969 that absent a learning community in which we exchange ideas about what we're doing, "a collection of coherent courses may be simply an incoherent collection."[7] That's just what happens with humanities graduate course offerings. Graduate-level humanities professors pay scant attention to our own faculty communities—and it's the students who stand to suffer.

Instead of engaging each other on curricular goals, we hide behind a microeconomic model in which we place rather too much faith. The rationale behind random course offerings is based on two assumptions. The first is that professors do their best work if they teach what they're interested in. The second is that if professors offer the specialized courses that they like, the collective diversity of their inquiries will give students a broad choice from which to meet their own educational needs.[8]

That second assumption needs a hard look. The underlying concept goes back to Charles Eliot's late nineteenth-century introduction of electives at Harvard to replace a fixed undergraduate curriculum, but its graduate-level precedents extend even further back. The idea that graduate professors should teach what they want invokes the German value of *Lehrfreiheit,* the "freedom to teach" that prevailed (and mostly still does prevail) at German research universities. This ideal underpins the earliest conceptions of academic freedom in the United States, a legacy that began to coalesce into its modern form when Americans improvised their own version of the German model and started their own research universities.

But that second rationale for random graduate course offerings arises from something more than academic freedom. It also rests on the assumption that if professors act as free agents offering their own course wares, they will coalesce into a marketplace that will supply students with their learning needs.

Professors have long relied on this marketplace model of course offerings, and our faith in it replicates the belief in the invisible hand that dominates the American marketplace of ideas. But the invisible hand works perfectly only in theory. Anyone who's lived through recent times (or the Depression, for that matter) understands that marketplaces need regulation. Certainly economists accept the idea.[9]

The social sciences mainly depart from this free-market-based graduate-course-selection model. The curriculum builds vertically in most of those fields, and everyone has to begin by learning the same foundational concepts, even on the graduate level. Josiah Ober, a professor of political science at Stanford, says that course offerings must be dictated by the need for students to learn the techniques that they'll require for their research. "In the contemporary world of the social sciences," says Ober, "you have to get the methodological skills down and get a sense of what the literature is, and has been, in the field."[10]

Many humanities departments throw a methods course into their annual eclectic mix. (You can usually tell the professor who's teaching it because his arm is in a sling from the twisting required to get him to offer it.) But there's no consensus about what methods need to be taught in the humanities in the first place. Literary theory? Archival savvy? Book history? In the end, idiosyncrasy prevails there too.

Educators have a name for this idiosyncrasy: teacher-centered curriculum. It refers to course design that starts with what professors want to do instead of trying to figure out what students need. The results of teacher-centered course offerings disadvantage the students and professors together. For one thing, the potpourri of classes that the students take doesn't do enough to prepare them for the general examinations that the same professors demand after classwork is done. (I'll spotlight those exams in Chapter 3.) We ask graduate students to display foundational knowledge on those tests. How can we legitimately demand such preparation if we don't teach it?

When we don't teach what's necessary, students learn it on their own. Humanities graduate students are a bright and mostly enterprising bunch, and they figure out what they need to know. They sift it out of their specialized courses like miners panning for gold, and then they dig for the rest in the library as they prepare for their exams. Thus, teacher-centered curriculum tacks on extra time for graduate students to study for these tests—and that adds to the unconscionable nine years that it takes them to finish their degrees. "If you really want the students to take their general exams, and soon," demands Russell A. Berman, a former MLA president and professor of German and comparative literature at Stanford, "then offer the courses that prepare for them."[11]

There's a value when professors teach their current research, to be sure. Gerald Graff has written of how a course based on a professor's book can draw students and faculty into a kind of collaborative partnership.[12] But courses based on specialized books in progress are not the only component of a nourishing educational diet. Students might refine their palates by eating complicated dishes of anchovies and capers, but they also need a bowl of whole-grain cereal sometimes, even if it's not as fascinating to cook. Basic skills matter. Andre Soltner, the legendary owner and chef at Lutèce, is said to have auditioned his sous-chefs by asking them to prepare a plain omelet.

Andrew Delbanco, a frequent and thoughtful commentator on American higher education, has written about how those basic skills need to be taught again for each generation of humanities students. The "progressive power of science" allows us to require medical students to know more "about the genetic basis of disease or the management of organ transplantation than physicians knew twenty or even ten years ago," he observes. The humanities, on the other hand, "remain concerned with preserving truth by rearticulating it" instead of "discarding the old in favor of the new."[13] That means that certain kinds of humanities teaching need to be repeated for each generation. Delbanco is talking about undergraduate teaching, but his point holds equally true on the graduate level. We have a responsibility to teach our students what we expect them to know.

What students need to know has for years, on the graduate level, been a disciplinary matter. I have little idea myself what an anthropologist considers essential for a beginning graduate student to know, but that's not my bailiwick. Members of anthropology departments need to get together to have that discussion among each other.

Shared goals are essential, and not just for faculty collegiality, though that's worthy in itself. If we discuss our educational goals together and agree on them where we can, we should be able to create a more coherent educational plan for our graduate students. In particular, we have to bring the courses that graduate students have to take into coherent relation with the general exams we require of them. If a broad grasp of literary history is the goal of a literature department, for example, then the professors in that department should agree to offer survey courses at prescribed intervals. Thus may we deliver more coherent course offerings to the students who need them.

Berman calls on professors to become better "curators of the graduate programs we offer students." Scholars of education would describe this as "student-centered curriculum," in which the plan is designed with the student's needs in mind. But there's no reason to get technical. We can describe it in simpler terms as the flip side of academic freedom: doing right by our students is a form of academic responsibility.

CONTENT AND ITS DISCONTENTS

Academic responsibility doesn't end with balanced course menus, of course. We must obviously consider the content of the courses themselves. But not so fast. Graduate study in the humanities has for generations been relentlessly content driven. That content is usually historical, not just in history but also in the other humanistic disciplines, where graduate students are expected to cover the history of what it matters for them to know.

This coverage metaphor has proved harder and harder to sustain, particularly as literary canons have expanded and reading lists with them. Departments may no longer expect to have an expert in every subspecialty, and graduate students can no longer expect to read everything. They specialize too, sooner than ever before. (Of course, the reasons that graduate students specialize are not limited to the unwieldiness of ever-expanding canons.) Because department faculties and student coursework cannot expand indefinitely, the coverage metaphor fails: the cover is too small to fit the bed.[14] It's time—past time, really—to think about the seminar from the student's point of view as well as the teacher's.

Student-centered learning is not a new idea—its beginnings may be traced back more than a century to the likes of John Dewey and Jean Piaget. Its application to undergraduate education came later. But student-centered learning has not, for the most part, reached graduate school yet. "We think very little about the scholarship of teaching and learning," says Jim Grossman, executive director of the American Historical Association, and we don't think about how to apply it in a discipline-specific context.[15] The result is content-driven graduate teaching that neglects the needs of students.

Content-driven approaches to graduate seminars suffer from teacher-centeredness. If the professor insists on plowing through eighteen weeks of content in fourteen weeks, that doesn't mean that the students can or will follow. What, then, does it mean when the professor insists, "I covered it"? Professors behave this way because they want to impart "mastery." But they do not think of what "mastery" means, let alone how graduate students might cope with a full course load, if each course is overstuffed. Such one-sided obstinacy leads to an academic version of Jim Bouton's baseball refrain, "I Managed Good, But Boy, Did They Play Bad."

Moreover, as the longtime university-teacher trainer Ed Neal points out, the content-driven model presents a built-in difficulty for students to find research topics late in the term. The consequent rush leads to slapped-together papers and also to incompletes that are pedagogically (for the teachers) and emotionally (for the students) both unpleasant and undesirable.

It's temptingly simple to design a graduate course around a chunk of disciplinary content. (I have given in to that temptation often enough myself.) Most professors need look no further for such models than the graduate seminars that we took ourselves. But the familiarity of that design doesn't make it a good one. "It is easy to imagine recent Ph.D.'s," write the scholars of rhetoric Peter Khost, Debie Lohe, and Chuck Sweetman, "finishing coursework and even leaving their programs having had interesting conversations but not quite knowing what they have been learning *to do*."[16] Confides one graduate student who asked not to be identified, "It's not really clear what one is supposed to learn *in seminar*. What one gets from the reading is obvious. But for the seminar itself, I'm not so sure." I believe that most graduate teachers aren't so sure either.

It's time to reconsider the content-driven mentality in favor of skills-based approaches. There's nothing new about this idea, really. Joseph S. Ames, president of Johns Hopkins, pointed out in 1930 that many Ph.D. students will not pursue research after graduation and will instead become teachers in colleges. He suggested that it was "the duty of the university to give them such a training that they will be better teachers than they otherwise would be."[17]

Before I proceed, I want to make clear that I am not suggesting abandoning content. Humanists have to read a lot, and nothing is going to change that. But they also have to be able to work with what they read. Specifically, they need to be able to create scholarship in some medium, whether it be publication, teaching, or some other outlet. Graduate-seminar leaders therefore need not just to "cover" material but also to set aside time for students to practice doing things with it—gaining what Gilbert Ryle more than seventy years ago called "workshop-possession" rather than "museum possession." Because, as Robert Frost says, "it's knowing what to do with things that counts."[18]

I'll detail what that approach might look like in the pages that follow, but before I get to the details, let's examine the principles that underlie them.

First and most practically, there is retention. It does no good to "learn" something if you don't retain it. Analysts of education at all levels take a jaundiced view of cramming for this reason: students retain the material for long enough to get through the test they're studying for and then they promptly forget it. Graduate seminars don't usually require cramming, but when they cover too much, they get crammed, with approximately the same results. The education scholar Barbara E. Lovitts quotes a graduate-seminar leader who complains, "Even as I'm teaching my graduate class right now, people have forgotten what they learned the semester before, which is very surprising to me."[19] He shouldn't be surprised. Most graduate seminars jam too much information into a brief time and provide little opportunity for students to retain it.

"*The purpose of formal education,*" write the education scholars Diane F. Halpern and Milton D. Hakel with emphasis, "*is transfer.*" In other words, we expect students to be able to use what they're being taught when the class is over. Indeed, Halpern and Hakel observe that the entire justification for higher education itself rests on that premise. Accordingly, they argue that the "first and only goal" of professors should be to teach for "long-term retention and transfer."[20] The rationale is obvious enough: your learning benefits your career only if you can draw on it while you work, not just for a brief period of your training. No one should object to such a goal.

The problems arise when we consider how to reach it. How might graduate professors teach in order to promote retention? One effective way to do so, say Halpern and Hakel, is to have students "take information that is presented in one format and 're-represent' it in an alternative format."[21] That might mean taking information presented in the form of a chart (such as a time line) and explaining it verbally. It's possible to see such an exercise taking place within a graduate seminar, but I doubt that it happens very often. I know that the last time I gave out a time line in a seminar, I referred to it briefly in a minilecture and trusted my students to take it home and study it at leisure. I meant to save time so that I could cover more content.

By skipping classwork with the time line that time, I failed to meet the requirements of "active learning," a practice emphasized by the authors of the aptly titled study *How People Learn*. Active learning demands not only a foundation of factual knowledge but also—and crucially—the ability to understand facts and ideas within a conceptual framework. That especially entails the ability to organize knowledge in ways that facilitate retrieval and application.[22] Teaching to such student-centered outcomes demands backward design—that is, designing a course from its goals backward. If the end is retention and the means to reach it is application of concepts, then the professor needs to invent applications that will serve that goal.[23]

The authors of *The Formation of Scholars,* a Carnegie-supported study of doctoral education, speak in this vein of "integrative learning," in which doctoral students practice what they learn "across settings and over time," such as "from one course to another."[24] This is an admirable aim. Given the decentralized nature of graduate study in the humanities, it is only a theoretical goal for now, but it's an important one.

I have been speaking mostly abstractly so far, but teachers know that the abstract requires the concrete in order to be understood. Examples of "experiential learning" are easier to find in the social sciences and sciences than in the humanities. The sociologist M. E. Kelleher, for example, writes of how to run a graduate proseminar according to this principle. In one example she cites, "most of the syllabus" was "emergent" (though the professor made sure that "certain 'core' topics" were included). The arc of the course instead grew "organically from the needs of the . . . students." For Kelleher, this collaborative "experiential" process "addresses a primary need of professional education by integrating students "into the values and authority of a larger occupational community."[25]

Such student-centered approaches may result in seeming detours from disciplinary content, but that impression results from teacher-centered dogmatism.[26] The literature on how to lead graduate seminars is thin on the ground, but a fine essay by Ed Neal offers some useful guidelines. Neal encourages professors to "think of a seminar as a course in which students practice critical thinking about the discipline and learn about research methods commonly used in the field" rather than as a vehicle for a student to produce a long research paper. Neal proposes that professors plan the seminar by considering a set of questions and develop the course out of the answers—and he raises the possibility of "cooperative learning," meaning that the professor and the students shape the objectives of the course together "within parameters provided by the instructor."[27]

Consider in this light historian David Gerber's effort to improve on the traditional model. I mentioned Gerber's experience as a student earlier in this chapter: he was the one with the professor who read from his own book-in-progress and strong-armed his students to write papers related to it. With that bad memory in mind, Gerber designed a paper-centered course that he hoped would foster independence and intellectual community among students—and he watched it fail. For one thing, he ran into a consistent problem in humanities graduate seminars that I brought up earlier: it often takes students so long to come up with a topic that they can't do justice to it. A semester proves not very long a period to complete a work of original research. Also, Gerber found that his students often lacked basic research skills—which in history include efficient note taking and organization of files, among other things. "It had never occurred to me," Gerber wrote more than a generation ago, "to set time aside to teach these skills."[28]

So Gerber adjusted. Using a student-centered approach, he scrapped the seminar paper. Instead, he assigned what he called "research reports" that were based on clusters of sources that he gathered beforehand. In other words, he substituted a research training exercise for a fully independent plunge into independent historical research. "I wanted to provide actual instruction in research," he said, "not merely individual guidance in choosing a topic," along with a chance to discuss together the historical work that follows.[29]

John Dewey argued that learners need to create knowledge firsthand in order to really experience it. He taught chemistry to primary school students by having them cook eggs and observe the way that heat led to changes in the texture of the whites.[30] Gerber's reworked seminar offers an analogous experience to apprentice historians.[31]

Gerber's work anticipates some recent pedagogical research into the goals and assignments of graduate seminars. Khost, Lohe, and Sweetman observe that "graduate courses produce plenty of writing but often fail to teach it very well." Responding to the same need, the rhetoricians Laura R. Micciche and Allison D. Carr argue that explicit writing instruction belongs in graduate seminars. They suggest a "comp for grad students" course, designed to create the "rhetorical awareness/flexibility" to "sustain a wide variety of critical writing projects."[32] This idea makes sense, but it also carries the dangerous possibility of shunting all graduate writing instruction into one course, If a department were to offer such a course, it's possible that its members could use it as a license to keep their own teacher-centered blinders firmly fastened. So even if graduate students benefit from such a course (and they likely would), their other professors would not. Consequently, seminar paper assignments would continue to go unexamined, and absent the will of professors like Gerber to perform self-critical course overhauls, graduate student writing will continue to fail—as it does too often—to advance graduate student learning.

Professors simply must take a more active role in promoting not just formal knowledge but *learning*. That's partly because graduate students are not always in a position to take advantage of "positive" freedom (that is, "freedom to" rather than the negative "freedom from"). Specifically, graduate students won't always accept an open invitation to identify their own weaknesses and work on them; one of the reasons that they're in training is that many of them don't recognize those weaknesses. For example, I've tried offering students an option of writing two medium-sized essays in a graduate seminar rather than the classic, stress-inducing long paper due at the end when they're itching to check out and move on. I think students benefit from two assessments of their writing instead of one, especially when one comes in the middle of the course, allowing the opportunity to practice what is being taught. That said, my students almost never choose this option when it's offered to them. They too have been socialized according to the old ways.

Lohe and Sweetman have experimented with placing students into the teacher's place, asking them to write lesson plans on a chart that "represents the dual perspectives of student and teacher." They wanted the students to "uncover the implicit choices they were making, helping them to be more intentional about those choices." Khost describes his practice as "unteaching" the seminar paper. He uses the genre of "autoethnography" (in which students write about themselves in relation to how they are seen) to get students to reflect on their identities as novices or apprentices. This self-conscious reflection then informs their conventional research. The combination "may or may not make the individual pieces more publishable," writes Khost, "but it does benefit the students' development as learners, writers, and professionals."[33]

The overarching goal of graduate small-group coursework, says Neal, is for a seminar to function as "a community of scholars." But to get there, "we must re-think our standard approaches to seminar teaching and adopt techniques that foster collaboration, cooperation, and critical thinking."[34] Seminars are for graduate students, not professors. To meet their needs, we have to invite them into the conversation.

I do not address graduate student teaching of undergraduates very often in this book, largely because it is considered in such detail elsewhere. But graduate student teaching is an important vehicle for graduate student learning, too—if we recognize and exploit its possibilities instead of simply treating graduate students as galley slaves who labor below decks in beginning courses.

Teaching can take place through the sharing of teaching itself, not just through classwork. Stanford University, for example, used a 2010 Teagle Foundation grant to set up a collaborative-teaching project that annually paired eight senior professors with graduate student teachers. The two-person teams, all drawn from humanities departments, each devised and taught an undergraduate course together. The eight teams—new ones are named each year—come together several times each quarter to discuss their experience and assigned readings on teaching and learning. The emphasis is on horizontal partnership: the professor and the graduate student are supposed to work together as equals, as nearly as possible, despite their vertical differences in rank and status. The program has been a success, so much so that the Stanford administration seems poised to pick up the cost of the program after the Teagle grant runs out. Indeed, other universities might try this even without foundation grants. Stanford is a rich university, but this particular program is not expensive to run.

Russell Berman, who helped to organize the initiative at Stanford, has urged that we stop "assuming that graduate education is a series of seminars and move toward a model of collaborative teaching." That vision gains further persuasive force from the shrinking of some Ph.D. programs that I noted earlier. Fewer graduate students may mean fewer seminars, but smaller student cohorts also offer more opportunities for creative partnerships, pedagogical and otherwise—and a more expansive view of outcomes.

We should consider the graduate assistantship as a site for collaborative teaching and learning in general terms. Many graduate students work as research or teaching assistants, and in those capacities, they're often expected to make scans, reserve library books, and grade papers on their own time. Such busywork (some of which is mindless) represents a lost opportunity: professors could be engaging their graduate students and really training them through those assistantships. The graduate student's classroom is a wide one, and this corner of it needs our participation. Therefore, a recommendation: we should shift the meaning of assistantships from professorial relief to teaching. In fact, we should think about who should be assisting whom—because our students need our assistance more than the other way around.

In fact, this is less a question of assistance than of partnership. We need to recruit graduate students as partners as well as apprentices, for when we work with them as partners, we enrich their apprenticeships. "Departments in which classroom doors are open (metaphorically and otherwise)," say the authors of *The Formation of Scholars,* become sites for "a teaching commons," a community that we all benefit from belonging to.[35]

TEACHING CAREER CHOICES

It seems a simple notion that graduate courses should reflect the needs of the people who take them. Well, maybe that's not so simple—because it forces us to question those needs, including the assumption that all graduate students are professors-in-training.

That assumption was once so entrenched that one Ph.D.-carrying lawyer (who asked not to be identified) recalled that when she first decided to apply to law school more than thirty years ago, the director of her graduate program actually refused to write her a recommendation because he disapproved of her decision to leave academia. Although the director's stubbornness was ridiculous even at the time, the story is less laughable than it seems. Too many professors still view nonacademic professions as a distant second choice for graduate students, and they show it in all kinds of ways, from the furrow of the brow that might result when a student suggests a nonprofessorial job prospect to the department placement list that omits any detail of nonacademic employment of alumni. If we are to welcome Ph.D.'s to venture outside the academy, we have to prepare them for that possibility inside as well as outside our classrooms.

The good news is that professors have begun to face that possibility. One notable example is Anthony T. Grafton and Jim Grossman's "very modest proposal" in 2011 to reexamine graduate training from that perspective.[36] As the president and executive director of the American Historical Association, the two mounted history's official disciplinary pulpit to endorse a new way of looking at graduate education in the field.

"Many of these students," the authors write, "will not find tenure-track positions teaching history in colleges and universities"—and it's time to stop pretending otherwise. The job market "is what it is." We face no "transient 'crisis'" but rather "the situation that we have lived with for two generations." That's a refreshing assertion and an encouraging sign that the graduate-school-industrial complex is beginning to embrace not just the not-so-new economic reality—which has, after all, been apparent for a long time—but also what that reality means for the future of graduate programs.

"A Ph.D. in history opens a broad range of doors," write Grafton and Grossman, and graduate programs should prepare students for an "array of positions outside the academy." It's not the first time such ideas have hit the open air, but in this instance we need to consider who's airing them. This is an important statement for the official leaders of a discipline to make, and a necessary one.

Grafton and Grossman's statement generated plenty of response after it first appeared in *Perspectives on History*.[37] Most of the response centered on outcomes—that is, the implications of the fact that most Ph.D.'s won't become professors—and the authors' call to prepare historians for a range of employment.

But graduate students aren't the only ones in need of refashioning. Grafton and Grossman made a second, more ambitious exhortation that was mostly ignored at the time: history professors, they write, need to "examine the training we offer. . . . If we tell new students that a history Ph.D. opens many doors, we need to broaden the curriculum to ensure that we're telling the truth." Right now, Grafton and Grossman observe, graduate school in history is designed "to produce more professors." If graduate programs embrace the idea that they should aim to produce other kinds of historians as well, it follows that students' training must change.

And so we arrive at the graduate classroom. What should graduate teaching look like when it aims to prepare students for a range of careers? "We need different kinds of training ourselves," declares Leora Auslander, a history professor at the University of Chicago.[38] But that training is in short supply, because professors live inside the box that we want to teach outside of.

I'll take up the problem first from the individual faculty member's perspective and then on the curricular level (that is, from the point of view of departments and programs). As I said in the introduction to this book, the assumption that graduate students should become professors arose relatively recently, during the postwar expansion of higher education. Any movement away from those assumptions must begin with a concerted refashioning of what it means to be a professional intellectual—and how to teach someone else how to become one. It's seamless to teach someone who wants the life of her teacher when she grows up: you teach the skills and model the life, and voilà, the student has the tools and the expectations together. But that has never been sound graduate-teaching practice because graduate school professors' jobs aren't typical. It's harder for a professor to teach graduate students to prepare for a range of possible employment—but not much harder. After all, professors already do that routinely in their undergraduate liberal arts classrooms. Sociologists know that most of their undergraduate students aren't going to become sociologists, but they manage to design courses that will place the skills of a sociologist into the context of a larger education that leads students in myriad directions. Graduate teachers need to do just that.

There's a way that I'm arguing that graduate education should provide more of a liberal education than it does now. In this case, the rationale is practical before anything else: the new realities of graduate education in this country require new designs. In particular, how can we design graduate courses that aren't just for future professors and other academic researchers? We need to adjust our goals in the classroom to accommodate different kinds of students. There has been some auspicious movement in that direction in recent times. In 2014, for example, the Mellon Foundation funded a pilot initiative in four history departments to develop a curriculum explicitly designed to prepare graduate students for a range of possible careers.[39] The results of that project will surely be useful, but we can't wait for them. Programs and professors need to change their teaching ways right now.

A history professor, for example, might acknowledge the fact that many of her doctoral students will teach below the college level by devising different kinds of teaching exercises to accompany the historical scholarship she covers. That doesn't mean she should transform her seminar into an education course, but it does mean giving students ways to approach the material as apprentice teachers as well as apprentice scholars. To move students away from thinking about their possible futures in purely professorial terms, Auslander suggests that graduate seminar leaders "teach from unconventional stuff." She particularly stresses the need to get beyond books to other media, which she has been doing in her courses, but she also admits that teaching to a new set of goals involves things she "can't think about yet."

How to embrace those unknowns depends greatly on the discipline, of course, but here's one overarching pedagogical guideline: we need to promote more collaboration in graduate education. I've already mentioned the Stanford model of professors coteaching with their Ph.D. students, but it's also possible to collaborate within a more traditional setup. Consider the pedagogy envisioned by Edward Balleisen, a history professor at Duke University who has been thinking about these issues in practical terms. Balleisen aims to reconceive the boundaries defining discipline and authorship. He suggests that we "imagine interdisciplinary seminars around a given theme," in which history graduate students would work "with grad students from other disciplines, as well as professional students." Balleisen himself taught such an experimental seminar in 2012 with Jonathan Wiener, a Duke Law School professor, on "regulatory governance." The course, says Balleisen, had "readings from sociology, political science, economics, and cognitive psychology, as well as history and law."[40]

The very nature of that idea points to its applicability to other disciplines. Its value goes beyond cool-looking seminars to the cultivation of a wider professional ethos. Such courses allow graduate students to imagine their work outside the contexts of their own specialties. In fact, the central virtue of the whole approach lies in its endorsement of a move away from the sort of niche specialization that creates scholars whose work is far deeper than it is wide.

The work in such settings also challenges the idea of solitary authorship that prevails in the humanities and some of the social sciences. In particular, Balleisen encourages graduate students to collaborate on projects such as "a global history syllabus or a Web site of some kind, which would cultivate technical skills as well as historical analysis and innovative presentation, with some consideration of how to reach out to nonscholarly audiences."

Such ideas deserve traction because work outside academia requires certain kinds of collaboration that pure scholarship does not—and because such projects develop skills that transfer easily outside the university. Michael A. Elliott, an English professor at Emory University whose scholarly interests encompass public history, experimented with such techniques in a graduate course on "historical tourism" that he taught in 2007. Elliott departed from the traditional seminar-paper requirement and instead assigned collaborative projects to be performed by student groups on historical sites of their choosing. "I formed the groups from their stated interests," Elliott recalls, "and allowed them to come up with the format." The results were wide ranging: "One group produced a Web site on the World of Coke; another produced a curriculum for high-school teachers on using a historical cemetery as a teaching school; a third worked on an article together; another wrote a series of short papers that could have been a conference panel." These widely varying responses suggest some of the possibilities that can ensue when teachers give creative intellectuals the opportunity to think in new ways. "I enjoyed these projects much more than the usual batch of seminar papers," Elliott says, "and I think the students learned more about research and design that could be transported outside of the academy."[41]

Balleisen further suggests that departments create the option for graduate students to pursue an outside field that would orient them toward nonacademic careers. He notes that Duke's School of Public Policy has been considering a "policy history" track as an option not only for its own Ph.D. students but also for history Ph.D. students. "It would allow them to put together a cluster of courses, some unambiguously involving history, and others involving 'policy' methodologies from economics and other disciplines," says Balleisen, "possibly including some kind of internship experience with a policy institution." With these comments, Balleisen points from classroom to curriculum.

In practice, such ideas work best when they go from the top downward. That is, innovations in graduate education are best implemented when they're organized and supported by departments and programs—not just proposed by a clutch of academics talking at a conference. As many educators have pointed out, it's one thing to speak hopefully of such programs and quite another to actually create ones that work.

How, then, do you put together a program that will prepare graduate students for nonacademic careers? History will again serve as my case-study discipline. It's "ethical and practical" to prepare history Ph.D.'s for careers outside the academy, says Julian E. Zelizer, a professor of history and public affairs at Princeton University, "but it's not as easy as it sounds."[42]

Consider the possibility of training history graduate students to enter Zelizer's own field, public policy. First, it would be practical to equip them with a recognizable credential, such as a certificate that they could earn by taking a certain number of courses. It's likewise practical to steer those who are interested toward a public-policy-friendly dissertation topic. But "if we really want graduate students to do that," Zelizer says, "we'll need a different curriculum," because the study of public policy "is extraordinarily different from what you do to get a doctorate in history." Public-policy students, he notes, receive more quantitative training in both economics and statistics than history students do, which gives them the tools to do budgeting, among other skills.

If doctoral programs in history are to credibly prepare interested graduate students to work in public policy, Zelizer says, departments will have to blend their own requirements with those of a policy degree to establish a public-policy track within the Ph.D. program. That will either add some course-work or mean that some other courses may have to be eliminated. Graduate students in history who are considering public-policy jobs would need to make room for that possibility early on—concentrating in U.S. history, making time for that extra coursework, and doing a nonacademic internship. Internships are "really important," asserts Zelizer, "not just for experience but also to get a reputation so that students can break into the field."

For the graduate educators who would design such programs, those various needs point to two main structural guidelines:

- Professors need to identify specific employment goals for graduate students and work backward to structure a curriculum. That may seem obvious, but it's not what we usually do. In a world of esoteric graduate seminars, the student's foot is much more often forced to fit the professor's already-designed shoe.
- Faculty members would have to actively intervene in graduate students' training in order to equip them to pursue those career goals themselves. The intervention, Zelizer warns, "needs to be specific, targeted, and early." Again, that seems basic, but new graduate students frequently go for months without anything more than a few words of advice about which courses to take—and maybe not even that.

Putting new programs like these into effect will require a kind of enterprise that doesn't come naturally to academics. Moreover, professors' horizons are understandably bounded by the conventions of their own entry into the profession. Graduate students have different horizons, though, and their teachers need to learn more about them. If professors know that their graduate students may head toward public administration, government, or some similar nonacademic direction, for example, we can adjust our own teaching to embrace those possibilities.

That will mean more than thinking. Professors are great at thinking—that's how they got to be professors. I've seen a lot of grant money get spent by groups of people who first talk to each other about how to spend the money and then decide that the best thing to do with it is to stage a conference where they talk to each other some more. The problems facing academia—and graduate school, in particular—demand concrete plans for trial and testing. We need to think but also to do. "Instead of taking conundrums that we might chew our cud over," says classicist Peter T. Struck, we should "design tasks."[43]

"Design" is the keyword to turn ideas into policy. "Great design," said Zachary First, the managing director of the Drucker Institute, "is feasible (can it work?), viable (can it spread?), and desirable (do people want it?)."[44]

Sometimes it's the students themselves who design the way. A new public-humanities initiative at Yale University originated in the American studies department through the parallel efforts of students and faculty members. The "public humanities" are just that: scholarship and teaching that go on outside university walls. For historians, the discipline usually points toward museums and historical sites. Public history—long viewed as a way to make money off master's students—has had an unfortunate reputation as a low-rent alternative to academic history.[45] But that's changing.

A number of universities have been teaching public history, usually at the master's level, for a while now. The Yale initiative is notable not because it invents public history but rather because it shows what can happen when professors respond to students' concerns and adjust their pedagogy accordingly.[46]

Lauren Tilton, a doctoral student in American studies and founding co-chair of Yale's student working group in the public humanities, describes herself as "passionate about bridging the gap between the ivory tower and the public at large." She recalls that the Yale student initiative arose a few years ago out of a collective desire for a "sustained dialogue about the public humanities" and that the group "started reading in all directions."[47]

Matthew Jacobson, a professor of history and chair of American studies at the time, agreed to direct the students' efforts. With Laura Wexler, another professor of American studies, he helped put together a certificate program in public humanities, a four-course sequence that is open to students from all departments and that can be completed as part of their M.A. coursework. Jacobson, who has taught in the sequence, reports that the students brought "amazing skills" that they don't get to use enough in traditional seminar paper writing.[48] Indeed, says Wexler, "the crux of the program" is to get both graduate students and faculty outside academia. "Students have to invent their own jobs" for themselves, which they have proved most adept at doing.[49]

Meanwhile, some Yale historians have been involved in a similar project. David Blight, a professor of history and director of Yale's Gilder Lehrman Center for the Study of Slavery, Resistance, and Abolition, says, "Historians have to get out and reach the broader public," which he describes as "the ultimate audience."[50] Dana Schaffer, former assistant director of the center, believed that students were clamoring for more experience in this realm.[51] Responding to public need and student demand, the Gilder Lehrman Center held a summer institute in 2012 that brought graduate students and museum professionals together for a week of lectures and team workshops—and, not incidentally, networking—followed by a year of collaboration. Financed by Yale and the Smithsonian's new National Museum of African American History and Culture, the institute cost less than a tenured professor's salary for one year (and I'm not talking about a Yale professor's salary, either).

These parallel Yale programs braid a lot of threads together. They identify a need for accomplished public historians. They create cost-efficient educational frameworks within which to educate graduate students about public history. And if the students show interest, the programs provide possible entry into the field. It's one thing to take some extra courses, cautions Princeton's Zelizer, and another to have those courses add up to recognizable qualifications for a specific kind of job. "We need to do this well so that it will mean something," he says. Professors in other fields can, and should, carve out their own versions of the path that history is trying to blast here. The approaches will naturally differ from discipline to discipline. But one thing is certain across the disciplines: in the words of Auslander, "If we continue to behave like ostriches, we're dead." Forget the idea that "it will be better tomorrow," she says. If there is to be change for the better, professors must be "willing to be influenced." That influence should connect professors to other professors, and to their students. We need to connect the way we teach to what graduate students will actually be doing with their degrees. Teaching, after all, is another of the collaborative arts. Graduate teachers have to start thinking together.

CHAPTER THREE

The Comprehensive Exam: Capstone or Cornerstone?

I HAD A math teacher in high school who could be fairly described as abusive. He would cut weak students out of the herd and verbally eviscerate them, as if public excoriation could somehow impart knowledge of the subject. I hated that teacher and still do, but now I wonder about him, too. If he actually cared about teaching math (and I believe that he did), what purpose could he have seen in his own pedagogy? He had to believe that fear was the greatest motivator.

With that dark thought in mind, let me turn to Ph.D. comprehensive exams. Everyone who has ever taken comps recalls something about the experience—the exams are a fertile source of graduate school war stories, not least because they inspire so much fear. Is that fear purposeful? Perhaps. Initiation rituals are often painful, but they suggest a certain utility that comes with showing oneself and others that one may leap a flaming hurdle without actually dying. But we may overdo it in the case of these exams. It's unreasonable to expect that we can fully free graduate students of professional anxiety, but we can deaden it more than we do. The tests we make them take are focused too much on theatrical torture and not enough on professional purpose.

So if the exams are not simply to instill fear, then what is their purpose? And how do they meet their goals? Let's look at what we're doing and ask why we're doing it. To begin with, let's consider the names given to these tests. "Comprehensive exam" is a content-based handle that suggests full knowledge of a field of study. "General exam" (also in use) is similar. The other usual name for the ritual is "qualifying exam," a term that connotes reaching a set goal by performing to expectations.[1] The lack of a clear title may suggest the lack of a clear purpose. In any case, I use all of these names in what follows because I'm concerned with all of these connotations.

These exams seem as old as graduate school itself, so that tampering with them might appear the equivalent of rewriting the sacred scrolls. But qualifying exams in the United States date back only to the late 1930s. They were instituted toward the end of a generation of steady growth in graduate education, when graduate school began to take on its familiar modern contours. The exams proliferated when student populations grew too large after World War II to manage by dissertation alone.[2] Fueled by Sputnik-related research spending, the number of Ph.D. students tripled in the United States during the 1960s. With demand for professors also at an all-time high during this brief but memorable halcyon time, dissertations were being mass-produced by teeming masses of graduate students rather than handcrafted through close adviser-student supervision. (The history department at the University of Wisconsin, for example, admitted over two hundred graduate students each year during the early 1960s. Imagine!) At the same time and for the same reasons, the dissertation defense became more of a formality, creating a need for so-called barrier exams beforehand.

The Ph.D. comprehensive exams form the barrier that separates graduate coursework from the dissertation stage. The root purpose of the exams is to determine whether a student should be permitted to "advance to candidacy," or "qualify" to go on. Whatever it's called, success certifies the student to go on and write a doctoral thesis. That basic fact is worth keeping in mind as we look at what the exam means and the purpose it serves.

A recent study of time to degree in U.S. graduate programs found that only half of all attrition from humanities graduate programs takes place in the first few years. In most math and science fields, the students who leave are usually gone by year three. It's a different story in the humanities, where half of all noncompleters depart over the following *seven* years.[3]

That is, advanced students who are hopelessly tangled in their dissertations turn out to be *less* likely to withdraw from graduate school than their unsnarled colleagues at the beginning of their studies. It's not hard to infer why: lots of people throw good money after bad. In this case, that cliché is literally true—noncompleters tend to carry heavy loan debt.[4] Yet they feel too committed to walk away. (I'll have more to say about these "stuck" students in Chapter 5.)

Ph.D. programs need to use the qualifying exams to try to preempt that unpleasant possibility of long-term noncompletion. Bureaucratically speaking, the comprehensive-exam stage represents the last procedural chance to dismiss a graduate student whose competence is in doubt. That's one reason it's called a "qualifier." I've seen lots of professors (including, regrettably, myself) give a weak candidate a break on the comps, only to see that candidate struggle horribly afterward. Mercy does no favors in these cases. To pass a weak student is essentially to deceive him or her—because, as any parent can tell you, the action (awarding the passing grade) matters more than the words ("We were going to fail you, but we gave you a break so you could shape up").

Easing weak students through a graduate program that makes its most onerous demands during its end stages (dissertation and job search) is a kind of torture. If weak candidates do finish somehow—and they are often borne to the finish line leaning heavily on the shoulders of committee members—they usually take a long time and invariably arrive underprepared to seek the jobs they want. Such endgames are a mortifying spectacle, and they don't serve the students.

It follows that professors should use the comps for what they were designed for: to identify students who are best suited for dissertation work along with those who are not. Those who can thrive should go on. Those who cannot, should not.

But what's the best way to identify good dissertators? Subjecting them to an oral inquisition under immensely stressful conditions, an exam that covers everything they've ever learned in the field, has little to do with the act of dissertation writing. It's like having to clear a high jump in order to qualify for a marathon. Given the scope and importance of the comprehensive exam, it should bear a concrete relation to the dissertation and the work—

that is, the research methods and practices—that will be required to complete it.

In sum, the qualifying exam lacks pedagogical imagination. Centering it on a long-prepared recitation fails to bring students into what was once a reservoir of understood common knowledge. This practice limits what students can learn from the experience. Writing teachers spend a lot of time teaching their students something that all writers know, namely, that writing is thinking, not simply a record of what has already been thought. Similarly, an exam is a kind of teaching, not just a way for a student to demonstrate what has been taught—and right now most comprehensive exams in the humanities don't teach very well.

Most Ph.D. programs in the humanities don't even try to exploit the teaching potential of the comprehensive exam. In particular, the "tell me what you know" model runs contrary to the principle of "backward design" that I introduced in Chapter 2, in which teachers start by identifying their goals and then design teaching and learning tasks to meet them. Two educators who advocate this approach, Grant Wiggins and Jay McTighe, cite the "twin sins" of "activity-focused teaching" and "coverage-focused teaching."[5] The former refers to tasks without a clear learning objective, while the latter (which I discussed in Chapter 2) centers on "covering" material without actually checking to see if it has been learned. These sins apply readily to different forms of classroom teaching, of course, but they also apply to comprehensive exams—because testing is a form of teaching.

Dissertations require research and synthesis in the service of something new. How does the ritual torture of an oral exam (or a grueling sit-down written test) serve that goal? The fact-based, "tell me what you know" exam encourages neither experimentation nor synthesis. The authors of *How People Learn* caution teachers against creating an environment that tacitly says "don't get caught not knowing something."[6] Instead, they exhort teachers to encourage risk-taking, for only by making mistakes can students learn to apply what they know. Qualifying exams send the "don't get caught not knowing" message in an unqualified way. They encourage the very conservative and defensive approaches to scholarship that vex dissertation directors later on. Put simply, I am suggesting that the bad design of the comprehensive exam does something worse than spend students' time poorly (though that is bad enough). The habits of thought encouraged by these old-fashioned exams actually make it harder for students to write good and timely dissertations. So the problems with general exams ramify outward; they're about more than just the exam itself. You might say that the problems are comprehensive.

Such disjunction between process and goal unfortunately proliferates in higher education, where captivity in disciplinary silos leads college professors to "teach the way they were taught." That means that most professors are rarely schooled in how students learn. As a result, say Halpern and Hakel, "it would be difficult to design an educational model that is more at odds with the findings of current research about human cognition than the one being used today at most colleges and universities."[7]

The main problem, according to sociologist David Jaffee, is instrumentalism: professors demand that students learn to meet narrowly construed goals (like big exams), not to retain the material for future use. As I noted in Chapter 2, "retention and transfer" is the gospel preached by education researchers, meaning that students should be taught tools that they can use outside the immediate context (the course, the exam) in which they learn them. Halpern and Hakel complain that professors claim to be interested in this goal, yet they teach "as though the underlying rationale for education were to improve student performance *in school*" only.[8]

I don't mean to suggest that the traditional general exam can have no purpose. I read plenty of interesting books in the months preceding my orals, but I was already doing that. My orals didn't require me to develop or demonstrate any sort of competency that might have helped me with the dissertation to follow. Nor did the exam permit me to show much more than evidence of my wide reading, coupled with a certain verbal agility under pressure. Moreover, two hours of conversation proved a real letdown after six months of study. I shook hands with the members of my committee and thought, "Is that all?" I was left feeling that I needed to get away, to purge myself of an unpleasant stage of graduate school in order to start the final one, so I decided to go traveling for a year.

English professors Cary Nelson and Stephen Watt ask what such exams accomplish that the courses do not.[9] Or as one present graduate student (who has not yet taken his comps and asked not to be identified) put it, "If I'm doing all this work, how could it become a chance for me to learn (not just memorize) something, try out a new idea, become hireable, distinguish myself? How can this be useful for *my* purposes?"

Most qualifying exams are not very useful for anyone's purposes. Education scholars John H. Williams and William J. Berg argue that the tests are "formless monstrosities set up by departments merely as barriers to the degree in question" that do nothing to further the student's education. They also suggest that the exams distract students from their research focus.[10] This all sounds very familiar, but it was written in *1971*. Not much has changed in more than two generations.

The distinction between teacher- and student-centered learning offers another way to look at this problem. Exams involve an exchange between professors and students. Each needs to gain something from that exchange. Right now, neither gets enough. The professors, as I've said, need to use the exams to identify likely noncompleters of the program—but judging by the high attrition rates of advanced humanities graduate students, they aren't succeeding. But graduate students have needs too, and an exam as time-consuming, significant, and, well, comprehensive as this one should identify and meet the students' needs too. So what's in it for them? Let there be a barrier, but it should have pedagogical purpose too. That, in essence, is the problem.

Solutions are already out there. Comprehensive exams in some nonhumanities fields already meet students' needs well. Many biology programs, for example, require students to defend a research proposal of their own authorship before a committee of faculty members. The purpose of such an exercise, declares the website of the University of Tennessee's biology department, is to "simulate, as much as possible, the professional demands that a scientist will face while pursuing a research career."[11] Daniel Simons, a psychology professor at the University of Illinois at Urbana-Champaign, makes a similar point about exam practice in his own discipline when he says, "We don't want students to stop and just read. They should read as they research."[12]

One very important difference between the exams in the sciences and the humanities is that qualifying exams in the sciences emphasize professionalism—that is, they test the skills that scientists use in their jobs—but those in the humanities mostly don't. By this I mean that scientists test their students in ways that allow them to develop the skills of professional scientists, and the certification of those skills later allows them to enter their scientific disciplinary communities. That's a model that humanists need to adopt.

Approaches to the comps in the social sciences and humanities vary widely, but old-fashioned written and oral exams still abound. Those exams look almost entirely backward. Their underlying commandment is, "Tell me what you know." It helps to know things, certainly. It's hard to succeed as a humanist without having read a lot. But professional humanists need to do more than read. As I stressed in Chapter 2, they must eventually apply their knowledge to their teaching and research. Just as we too often teach seminars without thinking about the students' takeaway, so do we insist that students learn content for their exams without asking them to apply it. In this way, humanities programs act unprofessionally—because they don't develop the capacity of their students to enter their professional communities.

Moreover, the changes in the humanities during the past two generations, particularly in the area of opened and dynamically shifting canons, have made it harder for humanists to agree on what foundational knowledge is. Reasonable people disagree about what graduate students should know, and that disagreement is reflected in real, substantial variation in the structure and content of exams within the same discipline. With little uniformity to the qualifying exams in humanities fields, it's hard to generalize about comprehensive exams in ways that are useful to students. This unusual level of variation underscores the uncertainty about what these exams are meant to be and do.[13]

I've spent a lot of time explaining why most comprehensive exams in the humanities don't make any sense, how they've outlived their original purpose and today serve neither teacher nor student. The reader might fairly conclude that I'm calling for the comps to be done away with. Not so. But I am advocating a wholesale reform. Let's look at the keyword "exam." There are many ways to examine, not just with traditional tests.

Instead of structuring examinations in ways that encourage students to cram (and what is preparation for a traditional comprehensive exam if not one long cram?), professors would be better off designing tasks that would allow students "to use the repertoire of disciplinary tools—be they theories, concepts, or principles—to analyze and solve a realistic problem that they might face as practitioners in the field." Educators call this "authentic assessment."[14]

A collaborative approach to the comprehensive exam may help us to reconceive its purpose and orient it toward this kind of authenticity. If the exam is to be truly useful, it needs to meet the needs of the examiner and the examinee together—so why should they not talk together about how to structure it? Education scholars Robert E. Bargar and Jane Mayo-Chamberlain argued a generation ago that graduate education works better if it's seen as a developmental process—and the general exams stand as a key stage in that development. "It is crucial," they write, "that a student and committee arrive at a *mutually shared* perception" of what the exam—*"their* exam"—should look like.[15] If both parties explore their needs and goals for the exam together, the "qualifier" may turn into an actual learning experience. Thirty years later, a small number of doctoral departments in the humanities are finally beginning to pursue that goal—but not enough of them.

Central to this teacher-student collaboration is the question of where the general exam should fall on the continuum from capstone to cornerstone. Does it come at the end of coursework as a testament to a student's general knowledge? (This would be the capstone.) Or should it signify the beginning of the dissertation phase as an indication of the student's ability to move from general knowledge to specific topic? (That's the cornerstone approach.) We have too long employed the capstone model. It's time to move toward the cornerstone.

Comps need to look forward as well as backward. Some humanities departments have devised exams that do just that, and they should be models for the rest of us. The University of Maryland's department of American studies, for example, has a comprehensive exam that includes an "interdisciplinary synthesis paper" based on the student's own research, and it's explicitly designed as a segue to the formal dissertation proposal. The English department at the University of West Virginia administers an exam drawn from a reading list based on the student's dissertation topic, with works selected by the student in consultation with faculty members. Written and oral exams built from that list direct students toward the questions that their dissertations will later raise.

Those are good examples of what can be done, but it's possible to go even further. Comprehensive exams take a long time to prepare for, after all, and may add significantly to a student's time to degree. In the humanities, it now takes about nine years to earn the Ph.D. One way that we might save students time (and money) is to streamline the admission to candidacy.

Accordingly, some departments have adopted portfolio-based systems that unfold in a series of stages rather than building to one anxiety-filled, watershed moment.[16] The American studies department at Saint Louis University, for example, administers a written exam early on, but assessment of a student's candidacy rests more fundamentally on a research paper ("worked up into publishable form," adds Matthew Mancini, chair of the department), followed by a literature review of three fields that the student chooses with a dissertation topic in mind. The system is "forward-looking" as well as developmental, says Mancini, and "rigorous without being inhuman."[17]

A number of programs have incorporated preliminary dissertation work right into the examination. The English department at Indiana University has incorporated a semester-long workshop for dissertation prospectus development into its comprehensive-exam design; early data suggest that this combination is reducing time to degree by about eight months. The English and film studies department at the University of Alberta similarly centers the qualifying exam on the dissertation proposal, as part of a newly streamlined curriculum that has students advancing to the all-but-dissertation stage by May of their second year. The Division of Spanish and Portuguese Studies at the University of Washington still has the old oral, but it's only one of three exam components. The others are an annotated bibliography and a dissertation prospectus. The exam at the English department at the University of Pittsburgh is a "Ph.D. project" in the form of two thirty-page papers—not quite a thesis prospectus but instead a homing in and honing down that typically leads right to one.[18] The history department at Duke University also moved a few years ago from what a former graduate director, John Thompson, calls "the big, scary exam sometime in the distant future" to a similarly phased model. It moves students along faster, he notes, and avoids "postprelim depression"—another contributor to lengthened time to degree.[19]

So who needs big, scary exams, anyway?

When we examine prospective dissertators, we are looking for a certain kind of fitness for the task ahead. The comprehensive examination is a rite of passage, but that doesn't mean it should scare the hell out of everyone who takes it; nor should it add unnecessary time to an already long passage to the Ph.D. We need less hazing and more learning.

Comps need to make sense. Let's examine our graduate students, by all means, but let's also examine what we do ourselves.

CHAPTER FOUR

Advising

UNIVERSITIES HAVE A LOT of names for the professor who works with a graduate student on a thesis or dissertation and later signs off on it. The main titles are adviser, director, and, more rarely, sponsor. Some universities, including my own, call a professor in this position a mentor, a term whose general use I dislike. (I'll explain why later on.) I like "adviser" because I think that's the best description of the job when it's being done well.

These terms are sometimes used interchangeably, but their connotations launch their meanings in wildly diverse directions. Whatever you call the relation, it's the longest and most important one in a graduate student's formal education, a unique blend of the professional and the personal. It's a relationship with consequences.[1] When it's forged and maintained the right way, it turns into a lifelong, productive, evolving relationship of mutually rewarding collegiality that often levels off into a friendship between peers. When badly handled, the connection can breed anger, resentment, bitterness, and an unfulfillment that extends far beyond graduate school itself. The tie binds like family, and genealogical metaphors for it abound.[2] Family relations aside, though, it's still a connection between a worker and a boss.[3]

What, then, do we call the professorial member of this meaning-laden partnership? The nineteenth-century term was "master," with all of the connotations that the word carried. The student would enter the master's orbit through the seminar, drawn by the gravitational pull of what was later called "charisma." The idea of the guiding master originated in Germany, but in the United States, the relation quickly translated into an "intensely personal," almost cultish, tie of admiring loyalty. So powerful was this tie that it was once proposed that one's Ph.D. carry the name of one's master rather than the university the student attended.[4]

All of this may seem extravagant and excessive to us today, but it's really not all that different from the situation that prevails now. Today's "masters" still attract students through charisma, and their recommendations still exert major control over the fate of those students who enter the academic job market. Minus the affectations, not much has changed—and that ought to make us nervous.

For that reason, I prefer the title of "adviser." I like it much better than "director" in particular, because it's less authoritative. Graduate students need to write their own dissertations. Professors have a job to help them. Certainly that help will entail some guidance, and some of that guidance may reasonably be described as "direction." But the fact that I offer direction doesn't make me the director. The director of a movie runs the whole set. Dissertation advisers shouldn't try to do that; it's not their project.

"You are the CEO of your own graduate education," I tell my advisees. I like this phrase because it conveys managerial duty and places responsibility where it belongs. Graduate school is professional school, and college graduates are not babies. It's a graduate student's job to complete the requirements for the degree.

But it's not quite as simple as that. My task may be to give advice, but my approval is required for the thesis to pass and the degree to be awarded. It's the graduate student's dissertation, but the imprimatur belongs to me, so perhaps the process belongs to both of us. To return to the direction metaphor, perhaps it's more precise to say that the graduate student is the director of the project, but everyone involved does well to remember that directors don't always have the final cut.

Graduate students do have the final cut on their own lives, however. They choose their goals, and they commit their own resources to pursue them. Within that context, the adviser should make sure that the goals are rational and the plans to reach them sensible. And there's the rub. Based simply on the numbers, chasing a professorship in the humanities (or the social sciences, or the sciences) is not exactly practical. Is it rational? That depends on how sensible the planned pursuit turns out to be.

It's vital for professors to prepare students for the jobs that they can actually get. That includes professorships, but can't be limited to them. To pursue a professorship at the expense of all other options can hardly be called rational. Thus arises the first problem of advisement: how can professors prepare students to seek jobs that they don't hold themselves and therefore don't know much about? That problem is not as unfamiliar as it may seem (we face it all the time with undergraduates who have no interest in becoming professors, and no one complains), but it does require thoughtful and practical solutions.

But the need to prepare graduate students for a range of jobs raises a related problem that is perhaps more vexing. Call it "the role model problem." The case of Rebecca Schuman, Ph.D., exemplifies it. Schuman graduated from college in 1998 and worked for seven years afterward, in media and as an editor. But her work didn't satisfy her; she "couldn't relate to conversations" at her job with the same pleasure that she brought to her reading of German literature. She therefore decided to enter a Ph.D. program in German. Why would she make such a choice in light of the terrible job prospects? As she tells it, her decision resulted from a combination of self-awareness and self-suggestion. She inoculated herself against the woeful academic job market, she believed, by telling herself that she "would complete the doctorate purely for my own edification."[5]

The vaccine didn't take. Schuman completed her degree in an expeditious five years (almost twice as fast as the national average in the humanities), but by the time she graduated, her defenses had somehow been overwhelmed: she wanted a professor's job badly. She did all the right things to get one, too. She got a prestigious postdoctoral fellowship at a major university and revised her dissertation into a book manuscript that was accepted by a well-respected university press. But in four years on the market, a tenure-track offer never came.

Schuman's lack of success not surprisingly frustrated her. She left academia—a rational response, certainly—with understandable regret and bitterness. Her exit was more inflamed than most. It left a wide wake, largely due to a much-publicized 2013 sign-off called "Thesis Hatement," in which

Schuman advises would-be applicants to graduate school to save themselves the disappointment and simply not apply in the first place. "Don't do it," she writes. "Just don't." Her article is perhaps the angriest entry in the "don't go to graduate school" genre that has emerged in the past generation. In just a few months after its publication in *Slate,* Schuman's furious protest received nearly two thousand reader comments.[6]

Some of the attention Schuman has received surely results from her spectacle of professional self-immolation in the public square. However, I'm more interested in her self-analysis, which she elaborated in another article published in the *Chronicle of Higher Education* a few weeks later. Here Schuman explained how she turned from a young scholar determined not to be seduced by a terrible academic job market into a postdoc whose job-market forays led to "four years of anguish intense enough to induce a fugue state." What, she asked, made her so single-mindedly chase an improbable goal that she knew all along was exceedingly difficult to attain?

Her answer is that she was the victim of a cult. Inspired by a formulation by William Pannapacker, Schuman describes academia as "cultlike," right down to its procedures of indoctrination and reeducation.[7] "First," she says, the tenured cult leaders "isolate graduate students" within the university walls, and then they break them down with exams and dissertation rituals. Once their charges have become malleable, the faculty cult leaders "fill their heads with dreams of R1 glory." ("R1" is shorthand for "Research 1," a reference to the Carnegie Foundation's longtime university classification system. The R1 category contains the largest and best-funded universities, which typically boast the most extensive graduate programs. The foundation has since moved on to a different taxonomical system, but the old one still endures in common usage.) Once inculcated with R1 ambitions, says Schuman, graduate students "do what we've learned," which is publish, go to conferences, and "expect a job." After those expectations get dashed, the inductees then "just hope" that a job will somehow come their way—and they hang on that way for years. When Schuman writes of such outcomes today, and of those who wait hopefully as she did, her anger mixes with her pain into a volatile and acidic rhetorical potion that incinerates more than it enlightens.[8]

Schuman's description of herself as a cultist is hyperbolic, of course, but it conveys an important truth. Graduate school professors possess considerable power to change minds—and lives. Moreover, *they exert that power constantly*—it can't be turned off. Role models are role models all the time, not just when they're walking the classroom runway before their public. And the role that graduate school teachers model first of all is "professor at a research university." That's how graduate students see their advisers first of all, and that's the role that they measure for themselves. In other words, if you leave graduate students alone, the chances are good that they will decide that they want to become professors at research universities.

We might say that graduate students have a default career-goal setting. It's a switch that moves a little bit at a time while they stay in graduate school, gradually moving toward desire for the kinds of jobs that their advisers have. Left untouched, that switch will slowly reach the professor-or-bust position. Not many people can reach their own switch to adjust it, but graduate advisers can affect its setting. When they don't take advantage of their reach, advisers in effect teach graduate students to want the kinds of jobs that most of them won't ever get. Thus do we socialize them in a way that disadvantages them in the larger professional world that they will one day enter. Schuman's adviser is conspicuously absent from her personal account, and that's a telling lacuna. She indicts the whole graduate school establishment, but she doesn't mention any conversations with her adviser that might have helped her shape her goals so that her job search might have been less painful.

Professors—and especially advisers—need to help graduate students see graduate school as an incubator (not a crucible) for a variety of goals. How to help students gain skills and realize their own options at the same time is not just a form of teaching. It is perhaps the most important teaching that takes place in graduate school. To teach effectively in this way, graduate professors need to understand the power of the student-adviser relation and then use it.

With that in mind, I'd like to look at the student-adviser connection from the ground up, eventually arriving at how it may be used to expand graduate students' understanding of their work and career choices.

THE STUDENT-ADVISER RELATION: BASICS AND GROUND RULES

Years ago, as part of a teacher-training workshop, I was asked to recall the most memorable comment I had ever received from a teacher. A trenchant criticism immediately came to mind: in my junior year of college, a teaching assistant in a course on twentieth-century British literature wrote in the margin of my paper on T. S. Eliot, "You retail clichés that you've bought at wholesale, but why should your reader have to pay more for them than you did?" That comment stung, but it jolted me out of smug writerly complacency—and it goads me still, more than thirty years later.

Most other participants in the workshop also remembered negative comments from their teachers. Only a few recalled positive remarks. Well-aimed criticism can stick like a burr, and for that reason alone, it has great power to teach. Nevertheless, as teachers, we learn early that we can't rely on the negative alone. There's a reason that "Look for something positive to say" has become an old saw in learning how to grade papers. It's entrenched wisdom because it's entirely correct. Well-placed compliments provide the proverbial spoonful of sugar.

Graduate students, too, need that sugar—they have a bigger sweet tooth than undergraduates in some ways. I once gave one of my dissertation chapters to a visiting professor I had become friendly with, and he returned it with margins overflowing with criticism. My first impulse was to put the manuscript aside, far aside, where I would never see it again. I knew I had to read it, though, so I did. It took all of my patience to get through his comments. That professor remains a friend, and when I asked him years later why he hadn't leavened his criticism with any praise, he was surprised. "I thought you understood that I liked it," he said, pointing to his thorough engagement with my ideas. I did understand—intellectually, at least—that his attention was itself a compliment, but I still couldn't bear to return to his comments to read them a second time. They needed balance.

That need for balance extends to the relationship between advisers and their graduate students, but it's not always easy to find. In master's programs, and especially at the doctoral level, graduate students depend on their advisers more than anyone else in their careers. Students do more work for their adviser's eyes than for anyone else's, and the adviser's approval is usually the key to the door that leads to the next place, whether full-time employment or more school.

For those reasons and many others, graduate students spend a lot of time watching and thinking about their advisers. They may not sit down with their teachers all that often, but we're on their minds. Graduate students gossip about their advisers. They read their advisers' writing and may even be inspired by it. And they follow their advisers' moves. I know a professor who quotes from books during his lectures with the same flourish employed by his adviser, who had borrowed it from his adviser, who may have borrowed it from his.

So an adviser's criticism of a graduate student's work can pierce deeper than the tiny hooks on a burr. Criticism from someone so important can wound, and it can impair a student's progress. And the adviser may not know it.

I'm not saying advisers shouldn't criticize students. How can they get better if we don't criticize them? If you're the CEO of your career, you shouldn't let criticism derail you, either—criticism is part of adult life. "Don't be judgmental" has turned into a popular axiom, but the phrase irks me whenever I hear it. How can anyone navigate the world without making judgments? Professors especially can't. As members of a culture of evaluation, professors make judgments for a living (not only of student writing and speaking but also of book and article manuscripts, tenure and promotion files, grant proposals, and on and on).

To be clear, I'm not suggesting that we coddle our students. But we should be aware of when we mean to criticize. Advisers may make certain comments that hurt, but it's impossible to know which comments will hurt which students (and perhaps hold them back)—until we get to know them. What's the best way to do that? One of the few investigations into this subject, by Robert R. Bargar and Jane Mayo-Chamberlain, emphasizes the "developmental" nature of the adviser-student relation—meaning that it's a connection that evolves over its duration. The students themselves develop, of course, as they move through a graduate program, and the adviser needs to adjust to the needs of their different stages. Advisers and advisees need to maintain open lines of communication, not only about the work that they are doing together but also about any potential emotional pitfalls that may attend that work. It's better to defuse an explosion than to deal with the fallout afterward.

Advisers, say Bargar and Mayo-Chamberlain, should create a "positive environment" for students by "showing interest" in their "work and welfare." The authors suggest "open discussions" and "direct programmatic activities."[9] All of which sounds very blurry. Instead, a good, concrete example comes from outside the university. A 2012 article in *Sports Illustrated* described the relationship between Tony Parker, the star point guard for the San Antonio Spurs basketball team, and his coach, Gregg Popovich. The coach ripped into Parker relentlessly when he joined the team, yet a few years ago, Parker signed a long-term contract extension to keep him on the receiving end of his coach's criticisms for years afterward.

Popovich's teaching presumably makes Parker a better player, but what allows the coach to ride his player so hard? Modern professional basketball is filled with stories of star players who flex their box-office muscle and get their coaches fired by threatening some version of "him or me." The Spurs' coach long ago sought and found his balance with Parker. Breaking bread lies at the center of their relationship. Coach and player share fifteen to twenty dinners a season. "You can't get on a player and ignore him until the next time he plays a game," said Popovich, "or all of a sudden he's chattel."[10] Popovich and Parker may have become friends after more than a decade together, but that's not the point. Each understands that their personal time together strengthens their shared professional goals.

Graduate students work for themselves and not a coach, but the sports analogy is useful nevertheless. It was with Popovich's teaching in mind that I instituted a rotating lunch schedule with my own dissertation students. I now try to eat lunch with one of them each week when school is in session. The agenda depends on the student. Work naturally figures in the conversation. With one student, we might talk about a chapter in progress. With another, the subject might be a larger discussion of potential career paths. But we also talk about lots of topics that have nothing to do with school: travel, books, children, politics (though here I'm especially careful), or sports. I've learned, though, that what we talk about is not the most important thing. What matters is that we spend time together as people rather than as academics. We already spend a lot of time relating professionally, in what amounts to an exchange economy (in which they provide scholarship and I give them credit). The lunches broaden our shared foundation.

Because the adviser-student relationship inextricably combines the professional and the personal, I'm finally suggesting that graduate students will be better scholars or scientists if their advisers sit down with them now and then and simply say, "How's it going?" or "What's up with you?" If we do that, then there's much less chance that our criticism will come flying around a corner like a grenade. It will have less chance to wound—because it won't feel impersonal—and much more chance to correct and motivate instead. By treating my graduate students as people and letting them see me as a person, I try to balance my professional demands of them. By paying attention to their personal side, I can best cultivate their professional work.

But there's a caveat to all of this: I have to be careful not to get too close. I've focused for the past few pages on what an adviser should do, but what an adviser should *not* do deserves attention too.

Elizabeth Leake, a professor of Italian literature at Columbia University who advises many Ph.D. students, told me once that doctors of philosophy should borrow an idea from the other kind of doctor: first, do no harm.[11] Borrowing from the Hippocratic Oath makes sense because doctoral advisers have the capacity to do plenty of harm. The ties between graduate students and advisers are both professional and personal and therefore uniquely strong—and tense. So advisers need to cultivate graduate students as professionals, but they need to maintain their distance from them at the same time.

Part of what I mean is obvious. Advisers shouldn't make their students into flunkies, for example. That ought to go without saying, but I've known graduate students who have picked up their adviser's dry cleaning. That kind of intentional exploitation disgraces the whole profession, but it's also possible to take advantage of graduate students inadvertently. We may think it's a gift to offer an impoverished advisee a chance to earn some money doing research for our latest articles or books, but remember that students may assume that they refuse at their own risk. Of course graduate students should be invited to collaborate on projects that might advance their training or careers, but an adviser has to be careful to offer them graceful ways to say no.

Advisers need to treat graduate students as people without getting overly personal. Why the caution? Because graduate students are already so close to their professors, closer than the teachers sometimes realize. They think about their advisers, and they care about what their advisers think in ways that can be hard to believe. One professor told me that when she was a graduate student, she once ran into her adviser at a supermarket. He made an offhand remark about what was in her shopping cart. She turned that remark over and over in her mind for months and remembered it vividly more than two decades later. Most graduate students will become as well versed in their adviser's personal life as the adviser allows—and when the adviser needs to criticize students' work, too much personal involvement can swiftly complicate the transaction. All of that was true before the well-marked minefield of social media. Such interactions are much easier now, but just as cautionary.

Don't brag about your job—that's another obvious one. But here's one that's perhaps less obvious: never complain about your job in front of graduate students, either. It's in the poorest of poor taste to do so. Most of our students aspire to jobs like ours, so our complaints disrespect their goals. They also make us look spoiled and unappreciative of what we have, regardless of the righteousness of whatever we might want to grumble about. (Complaining about money is especially bad behavior. Yes, many professors are poorly paid, especially in the humanities. But most graduate students live below the poverty line.)

Here's the overarching point: many adviser-student relationships—especially those centered on a dissertation—involve a transference. As Freud outlined in his writings on therapeutic technique, transference involves the projection by the patient onto the analyst of "some important figure out of his childhood or past," so that the thoughts and feelings of the earlier relationship (perhaps with a parent) affect and inform the interactions with the therapist in the present.[12]

I don't mean to suggest that teaching graduate students is like psychoanalysis. It isn't. (If students need therapy, it's our job to refer them to counseling.) But I am suggesting that the long-lasting hybrid relation between graduate student and adviser—professional and personal at the same time—invites the kind of projection that characterizes transference. Many Ph.D. advisers think of their dissertators as their intellectual children, so why shouldn't Ph.D. students experience some filial feelings toward their advisers? It's no coincidence that the German word for adviser is *doktorvater,* or "doctor-father."[13] When I learned some years ago of the death of the last of my two graduate school advisers, a man I'd not been in contact with for some years, I immediately thought of myself as an academic orphan.

With transference comes countertransference—that is, the identification of the therapist with the patient—or, in this case, the teacher with the student. It's a basic tenet of psychotherapy that the therapist needs to manage the countertransference. The task can be difficult. There's an interesting example of that in the 2010 movie *The King's Speech*, one of the best teaching movies to come out in a long time.[14] The story, based in fact, centers on the efforts of

King George VI of England to conquer his stammer with the help of a speech therapist, Lionel Logue. When Logue pushes too hard at one point, he drives the king away in anger and frustration. The disappointed teacher then realizes that he had tried to project his own ambitions for his student onto an unwilling recipient. That's an example of badly managed countertransference, and Logue apologizes for it to his royal student the first chance he gets.

"Not too close" serves as a professional caution as well as a personal one. Countertransference can transform teachers into nannies who worry more about a student's deadlines than the student does. That can never do. Graduate students are in the final stage of becoming professionals, and they have to figure out their professional identities for themselves. Advisers can also turn into mad scientists who seek to clone themselves. Graduate students know the difference between advisers who want to reproduce themselves and advisers who help students to know their own minds. That difference obtains even in science labs, where the adviser approves and pays for graduate-student experiments and places his or her name on all student publications that come out of the lab.

So don't get too close, but don't stray too far either. How to maintain that delicate equilibrium will vary with each graduate student.

RECOGNIZING STUDENT DIFFERENCES

Graduate advisers should have two main goals. First, they need to help their students finish their degrees if possible, or else help them to leave the program. Second, advisers should prepare students to compete for employment afterward in their chosen field, whether that field is academic or not. Career preparation is, as I have emphasized, a form of teaching. I've been calling in this book for student-centered instruction in graduate school—so how do professors make advising student centered?

First of all, it's important to recognize differences among students. Racial difference is a good case in point. Race receives much more attention on the undergraduate level than in graduate school, but graduate students of color face obstacles too. Though professors as a whole tend to be politically progressive on matters of race, graduate school remains a mainly white enterprise. Nonwhite graduate students have not exactly proliferated at any point in its history. In the 1950s, when the postwar university grew and democratized, graduate school administrators sought to overcome the "background deficiencies" of black students but continued to have trouble dealing with the fact that minority students tend to be at an educational disadvantage.[15] Not until the 1960s did a small number of graduate schools attempt to recruit minority-group members who did not meet the formal admissions criteria generally imposed; universities "gave the benefit of the doubt" to black, Mexican American, and Native American students—but this in turn raised many questions about the selection process.[16] Notwithstanding this initiative, recruitment of minority candidates has rarely been much of a priority for graduate schools in the United States. Currently there is a "woeful underrepresentation of populations of color" in doctoral programs that results from a general deficiency of attention and resources.[17]

When graduate students from minority backgrounds do find their way to graduate school, the good intentions that may accompany their arrival often end at the gates of the university. That is, once nonwhite students enter, any extra attention given to their candidacy falls away like temporary scaffolding, and the student is immediately expected to succeed without support. That's dangerous neglect: research has produced the telling finding that "the greater the differences" between the student and the department or institution, "the greater the difficulties in successful socialization."[18]

Scholars have concluded that "Black PhD students face isolation, lack of social support, difficulty navigating the system, and few role models or peers who look like them"; they "reported lower levels of social interaction" and "had more difficulty finding a mentor."[19] Research has not surprisingly recommended that multicultural graduate students need "more effective mentoring." Martin Davidson is one of many observers who argue that the definition of mentoring must be broadened to include issues specific to the preparation of a culturally and ethnically diverse population of doctoral students.[20]

I have neither the space nor the expertise to unfurl the literature in the field of socialization of minority-group members into university culture. My point is that graduate advisers need to recognize that where there are differences, attention must be paid. Davidson notes that "the framing of race in a cross-race mentoring relationship determines the effectiveness of, and satisfaction with, the relationship." One message conveyed by that finding is that white advisers should engage the issue rather than let it become an elephant in the room, but, as Davidson observes, most of them avoid it.[21] Graduate programs—and especially advisers—cannot afford to ignore the needs of students who belong to minority groups in this way. Marissa K. López and Daniel Heath Justice have written a good brief guide, "On Mentoring Graduate Students of Color," that contains useful references. It's worth reading for the suggestions in it, but perhaps the most compelling section of their essay is the opening, in which López recounts their difficulty in publishing it in the first place.[22]

Women provide another case in point. Statistically speaking, they are not a minority; at this writing, women receive a majority of the doctorates conferred annually in the United States.[23] Despite their numbers, they still present a nonnormative case—because the norms that govern graduate school need correction.

A story of one of my own advisees makes this point clearly. Let's call her Diana. She's the only graduate student who ever interviewed me for the job of dissertation adviser. She and I knew each other already, of course. She had taken one of my courses and done well. I was excited at the prospect of working with her.

One moment stands out from our conversation. I was telling Diana that she would be the CEO of her own dissertation—and of her whole graduate education—and I would do my best to support her and guide her through the decisions that she would have to make over the coming years. "You may choose to start a family while you're in graduate school," I said to Diana, "or you may not. Whatever your decision, my job will be to support you and help you reach your goals."

I saw that comment register on Diana's face. A few days later, she officially chose me as her adviser. Diana told me a few years afterward that my willingness to raise the question of children had helped her make up her mind. I try to initiate that sort of honest exchange with advisees from the start, because I believe that I have to. The length of graduate school, coupled with where it usually falls in students' lives, makes raising the issue a necessity. The nine-year average time to degree for a Ph.D. in the humanities is staggering and disgraceful, but it's also a reality. If students start graduate school right after college—which I do not recommend, by the way—then they will finish in their thirties.[24] People have important life decisions to make during that time, and it's artificial to pretend otherwise, not to mention ethically questionable.

There has been much salutary discussion recently about how graduate students who want to have families should confront those logistical difficulties and do what's right for themselves.[25] Amen to that. But that conversation—started, I should note, by graduate students—generally avoids the question of what the adviser should do when graduate students face these life questions. There's almost an implicit assumption that advisers, acting out of either malignity or ignorance, will sabotage their students' best-laid family plans.

There's much that advisers can do to help graduate students who decide to become parents. Telling them that it's okay, however silly it may feel to say so out loud, is important. But that's only a first step. Advisers can also help by alerting students to any university benefits available to them, such as parental leave. (You might think that students would know of such things, but that's not always the case.) The authors of the recent and already influential book *Do Babies Matter?* show that awareness and enforcement are key. Graduate students are often unaware that if their institutional policies don't provide basic provisions and protections, they are entitled to unpaid leave and job protection under the provisions of Title IX. Likewise, faculty often don't know that entitlements such as family leave, teaching relief, and stopping the tenure track are on the books at their institutions.[26]

For my own part, I believe that most advisers mean well. But that doesn't necessarily mean that they know what to do. The life decisions that my advisees face, including whether (or when) to have children, ought to be none of my business. That's essentially what I told Diana. Of course, I could have just said nothing at all about it. One might argue that keeping silent would have been the best way to show that such things are not my affair. But that passive approach feels wrong—and the reason has a lot to do with the shape of the adviser-student relation.

I chose to speak up because, like it or not, I play a role in my graduate students' whole lives, not just the dissertation part. Diana depended on me in a way that was professional and personal at the same time. Her thesis—and her long preparation for the job market, including the familiar decisions about what to publish and how to balance article and dissertation writing—took up a large chunk of her existence. So my actions as her dissertation director affected her whole life, not just her thesis.

Acknowledging that fact is part of my job as a student's adviser. Just as second-wave feminists recognized that the personal and the political could not be separated, graduate advisers should likewise accept the inextricability of the personal and the professional, which is really the same thing. If I fail to recognize that my students' personal decisions are marbled together with professional ones (by saying nothing about the possibility of children, for example), I'm not making those personal issues go away. I'm just avoiding them. Moreover, students like Diana wouldn't know the reason for my silence, so questions would still hang suspended between us.

Thus, a paradox: even though Diana's decision about whether to have children was none of my business, I had to make it my business to tell her so. That's because my support is important to her emotional well-being, and therefore to her professional progress. It's a sorry statement about the professional world of graduate school that I have to go out of my way to state something about someone else's personal life that ought to be obvious, but the situation is hardly unique. Other professions in the United States are likewise unevolved. The only difference may be that we professors think that we're more progressive than we actually are, at least in this area.

Diana later described my statement of support as "contractual." That may sound dry and businesslike, but it's exactly what I'm looking for. My professional commitment to support Diana's personal decisions cements the relation between us in a way that is both professional and personal. Diana went on to have two children, one on each side of a dissertation fellowship that she won. She defended her excellent thesis, one of the best I've advised, and at this writing is conducting her job search. Her story isn't over, nor is my part in it. But I believe that neither of us harbors any significant regrets about how we've together shaped the professional—and personal—arc she's chosen.

The choices now before Diana—and so many other graduate students— are polarized in ways that most of us take for granted. The world of professors' jobs is split between "serious," all-consuming, tenure-track jobs, the growing second tier of full-time, non-tenure-track jobs, and poorly paid, contingent adjunct work.[27]

That split is thoroughly gendered. The authors of *Do Babies Matter?* unveil a disturbing picture of gender and family in the ivory tower. The authors found that women make up the majority of adjunct and other part-time faculty, and mothers of young children tend to remain locked in second-tier positions or leave academia altogether. Mothers of young children who aspire to tenure-track jobs are statistically very likely to be passed over. As a result, fewer women than men occupy the tenure-track ranks, and women are less likely than their male colleagues to be married and have children. In effect, men get rewarded economically for having children, while women pay a price.[28] Consequently, even though women make up a majority of the faculty in many fields (including Diana's and mine), the implicit professorial stereotype continues to be a man with children and a wife at home to care for them.

Professors mostly lean left, as I said, so I doubt that many of us are comfortable supporting a retrograde system that treats our graduate students so badly, but we do anyway. We have to change it not only administratively but also at the ground level of the adviser-student relationship itself. Advisers who don't acknowledge the personal aspects of their students' lives are (and here's that paradox again) acting unprofessionally. We need to support graduate students as they seek different kinds of lives. They make life-altering decisions and balance competing responsibilities on the long road to their degrees. Advisers need to be aware of those personal pressures and make a point of raising them, even if—and perhaps especially if—their advisees don't. Parenting is only a case in point. The larger point is that graduate education needs to shed its one-mold-fits-all design, and advising, if it's to be worthy of the name, must avoid the dogmatic form that follows such inflexible design.

"Meet your students where they are" may be a pedagogical cliché, but it applies here. You don't have to teach or advise graduate students to know that they don't all have the same talents. That's obvious. But they don't all have the same professional aims, either, and that's less obvious because most graduate education is designed as though they did. Not all graduate students want to be professors. And some of those who do also want to become parents. I began this discussion with the legally recognized forms of diversity, and it's important to recognize how those differences affect the experience of graduate students. But my larger point is really that graduate students are different in all kinds of ways—and we should recognize their diversity in order to advise them properly. Our job is to shepherd them through the liminal space that is graduate school, to show them what they can do, and to give them the tools to do it. They will progress differently and need different kinds of attention. Treat graduate students as adults with lives, suggests Bruce M. Shore. His call for "student-centered advising" is simple: "It's about them."[29]

STUDENTS WHO PROGRESS AND STUDENTS WHO DON'T

What should advisers do when graduate students stall? There are essentially two choices: help them stay, or help them leave. The first is simple enough to understand, but the second may go against the grain. I'll treat each in turn.

There's already a lot of literature out there on how to get Ph.D. students through their dissertations. Books with titles like *Authoring a Ph.D. Thesis* and *How to Plan, Draft, Write and Finish a Doctoral Dissertation* amount to coaching. They command the student to "teach thyself" and convey the implicit assumption that the dissertation adviser will offer no help.

Advisers can—and should—do plenty when their students struggle. But because we don't talk enough about how to teach graduate students in general, let alone at the dissertation stage, there isn't a lot of pedagogical guidance out there.

Perhaps the first item on the discussion agenda should be a reexamination of the dissertation task itself. This seems a particularly propitious time to do so. New media and new economic realities are, after all, reshaping our own information business. Sidonie Smith, during her 2010 term as president of the Modern Language Association, called for "expanding the forms of the dissertation" to encompass digital and public scholarship, among other possibilities.[30] The Association endorsed this sort of experimentation in its 2014 *Report of the MLA Task Force on Doctoral Study in Modern Language and Literature*.[31]

We may be contributing to our students' difficulties in finishing by taking the parameters of the dissertation for granted. Graduate students already question the shape of the dissertation. Their professors are beginning to do so too. Rather than hewing to old-fashioned models of what a dissertation has been—models that have been distorted by the demands of a contracting academic job market—we might cut down on our students' struggles if we reflect on their tasks together with our own. The question of what to do with the dissertation encompasses teaching and administration together. In keeping with the contiguous nature of the problems facing American graduate school today, the issues raised by the shape of the dissertation encompass completion rates, time to degree, and the rethinking of graduate students' goals. A widely scoped conversation about how to teach dissertation-stage graduate students better has begun and needs to continue in earnest. But while graduate programs everywhere work it all out, graduate students still have to write dissertations, and their advisers have to advise them. With that practical brief in mind, I return to the work being done on the ground and will describe a few common problems that slow—and sometimes stop—dissertation writers, along with some possible solutions. Consider what follows as advice to advisers.

Use your fellow committee members. All dissertation students have a committee as well an adviser, but they don't always know what to do with it.

Sometimes the adviser doesn't, either. What is the role of the committee compared with that of the adviser? The answer is not at all clear. "We don't know as much about the adviser-committee relationship as we should," says Daniel Denecke, associate vice president for programs and best practices at the Council of Graduate Schools. "It's an area of graduate study that deserves more attention."[32] We worry a lot—and rightly so—about dissertation writing becoming too solitary. The same concerns should apply to dissertation advising.

In *The Graduate Grind,* a good book on graduate school from the student's point of view, Patricia Hinchey and Isabel Kimmel observe that "while all faculty members have power over students, they also have unequal amounts of power among themselves."[33] That imbalance is highly field specific, and it can cause problems. In the laboratory sciences, the adviser owns the means of production of the thesis. Students work in their advisers' labs and are financed by their grants. The student's name goes on any publications that result from the experiments done there, but so does the adviser's. The dissertation, usually a collection of experimental results, goes out under the student's name, but it's thoroughly underwritten by the adviser's money. Given that setup, we might expect the committee's role to be limited—and it usually is. Just as the U.S. Senate provides "advice and consent" before ratifying treaties, members of dissertation committees in the sciences typically offer broad oversight to the work that the adviser is managing in detail in the laboratory.

The humanities are organized quite differently. Again, we can follow the money. Doctoral students are usually financed on the departmental level, through either stipends or compensation for undergraduate teaching. The adviser has no financial stake in the student's dissertation work, and the adviser's name appears nowhere within any publications that result, except maybe in the acknowledgments. Instead, the adviser's investment in the student's research takes the form of time. A good adviser in the nonlaboratory fields (including mathematics and some of the social sciences) will read multiple drafts of a dissertation and meet with the student regularly.

In nonlab fields, too, the committee does less than the adviser. I tell my advisees that they may, as a rule of thumb, count on each committee member for one close reading of each chapter. Further readings by committee members (such as the one at the very end, when the whole thesis is turned in) are usually more cursory, more in the nature of ratification than detailed engagement.

So when is the best time for students to cash in that one careful reading? It depends. Students should obviously aim for the moment when they will get the most out of each committee member's particular approach and expertise. That might come near the beginning of the process: maybe the student needs help for a piece of writing to find its way, or maybe the close reading would be more helpful once the chapter is mapped out, the research is done, and the findings need critical evaluation. Part of a student's job as CEO is to decide (with the adviser's guidance) how deeply to involve the committee at each stage.

Committee members, for their own part, need a middle ground between presumptive deference to the adviser and an unpleasant demonstration against a graduate student's nearly completed dissertation. Where might that middle ground lie? Some years ago Columbia University's English department did away with the position of adviser entirely and mandated that each committee member (there are three) hold equal sway. That arrangement, which was designed to limit the imperial power of the adviser, theoretically levels any power imbalances at the outset. In practice, though, students seek a main point of contact. Moreover, the outside world expects them to have an adviser, especially when they apply for academic jobs. A three-headed adviser ought to confer an advantage, but not when each head expects one of the others to take the lead. Such a system requires a lot of collegiality of its participants, maybe too much.

Instead, this is an area where the humanities might take a cue from the sciences, where many departments demand that Ph.D. candidates give periodic semiformal presentations to their committees. Some humanities departments already require that Ph.D. candidates formally defend their thesis proposals before their whole committees. Surely that's a good thing: the student gets more input, and the committee gets to witness the project's liftoff. But such close monitoring needs to extend beyond takeoff. Professors need to regularly check graduate students' work as it progresses, and they need to do it together.

Lots of Ph.D. programs in the sciences require such group checkpoints.[34] That approach would translate readily to nonscientific fields as well. If a doctoral student in the humanities presented an annual progress report in the form of a twenty-minute talk to his or her committee, everyone on the panel would be informed together about the state of the project and could share suggestions (and/or cautions) about how to proceed. In addition, the important decisions about when to have committee members look closely at each chapter could be planned out thoughtfully.[35]

Create a collaborative environment. Life for advanced graduate students is inherently isolating, and that isolation can easily stall a dissertation. Consider that a graduate student goes from taking courses (where everyone reads and talks about the same texts) to studying for comprehensive exams (where candidates often work together in reading and study groups). Then it's time for something completely different: writing a dissertation that's supposed to be creative and original, that takes each student into a specialized world uniquely his or her own.

That's a jarring transition, and it has only recently begun to attract the attention of scholars of education. "Being a good course-taker is not enough" to make a graduate student into an effective dissertation writer, declares Barbara E. Lovitts. "When they embark on the independent stage of their education," she says, "graduate students are asked to be creative and original, and otherwise think in ways that they have not been conditioned to think in the previous 16+ years of schooling."[36] Moreover, faculty are aware of the disjunction; they know that undergraduate and graduate coursework are not consistent predictors of who will make a smooth transition to the dissertation. The students know it too. Studies show that roughly one-third of graduate students don't believe that their courses provide an adequate foundation for independent research.

What is needed, says Lovitts, is a combination of creativity and "practical perspective"—and she argues that both can and should be taught. She theorizes that creativity amounts to a relation between the raw materials (a body of knowledge, rules, and methods), the individual who manipulates those materials, and the field (the gatekeepers who decide whether those manipulations are valuable and worth endorsing for others to build on). It's perhaps more difficult for humanists (as opposed to scientists) to develop the practical and instrumental view of creative work that will best serve them at this point in their scholarly lives. "During the independent stage," Lovitts observes, "humanities students are more likely to work in isolation and, consequently, their advisors do not see their daily struggles." The students themselves complain that the problem is "not having structure."[37]

It's up to advisers to provide this structure. It can take myriad forms. An adviser might meet monthly with students to go over their notes or set deadlines for students to produce drafts or have students meet in groups to go over work in progress. An adviser might assign bibliographies or suggest topics and so on. The overarching point is that the movement from coursework and exams to dissertation scholarship is arguably the single most crucial pivot of a doctoral student's education. It requires a new set of survival skills—and it's the job of the adviser to teach them. We can't simply assume that students already know how to make the transition or will learn on their own in the course of dissertation work. It's the job of students to acquire a new set of skills and the job of professors to teach them.

Advisers need also to encourage dissertation writers to expand their worlds, not only at professional conferences but also at home. In particular, all-but-dissertation (ABD) students need different audiences for their work in progress, not just their faculty advisers. Faculty can encourage dissertation students to form peer groups within their discipline (yes, an apprentice American historian can be a good audience for a specialist in the British early modern period; after all, they originally trained alongside each other). Or we can promote the formation of dissertation groups in various subfields. (I convene my own dissertation writers in a group each month.) There are lots of possibilities—and some departments are experimenting with new ones. The larger point is this: dissertation students should not feel that they're working all alone.

Managing the dissertation proposal. Graduate students may fall into solitary solipsism as they write the dissertation proposal, which necessarily sits at the junction point between group projects (coursework, exam preparation) and individual project research. It's a common mistake for a proposal writer to fall into writing the actual dissertation in the process of laying it out. That's not entirely a bad thing: it gives students a head start. But because students and faculty members too often misunderstand the nature of the project, most dissertation proposals take too long to complete. Graduate students in the humanities should ordinarily finish writing the proposal in three to six months, and their advisers need to recognize the point at which students should be turned loose to work on their actual dissertations. It's far too common for advisers to put students through needless extra drafts, perfecting a document that doesn't need to be perfect because it's just a step on a long road. Extending the proposal stage only makes that road longer and more costly. Students, for their part, generally don't recognize the proposal for what it is, either: a provisional document that marks a point of transition, not a polished work of compressed scholarship that need only be inflated to become a dissertation. Ideally, it's a writing assignment that points graduate students toward the world of inquiry and turns them loose.[38]

What is your student really interested in? Good scholarship is usually auto-biographical in some way: it tells the story of the writer's interests, refracted through the work of others. But a dissertation is a work of discovery as well as a demonstration of mastery. The writer's passions and commitments may change over the course of the writing, sometimes leaving the student in the middle of a dissertation whose topic no longer stirs his or her passion. That can turn the thesis into a long slog, and a student may get bogged down.

It's useful to sit down with struggling graduate students to see if they still care about what they're writing about. Such students may need your encouragement to follow their own interests, for most fear the disapproval of their advisers. A low-key conversation may be all it takes to begin the process of reconfiguring a research plan and rethinking a topic to turn it into one that the student is eager to return to. Since new topics are often contiguous with old ones, it's usually possible to redraw them to preserve already-completed work.

The trigger can be an ordinary observation: I recently had a student point to an offhand comment that I made years earlier as the key to her reconception of her now-completed dissertation. I would never have remembered what I said to her if she hadn't repeated it to me.

Steer dissertators away from the beginning. Too many students enter the dissertation phase with rigid rules of composition. Left to their own devices, too many start at the beginning of a paper and doggedly work their way through it—as though the writer were an artist who decides to start a picture at one end of the canvas and work steadily toward the other. But that kind of writing process requires you to envision the whole paper before you begin, for how else can you write the introduction to something that does not yet exist?

It goes without saying that such a convoluted method won't work for a chapter, let alone a whole dissertation. Students quickly become paralyzed before an empty page or a repeatedly rewritten opening paragraph. An adviser can snap students out of it by getting them to start writing at any point in the middle where they know what they want to say. After writing that part, they can turn to another. The missing chunks will find their places later. In the meanwhile, the student is actually writing, employing an organic writing process that makes for a much less stressful experience.

Perfect is the enemy of done. Graduate students often think of their dissertations as polished displays of learning. That's not exactly a fallacy, but it's a dangerous habit of mind. The dissertation is part of a graduate education, and students need to see it that way. Not simply product, the thesis also displays a process of learning—and teaching. So, yes, a dissertation has to be good, especially if its writer wants to compete for an academic job. But a thesis has to reach that level, not start there. The thesis—and its writer—need time and space to evolve in a scholarly environment. If everyone involved understands that, then the writer can proceed with less stress. We also need to remind our students that even a finished dissertation (one that may already have yielded publications) need not be camera-ready. We need to leave them with something to do after they graduate, after all.

A time to read, a time to type. Too much research is one of procrastination's most elegant disguises. There's always another book or article to read and then another two after that. Students who are nervous about beginning a chapter (or a dissertation, period), or are stuck in the middle of one, can easily be seduced by the siren's song that calls them to additional learning.

When is the right time for students to write? When they know enough to put fingers to keyboard. What's the adviser's job here? When you see students doing research instead of writing, give them writing exercises that break up the job they're shying away from. Annotated bibliographies are a good example. Few graduate student writers, no matter how anxious, find themselves unable to take notes or to redact sources—and a teacher knows that it's just a short leap from there to full-blown composition. I thought I was taking notes for my own dissertation until I realized after a few weeks, to my delight, that I was writing it. Sometimes it's that simple.

Don't let your students teach too much. When I directed my department's graduate program, I would convene the students at the beginning of each year and say to them together, "Your most important job is to finish your own degree, not to teach the department's courses." Most graduate students in the humanities love to teach, and their energy and enthusiasm buoys them. But teaching is only one skill of many that they must acquire, and they can't let it block their research—because their research is what they must complete in order to graduate. I will allow that regulating the amount of time that graduate students spend on teaching is easier said than done. Sometimes graduate students just need the money. But it's an adviser's job to weigh in on this topic. It's a form of professional hygiene that students need to learn in order to avoid dissertation struggles. Advisers who don't teach these work habits become complicit in the dissertation problems that their students experience later on.

This list can go on. Perhaps the reason why so little has been written about how to teach advanced graduate students is that the process is so individual, with each doctoral student's path as distinctive as a fingerprint. A practice that helps one dissertation student over a bump might only irritate another.

Some general principles emerge nevertheless. The most important one is that dissertation writers are still students, and students need thoughtful instruction. Dissertation advisers usually behave like gardeners, training our plants to grow upward, bending them a bit here or there, always along the established lines of their growth. But if they stop growing, we need to turn arborist and try to figure out the reason.

Some of the students who stop are showing that they no longer want to write a dissertation. Not every graduate student will finish a thesis; we know that truth to be self-evident. Nor *should* every graduate student finish. Some would be better off doing other things with their lives. Others simply can't complete the project. A former graduate student wrote me a note a few years ago to thank me for helping him drop out. What's wrong with that picture? Nothing, except that we don't see it often enough.

The problem is that academic culture doesn't credit the decision to stop writing a dissertation as legitimate on at least two levels. Institutionally, graduate schools measure "completion rate" and use it as an indicator of the overall success of a program. That's not a bad idea in theory, because attrition is too high. But this policy may translate into pressure on students to stay in school for the sake of the program's numbers—as, for example, when laggard progress triggers mechanisms to rescue students who might be better off with counseling that could help them decide to cut the cord.

For students, leaving graduate school has a reputation a lot worse than completion rates can ever measure. I've met many people over the years who have dropped out as ABDs, and none has ever presented the decision better than apologetically. Many see it as a personal failure—like the student who confessed, "I haven't lived up to the investment that the university made in me." Graduate schools collect untold fortunes in "open file fees" from people who pay to keep their student status alive for five, ten, even twenty years after they've left the university, all in order to say (mostly to themselves) that they're still at it.

They stay because the unfinished dissertation is like the wound of Philoctetes in Greek mythology, a festering sore that never goes away. No mere albatross, it stigmatizes its owner in ways that usually leave permanent scars. Philoctetes himself was ostracized, and he became a suffering hero of tragic theater. Shame, the sociologist Erving Goffman reminds us, accrues to stigma.[39] Graduate students are already marginal by virtue of being apprentices, but a foundering dissertation compromises their status even further. No wonder struggling graduate students rarely consider leaving. Watching someone tread water in Lake Dissertation (as one clear-eyed student aptly put it) is one of the more painful sights in academia, but it will remain an all too common spectacle given the stigma attached to the alternative.

Attrition, past and present. The good news is that Ph.D. completion and attrition rates have gained more attention in recent years. The bad news is that the problem is still being viewed almost entirely in administrative terms. If we are to take the full measure of the situation of struggling doctoral students, a few words about attrition are in order.

Perhaps the most important observation about graduate school attrition is that few observers care about it, so the problem goes largely unnoticed. Those who do notice it often blame the students themselves for leaving.[40]

Doctoral program attrition today stands at about 50 percent.[41] We might expect that figure to perturb, disturb, and reverberate everywhere. It's obviously way too high, but it hasn't exactly inspired picketing on the graduate quad. Why not?

First, there's a historical reason. When graduate schools first started to grow during the 1920s and 1930s, they became "open," as Roger Geiger puts it. Almost everyone got in—including many "undistinguished students." A 1933 study of the leading graduate schools revealed that the proportion of graduate students who had received high undergraduate honors (or the like) was less than a third. At Wisconsin, a quarter of graduate students graduated in the top 10 percent of their undergraduate classes, but 40 percent finished in the lower half of theirs.[42] In these times of essentially open admissions, many students left early on, not always voluntarily, leading to high attrition rates. These practices of open admission and high attrition continued for decades. Bernard Berelson's 1960 study found that the most selective graduate schools admitted about half of those who applied. Schools further down the food chain turned almost no one away.[43] So graduate school hardly stood out as an aerie where came to rest only the best and brightest.

The large disparity in graduate students' qualifications suggested a wide spectrum of ability among those entering cohorts from decades past. A demanding curriculum would presumably result in high attrition—and that's just what happened. In effect, selectivity was practiced not at the point of admission but after students had already enrolled.[44] So high attrition rates were enshrined as part of the status quo during the era when American graduate schools took on a recognizably modern scope and structure.

As with so many institutional practices in U.S. graduate education, this one showcases teacher-centered motivations. The economist David W. Breneman observed in 1970 that graduate students may be viewed in this high-volume, high-attrition system as "inputs" and "outputs." As inputs—that is, admitted students—their large numbers could justify large departments with lots of graduate courses for professors to teach. As outputs (or graduates), their placement in prestigious jobs conferred glory on their home institutions and on their advisers. But only a small number of the very best Ph.D.'s could deliver this prestigious return. The others, who might be employed at down-market institutions (or, worse, not in the professoriate at all), could detract from a program's overall reputation, so it was better to get rid of them ahead of time—hence, high attrition rates. The national attrition rate in humanities doctoral programs during the 1960s stood at 75 percent.[45]

That story helps to account for a habit of attrition in American graduate school, but it remains to explain why still-high attrition rates do not cause more alarm today. To consider that question, we have to dispel the cloud of connotation that surrounds the term. "Attrition" is something of a dirty word in higher education. No one likes it: not graduate schools, which prize their completion numbers; not departments, which prize placement of Ph.D.'s; and presumably not students, who invest time and money and then don't complete their programs. Attrition carries the taint of loss, failure, and despair.

Current scholarship on graduate school attrition conveys the assumption that each departing student represents an avoidable loss. A big reason for that is because graduate programs do such a bad job of retaining their students. The culture of graduate school, says Barbara E. Lovitts, cultivates a "pluralistic ignorance" in which everyone involved—deans, faculty members, students themselves—tend to blame the departing students for leaving.[46]

The Ph.D. Completion Project, a valuable study sponsored by the Council of Graduate Schools in 2010, also points to the general culpability of faculty and administration. The study focuses on time to degree as well as attrition. To limit both, it suggests a set of "promising practices," such as early and regular progress review, better financial support, and a more encouraging "program environment."[47]

It's only logical that the culture—or environment—of a graduate program affects whether students stay in it. Professors and administrators do more than students to create that environment, so it follows that we need to pay more attention to our role in student completion and attrition. But the students have a responsibility too. A prospective graduate student who's thinking of enrolling in a master's or doctoral program should look closely at its attrition rate. But what conclusions should be drawn from that information?

Let's envision the optimal rate of attrition from a graduate program. Of course it should be lower than it is now, but it should not be zero.

By way of explanation, let's first compare master's and doctoral programs. The appropriate attrition rate for master's degree programs should be minuscule. Rare is the program that lasts longer than two years, and if students succeed in getting admitted and then commit their time (and, for many, their money), they should expect to graduate. Doctoral programs present a different profile. Not all Ph.D. candidates will finish—nor should they. Doctoral students fall into three groups:

- Those who can't get it done. Perhaps they lack the temperament to work on their own (which undergraduate work does not test as severely as graduate school does), or perhaps they lack, say, the mathematical chops necessary to succeed at advanced physics. But there will be a number—and if admissions committees do a good job, it will be very small—who won't be able to finish because they're not up to the demands of the task.
- Those who have the ability to finish but choose not to. Some may seek alternative academic careers. Others may try to become entrepreneurs, sailors, or artisans. Some may leave for personal reasons. We may reasonably expect, especially in these straitened times, that a certain number of people who initially aspire to become academics may choose other courses in life.
- Everyone else—that is, those who complete their doctorates.

In well-run graduate programs (that is, where advisers work hard and avoid malpractice), that third group will be the largest and the first the smallest.

But what of the middle one? It's unreasonable to suppose that all doctoral students will proceed through the long gantlet and emerge with the degree. Not only is that outcome not credible, it's not even a desirable fiction.

Let's try imagining it, though. Envision a class of Ph.D. candidates with the highest probability of getting the degree. Admissions committees can readily pick out applicants with both high competence and motivational infernos in their bellies. To borrow a phrase from sports radio, those are the stone-cold, lead-pipe locks. There are bound to be very, very few of them in any applicant pool, and they're not hard to spot.

But what about those with demonstrated talent who aren't sure that graduate school is for them? (Let's assume for the sake of argument that they're well informed about their employment prospects and remain curious about doctoral study.) Given the state of the academic job market, we ought to honor such circumspection. The bellies of this applicant group will house not roaring fires but uncertain, guttering flames, which might get hotter but also might flicker out. Don't those students deserve a chance to check out graduate school if they so choose?

If we admitted only lead-pipe locks, we'd get very high completion rates (i.e., negligible attrition), but we'd also be excluding that second group, barring them from a journey of self-discovery that could lead to a Ph.D.—or not. Full disclosure: I was a member of that second group. I applied to graduate school uncertainly, comfortable with the knowledge that I might not get a Ph.D. (I intended to get a master's degree at the least.) I knew that even if I did finish, I wouldn't necessarily end up as a professor. The academic job market was lousy in my day, too (though not as bad as now). Yet I wanted to give graduate school a try. I assumed that I would learn more about whether to continue once I was there. And once I did get there, I discovered that I liked teaching a lot. By the end of my third year, I knew that I would aim to finish.

Others take longer, way too long, to make that decision. One of the key statistical measures of doctoral attrition is when it occurs—that is, at what point students depart. The Council of Graduate Schools (CGS) reports that in most math and science fields, the students who will leave are usually gone by year three. The humanities are another story and not a happy one: only half of all attrition takes place by the third year. The other half of the humanities noncompleters—fully 25 percent of those who enter graduate programs—trickle out over the following seven (!) years. That's a horrifying finding. Worse still, as Lovitts notes in her pioneering study of graduate attrition, non-completers are more likely than completers to carry heavy student-loan debt.[48]

So what should we do? The possibilities include carrots and sticks. Derek Bok suggests a simple stick: make acceptable completion rates an incentive for departments. For example, more noncompleters would result in fewer slots for incoming students.[49] The CGS study calls for a global approach to limit attrition. That approach begins with thoughtful admissions practices—which emphasize "fit" between student and program—and extends through assessment, advisement, and financial support. That's a sound plan, but it means that we have to do plenty—and, worse, we have to do it together. Professors are like pianists; we rarely play together, nor do we usually want to. Maybe the 50 percent attrition rate hasn't inspired more alarm because everyone knows that it will take collective action to repair. Professors have to form a piano orchestra for the sake of our students, with dissertation advisers as the soloists, because this is an advising issue at the core. High attrition bleeds the professional lives we have agreed to help develop. It's grossly irresponsible for us to tolerate so much of it, especially at the back ends of humanities programs. Not all graduate students will stay the doctoral course, but more of them should—and when half do not, it's our fault.

We can only benefit from examining our degree-granting practice to reduce attrition, but let's not forget that this is foremost a teaching task. Many educators see this as a question of "soft" versus "tough" treatment of lagging graduate students, but that assessment overlooks the goal, which is for struggling students to choose to do what is best for themselves.[50] Graduate students will never see leaving a Ph.D. program as a viable choice unless their teachers honor that choice first. Right now we allow—and through our passivity even promote—the sense that someone who doesn't finish is a quitter.

This attitude amounts to an arrogation of duty. These are our students—all of them, including the ones who are stuck. We have a responsibility to teach them, so it's on us. Most professors recognize the graduate students who won't finish early in the game, but mostly we do nothing for them. Advisers need to talk to struggling graduate students, not treat them as though they were invisible. We need also to start a conversation *about* them.

How then should we teach the students who are destined to run aground? Students who aren't going to finish have certain specific needs that we can identify and try to meet. Here are a few suggestions to start: more advice for advisers.

If you love them, let them go freely. The adviser's job is to lead students toward the finish line, but it's also to let them choose their own finish line. Let's assume for the sake of this discussion that adviser and student have done all they can and that the dissertation is still foundering. In that case, it may be time to ask, "Are you having trouble hanging on or letting go?" I've asked that of graduate students more than once in my career, and the initial response is usually something along the lines of, "Wow, good question." Indeed, it is a question many graduate students should consider, and it can serve as the proverbial mustard seed.

Advise the student, not just the dissertation. Most graduate students are young grown-ups who are still making major life choices. Some of those choices, such as the need to support a young family, may lead away from dissertation completion. Sometimes I have to remind myself that it's the student's dissertation, not mine—another manifestation of the countertransference problem. We can often help students navigate past research or writing problems, and we should always try. But if the dissertation is not going to get done, the adviser needs to let go of it, no matter how significant a contribution the work might make if it were ever to see the light of publication.

Understand the power of your approval. "Who's your dissertation adviser?" is one of academia's frequently asked questions, but its outward benignity conceals the assumption that if you work hard and all goes well, you will be prized one day as your adviser's scion. Graduate students seek their advisers' approval all the time and invariably believe that if they leave the program without a Ph.D., they'll be letting their advisers down personally. I once sat a student down and told her that I would be as proud of her if she left the program to work full-time at the nonacademic job she loved as I would be if she stayed and finished her thesis. She looked stunned. When she recovered herself, she thanked me profusely. She hadn't felt free to choose before.

ABD does not equal failure. All graduate students embark on the dissertation with the idea of finishing it, but sometimes it's better for them to cut their losses. Erasing the stigma attached to the unfinished thesis starts with us. If we accept that leaving school can be a better decision than staying, we need to treat it that way.

There are abundant good reasons for putting a dissertation aside. One student might be unable to cure himself of perfectionism, while another might so dislike research that she can't make herself do it. Another might be put off by the terrible academic job market. Many students make those self-discoveries during the dissertation phase, but the insights can take a while to sink in.

Faculty advisers (particularly of fully funded students) sometimes compound the problem by choosing not to discuss with their advisees the signs of possible problems down the road. We think of mounting time to degree, and we say, "Onward, onward," no matter the cost or consequences, but we should check that impulse. Talking to students about their work can include asking them if they're having trouble doing it. Those conversations may give them their lives back, sometimes after years of unexamined suffering. If we teach students that leaving graduate school is a decision and not a failing, we can start to erase the stigma that so wrongly attends withdrawal.

Most of my advisees finish their dissertations and get jobs. I'm proud of them. But some walk away—and of that group I'm just as proud. Not everyone gets a Ph.D., but everyone who tries deserves our attention and respect. Teaching students how to leave graduate school is a task every bit as noble as shepherding them through it.

ADVISING GRADUATE STUDENTS WHO LOOK BEYOND THE PROFESSORIATE

Dissertation advisers sometimes want jobs for their students that the students may not want themselves or may not want to risk chasing. Lots of anecdotes circulate of advisers' disappointment at their students accepting jobs at small colleges instead of casting their eyes upmarket to research universities. That proposition seems so absurd to me that I thought these accounts were urban legends, but I've encountered too many that proved genuine to dismiss them. (Though it should be said that this particular narrative especially proliferates today in the sciences.) My belief in the overall truth of these accounts was further bolstered when I caught myself thinking something similar about a prize student of my own. His own evident pleasure at the job he got changed my mind quickly and made me feel ashamed of my first reaction. Advisers have to monitor their own feelings and especially their responses—and beware of that countertransference.

If a student's choice to take a position at a less elite college or university can inspire such a response, then what about the decision to leave academia entirely? "I have a more than vague feeling that I let my PhD advisor down by not going on the postdoc that awaited me," writes Dana Campbell, a scientist who left the university.[51] That story is familiar across the disciplines, and it grows from the quasi-familial tie between adviser and student.

Advisers have to treat their students as their own people, not as family members, or worse, as potential mini-me's. Given today's job prospects, many promising scholars and teachers will choose not to pursue professorships. That decision may disappoint an adviser, but it's the adviser's job to fight such feelings. "Be suspicious," says English professor Leo Braudy, of advisers who "stop you from making your own mistakes and finding your own path." We need to maintain professional distance from our students' choices—and that distance may be just what's needed to allow us to support those choices. A good adviser, Braudy says, "should make you free."[52]

What is the best way to support the choices that our students make? More specifically, how can advisers prepare graduate students to seek nonprofessorial employment? That question overlaps with the previous section, on students who struggle at the dissertation stage. Realistically, lots of stalled graduate students, even the ones who complete the degree, will wind up working outside the professoriate. (The ones who finish will, because of their struggles, typically lack the kind of professional portfolio that will allow them to compete strongly for academic positions in a buyer's market, so their options will likely lie outside higher education.) So an adviser who recognizes the decision by a student to leave without completing a doctorate is, by extension, contemplating nonprofessorial employment alongside the student.

The first and most important preparation that professors can offer students about nonprofessorial employment is to convey their own awareness and approval of this alternative. I said earlier that professors need to honor a student's choice to leave graduate school, and not just at the moment it happens, either. The approval must be displayed well beforehand, because the student needs to know that leaving is a reasonable and honorable choice. The same goes for the choice to get a doctorate but not to pursue a professor's job. Advisers also have to honor that possibility in advance in order for students to see it as a viable and valuable choice.

It's straightforward to give respect in this way, but it requires effort and concern. And it entails more than professors just telling students that they believe in the possibility: they also have to walk the walk. That means public demonstration. For example, a department might hold periodic symposia at which recent graduates who have found work outside the academy are invited back to talk about their jobs. (Some departments now do this; every department should.) "The personal story," said historian Jacqueline Jones has said, "is the best vehicle for change here."[53] It's very important for faculty to attend these events and hear these stories, if only to show their support for what they signify.

Such extracurricular activity makes up only part of the solution. Educating graduate students about the realities of job placement ought to be curricular too. It's an education that needs to begin as early as possible—long before the students are thinking about the job market in concrete terms. Given that imperative, it's hard to separate more diverse job preparation from the rest of a graduate student's education, especially the coursework that everyone begins with. Indeed, the role model problem that I described at the beginning of this chapter demands early intervention. If graduate programs are to prepare students to contemplate (and perhaps seek) different kinds of work, they have to expose them to that possibility early in the program. Otherwise the default takes over, and the role model problem kicks in.

Why should professors be the ones to do this? The graduate director of a large English department at a midwestern state university complained to me not long ago that he simply wasn't qualified to advise graduate students about how to look for work outside the academy. Being a professor, he said, is the only real job he's ever had, and he locates his expertise in his scholarly field, not in alternative career counseling. So how can he be expected to know about how to help students look for other jobs?

My answer was—and is—that professors have to do this because it's part of their twenty-first-century job description. An adviser in the 1960s, when the number of professors' jobs exceeded the number of Ph.D.'s seeking them, could make a reasonable case that knowledge of alternative academic careers was unnecessary. (Though this too might be debatable; attrition was high then, and programs had a duty toward noncompleters too, even if most of them didn't recognize it. The same holds true today.) Today, there can be no debate. What professor, asks Braudy, "would be so self-deluded as to offer his or her career as a model to anyone? We all know how what we've done is filled with happenstance, circumstance, and chance." To say (implicitly or explicitly), "Do the things I've done," Braudy says, is "totally unhelpful and, in some situations, perhaps even offensive."[54] If most graduate students will not wind up professors, we cannot lay moral claim to teach them if we're only concerned about the minority who wind up as full-time academics. We have a wider responsibility.

Then there's the difficulty of teaching a topic—outside employment—that one may not know. That's perhaps not as daunting as it may sound. We learn new topics to teach all the time. Professors have gotten where they are because they are professional learners. We are exceptionally good at finding, absorbing, organizing, and making sense of large amounts of information for the purposes of passing it on to others. (Dissertation students are good at those things too—in fact, those skills make for good arguments for hiring Ph.D.'s outside the academy.) Compared to, say, writing a dissertation, learning about diverse career options for humanists is not a monumentally difficult task. It takes thought, yes, and perhaps some creativity—but professors are paid for those skills, too. The bottom line is this: professors can learn how to help students get jobs outside the professoriate, and we have a duty to do so.

Luckily, advisers don't have to do it alone—nor should they. Dissertation advisers must shoulder a portion of the responsibility for teaching their students about the range of professional options, but before students choose an adviser, the department as a whole should meet this student need in the classroom. That's because programs must open the minds of graduate students as soon as possible to the jobs that they can get. That affirmation has to begin at the earliest stage of graduate school. Professors need to shape students' expectations as soon as they enter graduate school about what's waiting for them afterward—which means more transparency about their career options. Instruction about opportunities outside the professoriate must therefore begin before many graduate students even have an adviser.

Professional development seminars. Unlike many problems faced by the academy today, the alt-ac exposure problem can be solved in-house at modest cost, starting with the institution of professional development seminars. Professional development seminars offered by Ph.D.-granting departments and required of all Ph.D. students early in their careers can do wonders to orient graduate students to their larger milieu at a time when it's rapidly changing. Some departments have begun to offer such seminars, and they're an example worth following. A professional development seminar may be woven into a beginning graduate student's early coursework, or it can serve as a capstone class before a Ph.D. candidate advances to the dissertation phase—though my vote goes to earlier.

Professional development seminars socialize students into their disciplines. As such, they should cover both intra- and extramural practices. It's widely accepted, of course, that graduate programs need to teach students the content of their disciplines, but professors' jobs don't end there. We also need to teach students *about* their disciplines. That means teaching them what the professional world of their field looks like and how it works, both inside and outside the university. In other words, if we have to prepare graduate students to seek jobs of all kinds, then that means more than simply credentialing students to seek those positions. We also have to show them what those jobs look like, so they won't be shocked when they peer outside the research university's gates. In short, we have a responsibility to socialize graduate students in a consciously different way than most departments do now.

The mandate of a professional development seminar is to look around in many directions. For example, graduate students in the seminar offered by the geography department at the University of Minnesota are visited by a series of department professors who discuss not only conferences, research, and publishing but also choosing a career path, as well as gender and class issues that occur in some workplaces, and family issues that affect students' progress to and from the degree.[55] The University of Michigan's "Introduction to Graduate Studies" requires that beginning graduate students in English and modern languages interview a senior professor in the department— thereby offering a look upward at a role model's career. But the course also requires an outward-looking "Alternative Careers Workshop." Such workshops might take a number of forms, but I would endorse bringing in recent alumni who are doing jobs that they enjoy and organizing them into panels of two or three (not more, because there should be a chance for in-depth discussion of the work that these graduates are doing).

In short, the professional development seminar addresses the culture of the profession, broadly conceived, and it should leave graduate students with a broad sense of how that profession may be practiced both inside and outside the university—including the dismal academic job market.[56]

Career services partnerships. Departments and advisers should also partner with offices of career services, which have become increasingly sophisticated outfits on many university campuses. This change is way overdue. Right now we force graduate students to segregate their job searches. They look for teaching jobs through their professors and departments, but they have to go elsewhere—usually the career-services office—for assistance with the non-academic job search. Ne'er do the twain meet. If graduate students are to maximize their efforts, then academic departments and career services need to pool theirs. They need to work together.

Michigan State University is modeling just such a joint effort. Matt Helm, the director of graduate student affairs at the university, has designed an exemplary program that brings the campus career-services office into the lives of graduate students and academic departments early and often—and not just when students are about to receive their Ph.D.'s. The MSU program, known by the acronym PREP (Planning, Resilience, Engagement, Professionalism) expands and shapes graduate students' expectations.[57] Its overarching idea is to help shape their professional selves and lives before the tension rises and the panic strikes at job-search time.

I've said that graduate students need to be taught right away that they have a range of possible career outcomes. If you don't reach them with that message early in their training, the likelihood rises that they'll decide that they want only to become professors at research universities, because that's what they see around them. The career-services office at Michigan State takes an active approach. It aims to create an awareness not of "the job market" (meaning professor or bust) but of "the many job markets" that are out there, says Helm. He calls this "a more mature model." It's also a different and necessary kind of graduate education, to "build their awareness of the world of work."[58]

The program doesn't wait for students to become angry and despairing nonprofessors who feel that they've failed somehow. Helm exerts the influence of his office on graduate students from the beginning of their training, when they still have the time to be taught. "When they need you," says Helm, "you're already there." In keeping with his own split duties to the graduate school and to the student-affairs office, Helm uses PREP as a bridge to work not only with students on career planning but also with faculty members on the role they should be playing.

As a result of outreach by the career-services office, many of the university's graduate programs have customized the PREP program for their own students. For example, the chemistry department might hold a PREP-sponsored workshop on résumé writing with a leader who knows the specific needs of that young scientific cohort. Helm is aiming at a peer-led approach in the future, based on what he calls "strong graduate student organizations at the departmental level," with students doing the advocacy work. His overarching goal, he says, is for PREP to "become an organic part of academic life," not just a support alongside it.

Research shows that many graduate students have an interest in nonfaculty careers in their first and second years, Helm says, but they are often afraid to admit it. L. Maren Wood, a statistician and consultant for the American Historical Association, reported at the organization's 2014 annual meeting that some graduate students even harbor paranoid fantasies that they're being "tracked" by career services, which will then report back to their departments about their supposed lack of seriousness about professorial careers.[59]

PREP aims for a more coherent—and saner—approach. The program is structured around the early, middle, and later stages of a graduate student's career, with resources targeted to each level. For example, PREP offers a workshop for incoming students that's focused on the question of what a brand-new graduate student needs to plan to be successful in graduate school. Such planning won't be limited to preprofessorial training but will remind students that they face a myriad of possible careers. PREP, says Helm, sees graduate students' career goals as works in progress. The program is "built on the notion that what they came here to achieve may change"—and that the sooner one meets the needs that attend those changes, the better the outcome is likely to be.

Accordingly, the program focuses on giving graduate students "essential competencies" that are transferable outside of professorial settings. Helm's office conducted a study of Ph.D.'s employed in various career tracks—not just in academia—to determine what those competencies are.[60] These skills include not only teaching and proposal writing but also assessment, management and communications skills, business, and entrepreneurialism. Graduate students already have the basics of many of these skills, Helm points out, but they need to "develop consciousness" of what they can do.[61]

Graduate programs need integrative approaches like this. Why have they not sought alliances with career-services offices before this? Because we've generally assumed that we have no part to play in our students' efforts to train for jobs outside the professoriate. Our assumptions thus obscure our view of the range of our possible teaching practice.

Students want these programs, and they take advantage of them when they're offered. Our general failure to supply them also exemplifies the "information silos" that organizational experts deplore within academia. In this case, professors don't get lost in their own research so much as forget how the skills and information belonging to others might help them do their jobs better. Doctoral advisement should not, as I've said, collapse into a dyad between professor and student. The university contains many resources that may be brought to bear on it—and as in the case of offices of career services, bringing them into the process requires questioning our long-held assumptions about just what Ph.D. programs are preparing students to do. Whether students become professors or not, says Helm, they need to learn "how to use their research skills to learn about the world of work." Programs such as the one at MSU enable us to think more globally about the uses of graduate education and its broader social good. We can't do that unless we help our students to use their education in broad and global ways. That's not an add-on to a program of scholarship. It has to be a full part of what we do.

ON MENTORING

I talked to a lot of academics while researching this chapter. One question I asked was, what do you and your department do to promote the possibility of nonprofessorial employment for your students? I've set down some of the suggestions I've received here and in other chapters, but many of my respondents said that they were the ones asking for guidance. It's hard to answer that request precisely, because nonacademic job searches demand a different kind of creativity than academic ones: the box is wider, and the searchers have more freedom to roam—and to define themselves in different ways. For example, in 2014, Helen De Cruz interviewed seven holders of Ph.D.'s in philosophy who had lately left academia. Their positions are software engineer; television comedy writer; founder of a coaching and training company; professional "ontologist" working on information retrieval for a computer giant; quality assurance engineer for a network security company (testing software); statistical researcher at the House of Commons Library in England; and independent consultant in sustainability.[62] This spread points to the vast realm of possibility. It's true that the work that Ph.D.'s can do that's related to their particular training is invariably discipline-specific. Public history jobs will mostly be pursued by students in history. Those in English might compete best for jobs in advertising or public relations. Political scientists often work in government. A bank might not care what subject someone's doctorate is in, but that's because the work that the bank offers draws on the general doctoral skill set, not the specifics of a particular discipline. Any list is necessarily limiting.

Nor were lists publicly available for a long time, but that situation is now being remedied. New studies of doctoral placement are appearing, as the academy belatedly realizes the importance of tracking not only its professors but all of its graduates. This rise in institutional support of alternative- and nonacademic jobs for Ph.D.'s needs to be accompanied by a personal commitment by advisers. I realize that I'm essentially calling for a reexamination of the title and job description of "adviser." These times call for such reevaluations.

I began this chapter by talking about the other names that "dissertation adviser" might be called. The one that I like least is "mentor." The title of mentor carries extra weight for me. Not just anyone who sponsors a dissertation deserves to be called a mentor. In Greek myth, Mentor earned the trust of Odysseus, and Odysseus selected him to educate his son, Telemachus.[63] I can't use the word without acknowledging its legacy. So I think of "mentor" as a title that should be earned. It shouldn't be hung on anyone who sponsors a dissertation.

I've spent a lot of space in this chapter laying out a broad job description for thesis and dissertation advisers during these challenging times. One way to summarize it might be to say that they should try their hardest to act as true mentors.

CHAPTER FIVE

Degrees

EVEN IN THIS era of seemingly endless graduate education, after the advising is done and the students do their work, they do eventually get the degree. For the past three chapters, I've been tracing the development of a graduate student's career—from coursework through advising at the thesis stage—from a primarily pedagogical point of view. Working from the needs of the graduate students themselves, I've examined the work that professors do at these stages, and I've suggested more student-centered ways to teach graduate students at each point.

Now the perspective lengthens. Without abandoning this practical, teaching-centered approach, I return to a more historical view, beginning with the problems that attend the master's and doctoral degrees themselves. We can't expect to address the twenty-first-century troubles of American graduate school without an understanding of how they came about. The history of graduate degrees and the jobs that they've entitled their holders to seek offers clues to how we might proceed today. The stories of degrees and of the job market lead in turn to a wide-scoped account of professionalism and the caretaking ethic that will conclude this book.

I begin my story of degrees with the doctorate—not just the Ph.D. but also the main alternatives to it that have been suggested and tried over the years. Then I will turn to the master's degree.

THE DOCTORATE

Universities have been awarding doctorates for some centuries longer than the United States has been a sovereign nation, but graduate students have been writing dissertations for only the past two hundred years or so. The practice evolved in the late eighteenth and early nineteenth centuries in Germany, where so many of the customs and procedures that guide American graduate education first saw light.[1]

Once the doctoral dissertation was introduced, it quickly gained a central role. The United States joined the graduate community on the late side—the first American Ph.D. was awarded by Yale in 1861. The earliest American graduate degrees were granted by colleges, but the coming of the new research universities in the late nineteenth century soon sparked the founding of graduate schools. Only when the Johns Hopkins University set the tune after its founding in 1876 did most other American universities join the Ph.D. dance. Hopkins, says the historian Roger Geiger, did more to "standardize" the Ph.D. in the United States than any other institution, not least because it awarded more of them than any other school during the formative decades of the 1870s and 1880s. Hopkins Ph.D.'s in turn became Professor Appleseeds, planting doctoral programs at public and private universities around the country.[2]

Following the model set by Hopkins, the 1890s saw the founding of graduate schools at the University of Chicago and at institutions that were formerly structured as colleges in the English mold, such as Harvard and Columbia. These early graduate schools became industry leaders, manufacturing Ph.D.'s who joined faculties at other universities. Whereas ambitious professors once went to Europe to study, these new graduate programs now provided a domestic option, and college presidents encouraged their faculty to take leaves of absence and study for advanced degrees at these new American standard-bearers of the German university tradition. The founding of the American Association of Universities (AAU) in 1900 further encouraged this emerging division between the elite universities and everyone else. "By

1893," writes the historian Laurence R. Veysey, "it could be said that some amount of graduate work was required to win a permanent appointment at nearly every prominent institution. At the turn of the century the Ph.D. degree was usually mandatory."[3]

The familiar structure of graduate education was thus set in place more than a century ago. It has changed little since—at least partly because it suited the social and economic direction that the country has taken. The Ph.D.-centered academic hierarchy proved particularly well suited early on. The United States needed organizing markers for its rapidly urbanizing postbellum economy and burgeoning population of workers. Historian Burton J. Bledstein points persuasively to the confluence of the rise of the university with the rise of the middle class and the emergence of professional culture in the United States. Middle-class professionalism placed a value on credentials, and the university was well placed to provide them—and the first generation of university presidents quickly realized this. The founding of graduate schools enabled the streamlined production of M.A. and Ph.D. degrees, along with credentials in medicine, law, business, and other professions, and the general anchoring of the university as the source of the necessary badges of membership in the new professional bureaucracies of the postbellum United States.[4]

Following that quick origin story, let us take stock of the humanities doctorate now. It's a bad situation, deplorable and disturbing by any reasonable measure. At a staggering nine years, time to degree in the humanities is the highest of any sector of graduate education (with the exception of education, a field in which graduate students commonly work full-time). Here's one way to look at that amount of time: if a college student graduates at age twenty-one and goes right into graduate school without stopping (a bad idea, I believe), then he or she will complete the apprenticeship—for that is what graduate school is—and receive the Ph.D. after age thirty. We might agree that thirty is rather late to begin adult life, except that everyone knows graduate students who had to wait longer than that. Moreover, the prevailing 50 percent attrition rate means that only about half of all doctoral candidates will make it that far. (And furthermore, the miserable academic job market that most of them want to enter still lies before them.) So the road to the degree is fraught, perilous, poorly paid, and too long.

The structural center of the problem is the dissertation—both what it is and what scholars (both professors and the graduate students who follow their lead) believe that it should be.

So what is the dissertation then? In the humanities, it's a treatise that adheres to conventions established long ago and that have barely been examined since. It's a one-size-fits-all template for achievement, at its worst a procrustean bed. Graduate students in the humanities aspire to and get a range of jobs, but most of them write the same kind of scholarly dissertation.[5] (Other fields have their own established molds too—this is not just a humanities problem.) This prescriptiveness hurts the students, but the problems also go beyond them. Our collective failure to examine and assess the dissertation requirement has made the humanities vulnerable to the dubious contention that doctoral dissertations are too esoteric. This complaint forms part of a larger and often successful public argument that Ph.D. programs are part of an entrenched research culture that is undermining undergraduate education—simply put, that professors spend too much time researching and not enough time teaching.[6] So there's a lot at stake here. Like most problems facing graduate school, the effects of long-term inattention to the dissertation extend beyond the boundaries of graduate school to affect the position of higher education in society generally and its health prospects going forward.

What should a dissertation be, then? Let's start with what it should not be. Many graduate students in the humanities take too much time because they believe that their dissertations should be publishable. That means the work may be polished to a blinding shine and typically something more: in most humanistic fields, the desire for publication takes the form of a book. The bottom line is this: many graduate students in the humanities believe that they are writing books that they will incidentally submit as dissertations. They sometimes get such ideas from their fellow students, but those notions mainly originate with their professors.

It's a costly and misguided mistake to think of a dissertation as a book-in-progress. That's a graduate student lesson that I had to learn the hard way: a dissertation is a book-length project all right, but it's not a book that is just awaiting cover art. It's true that the dissertation showcases a student's original contribution to a particular field. That's an important (and honorable) accomplishment. But not all original contributions take the form of books.

Dissertations and books are destined for different markets, and so they have different purposes. The audience for a dissertation is the faculty committee that advises and credits it. Here's one way to look at the audience for a dissertation: I remind my advisees that excluding those with whom they share DNA or a bed, the number of people who will read their dissertations is ordinarily fewer than five. *Do not imagine that publishers will read your dissertation,* I tell them. The fact is, they almost never will—at least not before it has been revised significantly.[7] Instead, *the primary purpose of the dissertation is to get the student a Ph.D.* Or to put it in even more bluntly instrumental terms, the most important goal of a dissertation is for it to be approved by the student's committee.

Books have to reach a wider audience, of course, because publishers have to be able to sell them. What a scholarly publisher needs to sell a book (a focus on sex rather than bedroom architecture, say) may overlap with what a committee will credit, but they're not necessarily the same thing. Books are also more polished than dissertations, and they tend to be more complete. That's because a book is a display of learning, while a dissertation is part of the process of learning itself. *The dissertation is part of graduate education.* It's not just a goal of that education or its written result.

Not all dissertations are even publishable. Mine certainly wasn't. I thought I had written a book-worthy manuscript when I turned it in and got my Ph.D., but I was soon disabused of that illusion by rejected grant applications and tepid responses from academic publishers. My autodidactic enlightenment took a couple of years that I could ill spare. I'd like to say that the ordeal gave me wisdom, but what I remember best is the stress. Then I spent a few more anxious years writing a book based on a few ideas that were homeopathically distilled from my dissertation.

That was more than twenty years ago, but my experience remains sadly typical of the guidance (or lack thereof) that many graduate students receive when they enter the research and publication mill. Instead of advice, too many graduate students receive an imperative: write a book or else. The escalating demands of the academic job market and the tenure track (or the dream of the tenure track) force many new Ph.D.'s to seek book publication of their dissertations regardless of whether that is the best showcase for their scholarship. (I want to stress that these pressures are by no means reserved for those who are fortunate enough to be on the tenure track. Aspirants to tenure-track positions feel them too, because the competition for tenure-track positions is so intense that for some, a book contract simply serves to get one's foot in the door.)[8]

University press editors have been complaining for years about the flood of desperation-motivated book manuscripts that wash over their transoms. Lindsay Waters, executive editor for the humanities at Harvard University

Press, has pointed out that when a department requires books of its junior faculty members, it effectively "outsources" its tenure decisions to university presses.[9] Waters, a publisher of books, has ironically found himself a flag-waver in a movement to re-privilege articles.

Viewed from a wide angle, such complaints from publishers may appear a bit disingenuous. University presses are attached, after all, to the same universities that demand book contracts of their job and tenure candidates, and one of the original reasons that university presses came into being was to publish dissertations. But even if the problem is that the system is disordered, the hard and undeniable fact is that academic publishers find it harder and harder to sell scholarly monographs these days, so they're simply not publishing as many of them anymore. Editors are trying to publicize that shift, but knowledge travels slowly when it has to crawl over so many high hopes and expectations. Broadsides like the 2006 report of the MLA Task Force on Evaluating Scholarship for Tenure and Promotion advocated ending the tyranny of the book in tenure decisions, but the battle for awareness is still being fought.[10]

Given the battered state of the dissertation within this battle, we should not be surprised that reformers have been actively debating how the dissertation might change. But "change" is a word that can cause some adverse responses in academia, especially on the graduate side. Such chilliness is not automatically a bad thing; we would think a good deal less of higher education if it were buffeted about by every new trend. But the structure of graduate study in the arts and sciences in the United States has changed barely at all since it coalesced in the late nineteenth century. That suggests rigidity, not conservatism.

Such rigidity characterizes the one-size-fits-all approach to U.S. doctoral study that I described a moment ago. The sheer numbers alone force us to acknowledge that not every graduate student will become a professor at a research university, yet we design graduate study as though they were all headed down that path. And central to this narrow, unrealistic, and unreflective focus is the dissertation template that emerges from it.

That rigid dissertation format supports an implicit two-tier system in which there are the few who work at research universities on top and everyone else below. I will have a lot to say about two-tier systems as this chapter goes on, but here I want to note that this kind of thinking starts in humanities graduate school with the way that the dissertation is assigned in the first place. This unspoken two-tier system enshrines an inequality of work and especially reputation. Those who have research-oriented jobs teach less, publish more, and enjoy more respect for the work they do. Everyone else teaches more, publishes less, and is taught to wish that they occupied the tier above them.

One reason for the longtime conservatism surrounding the dissertation is because the dissertation is now required of doctoral students nearly everywhere in the world. Indeed, it has become the most sacrosanct of doctoral education requirements, and some distinguished observers of American higher education argue that we should be careful when we mess with it. Anthony T. Grafton, a professor of history at Princeton University who called for sweeping reforms of graduate education during his 2011 term as president of the American Historical Association, counsels caution when it comes to the dissertation. He advises that reform-minded humanists learn "how to combine the rigor of tradition with experiment and innovation."[11]

Any change in the doctoral dissertation starts at the intersection of two questions: first, what should a dissertation be? Second, how long should it take to write one? These questions are interdependent and inseparable. Most historians, for example, agree that a history dissertation should be an extended work of original, typically archival, scholarship. Given how long it takes to produce something like that, it is understandable that historians have been slow to embrace a reduced time to degree. Most scholars of literature and language, on the other hand, have proved more willing to consider a shorter time to degree—and they are therefore more open to alternative dissertation formats. (Though perhaps not to Louis Menand's radically functional suggestion that one peer-reviewed article substitute for the dissertation.[12] Because Menand's suggestion goes so far beyond conventional practice, it is presumably polemical, and as such, it serves the salutary purpose of exposing some of the sketchy ethics underlying the current time to degree.)

These differences between the two largest humanities fields show that the two central issues (the shape of the dissertation and the time it takes to write it) can't be considered separately, and that the answers are likely to be discipline-specific. I emphatically do not presume that there's a single standard for what a dissertation should look like. The only right answer is to have open conversation about dissertation structure and goals within and across disciplines. One-size-fits-all changes are no more likely to make sense than the one-size-fits-all dissertation requirement that currently prevails. The necessary conversations about the shape of the twenty-first-century dissertation have begun, and must lead to reform.

Multitrack Models

Broadly speaking, graduate education needs to be more effectively tailored to fit the graduate student. Graduate programs aren't admitting armies of Ph.D. students anymore, so it's eminently possible to contour humanities doctoral education to the individual—and evolving—goals of those who seek it.

For example, the German and Slavic Languages and Literatures department at the University of Colorado has balanced its Ph.D. program on the twin pillars of radically reduced time to degree (the plan is for only four years) and a flexible doctoral dissertation format to match. Designed for those who are "interested in an academic career but also applicants who may want to pursue careers in government, business, and the not-for-profit sector," the program's guidelines state that students will spend a year writing the dissertation following two years of coursework and a year of research (either at home or abroad, presumably in Germany).[13] Attentive advising is built into this goal: the plan is to admit only four students a year.

At this writing, the Colorado program is still quite new—it has not yet graduated its first cohort. It therefore remains to be seen not only whether students and faculty can fulfill the ambitious plan of graduating students in just four years. Also—and as important—it's not yet clear how those students will fare. The attainments of a student who finishes in four years will look rather different from those of a student who finishes in eight, but will employers recognize the faster finishers as different, or deficient? The new program, says the Colorado German professor Helmut Muller-Sievers, represents "an effort on our part to shape the market."[14] Indeed, they are trying to shape it so that it will value potential instead of demanding achievement. (I have much more to say about the choice between achievement and potential in chapter 6.) For those who want to pursue it, the new Colorado German Ph.D. entails a risk, but a worthwhile one.[15]

The Colorado example points to the importance of matching Ph.D. requirements to the career needs and goals of the individual graduate student. If graduate students' careers are going to be diverse, then we—and they—need flexibility in the format and requirements of doctoral dissertations to accommodate that diversity. That doesn't mean that anything and everything should count as a Ph.D. dissertation, but it does mean that we need more imagination when it comes to deciding what does. And we need to eliminate the swollen requirements that govern doctoral education now— what Derek Bok calls "thesis creep."[16] The MLA, for example, now urges graduate programs to "validate diverse career outcomes." That can't be done except in concert with another of its recommendations: to "reimagine the dissertation."[17]

We can start by reimagining its size. Most dissertations in the humanities are four-chapter affairs, with some coming in early at three chapters or running longer to five and occasional outliers at six or more chapters. There is, in other words, a fairly tight window for current graduate students to imagine and execute the structure of their dissertations. This isn't necessarily a bad thing; the worst anxieties for graduate students are caused by expectations without instructions. At least in the case of the dissertation's structure, students rarely fret, for they know that if they write four chapters, they will have one less thing to worry about. That allows them, one would hope, to put their energy into those four chapters.

But there are certain cases in which graduate advisers may usefully offer students the option of scaling back to a three-chapter dissertation. The three-chapter dissertation is nothing new. Humanities students have been producing them for a long time and continue to produce them, though without much guidance from advisers.[18] But students should know, at the least, that a three-chapter dissertation is an option. So are dissertations that do not necessarily fit the shape of proto-monographs.[19] And they should know that a five- (or six-) chapter dissertation is likely more work than they need to do at this stage and adds months or years to their time to degree with few professional advantages in exchange.

Questions of length and time have always been relative anyway. There was a "debate over the dissertation" that was raging in 1960, and at the center of that debate was "the time it takes" to write it. At that time, when demand for Ph.D.'s in the growing academy was high, time to degree was low. The median period of time "spent working directly" on the dissertation in the humanities was 1.3 years.[20] We don't have a tradition of long dissertations so much as a tradition of letting the shape of the dissertation reflect the state of the academic job market, regardless of whether a student is planning to enter it. A small first step toward reform might be just to honor this tradition of flexibility—and expand it.

In essence, we need to build the shoe to fit the foot, not the other way around. While those who plan to seek positions at research-oriented universities are probably well served by some version of the traditional doctoral dissertation (though it's easy to envision this expectation changing), those who seek positions at teaching-intensive institutions (including community colleges) are not. When they apply to such institutions, students are routinely advised to shrink the descriptions of their dissertations and bury them at the end of their job-application letters. Why? Because the hiring committees at these institutions are interested in the applicant's experience and commitment to teaching much more than they are in the details of their research. Indeed, a commitment to research above all often raises a warning flag that the applicant ultimately wants a position at a research-intensive institution and won't be happy for long at the teaching-intensive school he or she is applying to. It makes more sense to revise the scope of the doctoral dissertation for such students so that its contents more directly relate to the teaching-centered jobs they are being recruited for. Ph.D. students in English at Idaho State, for example, include in their dissertations "a chapter-length essay that discusses the implications of the dissertation research for teaching" in order to prepare students for such positions.[21]

It is similarly imperative that some flexibility be built into the dissertation requirement for graduate students who will look for positions outside academia. New surveys show that many students actively seek such jobs (as opposed to settling for them as a poor second choice to teaching), and their dissertations ought to help them pursue those jobs, not get in their way.[22] They ought to be able to write doctoral dissertations that will help qualify them for such positions (for example, by including pedagogically centered analysis, as at Idaho State), and the structure of the traditional dissertation may hamstring them in this pursuit. In essence, the dissertation should be made flexible enough to make its pursuit worthwhile for the wide range of intellectuals who seek it.

The Colorado German department's experiment is admittedly small-scale. A bigger sign of collective awakening on the graduate school landscape is a 2012 white paper titled "The Future of the Humanities Ph.D. at Stanford."[23] Written by Russell Berman, a professor of German and a past president of the MLA, together with five other Stanford faculty members, the document presents the best specific proposal for more flexible doctoral instruction that I've yet seen. The Stanford model is based on admitting students in one group and then allowing for them to disperse later on into different tracks aimed at their different career goals. The Stanford group wants to reimagine the whole graduate curriculum in the humanities. If their proposal is approved—and that's a big if—then humanities Ph.D. students at Stanford will submit a ranked list of their career preferences to their departments at the end of their second year of doctoral study. The rest of their time in graduate school would then be customized according to those preferences, with the remaining requirements (such as the comprehensive exam) prepared with their particular career goals in mind.

The dissertation figures prominently in this vision. The Stanford paper focuses on the unconscionably high time to degree and the failure of graduate schools to prepare students for a "diverse array of meaningful, socially productive, and personally rewarding careers within and outside the academy"—the two variables that also define what a dissertation will look like. The authors note the demand for "efficiency" and "broader professionalization opportunities" at the same time, Berman says.[24] The new plan is designed to resolve the incompatible demands for both "faster" and "more."

The most important requirement, the dissertation, has to be included in this practical calculus. The Stanford document doesn't traffic in details, but it envisions "alternatives to the traditional dissertation format" that would serve a student's individual career goals. Jennifer Summit, one of the authors of the document, suggests that students might turn in a "suite of essays" instead of a monograph.[25] That idea of breaking up the dissertation has a lively recent history. The phrase itself is borrowed from Sidonie Smith, a professor of English at the University of Michigan, who invoked it when she was president of the MLA, in 2010. But David Damrosch, a professor of comparative literature at Harvard University, campaigned for a version of the same thing much earlier, in *We Scholars* (1995). The 2014 *Report of the MLA Task Force in Doctoral Study in Modern Language and Literature,* also chaired by Berman, offers somewhat more specific suggestions along these lines. An "expanded repertoire" of dissertation possibilities would include not only the suite of essays but also "Web-based projects that give evidence of extensive research; translations, with accompanying theoretical and critical reflection; public humanities projects that include collaboration with people in other cultural institutions and contain an explicit dimension of research; and the treatment of texts in terms of their pedagogical value in classrooms."[26]

These proposals would expand what is possible for a graduate student to do, but they also question the traditional idea of who a graduate student *is*. That's important, and it needs our atention. A more flexible view of the dissertation offers to expand our definition of "scholar" (and "scholarship"). Or else it may lead to the argument that some graduate students are not scholars at all.

We have to oppose such a narrow definition of "scholar." To do otherwise would show a lack of imagination about what we do, to say nothing of a lack of concern for both its past and its future prospects. This idea is not exactly new. In a landmark 1990 essay, Ernest Boyer distinguished what he calls the scholarship of teaching, the scholarship of integration, and the scholarship of application from the traditional scholarship of discovery.[27] Boyer's ideas resonated—his essay is still cited often—but they haven't taken root where they most need to. Professors have operated for too long as though "discovery" were the only kind of scholarship worthy of the name. Even those who teach heavy loads accept the prevailing value system that places the scholarship of discovery (and the publication industry that is built on it) at the top of the heap. And these beliefs all support the idea that everyone should write the same kind of doctoral dissertation.

Dissertations like the ones being written at Idaho State suggest that many graduate students will benefit from a wider approach to scholarship than that. A broader definition of scholarship need not connote a lack of commitment to research (and the MLA's suggestions for alternative dissertation formats carefully emphasize a research component in every case). These different approaches don't equate to a lack of research or rigor. They simply mean that students will ask different kinds of research questions.

It's useful and valuable for suggestions like this to emanate from elite universities at the top of the food chain. When top-ranked institutions make policy that might be attacked as less rigorous—say, by making the Ph.D. appear less scholarly—they give cover to everyone else to do the same. I'm choosing my words carefully here: the Stanford idea isn't less rigorous. (Rather, I can imagine Stanford graduate students working harder than most of their peers at other institutions to finish their degrees ahead of their fellowship deadlines.) Instead, it's more realistic in that it corresponds to the world that graduate students actually live in, and contours the Ph.D. degree to fit it.[28]

A broader definition of scholarship also helps to avoid the biggest danger facing new dissertation formats: the two-track Ph.D. The two-track model of education echoes the two-track employment system that I described earlier, which divides research universities from all other postsecondary institutions. Importing that value system back into graduate school would mean dividing the "scholars" from the "teachers" by granting them separate versions of the doctorate. The motivation to separate the two has generated a number of initiatives over many years. Because most graduate students won't get jobs that emphasize research, the two-track argument goes, why should they write esoteric scholarly dissertations that take years and years to finish? Let them get some kind of "professional doctorate" that will prepare them faster for the teaching that will occupy more of their professional lives. This idea of different pathways is logical, and it has notable proponents.[29] Psychology, which grants both the Ph.D. and the expressly clinical Psy.D. (a three-year degree), already does this. Why can't other fields?

Perhaps they can. But it's not as simple as all that. The two-track model has practical appeal, yes, but it relies heavily on binary thinking—the "us" and "them" problem. It's easy to imagine this bifurcated model of scholarly and clinical Ph.D.'s creating not different paths but different tiers, with one entrenched higher than the other. Put simply, the danger is that it would enshrine a caste system. (More than a taint of caste already pervades psychology, but because most Psy.D.'s go into clinical practice, there exists an escape valve of sorts that keeps the Ph.D. and Psy.D. populations separate in certain academic settings.) Moreover, a two-tier model would reduce the time to degree only for those who choose the teaching-intensive option. It would do nothing to speed up the progress of would-be scholars. But the biggest problem is one of attitude: two-tier models focus on cleaving the whole and exiling the less prestigious portion to some other place that would become a place of exile. We've already seen how that sort of thinking helped build the graduate enterprise, starting with admissions, and the story wasn't pretty.

The Stanford plan is a multitrack model, not a two-track one. Most important, the proposal requires that all students be admitted according to the same standards—no first- or second-class tiers obtain. Once admitted, they wouldn't have to decide on their career paths within the Ph.D. program until they got a close look at the scholarly option (for which their own professors would serve as role models). They would also have the time to look into other career tracks—and one presumes, or at least hopes, that the departments would make information (and role models!) available about the non-faculty options, too.

I particularly appreciate the timing of the choices contained within this plan. Why should students have to self-identify as scholars or teachers before they even enter graduate school? It's true that some humanities Ph.D.'s will go on to teach two courses a term, while others will teach three, four, or five. (Professional adjuncts often teach more. Their horrifying situation tasks us all, but it deserves a book of its own.)[30] Some will choose not to teach at all. Graduate students obviously don't always get the kind of job they want, but graduate school is the time when they choose what goal to chase. It's much more sensible for them to make an informed choice of career path on the basis of a few years' experience in a Ph.D. program, as opposed to taking a guess before ever doing graduate-level research or standing in front of a college classroom. The question that programs must ask of graduate students is not, in effect, "Which level do you choose?" Rather, it's "How may we help you discover and work toward your professional self?"

The Stanford proposal coheres around the goal of reduced time to degree. Its authors note that the new plan would require a "substantial buy-in" by the administration and the departments that adopt it. Professors would also take on new duties under this new regime. Pre-thesis advising would surely become much more involved (and thus time-consuming), in contrast to the perfunctory form that it often takes now in the years before students choose a dissertation topic. In the new model, the dissertation adviser would take a much more active role in setting and maintaining a student's completion schedule than we usually see these days. Progress toward the Ph.D. would be assessed every year (with "benchmarks") as students, professors, and administrators aim together for faster graduation. Advisers would thus become taskmasters.[31] Or perhaps we could just say that they will teach more than they do now—because advising is a form of graduate teaching.

Two-Track Ph.D.'s in the History of Higher Education

Educating Ph.D. students, according to Fredson Bowers of the University of Virginia English department, is vexedly difficult when they have to "work for a living" as teachers while they "stagger along on loan funds, partial fellowships, student instructorships." No wonder, Bowers laments, that time to degree is so high. These complaints sound like they might have been made yesterday, but they're about fifty years old, dating from the brief postwar generation when professors' jobs were being created faster than they could be filled. Bowers made his remarks in 1965, as part of an argument for a "learned but non-research degree" that would, in three years, prepare its holders to be "well-trained and informed collegiate teachers of English" at undergraduate institutions, where they were badly needed at the time. Staffing this second track would, he argued, allow an elite minority of Ph.D.'s to concentrate on research.[32]

Bowers's proposal was a small entry in a larger and still-ongoing story of dual-track Ph.D. ideas. These ideas occupy important branches of the larger history of higher education in the United States, and new two-track models are still being proposed now. The two-track story is persistent, and therefore worth tracing. It is an important cautionary tale.

The doctoral dissertation isn't that old, at least not compared to the doctorate itself. The new academic traditions of the Ph.D. and the dissertation quickly entrenched themselves in U.S. academic culture during the late nineteenth and early twentieth centuries, when the university remained small. (Not many Americans went to college in the early twentieth century—fewer than 5 percent of those of college age attended. Even the new state universities, which were founded shortly after the first wave of private research universities, had enrollments in the low four figures; unlike now, their numbers were comparable to elite private universities at the time.)[33]

The Ph.D. became a symbol of pure intellectual inquiry during this early period—but at the same time, it possessed an accompanying practical application: its holders also taught at the postsecondary level. In the view of many traditionalists, that need to teach was like a tin can tied to the tail of research. Howard Lee McBain, dean of the graduate school at Columbia, complained in 1932 that every graduate school in the United States had become "in essence . . . a teacher's college." In this respect, he said, American graduate school refuses "to confess or even to face its nature." But McBain wasn't ready to give up the effort to reform that nature. He suggested that doctors of education (about which more presently) might be prepared to handle the teaching that currently burdened Ph.D.-holding scholars.[34]

McBain's view was common in his time, and its vestiges still linger. The Ph.D. had many adherents who were eager to nurture and protect it from any association with practical application—including direct preparation for teaching. (It was considered acceptable—if not desirable—that Ph.D. recipients teach below the graduate level but not that they be explicitly prepared to do so.) Lower-level teaching, then, was widely considered to be beneath Ph.D.'s, even if they did occasionally have to engage in it.

As we've seen, such efforts to separate research and professional practice have deep roots. The early leaders of elite universities (and aspirants to that elite status) supported research but also saw the value, financial and otherwise, of training practitioners. Early graduate-admissions practices thus entailed accepting a lot of master's degree students, while also trying to keep these teachers-in-training separate from the apprentice scholars who were studying for the Ph.D.

Universities increased in numbers and size during the early twentieth century, but graduate schools grew at a disproportionately higher rate, much faster than their surroundings. Though the size of the national college-age population did not even double between 1900 and 1940, reports Bernard Berelson, "institutions offering the doctorate more than tripled," and "college faculties became five times as large." College enrollments increased sixfold, but their gains paled beside graduate enrollments, which rose by more than double that ratio. By every measure, graduate school was booming.[35]

By the 1930s, the increased size and scale of graduate education led to calls for a separate professional doctorate that would meet the demand for college teachers without tainting the mission of scholarly researchers studying for the Ph.D. The idea of professional doctorates was not new to the American higher-educational scene. Medical schools and law schools have been turning out professional doctorates for generations, though we are no longer accustomed to thinking of them in those terms.[36]

Two specific initiatives eventually resulted from the call for professional doctorates: the Ed.D. (or doctor of education) and the D.A. (doctor of arts). Each centered on training practitioners, as opposed to scholars. The fates of these degrees are instructive, for they illustrate the risks of the two-track approach that some commentators want to revive today.

The Ed.D. was a degree intended as preparation for practitioners in the field of education, such as principals, curriculum specialists, teacher-educators, and evaluators. It was difficult from the beginning to distinguish the Ed.D. from the Ph.D. in education, and that problem has never been solved.

The first Ph.D. in education was awarded by Columbia University's Teachers College in 1893, while the first Ed.D. was granted by Harvard in 1920.[37] The Ph.D. in education was considered to be a traditional academic degree that prepared teachers, faculty, and scholars, often from the perspective of a particular discipline. In reality, its distinction from the Ed.D. proved minimal. Ed.D. programs tended to require research work—including a dissertation—similar to what was performed in Ph.D. programs but with fewer other requirements. Consequently, the Ed.D. wound up looking like a "low-end Ph.D."[38] Lee S. Shulman, president of the Carnegie Foundation for the Advancement of Teaching, not long ago called it a "Ph.D.-lite."[39]

In 1931, a study was conducted on the wisdom of granting the Ed.D. as opposed to the Ph.D.[40] No red flags went up, and by the 1950s, ninety-two universities were awarding one or both of those degrees. The Ed.D. witnessed a decline of popularity in the 1960s, but by 1983, the number of institutions awarding either the Ed.D. or the Ph.D. in education (or both) had risen to 167.[41] The Ed.D. had achieved distinction, if not distinctiveness.

The doctor or arts degree was first suggested at the same 1932 meeting of the AAU at which Columbia's Dean McBain accused American graduate schools of being teachers' colleges in disguise. The D.A. was not adopted at that meeting, but it was proposed again during the 1960s, around the time Fredson Bowers touted it. Its main purpose was to meet the shortage of college teachers during the postwar generation. During this period of academic abundance, baby boomers crowded into universities, which were themselves enriched by federal money that started to flow due to the demands of the Cold War. Ph.D.'s were badly wanted for teaching jobs; when Bowers worried that there were "not enough to go around," he was talking about people, not professorships.[42] This time, the new degree caught on. The first D.A.'s were offered in math, English, history, and fine arts by Carnegie Mellon in 1967.

Intended as a shorter alternative to the Ph.D., the D.A. was designed to cut time to degree (which even in the 1960s was thought to be excessive, as

Bowers's assessment suggests). Supporters of the D.A. noted that the lengthy and specialized nature of Ph.D. dissertation research ill prepared students for college teaching. The new degree would take only three years because it would eliminate the dissertation. Defenders of the traditional Ph.D. and proponents of the new professional degree agreed that Ph.D.'s should be shifted out of undergraduate classrooms and replaced with professional D.A.'s who knew what to do there. (Unimaginable as this suggestion seems today, let us remember that it was a time of unprecedented academic prosperity in the history of the United States and also the world.) As the "degree of the practitioner, the college teacher," rather than the longer and more specialized training of the researcher, the D.A. was envisioned by its proponents as the solution to the teacher shortage in U.S. higher education. The Council of Graduate Schools (CGS) endorsed the D.A. early on and suggested that its standards ought to be as rigorous as those of the Ph.D. (Here, though, we may see a glimmer of concern. The CGS must have been worried that observers might view D.A. standards as less demanding, or else they would not have mentioned them.)[43]

The D.A. gained noticeable traction for a brief period. The Carnegie Foundation provided seed money to fund D.A. programs during the 1970s.[44] "At its zenith," report Stephen R. White and Mark K. McBeth, "the Doctor of Arts degree was offered in forty-four interdisciplinary fields at a total of thirty-one institutions of higher education. In a brief fifteen-year period, over 1,943 Doctor of Arts degrees were awarded."[45]

Flash forward to the present. The Ed.D. and the D.A. are in scarce evidence. They have not entirely died out, but they both have dwindled and withered to virtual irrelevance. Various reasons have been given for why they receded, some of them reasonable, some perhaps disingenuous.

The insufficient separation of the Ed.D. and the Ph.D. in education surely contributed to the struggles of the former. That problem, which was present at the birth of the Ed.D., has never gone away. The Ed.D. now survives entirely in the field of education, at a relatively small number of universities—and members of that field remain confused about how to distinguish it from their Ph.D.[46] A 2007 initiative to reinvent the Ed.D. found educators muttering the same complaints as they had generations earlier about the resemblance between the Ed.D. and the education Ph.D. We need, said one, "to invest the time to really look seriously at the distinction between them." To the extent that the two degrees could be told apart, the only difference people perceived was that the Ed.D. was not as good. The problem, said the dean of the College of Education at the University of Florida, was that the Ed.D. had no respect: students were drawn to the Ph.D. because it had "more prestige" than the Ed.D.[47] *Plus ça change*. In 2012, Harvard University, the owner of the oldest Ed.D. program in the nation, announced that it would discontinue the degree and replace it with a Ph.D. in education.[48]

The D.A. suffers from a respect problem too. Its capital as a teaching-centered alternative to a Ph.D. evaporated as a result of two related developments. First, the academic job market tightened, reducing the demand for college teachers that brought the D.A. into being. Second, the increased competition for the professorships that remained led Ph.D.'s to become less fussy. Defenders of the Ph.D. had haughtily claimed that undergraduate teaching was below them, but they now claimed that same teaching as their due.

Professional doctorates thus dwindled, as Ph.D.'s—who were now being trained to teach also—outcompeted them in the undergraduate teaching market. True, Ph.D.'s still saw their real calling as research, even if its price was undergraduate teaching. Many of them still feel that way. And why shouldn't they? Academic culture consistently rewards the "scholarship of discovery" and publication over the scholarship of teaching. Nevertheless, virtually all Ph.D. programs in the humanities now incorporate some form of teacher training.

The case of the University at Albany, one of the flagships of the New York State system, shows how the D.A. has been pushed off the plank. Increased emphasis on teaching in Ph.D. programs, said administrators at the university, resulted in a greater "possibility of accommodating the interests of DA students in existing MA Programs or PhD Programs"—meaning that the D.A. no longer offered anything distinctive. But the Albany administrators also noted that the D.A. "is not usually a competitive degree for positions leading to tenure at research institutions," demonstrating their continuing focus on these unlikely outcomes even though such positions are few. This concern is absurd because D.A.'s were never explicitly designed to compete for such jobs in the first place. These statements formed part of a 2004 administrative move to cancel the university's remaining D.A. program.[49]

The National Board on Graduate Education, after a 1973 conference devoted to the D.A., described three reasons why the degree stumbled. First, they said, it was instituted too fast, before there was consensus about it among the faculty—who were, after all, the ones who would support and staff the courses that led to the degree. Second, there was never enough money for it, and third, the D.A. was causing an incoherence of mission in graduate education.[50]

But these accounts elide the overarching and most important explanation: the Ed.D. and the D.A. never escaped the shadow of the Ph.D. generally, so they wound up looking like second-class Ph.D.'s. If we return to the endorsement of the professional doctorate by Virginia's Fredson Bowers with which I began this discussion, we can see that he offers backhanded support. Bowers may have called for the D.A., but he effused about Ph.D.'s. He compared Ph.D.'s to fine wine, "aged-in-the-wood, and need[ing] to mature slowly before bottling." The result was an "elite group" that made up a "distinct minority" of the academic population. Bowers endorsed the D.A. as a solution for the masses that would not only give them employment but also stop them from "weakening the Ph.D. to make it more a teaching degree than the research degree for which it was instituted."[51] It's easy to see which program Bowers would have saved if the institution were on fire and he had room for only one on his back.

Other supporters of the D.A. also recognized the risk of second-class status. One early backer anticipated opposition from those who were worried that the D.A. would simply attract those who fail to get into Ph.D. programs.[52] From the outset, there was concern about caste.

That specter of lower status has stuck to every two-track alternative proposed to the traditional Ph.D. Instead of trying to unify the mission of higher education, supporters of the Ph.D. have often tried to divide it for their own benefit. But even though the Ph.D. defenders have been consistently arrogant about their research mission, the rest of American higher education joined them early on and bought into the same view. As a result, the Ph.D. establishment has kept the grip on teaching that it needs in order to maintain its position at the top of the academic pile—even though advocates of the Ph.D. have never fully embraced teaching as a full partner of research. As a result, doctoral alternatives (such as the master's degree, which I consider next) have always looked like thin gruel: second-class, second-choice fill-ins, and poor substitutes for first-class education.

American Ph.D. programs have long harbored this conflicted relation to teaching. It's an ambivalence we can no longer afford, so it has to change—especially in the humanities fields, where teaching and research may so easily and productively intertwine. For this reason, I believe we must beware of two-track Ph.D.'s. For doctoral reform to work, it has to take place under the aegis of the original, genuine, first-class article. Dignity is important, and so is honesty.

Reforming the Ph.D. must advance a socially conscious, ethical way of recognizing the importance of teaching and research as two sides of the same enterprise. There's evidence for that in this very chapter, in fact. The example of dissertation reform at Idaho State—the department's "Ph.D. in English and the Teaching of English"—is an overhauled version of a D.A. program. Under the Ph.D. banner, it evidently sells better.[53] It therefore seems to me that any reforms of the Ph.D. will have to happen under that banner—and these reforms will have to avoid creating a second class that no one will want to enter.

THE MASTER'S DEGREE

Some people say that we already have a credential for people who don't want a full-blown scholarly Ph.D.—it's called a master's degree. Instead of reforming the Ph.D. to make it more relevant to different career choices, this argument goes, we should just direct undecided graduate students into master's programs. After that, they can either go to work at something or—if they're told the score and still want to go for it—enter a Ph.D. program. Why worry about two-track Ph.D.'s when that's what a master's degree is for?

If only. It's convenient to think of the master's degree as a carefully crafted educational stage that prepares graduate students for either related employment or further scholarship. The problem is that no one actually crafted it that way, at least not in the humanities. It's not even clear whether a master's degree stands for "mastery" in a general sense. Writing in 1973, historian Richard J. Storr described the master's degree as a mark of "completion of a program of studies" that took the student beyond college "but still not to full competence." Storr held out the possibility of stiffening master's degree requirements with an eye toward creating a "professional orientation," but he wasn't very hopeful. Such models, he suggested, would be "mere exercises in futuristic design."[54]

Reformers after Storr have shown more optimism. They have held that the master's degree in the arts and sciences might be directed for use as a tool rather than tossed off as an afterthought. The thriving "professional master's" initiative in the sciences, started about a generation ago, is a prominent recent effort to give the master's wider relevance in the world of nonacademic employment. This plan gained early influential foundation backing that put wind beneath its wings. Its success led to a similar effort in the humanities. The outcome of that initiative appears less promising, but before we can assess its flight trajectory, we need to look at the wider landscape in which it's flying.

A Brief History of the Master's Degree

The master's degree gets lost easily in discussions of graduate school. It's not so much that the master's degree lacks meaning as that it has too many meanings—though in the end, that's much the same thing. Some master's degrees carry considerable prestige: the M.B.A., for example, is a well-respected terminal degree. Others offer a necessary credential, most commonly to teach public school. Still other master's degrees offer mostly consolation, such as those handed out to students who fail to qualify for certain Ph.D. programs. Significantly, most master's degrees in the humanities are unfunded—which gives an important clue to the purpose that the degree serves in today's graduate school universe.

The master's degree has a long history as a teaching degree, an in-between degree, and a professional degree—often in bewildering combination. In medieval universities, *magister* was one among several synonymous titles given to graduates when they began to teach. (*Magister* means "teacher" in Latin, though it should be noted that teachers were also known as doctors and, more rarely, professors.) Taken from the trade guilds, the title "master" did not then signify that one had passed certain exams, but it did mean that one was actually a teacher. By the end of the Middle Ages, the master of arts had become established as a degree acquired "in course" by students who continued their studies after the baccalaureate.[55] The library science scholar Jean-Pierre Hérubel says that the "protean nature" of the M.A. "can seemingly accommodate almost any professional justification," but it's clear from the degree's early history that the myriad meanings and uses that we attach to the degree today have longtime precedent.[56]

The M.A. has always meant a variety of things to a variety of people. That's because there has been little conversation about it—it tends to come up incidentally. Educators "want to talk about Ph.D.'s," says Carol Lynch, a former graduate school dean and program officer at the Council of Graduate Schools. "They don't want to talk about master's degrees."[57] It's hard to even start a discussion about master's degrees, let alone do anything about them.

The idea that an earned M.A. indicates advanced study in a particular discipline dates from relatively recently, no earlier than the 1870s, which is the same time that the modern Ph.D. degree was instituted in the United States.[58] But how advanced was that disciplinary study? Some of the earliest justifications for the M.A. centered on the simple notion that it was something less than a Ph.D. The Johns Hopkins University, for example, instituted the M.A. in 1908 on the grounds that it "would meet the wishes of those graduate students of the University who, for good reasons, cannot spend the necessary time for completing the work for the degree of Doctor of Philosophy." That's not exactly a ringing endorsement of the value of the M.A., and Hopkins president Ira Remsen knew it. His annual report continued in a defensive crouch: "It is believed that this degree is sufficiently protected to prevent any abuse. It is not a cheap degree."[59] Remsen's successor, Frank J. Goodnow, went further in his deprecation; he crossed the line to contempt. M.A. candidates, he declared in 1923, "are not graduate students in the sense that we use the words." They have "little inclination and less capacity to train themselves in investigation and research."[60]

With characterizations such as this, it's not surprising that locating the M.A. within the disciplines didn't solve the problem of the degree's indeterminacy. Into the 1890s and beyond, the master's degree still seemed "an object of deserved ridicule and . . . an ill-defined being."[61]

This muddiness persisted until the 1930s, when the continuing neglect of the M.A. by the Ph.D.-granting enterprise opened up the field for others to define and shape the meaning of the degree. Graduate schools of education emerged in the United States beginning early in the twentieth century. These schools professionalized the field—invented it as an area of study, really—at a time when more Americans were going to school for longer and the population was becoming generally more educated. (Public high schools became widespread in the United States during the early twentieth century, for example.) As with many other fields during this period, the professionalization of education led logically to a credentializing process. Teachers were once local employees with local reputations, hired and fired by towns on an ad hoc basis. Washington Irving dramatized this situation in 1820 in the famous story of the itinerant schoolteacher Ichabod Crane in "The Legend of Sleepy Hollow." Crane's continuing employment as the local schoolteacher depended solely on his remaining in the good graces of the town fathers, a prospect complicated by his attraction to the daughter of one of them.

The professionalization of education meant that teachers now needed a mark of validation that could be recognized across community borders. The M.A. was co-opted for that purpose, and many states began to require that secondary-school teachers attain the degree. These requirements prompted a huge proliferation of M.A. students. The number of American M.A. recipients jumped more than tenfold to nearly twenty thousand between 1900 and 1932.[62] Due to the newfound importance of the master's degree as a professional certification, some scholars came to regard the degree as possessing the same status as the old B.A.[63] This assertion that "the master's is the new bachelor's" was repeated often, and has persisted into the twenty-first century.[64]

Academics in the 1930s attempted to create better standards and a coherent definition of the master's degree. A report of the AAU prompted most universities to require a thesis of their M.A. candidates, while in general, scholars came to agree that the M.A. should require at least one year and that a student should demonstrate proficiency through an exam.[65] The modern M.A.—defined by its standards and requirements—thus developed in response to the degree's mainstream use as a professional certification in other fields.

During the 1920s and 1930s, when the master's degree was awarded on an expansive plane, the M.A. represented a kind of commoditization of learning that offended many high-toned humanists of the day.[66] These contemptuous attitudes persisted. In 1959, Harvard graduate school dean J. P. Elder described the master's degree in simultaneously vulgar and biblical fashion as "a bit like a streetwalker—all things to all men (and at different prices)." Elder argued that the M.A. should be revamped to serve as a certificate for college teachers, a low-status fate indeed.[67]

Today, the meaning of the M.A.—especially the humanities M.A.—remains confusing. Apart from the fields of engineering and education (and, of course, business), the master's degree is misbegotten. It also retains a stigma because of its continuing association with lower-level teaching. Recent surveys of students in the CUNY, SUNY, and California state systems suggest that many, if not most, M.A. students pursue the degree as a teaching credential, for both secondary schools and community colleges.[68] Students also reported that they sought the degree for professional growth, and as preparation for the Ph.D. A number of universities have sought to tap the "personal growth" market with M.A.'s in "liberal studies" and other broad designations. From the universities' perspective, these programs are designed for a different kind of growth, the kind that you see at the bottom line. That's an important reason why most M.A. degrees are unfunded, perhaps their most telling contrast with the Ph.D.

In the case of doctoral candidates, some Ph.D. programs follow the medieval tradition of granting the master's degree in course, as a way of signifying successful progress toward a higher goal, while others have detached the M.A. from the Ph.D. to create, in effect, two separate student bodies who mingle in the same set of seminars. Besides functioning as a stepping stone leading to the Ph.D., the M.A. also serves as a balm of sorts for failed doctoral candidates. For this reason the master's degree is commonly associated with failure in many Ph.D. programs, where it functions as an ending point for students whose doctoral studies are terminated by their departments. Such genteel expulsions usually result from failure on the comprehensive examination or insufficient progress on the dissertation.[69] It's common to describe these master's degree recipients as having "washed out" of their programs. That phrase demands close reading: it figures such students as human stains. No wonder the master's degree has a respect problem.

Given these associations, it's not surprising that the M.A. also carries the taint of failure when it's awarded to students who leave their doctoral programs voluntarily. This deplorable connection is a bell-ringing example of the kind of indifference to the M.A. that led to its marginalization in the first place. Such treatment gave the master's degree the image as a throwaway consolation prize for Ph.D. students who had left their programs voluntarily ("quitters") as well as involuntarily ("failures").

But there's another reason that the master's degree fell off the radar and turned into a low-level afterthought. Its denigration arises paradoxically from the generous support lavished on the university enterprise during the academic profession's so-called golden age. The increasing support for Ph.D.-level education in the sciences that began in the 1950s and 1960s, part of an unprecedented expansion of U.S. universities generally, caused master's-level training to lose its importance.[70]

Demand for Ph.D.'s was at an all-time high during those years—not least because of the huge numbers of professorial vacancies being created by exploding student populations. Their numbers were driven up first by the G.I. Bill, and then by baby-boom populations reaching adulthood, coupled with post-Sputnik research-and-development investment in universities. This movement fueled the demand for the second-tier Ph.D. substitutes that I examined earlier in this chapter—and these second-level doctorates suppressed interest in the master's degree. (This general movement also contributed mightily to the fixation on tenure-track employment that so hinders U.S. graduate programs today—but that's a story that receives more attention elsewhere in this book.) For a brief halcyon period, the system could barely produce Ph.D.'s fast enough to satisfy demand. The sciences led the way.

The burgeoning availability of Ph.D.-level funding to meet the immediate need for research scientists caused educators' attention to drift upward and leave the master's degree behind. Master's-level training lost its direct funding lifelines, instead of receiving the runoff from Ph.D.-level funding. When overall funding of higher education waned in the 1970s and afterward, master's programs everywhere found themselves starved for support, because Ph.D. programs sucked up whatever was left once the flood of money slowed. Support for master's-level training per se diminished. Some science departments did away with their master's degree entirely, as did others in the humanities, and the value of the degree waned along with it. The indirect effect of bolstering the Ph.D. in the sciences, then, was to diminish the utility of the master's degree generally. Always hard to classify, it became a degree that the professoriate doesn't care about for the most part—and it shows.

The Professional Master's Degree

Change is in the air—we hope. The twenty-first century has brought a substantial recent effort to revitalize and to "professionalize" the M.A. In the 1990s, the Council of Graduate Schools pushed for the development of so-called professional master's degrees. Such degrees offer the hope of a solution to the challenges faced by doctoral students amid the economic climate.[71]

The professional science master's, or PSM, was the first master's degree to be conceived in light of its own goals. This notion is worth a pause to consider: it makes a lot of sense for universities to think about their offerings in terms of how people might use them, from the side of both employer and potential employee. Such unified thinking doesn't happen often enough because universities often overlook that connection to the world outside their walls, even though it's a world that they are part of and that funds them. (I have more to say about that connection in Chapter 7 and the Conclusion.)

This book focuses on the humanities, but the story of the professional science master's degree is worth telling because of the ultimate connection to other fields and other possible professional master's degrees. The PSM story begins in the mid-1990s. "We saw increasing numbers of science and engineering students getting M.B.A.'s," recalls Michael Teitelbaum, a senior adviser to the Sloan Foundation.[72] That's because there was a gap in graduate education in the sciences: a B.A. did not provide sufficiently advanced scientific training to enable a nonacademic scientific career, but the Ph.D. took too long and didn't provide enough specific training for the purpose.[73] Employers said that they wanted to hire people with graduate-level knowledge of science, but not Ph.D.'s and postdocs. What they wanted, says Teitelbaum, was "a different kind of knowledge."

Persuaded by this argument, development officers at the Sloan Foundation sought a solution. They initiated "lots of discussions with nonacademic employers." The employers were, says Teitelbaum, "surprisingly consistent" in their descriptions of their needs: they sought employees with depth in one field, along with a breadth that would allow them to communicate and work with people outside that field. Industry employers have a name for what they're looking for: a "T-shaped person"—a professional with a strong grounding in one area who can also reach out across a spectrum of related fields and responsibilities. Graduate training in the sciences, they complained, was instead producing "I-shaped people" who lacked the facility to work outside their own sometimes-narrow areas of expertise.

Without a T-shaped supply, employers would instead "hire people with graduate-level skills in the field," Teitelbaum says, but they complained, "We have to train them in the rest of the skills we need." Companies reported that Ph.D.'s might be great scientists, but they weren't educated for the nonacademic career path—"they wanted people who know how companies and business work," says Teitelbaum. Ph.D.'s didn't know how those workplaces functioned.

The master's degree offered a natural point of entry to try to meet the need that was being described. Master's degrees in business, health, and other fields were already enjoying high prestige and credentialing influence—why not the master's in science?

Sloan sought to rebuild the master's degree in the sciences according to a new template: the professional science master's degree, or PSM. Most master's degrees at that time took one year, but the proposed new PSM would take two years, so that it wouldn't skimp on rigor. At least half of the required coursework would be in science, so that the degree wouldn't morph into an M.B.A. with a dress handkerchief of science courses tucked in for show. PSMs would supplement scientific coursework with instruction in areas that were directly relevant to careers in business and industry. The "plus" courses (as in "science-plus") would attend to knowledge about management, communication, marketing, and finance that were not part of the typical Ph.D. or master's program in science. The PSM in pharmaceutical sciences, for example, would include courses to instruct students in the workings of regulatory agencies such as the Food and Drug Administration (the understanding of which are crucial to that industry), while a PSM in a relatively unregulated field like computer science would incorporate courses in patent law, marketing, and other entrepreneurial skills.

Sloan invited proposals to develop such programs, with the requirement of communication between academia and industry from the outset. "One of the hallmarks of the design of the PSM from the beginning," says Teitelbaum, "was for departments to talk to industry employers about the knowledge they would like to see in new scientific hires." (Some faculty researching the PSM proposals were "extremely uncomfortable" making cold calls to businesspeople for their input, Teitelbaum recalls; but they did it, and most of them said they learned a lot in the process.) Similarly, all PSM programs were required to establish a formal advisory board of employers in the scientific sector corresponding to the particular degree—a PSM in biotechnology, for example, would be advised by an external board of biotech-company executives.

This tie between the school and the workplace is entirely consistent with the history of the American research university, which has a long tradition of seeking justification for its existence in its social utility. But researchers have not usually been the ones making these arguments for usefulness. They've usually been on the side of pure research (or "inquiry").[74]

The Sloan Foundation initially funded PSM proposals at Michigan State, Georgia Tech, and the University of Southern California. Each department received a three-year start-up funding package, with the goal of moving to financial sustainability at the end of that time. This small group of institutions made up an unofficial pilot program during the years 1997–1999. These early PSMs proved successful, and they provided the models for the programs that followed.

Building on these gains, Sloan funded a slowly growing number of PSM programs from 2000 through 2007. About 120 PSM programs came into existence during those years, with the number growing steadily by about ten each year.[75] The degree programs thrived, and the signs augured well for further growth.[76] The foundation decided to continue the program for two years past its scheduled 2008 endpoint, because the degree seemed to be reaching a tipping point toward further expansion.[77] The goal was to stimulate the expansion of the PSM at large state university systems, where many such programs could be instituted at one time. That high-level stimulus proved good policy, and PSM programs immediately began multiplying exponentially. In 2013, the Keck Graduate Institute (which replaced the CGS as the external assessor of PSM programs) held a large event to celebrate the three hundredth PSM program.[78] Over five thousand students have graduated with PSMs at this writing. Most have found science-related employment.

One remaining concern for the PSM is limited support from federal funders, who remain focused on the Ph.D.[79] But the main risk that PSM programs face going forward is a happy one: overgrowth. The responsiveness of PSM programs, which were, after all, built to suit the market, has been good so far; but the spectacular growth rates of the PSM (20–30 percent annually) are unsustainable in the long run, and programs will have to adjust.

Nevertheless, the PSM is, in Teitelbaum's words, "a roaring success story." The degree stands as a joint achievement of the philanthropic, educational, and industrial sectors. It "has its own momentum now," says Carol Lynch of the CGS. "Institutions want to be part of the brand."

The success of the PSM led naturally to efforts to extend that success to the humanities and social sciences. Following on the early good fortune of the PSM, the CGS approached the Ford Foundation in 2001 about a version of the degree in the humanities and allied fields, to be called the professional master of arts degree, or PMA.

The CGS subsequently convened a group of humanists and social scientists to think through the design of such a degree and did a web survey to look for consensus on degree criteria. The Ford Foundation then funded some preliminary feasibility studies in 2003. When preliminary findings proved encouraging, the CGS put out a request for proposals for a second round of pilot degree programs.

At this point, there was a sense of growing interest in professional M.A.'s—and early assessments by the CGS bore that interest out.[80] The professional societies in history and geography, among other fields, took this initiative especially seriously and led their faculty in this direction. Some early PMA programs were established at eighteen campuses in fields like applied public history (at Appalachian State University) and applied philosophy (at the University of North Carolina at Charlotte). It was an auspicious beginning.[81]

But then the funding ended after five years. Carol Lynch, the CGS officer who was detailed to professional master's degrees, subsequently saw her position end in 2012. Part of the reason for the withdrawal of support, says Lynch, has to do with the difference between the Ford and Sloan Foundations. The Ford Foundation "didn't have the same kinds of resources as Sloan or the same philosophy" of how to disburse them, she says. The PSM benefited from "a consistency of support" from Sloan over an extended period, says Lynch—ten years of funding plus the two-year extension I mentioned. But "Ford is not used to the kind of sustained funding to get something like this going."[82]

The external support for the PMA ended at just the wrong time. As a result of the defunding of the PMA's central planning, there is no national leadership of the PMA idea anymore, and no national program for reform of the traditional M.A. Today the PMA exists only at individual campuses, in individual departments. New programs are not being created beyond the handful of pilot programs that marked the beginning of the initiative. If the PMA is not dead, it's on life support. But why? Lynch notes that the early years of the PMA program resulted in "an increase in professionalization" at those campuses where it was being tested. The degree was working. But its lifeline was cut off just at the point where it might have grown.

The PMA clearly didn't get the kind of support or promotion that the PSM did—and not surprisingly, it didn't grow like the PSM did. Lynch notes that the long-term support of the PSM helped the degree to grow roots. The PMA has none, and "without long-term investment and branding," says Lynch, "you don't get an organizational structure that would support reform at a national level."

The PSM, says Lynch, is a "proof-of-concept success story." But it has also been treated like a hothouse flower from the start. The PMA was a promising-looking plant left to take root in the cracks between the concrete slabs in the backyard, exposed to the elements, nourished only by the rain. Is it any wonder that it has withered?

The defunding of the PMA is a sadly lost opportunity. The degree might have performed necessary public service to the educational and employment communities together. It had a chance to offer useful alternative training for those who are interested in humanities but who don't necessarily want to work as professors.[83] At a parting meeting of the PMA leadership convened by the Council of Graduate Schools, Lynch recalls, people asked, " 'Where's our national movement? Where's our organization? Where's our support?' And I didn't have an answer to any of those questions."

The PMA languished from "benign neglect," she says. "There were no resources to keep it going." In retrospect, Lynch says, it may be that CGS got overtaxed—in part by the success of the PSM. But gone is gone. "Faculty are saying, 'there are some opportunities here,' " Lynch says sadly. "We really need to do something about this. Maybe the time will come when somebody will start thinking about the students."

Indeed, the students are the ones who lose the most. American academics at all levels need to think more clearly about the master's degree and about degrees in general. The PSM and even the failure of the PMA show that there is room for creative thinking. At Lynch's home institution of the University of Colorado (where she served as dean of the graduate school before moving to CGS), for example, she oversaw a move to five-year bachelor's/master's programs. These proved successful in departments like East Asian Languages and Literatures, she says. Students and faculty both welcomed these hybrid programs as "a stepping stone not to the Ph.D. but to the world."[84]

In the end, the M.A. needs respect and attention together. American universities lack a clear idea of what the M.A. is or what it ought to do. The variation of possible meanings persists and shows a lack of care for our own garden. Professional master's degrees offer an interesting possible path, but in the process, they highlight the need for wider discussion of the degrees we confer, and why we confer them. We need to spend more time thinking about what our degrees are for, and how they might be contoured to serve all of the people who use them. The master's and the Ph.D. both need clarification. In an academic world dedicated to separating the two wherever possible, that's something they have in common.

CHAPTER SIX

Professionalization

PROFESSORS USED TO be weirder than they are today. Specialized, solitary work doesn't attract the majority of the population to begin with, and professors' jobs used to be lower paying than they are now, even after you adjust for inflation. Once upon a time, fifty years ago, most scholars who wanted to become professors could. Even after the academic job market tightened, the chances were still better twenty years ago than they are today. Fewer people were discouraged because of eccentricity, so many eccentrics walked the academic earth. As I look back at my own undergraduate and graduate professors, I realize that some of them were pretty odd ducks.

That's not really true anymore. The more straitened the market for anything, the more requirements that the buyer can make. So too for professors, for whom the bar has been rising for years. It's a simple irony, really: the more withered the academic job market becomes, the stronger the job candidates who emerge from it. As a member of many hiring committees over the years, I'm used to feeling depressed at having to turn away so many dazzling applicants. Every year seems to set some kind of new mark. In such a market, eccentrics—literally, people who are off center—usually get left out.

When candidates pile on top of one another in pursuit of a few coveted professorial openings, they look for every opportunity to distinguish themselves. This selective pressure leads to greater and greater achievements. These achievements tend to be conventional, which should not be surprising: prospective professors know that it's most persuasive to distinguish themselves in the areas that the greatest number of their would-be employers will understand and appreciate. But academia is a distinctive market because employers (in the humanities and other fields too) look for distinction within a very narrow band. Most particularly, they want to see publication. Today's applicants for beginning assistant professorships have almost always published, and the best of them have published as much (or more!) than their interviewers did in order to receive tenure.

This credentials inflation exemplifies the professionalization of graduate students that has become increasingly typical in the United States, especially during the past generation. Research multiplies at all levels. Though graduate students cultivate many skills, their consuming emphasis on research comes at the expense of other forms of scholarship. There are plenty of good intellectual reasons to oppose such professionalization. Specializing too early, for example, deprives students of a chance to explore and experiment widely with the topics and methodologies of their disciplines. It also leads them to resort to professional codes and conventions in their speech and writing that, as a colleague in English lamented, makes them "sound awfully like each other."[1]

Professionalizing our youngest scholars in this way also has wide-ranging consequences for disciplines, institutions, and other faculty members. The pressure to publish causes a student's curiosity to conform early on to what the market will reward. Collectively, most graduate students and their advisers believe that great scholar-researchers will have more choices—and more different kinds of choices—than great young teachers or administrators. This assessment is at the very least questionable, but it guides a collective pursuit of research distinction. The uniformity of this pursuit also illustrates a central paradox that confronts graduate students when they professionalize: to demonstrate their individual creativity, they cultivate a sameness of achievement.[2]

That sameness could be expected. Professors, after all, are mandarins whose conventionality allows them to maintain consistency and stability in their institutions.[3] But professors also celebrate unconventionality in most of its forms. Maverick scientists like Richard Feynman are heroes to physicists. Humanists worship great artists who break molds. But even as they value such iconoclasm in their articles and classrooms, humanists maintain highly restrictive molds for themselves.

This contradiction exemplifies the tension between individualism and equality enshrined in the founding documents of the United States. Graduate students face some particularly steep banks as they navigate between them. To publish in the peer-reviewed journals that bring them the greatest prestige, graduate students (and other young scholars) have to be smart and creative, but only in ways that will be appreciated by their elders, who are the same ones who guard the norms that these new scholars are challenging. In practice, deference to those elders proves necessary. We may prize big new ideas that start conversations, but we mostly must learn to enter existing dialogues. More than any other skill, it is the ability to speak that language and enter that conversation that turns graduate students into professionals.

The simplest way to evade the pressure to conform in this way is to be established already. And by the time young professionals have carved out their own place, they are usually willing (if not eager) to perpetuate the values that earned them that place and maintain them in it. Such replication of the system of specialized research is part of the history of the academic profession—and of academic professionalism—at least since the nineteenth-century arrival of the university to the United States, and its installation of research atop the hierarchy of academic duties.

Bruce Robbins, one of the most astute scholars of professionalism, has observed that specialization isn't the only way to distinguish yourself. There is also the scholarship of synthesis and the scholarship of popularization (a form of the scholarship of teaching) as delineated by Ernest Boyer.[4] But these options aren't really available to graduate students: you need cultural capital to practice these arts intensively, because they don't bring much in the way of professional reward the way the system is structured now.

The need for distinction, coupled with the very narrow set of venues within which to seek it, is the defining condition of academic professionalism in the humanities. In other words, graduate students must publish because nothing else that they can do will bring them anything like the same amount of respect that publication will. Humanists certainly support pursuits other than research. But as a group, they don't challenge the hierarchy that marks research as the supreme exemplar of "professionalism."

Professionalism, in academic terms, follows this hierarchy. It means subordinating oneself to a set of norms established by disciplinary leaders. More bluntly, it means Doing What They Say until you become one of them, at which point you can tell other people to do what *you* say. Who has not heard the admonition, often delivered in sympathetic tones, to "just keep quiet until you get tenure"? Professionalization refers to the process of learning to observe the demands of a community that you want to enter. Professionalism, in short, demands conformity.

It's perhaps not surprising that "professionalism" is a relatively new word. The *Oxford English Dictionary* records its first use in an 1856 essay by the philosopher John Grote, who writes of "the placing of the growing human creature in such circumstances of direction and restraint, as shall make the most of him, or enable him to make the most of himself."[5] Like parenting, this description combines freedoms both positive ("direction") and negative ("restraint").

Conformity has its plusses and minuses. Learning to stay within the lines may increase productivity, because old and established ways usually promote efficiency. On the other hand, too much time inside the lines may lead you to forget that you can go outside at all—or even that there is an outside. The American view of freedom leads to an almost reflexive scorn for conformity, but the American culture of professionalism—which created the middle class—adores it.[6] But these contradictory views rarely converge to form ambivalence. Instead, they remain separate in the nation's cultural geography. They also remain separate in academic consciousness—and that inhibits our work.

That work, for both teachers and students, amounts to self-making. We want our graduate students to follow the rules, but we also want them to be creative and innovative. Rather than try to resolve that opposition, we tend to think about professionalization very narrowly. For graduate students, academic professionalization typically becomes a synonym for "learning how to publish." But professionalization for graduate students is far more than that. When graduate students acquire the desire to publish and the skills that allow them to do it, they are acquiring a professional identity. These desires and skills locate them in relation to the hierarchy they bid to enter. When we talk about teaching graduate students what we call professionalism, we're talking about teaching them about who they want to be.[7]

With that thought in mind, consider the important findings of the education scholars Chris Golde and Timothy Dore. Their research on doctoral students' experiences shows first that "the training doctoral students receive is not what they want, nor does it prepare them for the jobs they take," and second that "many students do not clearly understand what doctoral study entails, how the process works and how to navigate it effectively"[8] Those are powerful indictments of graduate teaching—that it's disconnected from its eventual uses, and that students don't understand it in the first place. Golde and Dore suggest, in essence, that graduate teaching does not help graduate students' lives. Moreover, because graduate teaching creates students' expectations without satisfying them, it may make their lives worse.

Golde and Dore's results are consistent with earlier research. For example, the sociologist Janet Malenchek Egan argued in 1989 that academic professionalization harms graduate students. Graduate programs resocialize students and expect them to reorganize their lives entirely around a new, professional lifestyle, says Egan, so that "a student may wonder whether the institution's regulations represent a meaningful way to fulfill personal goals or the unreasonable, arbitrary demands of a faceless bureaucracy."[9] Therefore, she says, professionalization turns graduate students into people "who define themselves as capitulating to the organization by following its rules." This surrender translates into self-denial—not being the kind of person one wishes—and compromises one's sense of individuality.[10]

A survey of doctoral students published in 1999 bears out these assessments. Surveyed students said that the professionalization process takes away the "inherent passion and joy in discovering more about one's field and sharing it with others" and installs "resignation and disappointment" in their place.[11] So a doctoral student's own aspirations might be replaced, through doctoral education, with a new and inferior sense of self.

Surrendering to rules that you don't understand or endorse means that you're not becoming the kind of professional, or the kind of person, that you wish to be. In other words, the push toward professional conformity in graduate school (expressed especially through the drive to publish) threatens to stifle the creative soul and turn young minds into reflexive followers of authority. At the least, it creates incoherence in graduate students' lives. That incoherence comes at the worst possible time: when they first start thinking about their professional goals. From graduate students' point of view, there is a strange and stony illogic to all of this. Graduate students have to individuate themselves, and the easiest way to do that is to hyperspecialize. Paradoxically, everyone tries to be special in the same way, and everyone is measured on the same yardstick. So when graduate students buy into the logic of "publish or perish," they are not just directing their time. They are creating their identities, their professional selves, according to a rigid and narrow set of guidelines.

One of my undergraduate professors counseled essay writers to follow the rules, so that when you break them on purpose ("as you must"), you will be presumed to have made a point rather than a mistake.[12] But that advice is premised on knowing one's place in the system. As Golde and Dore show, most graduate students don't understand the relation of their education to their future, or their own part in creating that future.

Graduate students have to learn to find their professional selves within a system that discourages the search. The kind of individualism that the scholarly world craves may be compared to writing a sonnet or a blues song. Both forms prize creativity within a defined set of rules, and they reward originality in conjunction with influence and imitation. The academy thrives when creative intellects communicate, so there needs to be a conversation. But conversations also chasten and "discipline" their participants. Indeed, that is part of the purpose of academic disciplines: to bring people into like-minded communities.

The word "professional" was once considered base in the arts and sciences, but that was when there were more professorships to be had.[13] That view is not sustainable in today's graduate schools. Graduate students can professionalize without becoming drones—but if their teachers are going to help them, it will require a certain rethinking of means and goals. In the end, we must keep socializing, and professionalizing, graduate students. Where there are professions, after all, their members have to be professionalized to enter them. But academic professionalization is deeply flawed right now. It teaches narrowness and neglects self-awareness. Graduate students need the precise opposite: a big and varied professional self and the reflectiveness to use it.

Graduate students need preparation to do more than one thing—and the consciousness that they can *be* more than one thing. Any well-connected

faculty member in any discipline will know which departments best prepare their graduate students for academic employment, because those students stand out when they apply for professorships. Certainly that's part of
professionalization.

Unfortunately, most graduate programs help graduate students seek professors' jobs only. That has to change, and at some far-seeing graduate schools,
it has. The solution lies in complementing the adviser's work and filling in
the rest of the picture.

A small number of graduate programs do this very well. The School of
Interdisciplinary and Graduate Studies at the University of Louisville offers
a great example. In 2012, the school instituted a comprehensive professionalization program for all graduate students called PLAN, an acronym for
Professional development, Life skills, Academic development, and Networking. Two of the program's architects, Beth A. Boehm and Ghanashyam
("Shyam") Sharma, describe these four areas as "rubrics for skills" that "students must actively cultivate."[14] Boehm's and Sharma's positions speak for
the value of such cultivation. Boehm is dean of the School of Interdisciplinary
and Graduate Studies and vice provost for graduate affairs at Louisville, but
Sharma, now an assistant professor of writing and rhetoric at Stony Brook
University, was a Louisville graduate student intern when he helped to develop the program. The collaboration between Boehm and Sharma helped
create the program, but it also defines it.

PLAN links its four main elements through a coordinated series of workshops, about twenty to thirty per semester. Offered by the graduate school
throughout the year, the workshops form a cycle that ranges over the graduate
student experience. There are workshops on getting one's bearings in graduate
school, teaching for the first time ("The Teaching Toolbox"), summer planning (through "Backwards Design"), preparing for different kinds of job
searches (including "Developing an Online Portfolio for the Job Search"),
and many other subjects in between. (Scholarly protocols and skills are in the
mix too: the program runs workshops on subjects like "Writing a Literature
Review" and "Argument and Evidence" in graduate student writing. PLAN
also houses a "Grant Writing Academy" for graduate students. Workshops on
job interviews and writing a job talk are on offer too.)[15]

"Our goal in developing the PLAN," write Boehm and Sharma, was to
equip graduate students with tools to get through their programs and get
their degrees. But it was also to "provide them with opportunities outside of

their academic programs to develop skills necessary to become successful professionals." The program, they say, was designed to help graduate students take responsibility for their careers. The means to that goal was, Boehm says, "to create a culture" that encompasses both graduate students and faculty.[16]

PLAN is a lean operation that's affordable for an urban public university like Louisville: besides Boehm, there are only three graduate school employees working on PLAN, and two of them work part-time. The small staff provides "the glue" that holds the culture together, says program manager Michelle Rodems. They publicize workshops, talk to presenters ahead to ensure continuity with program goals, and attend the workshops to maintain that continuity. The PLAN website, says Rodems, serves as a "central clearinghouse for all things graduate student."

Meanwhile, graduate students, faculty, and staff all step forward to run the workshops. "Getting people to volunteer for extra work is a miracle," says Boehm, but they do it, she thinks, because PLAN gives them a sense of community.

PLAN also sponsors faculty development. I attended a meeting of a reading group for graduate directors from different departments when I visited Louisville in 2013 to see PLAN in action. Not surprisingly, these directors shared different goals, including what to do when advisers oppose outside training (psychology), how to get additional teacher training (biochemistry), and how to introduce training for alternative-academic (alt-ac) jobs (English). Their collegiality was admirable, but I think it helps a university simply to gather a varied group like this so that they can listen to one another.

Programs like Louisville's PLAN point the way forward for graduate schools. Among ambitious graduate programs, broadly conceived professionalism can no longer be the sole province of "applied" fields like business or engineering. It's essential to graduate study in all fields. Professors "already think like entrepreneurs," says Eugene Krentzel, Louisville's associate vice president for research and innovation, but it's hard to train them to realize that. And if they don't know it, how can they teach their graduate students to think that way?

PLAN fills that gap at Louisville. Academics certainly need to gain entrepreneurial awareness—the beating that higher education is taking in the public square amply shows that. We might follow the lead suggested by Boehm: "Why not start with graduate students?"

THE TIME-TO-DEGREE CONUNDRUM

The collective academic obsession with qualifications has caused us to lose track of an ethical issue of great pragmatic importance: time to degree. In essence, we've gotten so interested in what young academics ought to be able to do that we've forgotten how long it takes them to learn how to do it. The contraction of the academic job market has led young would-be faculty members to present themselves at hiring time not as apprentices nearing the end of their term but rather as fully formed professors equipped with clearly delineated specialties and subspecialties. That translates into an unreasonable pressure on graduate students to seek achievements that ought to exceed their pay grade. They professionalize at the literal expense of their lives.

That ratcheting up of credentials has been going on for a long time. The concern about its effects has been going on for a while too. By steadily raising the research qualifications for entry-level jobs, academic employers have profoundly affected not just the job market but the entire workplace. To put the problem into perspective, let me turn the clock back a few years to tell a story about an influential foundation whose new leadership believed that graduate students were taking too long to complete their Ph.D.'s in the humanities and social sciences. "How might we help these students?" the foundation's leaders wondered. A major study had recently called for extra financial support aimed at finishing the doctorate. The research supporting that conclusion was thorough and respected. The foundation followed the study's broad recommendations.

So was born a major new program to shorten the time spent earning a Ph.D. The foundation would provide money sufficient to cover multiple years of generous stipends. Universities would be given the flexibility to award the money as they saw fit. The cash would free graduate students of financial burdens. Relieved of the need to teach (or shelve books or scoop ice cream) in order to make ends meet, the students would then motor through their dissertations. The foundation made arrangements with ten top universities to award this money to their best doctoral students. Eight more institutions were added a year later. Then the foundation leaders stepped back, rubbed their hands together, and awaited the results. It looked like a happy ending in the making, and a point scored for targeted higher-education philanthropy.

These events took place in 1967. The foundation was the Ford Foundation, newly led by McGeorge Bundy, a veteran of the Kennedy and Johnson administrations. The foundation adapted a recommendation made in 1960 by Bernard Berelson (in the Carnegie-financed study Graduate Education in the United States) that students should receive additional financial support at the end stages of their doctoral studies.

The Ford Foundation Graduate Program lasted seven years, and it failed utterly. According to historian Roger Geiger, from whose account I am borrowing here, the program yielded an outcome precisely the opposite of what was intended.[17] The added money drove time to degree *up* rather than down.

Let's consider the background for that unexpected finding. The Ford program began at a time when professorial jobs were in abundance, but paradise did not exactly reign on academic earth. For one thing, the fountain of tenure-track employment dried up a few years after the fountain of money started flowing. As Geiger points out, federal support for research also began to decline. The Selective Service was trawling for young men to send to Vietnam, and graduate school provided an official refuge from the draft. Even so, says Geiger, professional options proved the ultimate determinants of time to degree. The students chose to use their extra money not to get out of graduate school faster but rather to stay longer and do more while they were there. They chose "completion with distinction" over completion with alacrity.[18]

As an economic matter, the behavior of those graduate students should not have surprised the Ford Foundation. There's a body of economic scholarship, dating from the 1960s, that argues against the idea that giving students extra grant money makes them finish faster. Economists like David W. Breneman showed years ago that while a number of factors (such as clarity of personal goals) affect graduate students' time to the Ph.D., increases in their student income make little difference.[19] The behavior of Ford Foundation–aided graduate students in the 1960s and early 1970s followed this economic model. "Given a shortage of academic jobs," says Geiger, "it seemed better to acquire stronger qualifications than to acquire them sooner."[20]

Has the situation changed? Not in any way that matters. If anything, the incentives to stay in graduate school and amass credentials are even greater now. Michael T. Nettles and Catherine M. Millett observe that productive graduate students "are more likely to be enrolled longer," and a recent Mellon-funded study showed that guaranteed financial aid packages (still) increase time to degree.[21] Hiring committees now routinely choose among applicants who have accomplished much more than their interviewers had at comparable stages of our own careers. At the same time, though, we've been calling for reducing the time that graduate students take to complete their degrees. How can we square that imperative with our hiring practices?

Just about everyone agrees that graduate students—and academic culture as a whole—would benefit if our Ph.D. students could graduate in fewer years than they do now. Deans call loudly and frequently for streamlined degree programs, and many, if not most, graduate directors have been asked to figure out ways to reduce the amount of time students spend in graduate school.

Yet time to degree remains stubbornly high. It's lowest in the sciences, where students still take about seven years to earn a Ph.D., and highest in education, where doctoral students take about twelve years (though students earning education Ph.D.'s often work full-time while they study). In the humanities, graduate students average about nine years to complete the Ph.D.[22]

One important reason that graduate students take longer and longer to finish is because departments don't reward quick finishers with academic jobs. In fact, we do quite the opposite. In the search for the best candidate to fill an opening, hiring committees privilege the kinds of achievements that can be attained only when graduate students stay in school for more time, not less. We offer the highest prizes—full-time faculty positions—to the ones who stay longer.[23]

Let's compare two hypothetical new Ph.D.'s. The specs can be adjusted by field, but the gist of the difference should be clear. Candidate A completed her Ph.D. at a rapid clip and has emerged from her program with a passel of recommendations attesting to the publishable quality of her dissertation and to her creativity, perspicacity, teaching ability, and enormous upside potential. Candidate B, who took three years longer, is also coming out bedecked with praise. She's done more varied and advanced teaching than Candidate A, and she has placed a couple of articles in leading journals in her field.

We would naturally expect Candidate B to have more to show for the extra years she spent in school, and we see as much in the form of her publications, enhanced teaching credentials, and (depending on what field you imagine her in) perhaps work on grants or even some administrative experience. That extra expectation is amply reasonable: if you take more time, you should do something useful with it.

What happens when hiring committees compare the two applicants? This is not a hypothetical question. Hiring committees find themselves presented with versions of this A-B comparison all the time. And if you look at the profiles of the assistant professors who get hired these days, you'll see that the nod almost always goes to those who look more like Candidate B.[24]

Some of these more experienced Ph.D.'s have had postdoctoral fellowships. Postdocs became the norm in the sciences during the 1970s, when an excess supply of job candidates led to the creation of what Paula Stephan, an economics professor at Georgia State University, calls "a holding tank" (though a special one from which only the bigger fish emerge).[25] Postdocs have now become increasingly common in other fields, where they serve the same purpose.

In fact, many departments take it even further and hire assistant professors who have been out for two or three years or even longer. These midlevel assistant professors (who typically show up with an armful of publications and other achievements) for entry-level jobs are then encouraged to reset their tenure clocks backward. Although that adjustment is made postgraduation, it essentially converts an experienced faculty member back into a recently minted Ph.D. and thus contributes to the same overall trend. (You'd think that departments would instead bring such well-qualified new hires up for tenure early, but somehow that never happens.) To be sure, junior faculty members are themselves complicit in such retrograde moves. Most of those who sacrifice years of experience do so in order to rise up the academic food chain, move to a preferred geographical area, or both. But we can hardly blame them for choosing options that employers make available to them.

What does it mean for an institution to advertise an entry-level position and then pit new Ph.D.'s against applicants who have years more experience? To begin with, it amounts to a preference for concrete achievement over raw potential. It also creates inexorable selective pressure in that direction. After a couple of years on the market, Candidate A gradually metamorphoses into Candidate B.

Choosing experience over possibility can result from the lure of achievement—and the achievements of today's graduate students are indeed considerable. But it can also result from complacency: instead of relying on one's own judgment, one substitutes the judgment of journals and presses. An emphasis on attainment over potential further implies that an applicant needs to have experience in order to get experience: a classic Catch-22 that is bridged by the willingness of departments to employ their student apprentices far past the point of simply training them.

Intentional or not, such practices send a disturbing message that gets worse in light of the numbers: most graduate students won't get full-time academic jobs, so it's more than cruel to force them to wait many years to find out whether they'll be among the chosen few who do. To set up such a trial is thoughtless at best. But an alternative interpretation is that it's not thoughtless at all. In this more venal scenario, the unspoken goal is to keep graduate students around long enough for them to teach enough undergraduate courses or complete enough lab experiments to earn their keep.[26]

Graduate school lasts too many years. Regardless of what one thinks of graduate student professionalization, it's neither right nor fair to force our apprentices to become full-fledged professionals while they're still being paid trainees' wages.

If we truly want graduate students to finish their degrees sooner and start their lives, then we have to honor that goal. That will involve two major changes in how the faculty approach graduate training. First of all, we need to set appropriate standards when we monitor students' progress through a graduate program. It takes more time to write a camera-ready dissertation than it does to write one that might be published after future revisions. This round of revisions used to be the main occupation of untenured faculty members, but the timer starts earlier now. (The same goes for publishing articles from a dissertation in progress while still in graduate school.) If students are to publish their dissertations as articles and books while they're in graduate school, they need to stay longer in graduate school—and in genteel poverty— to write and polish them. That's not right, which brings me to the second way to meet the goal, which is to encourage these standards—and reward them.

Brandeis University, in partnership with the Mellon Foundation, has developed a model program to give graduate students an incentive to finish sooner. The university is trying to reduce time to degree by awarding generous one-year fellowships to late-stage graduate students in order to help them complete their dissertations. The program started in 2009, and for its fifth year, the stipend was raised to a remarkable $35,000. If this effort sounds familiar, there is a salient difference from the Ford Foundation's program of more than forty years ago: Brandeis and Mellon require a written commitment from the Ph.D. candidates and their advisers that the students will indeed finish in the prescribed year.

They do, mostly. The numbers show that the added money and the signed commitment have evidently enabled students to complete their degrees faster. As reported in the *Chronicle of Higher Education,* more than two-thirds of the fellowship recipients over the past four years have finished within the fellowship term.[27] (Job placement data for this group are not yet available.)

Students at top research universities like Brandeis understand that if they want tenure-track jobs, they'll have to publish. They need to go on the market with first-rate dissertations, yes, but also with major publications that meet the standards of their fields.

It follows that the Mellon completion fellowships have a serious possible side effect: the finish-in-a-year provision can drive students out into the job market before their résumés are market ready. That seems an unjust result, but it's already happened—not to everyone, certainly, but to enough students to constitute a genuine risk attached to taking the money. Jason M. Gaines, a Brandeis Ph.D. in Near Eastern and Judaic studies, finished his degree in 2013 with the aid of a Mellon fellowship grant. It took him just six years, well below the national average. "My adviser told me I was as strong a candidate that they could produce," he says, but potential employers didn't see it that way.[28] He had no success on the academic job market that year.

The problem, Gaines says, was his "time line." Because he didn't have his Ph.D. in hand at the time of the autumn 2012 job season, he believes that his applications may not have received full consideration. Nor had he published. "I was encouraged to focus on my dissertation," he says, and to "publish after I had established my credentials." Besides, he adds, if he had taken the time to publish, he would not have finished his dissertation as quickly as he did.

Early finishers such as Gaines have credentials that do not necessarily sell themselves. The Brandeis-Mellon program creates an unusual supply of quickly minted Ph.D.'s whose talents have been endorsed by their universities. It doesn't require a Ph.D. in economics to understand that supply does not create demand. If Brandeis and Mellon are going to generate a group of candidates who possess unusual credentials, then they must also stimulate demand for those candidates in every way possible. For example, Mellon-sponsored early finishers need special institutional support that will identify them to potential employers.

The rest of us, too, have a responsibility to support this effort, because everything about the Mellon fellowship program—from its generous payments to its well-intentioned goal of reducing time to degree—deserves our encouragement and help. We presumably want projects like Mellon's to grow and proliferate. So what can we do?

Hiring committees are the real proving ground for faculty commitment, for only in that setting can we personally endorse the actual results of a shortened time to degree. If we truly support the cause of reducing time to degree, then hiring talented early finishers is the only decisive way to confer that support. To do otherwise is to perpetuate a contradiction—a collective hypocrisy, even—from which we have no right to avert our eyes.

To hire early completers says, in effect, that we respect their achievements. It also says that we respect their decision to accept what the fellowship represents: that they have agreed to enter the job market early rather than hang back and amass further publications. They will publish, surely, but under the banner of the colleges and universities that hire them. And isn't that a good thing?

Time to degree is too high in many fields, but it's a travesty and a disgrace in the humanities. It's easy for us on the inside to denounce that, but if we really want to do something about it, we have to reward the exceptional graduate students who are trying to lower the average. If we don't, we're just talking the talk.

GRADUATE STUDENT DEBT MATTERS

The most important reason that we can't look away from our professionalization practices is because professors literally live off their students' money.

How many professors are aware of the amount of debt that our graduate students are carrying? I certainly did not consider that question until recently, but it marks a path leading to precincts that professors must explore. When we design curricula or set graduate-program policies, we need to think about how much money our students will one day owe. If debt affects our students' lives—and it obviously does—then it should affect our thinking about how we teach and about graduate education generally. And that includes how we professionalize them and the ways that we encourage them to professionalize themselves.

Like undergraduates, most graduate students take out loans to finance their studies. Their debt loads are increased by rising tuition costs, but without the same hope for a compensatory high salary that motivates millions of undergraduates to borrow large sums. The scandalously small percentage of Ph.D.'s who land tenure-track jobs is no longer news, of course. But even tenure-track jobs are not lucrative enough. For a would-be academic, grabbing the brass ring—that is, getting a professor's job or some other intellectually rewarding position—can lead, instead, to a lifetime of debt servitude.

Tuition used to be low, especially at public universities, so the federally supported student-loan industry initially cost little when it started in 1965. But it has grown exponentially, so that now one out of every three dollars that Americans borrow (excluding home mortgages) goes to pay for higher education, with a total principal of around a trillion dollars. Yes, that figure is inflated by for-profit universities, whose elaborate mechanisms to encourage their students to borrow federal money are relatively new on the landscape. But even if we exclude these scams (for that is what they are), the numbers have gone up so high that they represent a game-changing difference.

That difference results partly from decreased federal support to the institutions themselves. What universities don't receive from the government, they have to make up in other ways. Public colleges and universities—which enroll about three-quarters of U.S. students—depend more and more on tuition, a model that the political scientist Bob Meister calls "privatization." Where do the students get the money? Lots of them borrow it—and they're borrowing more and more. (The thriving resale market for these government-guaranteed, bankruptcy-proof loans contributes to what Meister calls "financialization.")[29] The more students borrow, the more they have to pay back—and, thus, the poorer they are. It follows that we're impoverishing our students at the same time that we're educating them.

Professors get paid in the form of borrowed money. In a speech to the demonstrators at Occupy Wall Street in 2011, Andrew Ross, a professor of American studies at New York University, deplored the fact that his salary is largely "debt-financed." He called the growing mountain of student debt "an unsustainable moral burden"—a reminder that we need to look at it in those moral terms. "Today's public universities are selling debt," writes Meister.[30] Private institutions, too, are selling debt. The average federal loan debt for a graduating senior in 2010 was more than $25,000. It's even higher now.[31] (And I'm not even including private loans and credit-card debt, which add thousands more.)

The appeal of loans lies in the assumption that they're an investment that will allow graduates to attain higher salaries. (As borrowing rose, college graduates did in fact receive higher and higher salaries at first, but for more than a decade, nearly all U.S. income growth has been restricted to the top 1 percent of earners.) This model of student borrowing is predicated on the assumption that the borrower will seek a higher salary to pay off the debt.

The model doesn't match the behavior of graduate students in the arts and sciences. They aren't necessarily seeking financial return on an investment, and they certainly are not primarily motivated by salary considerations. Many of them are simply trying to pay for their studies in the only way they can. Only a small percentage of graduate students receive full financial aid. Even if we keep that in mind, graduate student debt levels are startling: a 2012 study put the median debt level for holders of the M.A. degree at a knee-buckling $59,000, up from the 2004 figure of $28,000.[32] The 2004 figure for Ph.D.'s was $45,000.[33] Those totals don't even include undergraduate loans. (Note, too, that those figures are medians, which are more telling than averages in this case. Some graduate students, especially those at wealthy universities, finish with little or no debt, while others might carry $75,000 or more.) "I've got debts no honest man could pay," lamented a couple of desperate Bruce Springsteen characters in 1982. Many graduate students could sing the same song today.

The social implications of undergraduate debt are wide ranging and disturbing. More than one analyst has pointed out that student debt turns higher education into a tool to perpetuate inequality (by promoting the notion that people should invest in themselves to get ahead), rather than a comprehensive social good (based on the idea that an educated citizenry is good for the country, not to say the world).[34] Moreover, high undergraduate debt naturally discourages students from attending graduate school, in effect reserving advanced study for the economically privileged.

Graduate student debt encompasses those concerns, but the specific situation of graduate students—many of whom aren't seeking primarily to make a buck with their Ph.D.'s—highlights the constraining nature of debt.

Jeffrey J. Williams of Carnegie Mellon University persuasively compares student indebtedness to indentured servitude. For a new Ph.D. who is lucky enough to land an intellectually rewarding job in his or her field (whether in or out of academia), the burden of paying off student loans on a relatively modest salary means a life of poverty from which the gentility wears off like a cheap coat of paint. Economist Paul Krugman warned in 2005 that the United States is threatening to become a "debt peonage" society, in which borrowers work endlessly for creditors to service debts they can never retire.[35] The gigantic indebtedness of graduate students threatens to turn them into intellectual sharecroppers.

We can't talk honestly about professionalization—or the larger meaning of being a professional—without bringing debt into the conversation. Debt affects what kind of professional a student is or can be. Graduate students don't explore many of the assumptions that underlie their own professionalization, but they are unsurprisingly well aware of the onus of their loan debts. In this case, it's the professors who lack self-awareness. When professors and administrators countenance practices that maintain (or even increase) time to degree, we make ourselves complicit with a system that hurts our students' lives.

As paid representatives of the academic industry, professors therefore have a responsibility to face this debacle and do what we can. That starts with keeping the facts in front of our eyes. Our control over this issue may be limited, but there are things we can do. We can promote some of the current policy suggestions to do away with student debt and make higher education into a public asset again. That would be a salutary public debate to have.

But we can also view the time-to-degree question—and with it the idea of professionalism—through the prism of graduate student debt. When I complained in a newspaper column about how academic job searches tend to privilege candidates who stay in graduate school longer, some commenters disparaged my concern. "Who wouldn't hire a [more experienced candidate]?" asked one, while another declared, "Potential is just that" and called it a "risk" to hire a less experienced Ph.D.[36]

But if more time in school equals more debt, then a preference for more experienced Ph.D.'s essentially adds to graduate student indebtedness. If we ask for graduate students to acquire a hyperprofessionalism in order to get a professor's job, we're essentially asking them to buy that training out of their future earnings—which, given the shakiness of the job market, are uncertain at best. Put simply, we're asking them to spend money that they haven't got and that they can't be sure they will ever get, to acquire a specialized skill set (how to succeed in academia) that they may or may not be able to put to direct use. And we ask those who want to try for a professor's job to do this at the expense of shaping their preparation for other kinds of work.

Viewed thus, a preference for more experienced job candidates is not simply instrumental. It's also pernicious, and redolent of malign neglect of one of our most pressing, but least visible, concerns as teachers of graduate students. We can debate the intellectual pros and cons of graduate student professionalization (hyperspecialization, the utility of graduate student publication, etc.) until the next millennium; but let's not forget that money is at stake, and it belongs to the poorest members of academic society.

Humanities graduate students receive low levels of support and thus pay more dollars into the system. (Graduate students in the sciences receive the most financial support. They also finish their degrees the fastest.) Humanists finish more slowly and take on more debt. They also work longer for the university at apprentice wages, paying sweat into the system—without receiving any "sweat equity" in return—before they start writing checks to the banks that issued their loans.

Part of the reason that graduate students take longer than they should is that there aren't enough jobs waiting for them. (That's what led to the creation of postdoctoral holding tanks.) Educators need to adapt to that reality by changing our practices from stem to stern—including not only the leisurely way we prepare our students for the job market (and not just the academic market) but also the way we assess them for professorships once they are prepared.

Andrew Ross has suggested that students form a boycott and refuse en masse to pay back their loans.[37] That's a radical proposal, but my main problem with it is that it deflects the primary responsibility for solving the problem onto the weakest members of academic society. I don't mean to suggest that student protest isn't essential—it is. But faculty need to step forward and take our own stand against a cynical system that hamstrings our students before they take their first steps. That doesn't have to involve picking up a picket sign. It can be as simple as evaluating the professional training of graduate students differently.

We might start by looking harder at the demands of "professionalism." A. W. Strouse, a self-described "queer medievalist," writes, "[I have been] enjoined by my academic mentors to 'be a professional' with the same paternalistic tone that has so often commanded me to 'be a man.'"[38] He sees professionalism as threat to a queer identity. Queering professionalism thus shows how coercive it can be to people who don't quite fit its well-scrubbed mold. That's an important pragmatic and ethical issue because that idea of being molded is pervasive in a profession whose apprentices take so long to train. We might think of professionalization as a process that starts on the back end of graduate school, as students set their sights on jobs. But as Strouse suggests, it really begins much earlier, as soon as graduate students start to think of what graduate school might lead to.

Or it can start even earlier than that. I date the start of my own professionalization to a moment during my undergraduate years when one of my professors impressed me as someone doing a job. Though she was brilliant and charismatic, she didn't act like a god who had come down from Olympus for a few hours to speak to an audience of mortals (which was how my other college classes often felt). Watching her, I thought, I could do this job. I didn't think I could do it as well as she did, but I could imagine myself doing the work. From that point, I wondered whether I should try to.

That professor shaped my desire to follow her into the academic profession. My case is not unusual; surveys show that most graduate students in the humanities were drawn first of all to teach, and inspired in similar ways.[39]

It's hard to overstate the role of professors here—and of teaching. Graduate students come before us at a time when their professional identity is vague (in some cases inchoate) and parochial. A student like me may think he wants to be a professor, but all he may know about the job firsthand is watching his own professors teach. Graduate students are mostly better informed now than when I applied, but they still have a necessarily limited sense of professional identity. Because their professional self hasn't yet been filled out and formed, it's a swirl of ideas and possibilities.

Professional identity coalesces during graduate school, but not by itself. Professors look at graduate students, and graduate students look at us. Whether you take a graduate student aside to talk about the meaning of professional identity or not, they're getting some of their own identity—maybe a lot of it—from you. If they admire you, they'll draw more deeply from your example. Being outer-directed people, professors like attention and want to be admired. So we willingly place ourselves in a position to affect our students' sense of their professional selves.

Let us not put too fine a point on it: we shape graduate students' desires. The process is not simply of pecuniary emulation—that is, of wanting to be like the Joneses. Desire is deeper and more complicated than that, and professors plant themselves right in the middle of its formation in our graduate students. Notwithstanding what some critics of the academy say, professors can't make students want specific things. (If it were that easy, we'd bottle the formula and dose our own children with it.) But we can affect the choices that they make for themselves.

Throughout this book, I've been stressing the importance of teaching as a tool by which we can reconceive graduate school from the bottom up. We teach graduate students all the time, starting with the way that we model lives that many of them want. When it comes to professionalization, we should do our graduate teaching with the role we play firmly in mind. How we teach and what we teach both affect our students as they decide who they want to be.

We therefore need to teach graduate students a better and more sustainable form of professionalism. Their health, and the health of graduate school overall, depend on it. When we teach Ph.D.'s to be satisfied only with professors' jobs, we are, quite simply, teaching them to be unhappy. The data on alternate career outcomes (which are finally being collected) show that lots of people who get Ph.D.'s and work outside the university are actually happy in their jobs. And learning how to be happy in your work is maybe the most important—and most neglected—part of graduate education. That we must teach. It's our professional responsibility.[40]

That responsibility runs through all of our teaching—from curriculum design to conferral over résumés and manuscripts. We have to bring students' desires into line with students' possibilities. When they're out of line, students not only go unemployed. We also set them up to be unhappy. Let us professionalize the humanities then, but let us do so humanely.

CHAPTER SEVEN

The Job Market Reconceived

I BEGIN THIS inquiry into the academic job market by putting on my English teacher's hat to close read the phrase "job market" itself. Take the word "market" first. Academics have a strange relation to markets. Our politics generally lean left, so we're suspicious of unregulated economic markets in the national context. But we don't scrutinize our own markets the same way. The academic job market is another prime example of an unscrutinized market.

Marc Bousquet makes the important point that the academic job market is not really a market at all.[1] For starters, the university produces the supply and the demand at the same time, so you don't have economic free agents as separate producers and consumers. This is worth stressing: universities produce Ph.D.'s, and universities hire the same Ph.D.'s. When the producer and the consumer are the same entity, it ought to be easy to achieve equilibrium. You simply adjust supply to meet demand, and you won't have a lot of graduate students scrambling for a small number of academic jobs.

This hypothetical outcome rests on two main assumptions. The one that Bousquet examines is the notion that the university wants a market where

supply meets demand. Bousquet says that this assumption is simply wrong—
he argues that the university *wants* supply to exceed demand, because that
puts the whip into the hand of the administration. In practical terms, an
excess of supply means that there will always be plenty of extra graduate students and unemployed Ph.D.'s around to teach lower-level undergraduate
courses for low salaries. Bousquet argues that the university can and does
manipulate supply and demand to maintain a system that is nothing less
than feudal, with graduate students as the serfs.

But the model also rests on a second assumption that Bousquet
rejects—and that's the idea that the only viable or desirable employment
goal for a Ph.D. is to become a professor. I've questioned that idea throughout
this book, and now I view it through the prism of the job market. In what
follows, I unfold a series of widening views of the job market. I start with the
traditional equation of "job market" to mean "academic job market." Then I
broaden the field to encompass what "job market" ought to mean: academic,
alternative academic (alt-ac), and nonacademic jobs, taken together as one
contiguous range of opportunity.

COMMUNICATIONS PROBLEMS

Here's a true story of the job market. Once there was an academic I'll call
Jack. Jack got his B.A. from an elite college in the early 1980s and then began
graduate school at another elite university. There he exemplified the national
trend toward slow completion. He didn't get his Ph.D. until twelve years
later, in the mid-1990s.

Like many other young Ph.D.'s then and now, Jack had bad luck on the job
market despite a solid publication record. He didn't get a tenure-track job out
of the gate, so he took a visiting assistant professorship at a major state university. With that appointment, Jack began a career-long migration in search of
permanent employment. That passage took Jack from school to school, with
the two longest stops lasting four years each—once in the writing program of
a major private university, and then in another visiting professorship at a
different private university (this one a series of four one-year contracts, so Jack
never knew from year to year whether he'd be employed beyond May).

Through it all, Jack evolved from a committed teacher into a fantastically
dedicated one. He struggled with mixed success to maintain a publishing

agenda while testing the job market each year. After that last four-year stint ended, Jack failed for the first time to land on his feet at another school. Then, in what amounts to a cruel cosmic joke—or a cynical reading of the book of Job, perhaps—Jack got cancer. His diagnosis gave him a new job, as caregiver to himself. That job, like all the others, proved temporary. Jack died in 2010.

Why, at a time when graduate students are lucky if they get a professor's job at all, should I invoke the travails of an unfortunate graduate of a top program? Because that gap between Jack's expectations and his reality is full of significance for all graduate students—and their teachers. Jack's life and death generated no headlines, but when you look closely at his unfortunate career, his ups and downs say a lot about the way that we prepare graduate students for employment, especially in the humanities and some of the social sciences.

Like most people with the gumption to complete a Ph.D., Jack felt that he deserved a tenure-track academic job. His first mistake was to stake everything on his competition for one at a time when the chances for such prizes had gone into free fall. Coming out of a highly regarded Ph.D. program, Jack also felt that he deserved a job with a low teaching load and generous research support. Over the course of his years as a temporary faculty member, his sights gradually dropped—but his expectations always trailed them. In other words, the assistant professorships Jack most wanted were always a little more desirable than the ones he could realistically compete for. Graduate school in the humanities teaches students to want the kinds of jobs that most of them won't ever get. Jack was typical in this regard. Like most graduate students, he was socialized in a way that disadvantaged him in the larger professional world that he sought to enter.

None of Jack's teachers ever talked to him straight. They wrote him sincere letters of recommendation, but they never advised him in the literal sense of actually giving him advice. Consequently, he didn't learn what he needed to know, at least not when he needed to know it. This was a failure of mentorship, but unlike many alongside him in the contingent faculty trenches, Jack never became bitter.

In fact, Jack was a persistent optimist. I never knew him to get angry about his own circumstances. But we might forgive his peers if they don't feel the same way. There isn't any quantitative data about the views that graduate students (and former graduate students) have of the academic job market, but when I've discussed the subject in print, it taps a vein—no, an artery—that releases a lot of pent-up anger.

One of my readers, for example, lashed out at tenured professors who have "seemingly no clue about the realities of the current higher ed job market," while another complained that "the system wouldn't be in such a bad state as it is if faculty didn't blatantly mislead students, whether through their own ignorance or lying intentionally, about the actual value of a graduate degree."[2] Such comments fairly represent the views of many current and former students. Unemployed or fearful of becoming so, they're enraged at their advisers and their institutions for failing them. Have we?

Here's what we've done: we've failed to help graduate students in the ways that they have expected us to. There's a yawning gap between what professors have been doing and what many of our graduate students believe that we can and should do. That gap points to a failure of understanding. How many professors sit down with their graduate students and ask them what they want from them? The default assumption is that graduate students want to be like their teachers—but many do not, and most will not.

Most students know when they enroll in graduate school that the market for professorships is tight. Nevertheless, they expect that they will at least be able to compete for tenure-track jobs. That's becoming an increasingly irrational belief. In 1975, the majority of the classroom teaching at colleges and universities was done by tenured or tenure-track instructors. By 1995 (around the time of Jack's graduation), the figure had dipped to just under half, but that was just the beginning of a steady downward trend. A decade later, it had dropped to under a third.[3] Four years later, in 2009 (the last year for which figures are available), it had dropped below 25 percent, with no sign of slowing its plummet.[4]

Tenure, it's clear, is being whittled down to a symbolic nub: educators (and sometimes legislators) argue about its validity, while administrators quietly marginalize it. Tenured faculty are not being eliminated so much as outnumbered. It's a little-known fact that tenure-track professorial openings have remained relatively constant over the past generations of privation—but the reason it doesn't feel that way is because the number of enrolled students has increased by 1.5 million over that time, and the number of Ph.D.'s has gone up in the same period. All of those new students are being taught by part-time and full-time instructors who work off the tenure track. So the number of non-tenure-track faculty has gone way up, tenured and tenure-track faculty have been minoritized, and competition for tenure-track jobs is worse than ever before.[5]

The diminished chances for tenure-track opportunities create a huge backlog of recent Ph.D.'s who vie for them. Each year, more join the pool. To hold this growing population of eager and anxious job seekers, the humanities fields have collectively hollowed out a "postdoctoral space" where new Ph.D.'s can tread water while they try the market a few more times.

This postdoc space results from a long-term oversupply of qualified candidates for faculty positions. It evolved first in the sciences, where postdoctoral work long ago became an institutionalized leg of a scientist's career path. The postdoc essentially extends the apprenticeship. It stretches out the job-seeking process in order to fit more people into it at a given time. It also creates more assessment points at which lower-performing competitors can be weeded out. Perform poorly in a postdoc (by not publishing enough, say), and you take yourself out of the running for a professorship later on.[6]

Scientific postdocs tend to be more respectable than their counterparts in the humanities. It was the rapid tightening of the academic job market in the 1970s that created "an ever-widening 'threshold' stage" for aspiring history professors, said Princeton historian Anthony Grafton and Robert B. Townsend, of the American Historical Association, in 2008.[7] This "transition period" between degree and job has been lengthening over the past generation for Ph.D.'s of all stripes. In 2012, Townsend tracked the data from the mid-1990s till after the Great Recession. He found a steady rise in the number of historians who had to wait at least three years for their first steady job.[8] The problem is not limited to historians, of course—they just have the best data.

In the humanities, that "threshold stage" postdoc space has evolved over the past thirty years or so from a prestigious award designed to support research into an uncategorizable mélange of positions that range from low-teaching, research-oriented positions (a fortunate group that comprises only a small part of the postdoc population) to glorified adjunct work with a "postdoc" label pasted on it. In addition, the category of "intramural postdoc" describes numerous recent Ph.D.'s whose departments try to extend their job-seeking lives for an extra year or two by calling them "lecturers" or "preceptors." In essence, the category of postdoc has become undefinable in the humanities, leading to the worry that "the humanities postdoc is transforming from a training period into yet another non-tenure-track labor trap."[9]

We can follow this concern to those who do adjunct work without the postdoc designation—for adjuncting also amounts to a low-rent, teaching-intensive postdoctoral "fellowship" for those who still seek full-time academic jobs. If many Ph.D.'s are bound to be temporarily employed, then they should be in positions that give them hope and orient them toward future goals—as opposed to adjunct jobs, which promise neither. Visiting assistant professorships, now so common that they have acquired their own "VAP" acronym, offer no future either. Instead, they create a class of academic migrant workers.

To start with, programs, departments, and professors should acknowledge that our lecturers and preceptors are still our graduate students. (So too for visiting assistant professors, because the prospects of our recent graduates as well as our graduate students is a collective problem that we must own, wherever they may happen to live.) That means that departments should give to their postdocs the kinds of teaching assignments (and other work) that will enhance their credentials and help them continue to learn. And we should give that work to our Ph.D.'s even if it means that they get the "good" courses and we teach more introductory-level and survey courses ourselves.

But even more important than improving the amenities of the postdoc space is to advise graduate students about the reality of its existence, and the reality of the diminishing percentage of tenure-track jobs. Graduate students deserve to know the score before they commit to join the game. It's the job of their professors to provide it, even when we might reasonably hope that they would seek such knowledge on their own. We need to talk frankly to them about their goals and their chances of achieving them. One of the fundamental problems in graduate teaching right now is a failure of communication—and the results are hot to the touch.

That failure is absolutely on us. We're the teachers, and the initiative is ours. The communication gap between graduate teachers and graduate students is an intramural version of the crisis facing the academy writ large: professors are only lately waking up to the need to take their assigned part in the ongoing and necessary discussion of the role of the university in society today. Advisers need not only to advise but also to communicate in a general sense. We need likewise to ascertain our role in the education of our graduate students—and to explicitly assume that role. We shouldn't wait for students to ask what's out there. It's part of the job to tell them. To mend the gap, we must mind the gap—or else corrosive anger will widen it.

SELF-SABOTAGE VIA THE PERILS OF PRESTIGE

One problem with the awareness that I just called for is that lots of professors lack it themselves. If you're mistaken about what's going on out there yourself, then how can you advise graduate students about it? Moreover, what if professors' ignorance made the situation even worse?

I'm not being hypothetical here. U.S. academia is driven by a very conservative prestige economy. Prestige confers reputation, and its markers are very hard to change.[10] J. Douglas Toma points out that despite the diversity of the American higher-educational landscape, most institutions aspire to the same goal. Moving in "eerily similar" cadence, institutions are together "obsessed" with the same thing. It's all about "moving to the next level," and the way to get there is always to garner more prestige. Institutions articulate these ambitions using the same rhetoric and try to realize them through generic approaches that are all designed to move up the same prestige hierarchy: colleges seek to become universities by adding graduate programs, universities seek to become research universities by adding star faculty, and so on. You can see differences only if you squint at the margins.[11]

"Prestige is to higher education," says Toma, "as profit is to corporations." Increased prestige usually leads to increased revenue; but prestige isn't money, and universities don't behave exactly like manufacturers. Corporations, Toma says, will practice differentiation in order to increase competitiveness—that is, if faced with a stiff market for pens, a company might decide to make pencils instead, especially if it's headquartered near a coal mine. Universities don't behave that way. They tend toward conformity. Another difference is that a widget maker will try to gain a greater share of the market—that is, it will try to sell more widgets and make more profit. Universities don't want a greater share: you don't see Columbia accepting ten thousand students a year. Instead, universities focus on grabbing the most elite segment of the market.[12]

The benefits of elitism are psychological as well as economic. Professors and graduate students connect their own identity with the organizations they affiliate with.[13] Simply put, academics revel in reputation.

That concern with reputation—that is, educational pedigree—distorts the academic job market that graduate students face and limits their already-constricted opportunities even further. To explain how that can work, let me start with a couple of facts. First, an easy one: not all graduate programs are equivalent. The second is not much harder: different graduate programs have different strengths and weaknesses. Armed with these facts, let's turn to the academic job market for Ph.D.'s in political science, a field that I have selected because there is good recent data on employment prospects.

Those data come from a 2012 study of job placement in political science departments, and it showed that top-ranked Ph.D. programs in the field exert disproportionate influence in the academic job market. Robert L. Oprisko of Butler University, a coauthor of the study, observed that graduates of the top eleven programs occupy almost 50 percent of all tenured or tenure-track openings in the top one hundred departments in the discipline. That is, Ph.D.'s from the top tenth account for about half of the most competitive jobs. "Students who come from less-prestigious institutions don't really get a chance," Oprisko says.[14]

But it's too easy to dismiss low-ranked programs on those grounds. They may not do as well at placing their graduates at research-intensive institutions, and political science may be, as will become clear, an extreme case of that. But the influence of low-ranked programs isn't necessarily less. Instead, it's different.

Consider the issue of placement potential: A given Ph.D. program has the greatest influence within a certain range of its own ranking. So Ph.D.'s from Yale University, for example, are most employable from the top ranks of their field to, say, about halfway down the listings. Meanwhile, Ph.D.'s from Little-Known Regional State U. have the most appeal from the bottom of the rankings to around halfway up. A mid-ranked program may reach up and down from its position.

Data on overall Ph.D. academic job placement are too poor to support a data-driven graph, so I'm describing a necessarily rough and general idea.[15] Moreover, the forces affecting who goes where on the academic job market are myriad, and most of us can point to exceptions. Not every brilliant graduate school applicant goes to Yale or its epigone, and not every brilliant Ph.D. will be hired at a tony place after graduation. Princeton University's history department, for example, does a lot of junior hiring from elite programs (including from Princeton itself), but it also currently employs young professors with Ph.D.'s from places like the University of Minnesota, the University of Wisconsin–Madison, and York University in Toronto—fine universities, to be sure, but lower on the prestige ladder than Princeton. There is no monopoly on excellent work.

Geography also matters a great deal. Even elite universities will place more graduates nearby than far away. Networking plays a part here: lots of credentialed apples come to rest near the tree, so Ph.D.'s who compete for local jobs usually encounter some of their fellow alumni while they're looking. (An institution's religious affiliation, if it has one, can matter as well.)

It's also worth mentioning that while rankings encompass entire departments, individual programs within departments may have very different placement records from the departments at large. For example, the University of Notre Dame's political science department was ranked thirty-sixth in 2012 by *U.S. News & World Report* (whatever one may think of that authority), but some of that department's programs (for example, the one in religion and politics) are particularly well regarded. Perhaps for that reason, says Geoffrey Layman, Notre Dame's graduate director, "We have had some recent success in placing students in major national or regional research universities."[16] Along the same line of reasoning, a superstar adviser may enjoy a personal placement rate that exceeds his or her department's overall record.

Provisos aside, the main point is this: there are different kinds of jobs and different kinds of training. Rankings encourage us to think of a department ranked number 5 as "better" than one that's ranked number 35. And the number 5 department will certainly be better at some things. We may safely speculate that the research produced by its faculty is probably better known and more often cited than the research by the number 35 department. In addition, a fifth-ranked department would be better at training and supporting graduate students who commit to doing cutting-edge research—partly by giving them financial packages that free them from having to teach much.

But might we not also expect that the thirty-fifth-ranked department would be better in some ways? Perhaps in training its Ph.D.'s to be thoughtful and creative teachers? Rankings are ultimately guided by what you're looking to compare, and the influential NRC rankings are comparing research output: NRC stands for National Research Council, after all.

Research isn't a professor's whole job, though. And colleges and universities that hire new Ph.D.'s don't all privilege research in the same way. Many, if not most, institutions seek skilled and experienced teachers.

Political scientists at many Ph.D.-granting institutions wrestle with the need for good teachers out there. It's an inconvenient fact for them because it conflicts with their aspirations to occupy one of the top forty spaces in the research-based rankings—and that surely contributes to the discipline's top-heavy placement record. Political scientists, like AM radio disc jockeys of old, prize the top forty. The top forty political science departments amount to a charmed circle, and political scientists invest a lot of psychic energy thinking about that circle—more so than in some comparable disciplines. Those departments outside the circle closely watch the universities inside and look for ways to push their way in.

Some of the have-nots can get defensive. A graduate director at a southwestern state university outside the top forty sought to flatten out any differences between her political science program and those ranked above it: "As a Research I University," she wrote to me, "our students, for the most part, are very much interested in continuing to do research," and accordingly, they apply to research-oriented institutions. Only in recent years, she said, have they encountered trouble, which she blamed on "the economy."

A graduate director of a political science department at a midwestern state university—also ranked outside the top forty—wrote of how his program's recent external reviewers pushed his department to adopt a top-forty model. The external team made a number of recommendations for how his department could compete against higher-ranked institutions and, he said, "place our job candidates at schools that lean more on the research side." The examiners recommended specialization, but the graduate director worries that this move "could pose a risk" for his department's job seekers, the more successful of whom tend to be generalists.

That top-forty model has proved unusually confining within the political science field. One graduate director at a state university in the South (also outside the top forty) commented that "the model coming out of the top forty is very narrow." It's also pervasive. "Socialization within political science departments is guided by the behavior of the top programs," he said. One result of that mimicry, the southern graduate director continued, is that "most lower-tier programs aren't emphasizing teaching," even though the graduate students at those universities teach a lot. Thus, he said, "there is a void in the academy when it comes to socializing political science teachers." Political scientists are failing, he said, "to see teaching as an essential part of what we do."

But teaching is obviously essential to what faculty members do—not only within the top forty and the top one hundred but also beyond those ranges, at colleges and regional universities where good teaching is paramount and central. And the Ph.D.'s who get hired at those places are not the narrow specialists with the high-ranking degrees. To learn this, I contacted some political scientists at colleges and universities outside the top one hundred (that is, below the lower boundary of the recent placement study). Compared with the aspirations of the top forty and their wannabes, these professors might as well be inhabiting a different academic planet.

An assistant professor at a state university's branch campus in the South described a hiring bias against the fancier job candidates. "My colleagues tend not to favor graduates of elite Ph.D. programs," he said, because his institution is "a teaching-oriented school." When his department hires, it seeks "candidates who have experience and a passion for teaching students," and, he said, "unless a candidate from an 'elite' program really communicated a high level of interest in the position and our school, we probably wouldn't consider interviewing him/her." Another young political scientist at a college in the South pointed to the four-course-per-term teaching load that prevails at his institution. When his department hires, he wrote in an email, it prefers candidates "with more teaching experience and who present themselves as generalists rather than specialists."

In other words, elite Ph.D.'s with highly specialized research interests and limited classroom experience don't easily fit at teaching-intensive campuses. And "fit" is what departments at any level seek above all. Heather Hawn, an assistant professor at Mars Hill College in North Carolina, recalled that when she was hired, her "hiring committee was very focused on 'fit,' which is why I got the job, over many candidates who graduated from higher-ranked universities." Her department also attracts applicants with Ph.D.'s from elite programs, but, she said, "we do not gravitate toward them."

These examples, typical of a larger sample I collected, suggest that what's being produced at the top of the political science food chain does not meet the nutritional needs at the middle and the bottom. Meanwhile we teach our graduate students to identify with their disciplines, as in, "I am a professor of x, and my own work is in the special field of y." By working in narrow niches and consequently disrespecting teaching, we're not really training our students for the jobs they'll hold.

The programs in the middle and even the bottom are too focused on what's going on above them. Thus, the disproportionate influence wielded by the top-ranked political science programs may result from the blinkered efforts of so many others to be just like them. Instead of cultivating their own strengths based on their own resources, they aim their prayers—and the desires of their students—upward because that is the basis on which they are evaluated. But in the process, they ignore the work to be done on the earth below.

I did encounter one graduate director—at a lower-ranked state university in the Midwest—who admitted that his colleagues "spend additional effort training students as teachers, making sure they have lots of classroom experience before going on the job market." Not surprisingly, his department's placement record shows the benefits, but he still sounded chastened and dejected: we prepare students that way, he said, "because we know our place."

He shouldn't feel so bad. The Ph.D.'s who graduate from middle- and lower-ranked programs possess fewer airs than some of the professors who train them. The assistant professor at the branch campus said that his university was "certainly not the type of institution I had in mind prior to finishing graduate school" but that he had adapted smoothly: "I really love it and am seriously considering making a permanent career here."

The lesson is not new. The economist and cultural critic Thorstein Veblen wrote in 1899 that "the propensity for emulation is probably the strongest and most alert and persistent of the economic motives proper."[17] That propensity has a lot of political scientists by the throat—and many academics in other disciplines, too.

A BROADER VIEW OF COMPARATIVE ADVANTAGE

We have no time for such petty pecuniary emulation. If departments want to maximize their students' access to the small number of stable academic jobs that are still out there, they must examine their doctoral training and play to their strengths. Only twenty-five programs can make the top twenty-five—and that leaves many dozens outside. And no wonder: what the National Research Council is looking for—research output, chiefly—isn't necessarily what all programs do best. Rich research universities will produce a lot of research, but that's not the only way to make a scholarly life.[18]

Graduate students at less wealthy, lower-ranked Ph.D. programs may graduate with less specialized research interests than their more elite peers do, but they're still researchers. Boyer distinguishes what he calls the scholarship of teaching, the scholarship of integration, and the scholarship of application from the traditional "scholarship of discovery."[19] Compared with graduate students at top-tier departments, those at lower-ranked programs often receive wider preparation, combining the kinds of scholarship that Boyer identifies. Such students almost always have more teaching experience too, which can give them an advantage in the pursuit of professorships at institutions that emphasize teaching. Moreover, those jobs at teaching-oriented colleges outnumber the more visible, research-centered positions.

Which brings me back to the insights of J. Douglas Toma that I introduced a few pages back. Toma recommends that universities could get better results from their efforts if they stopped trying to get more prestige than the schools above them by doing the same things (as political science departments mostly seem to do) and instead paid "greater attention to real differentiation."[20] That requires a new strategy.

Some departments have caught on, and they are models to follow in the job marketplace of the present—and future. For example, Susan Welch and Christopher P. Long of Penn State did a commendably detailed placement study of humanities and social science Ph.D.'s at their university and published the results. They found that their graduates hold a wide variety of professorships, up and down the food chain.[21]

Jonathan Auerbach, an English professor and former placement director at the University of Maryland, observes that "large public institutions and small, regional liberal arts colleges are looking for different things in candidates because the situations there differ as to expectations for research and teaching and service and the balance among these three." In English, says Auerbach, the issue is "not the education of candidates but rather the amount and kind of teaching experience they have." At Maryland, he says, Ph.D. candidates "do a hell of a lot more teaching than most candidates with Ivy League degrees"—including designing courses independently and teaching different types of courses (not only composition classes but also courses in literature, film, and even seminars).[22]

That profusion of teaching experience is, of course, part of a larger ethical debate about the use of low-cost graduate student labor to sustain large universities. Auerbach and his like-minded colleagues look to turn that disadvantage into a virtue for job candidates: "The very fact that, for financial reasons, our students are compelled to do more teaching than their counterparts at wealthier places actually works to their advantage!"

Graduates of wealthy Ph.D. programs rarely show that range of teaching, because their fellowship packages release them from having to teach.[23] Graduates of more elite programs compete strongly at the top of the research scale, whereas Maryland Ph.D.'s typically do not. But graduates of Maryland—and universities like it, many ranked lower—prove more competitive at institutions looking for skilled and experienced teachers.

Katarzyna Jakubiak, a recently tenured associate professor in the English department at Millersville University of Pennsylvania, praised the similarly practical virtues of her Ph.D. program at Illinois State University. The breadth of her preparation—"We had to take classes in all areas of English studies," not just literature—gave her "a certain flexibility as a job candidate," she wrote to me. Although she taught fewer literature classes while a graduate student than her counterparts at the University of Maryland did, Jakubiak gained "both experience and theoretical preparation" in teaching freshman composition that served her well on the job market, and that experience also informs her research. By contrast, a New York–area community college professor wrote to me that most of the job applicants she sees from elite institutions "seem to think anyone can teach composition and rhetoric," so they don't get hired.[24]

How do graduate programs best position their students to compete for those jobs? To begin with, they teach their graduate students to value teaching. Elite Ph.D.'s often do not even bother applying to teaching-centered colleges and universities. "I'm sure that some Ivy League Ph.D.'s would rather repair dishwashers" than assume the teaching load at a community college, wrote one New Jersey community college professor when I asked him how many of them applied to join his faculty. On the occasions that such candidates do apply to community colleges or other teaching-intensive institutions, the departments may subject those applicants to suspicious scrutiny. Such places have sensitive snob detectors.

One reason for such aversion is the concern that elite candidates are "slumming" out of desperation for a job, any job, and will leave at the first opportunity. The suspicions can cut both ways. A well-known English professor with an elite Ph.D. recalled a job interview he had years ago with a teaching-intensive college: "they told me they didn't want to pursue my candidacy because they couldn't imagine keeping me." He subsequently endured a four-year job search before landing a position at a research university. "For all I know," he said, "I would have been happy teaching at that college."

That skepticism persists because Ph.D.'s from elite programs often don't fit the institutional culture of teaching-intensive colleges. "When we hire, we ask first: What kind of teacher will the applicant be?" said an English professor at the University of North Carolina at Wilmington. Stephen Spencer, the chair of English at the University of Southern Indiana, was more precise: "We are interested in candidates who understand who we are as a student-centered teaching institution and who are pursuing interesting, promising research," he wrote me in an email. "The standard form letter that is not individualized to our needs," Spencer continued, "does not get a candidate very far. We tend to get more of these kinds of letters from candidates from higher ranking Ph.D. programs."

Auerbach, of Maryland's English department, recently created a nifty acronym to help his department's Ph.D.'s prepare themselves for this very large segment of the job market. It spells DEVOUT:

- Diversity, both in texts and the kinds of students taught.
- Experience, the amount of actual classroom experience.
- Versatility, or being able and willing to teach writing, literature, film, and theory.
- Outcomes, for the "learning outcomes assessment" tasks. ("A big deal these days," said Auerbach. "Since older faculty are clueless, they want new hires to handle these increasingly important administrative duties"—to which I would add that another reason that assessment should be valued more is because the ability to assess what students learn offers the best potential argument against massive online open-enrollment courses, or MOOCs.)
- Usefulness, or being able to link your teaching to real-world issues in convincing ways.
- Technology, or using technology in innovative ways in the classroom.

The DEVOUT idea is more than a gimmick.[25] It illustrates a larger truth: that our profession is not so much a ranked hierarchy as an ecosystem. Ecology is a science of relationships—the relationships of organisms to their environments. But since the environment is composed largely of other organisms, you could say that it's also the study of the relation of organisms to other organisms. We can look at the job market as an environment—that's what I just did. It's a harsh environment, with lots of organisms competing for relatively few niches. (Graduate students: I beg your pardon for describing you that way, but we're all organisms.) In the academic ecosystem, different institutions occupy specific niches, serving different populations according to the colleges' strengths. The job market has niches, too. An intellectual in one niche of the market is not "better" than another, no more than a bird is "better" than a squirrel or a tree. As Darwin explained more than 150 years ago, it's a question of how well an individual is adapted to the surrounding environment.

Economists call these distinctions "comparative advantage," a term that refers to the ability of a party to produce a particular good at a lower opportunity cost than a potential competitor can. The theory of comparative advantage leads to the conclusion that producers should specialize in what they produce best.

Universities, of course, do not. The competition for prestige blocks us from seeing the workings of our own markets and, worse, keeps us from our actual educational mission. So instead of concentrating on teaching and learning, we persist in trying to understand everything in terms of top-down rankings. Hierarchical thinking warps our perceptions about what we do as professors and can prevent us from preparing our graduate students for the work that they can get. Can we change this restrictive prestige economy? It is to be devoutly wished.

KEYWORD: PLACEMENT

If we are to change, it has to start with a reconception of the whole idea of job placement. Placement figures exert a lot of influence in departments and graduate schools. But what do they mean? Professors don't examine them very critically.

"Placement" is a great keyword for the graduate school enterprise. The word offers a portal into our way of thinking about the success or failure of what we do. To illustrate what I mean, here's another real-life story. Nathan Tinker, a former graduate student from my own department at Fordham, received his Ph.D. in English in 2002. He started out doing communications in a public-relations firm and then moved to a public-relations company that focused on technology. From there, he specialized further in nanotechnology and went on to found a start-up trade association for nanotech companies. Nanotech then provided a segue into biotech, as he took a position with the Sabin Institute to help promote its search for cancer vaccines. After a few years, Tinker moved in 2007 to his present position as executive director of the New York Biotechnology Association, a nonprofit trade group for bioscience and life-science companies in the state.

All I knew about Nathan Tinker between 2002 and earlier this year was a brief notation in my department's placement records. That entry states simply that he "did not seek academic employment." I used LinkedIn to contact him and learned the impressive details.

I'm guessing that there are plenty of cases like Tinker's, in which a department knows little or nothing of the extramural achievements of one of its own graduated Ph.D.'s. That's why I used an example from my own workplace. To do otherwise would single out another department for doing something that just about all of us have done.[26]

Losing Nathan Tinker's trail for so long is an instructive mistake on at least two levels. First, it's a practical loss because we haven't been able to refer other students to him for information, advice, or networking. "I use the skills and tools of an English literature Ph.D. daily," Tinker told me, but he's never been invited back to our campus to talk about that or anything else. (He has been invited to other campuses, though, which compounds the embarrassment.)[27]

Second and more important, losing track of Nathan Tinker is a conceptual mistake. Angela Brintlinger, a Slavic studies professor at Ohio State, suggests that "we talk about outcomes instead of placements." If we do that, she says, "our students can take pride in their own talents and accomplishments," and we teachers "can work toward enhancing the value of the Ph.D. outside of academia, including educating ourselves about what 'alternative career' preparation might mean."[28] My department stopped tracking Tinker's career because it didn't seem to matter to our mission. The longtime absence of his employment from our records clearly shows what placement means in the academic workplace—and what it doesn't mean. And if we look more closely, we can also see what it *should* mean.

Graduate schools count academic (that is, professorial) placements more eagerly than any other kind. And why shouldn't they? The practice reaches down to the roots of the enterprise, especially the blinkered chase after "prestige" that eclipses the educational mission. Consider that academic placement drives the graduate school rankings that matter so much to everyone.

When the National Research Council tabulates the rankings of departments, it explicitly seeks records of "placement in academic positions (including academic postdoctoral positions)," and those placements alone help to determine the order of those pernicious lists whose effects ripple outward through our professional public square. So a graduate school dean who speaks sincerely about the need to encourage alternative academic careers still has to devote the bulk of his or her resources to help graduate students get the academic jobs that will bolster the university's NRC ranking.

Lets consider how that requirement be changed. It turns out that the path leading from the definition of placement to the NRC's questionnaire results that determine graduate school rankings, and from there to the institutional behavior that arises from those rankings, is circular. It's a well-marked loop. The NRC's criteria for ranking graduate schools originate in the organization's Committee to Assess Research-Doctorate Programs. That committee, made up mainly of present and former deans, provosts, and other administrators, followed a commendably transparent process laid out in its 2009 *Guide to the Methodology of the National Research Council Assessment of Doctorate Programs*. The committee first made up a draft questionnaire that it showed to a panel "consisting of graduate deans and institutional researchers." That group made suggestions, and then the next draft was posted on the NRC's website, which led to more suggestions. Then the questionnaire was finalized and distributed.[29]

So who determines the definition of "placement" that directs—and also constrains—the work of graduate deans? None other than their fellow deans and administrators. The problem is embedded in the foundation of the edifice itself.

Reform therefore depends on a more self-conscious definition of the word "placement." It should mean the jobs that graduate students want—not just the academic kind. A broader definition would overturn the common assumption that a Ph.D. is a pipeline leading to an evaporating pool of academic jobs.

How do advisers know what kinds of jobs their graduate students want? By asking them, and then by periodically asking them again, to see if the answer changes over time. These periodic check-ins are part of good graduate advising. It's common sense that teachers need to prepare students for the work that they can get. To shape their desires so that academic jobs are the only ones that they want hurts them professionally and personally. Or we might just call it bad training. Yet that's exactly what happens when we accept unquestioningly the traditional meaning of placement.

Successful placement of graduate students has never been harder these days and not just because the academic job market is a mostly dry well. As recent graduates know, the nonacademic market isn't exactly overflowing either. But we owe it to our students to expand our view of placement. It's been a long time since new Ph.D.'s could feel assured of a job after their graduation, but what professional obligation should professors have to them? Even though graduate students invest considerable time, trust, and money (both capital and opportunity cost) in the education we provide them, I see little collective responsibility on our side. (I often see individual professors helping individual graduate students, but I'm seeking a distinction between that admirable effort and the presence of a general ethic. For example, I might care about my own Ph.D. students, but what about my institution's graduates as a group?)

There remains a particular lack of concern for the prospects of Ph.D.'s who don't fit the traditional academic model, and it's reflected in the way that we track—and don't track—their placement.

We have a lot to learn about how to orient graduate students toward alternative academic careers. We also need to find out more about the ones who take this path. Social media make this data gathering easier on a departmental level, but there has long been a need for a more concerted sweep for information. The placement data for students who land outside the academy have been insufficient for a long time, which is disgraceful in light of the importance of the topic. As a result, discussion of nonfaculty careers for graduate students has often disintegrated into dueling anecdotes. (You have a story about someone who parlayed her Ph.D. into a great business career? Well, here's one about someone who had to drop his Ph.D. from his résumé in order to get a job at all.) The prurient interest of stories has helped them dominate the landscape, but they also rule because statistics have been in short supply.

The first serious study of doctoral career outcomes didn't appear until 1999, and it was limited to Ph.D.'s who had completed degrees between 1983 and 1985. (English was the only humanities field originally surveyed. The other disciplines in the survey were biochemistry, computer science, electrical engineering, mathematics, and political science.) The narrow scope of the study raised questions: What about ABDs, for example, let alone graduates from other fields? Still, the report—by Berkeley investigators Maresi Nerad and Joseph Cerny—gave quantitative backing to what was already common sense by the late 1990s: time to degree was lengthening, while the holy grail of a tenured professorship had become a more uncertain prospect.[30]

Incredibly, no significant survey of graduate students' career outcomes was published after Nerad and Cerny's for nearly a decade and a half—that is, until well after 2010. But now they're finally starting to appear in quantity, as researchers have moved to remedy a crying neglect.

First, the Council of Graduate Schools published a wider-scoped study in 2012. *Pathways through Graduate School and into Careers* focuses on the transition from graduate school to job. Its findings, based on consultation with students, deans, and employers, are now resonating in an academic culture that remains fixated on the tenure-track outcome. The CGS study found that professors don't talk enough to their graduate students about possible jobs outside academia, even though such nonfaculty positions are "of interest to students." That lack of guidance is particularly egregious in light of where graduate students actually end up: about half of new Ph.D.'s get their first jobs outside academia, "in business, government, or nonprofit jobs," the CGS's report says.[31]

Another welcome entry is *Humanities Unbound,* the Scholarly Communications Institute's survey of former graduate students who have (or are building) careers outside the professoriate—a career category now commonly called alternative academic, or alt-ac.[32] At the same time, the institute has built an alt-ac database called "Who We Are," in which people list their names, employers, and job titles. "One of the reasons we set up a public database," says Katina Rogers, a senior research specialist at the institute at the time, "is so that graduate students can get a glimpse of the kinds of careers in which humanities graduates are thriving."[33]

The institute's survey, conducted in 2012 and published in 2013, analyzes alt-ac employment data in this post–Great Recession era. Rogers, who designed and administered the survey and wrote the report, describes it as "an exploratory study" that's intended "to move from anecdote to data in conversations about career preparation in the humanities." The survey was limited to the humanities ("and allied fields") for practical reasons, Rogers says. The sciences already offer more varied possibilities of industry employment, so alternative academic careers can look very different in those fields. "The humanities," she says, "has a longer road to travel toward improved awareness of the variety of career paths available to graduates." Initiatives like these are finally lighting that road.

Last and perhaps most important, the two largest disciplinary associations in the humanities, the Modern Language Association (MLA) and the American Historical Association (AHA), have joined together to track nonprofessorial Ph.D. placements. Their formal collaboration began in 2013 with a grant to both associations from the Andrew W. Mellon Foundation to track the placement of Ph.D.'s over the past generation. Both organizations had previously maintained a blinkered focus on who got the professorships and ignored what happened to everyone else. This study is different: it's dedicated to the nonprofessorial outcomes that were elided before. The data gathering (from the years 1998–2009) and analysis is nearly finished as this book goes to press; the job is as large as it is overdue, requiring that many thousands of Ph.D.'s be tracked down. But both organizations presented preliminary reports at their annual meetings in 2014. Those findings showed substantial percentages of the Ph.D. work force employed outside the academy.[34]

The recent new data have planted some healthy good news in a bleak-looking landscape. From these new surveys, we're discovering that Ph.D.'s who leave academia (1) get good jobs and (2) enjoy them. I will refrain from providing anecdotal evidence after having earlier warned against doing that—the data show that while disgruntled adjuncts get a lot of the air time (and their cause is certainly righteous), they may in fact be outnumbered by a quieter group of Ph.D.'s who work outside the universities at jobs they like.[35] (And there is a growing body of knowledge and advice about how to look for such jobs.)[36]

Further, as I said in the introduction to this book, those gainfully employed Ph.D.'s have been successful at getting jobs that draw on their particular training. Megan Doherty, a history Ph.D. who leveraged an alt-ac-directed postdoctoral fellowship into a full-time position at the German Marshall Fund of the United States, is one of a number of writers who have pointed out some of the specific benefits of a Ph.D. in the nonacademic workplace.[37] Her teaching experience, she notes, translates into superior presentation skills, while analytical writing skills prove valuable in numerous institutional settings.[38] To this I would add an observation I've heard from people on both sides of the interview table: the ability of Ph.D.'s to organize, synthesize, and analyze large bodies of information is without parallel among credentialed degree holders.

Graduate programs are notoriously slow to change, but they need to acclimate to the fact that not all graduate students will wind up as professors. And "as graduate programs take this into account," says Rogers, they should "have access to a body of data that leaders can point to when they want to make changes in their programs." Career-decision points begin to appear during school. Graduate students know that they need to think about their specialties and skills in terms of what they're hoping to do with them. Is it a good idea to get involved with a particular grant proposal? To teach in that program outside your department? That depends on what you plan to do afterward.

THE ROAD AHEAD

It's part of a professor's job to open graduate students' minds to the range of employment possibilities—both academic and nonacademic—before them. Too many of us teach the same old way, to manufacture old-fashioned scholars as though the demand for them were still viable. When that happens, the professor's fantasy can become a student's fantasy through the everyday magic of role modeling.

Too many advisers are only selectively interested in what happens to their students afterward. Brintlinger remarks that when talk turns to placement, "we have a hard time resisting the desire to highlight that one alum" who landed a prestigious assistant professorship—which discredits all the others.[39] Some professors like to build mini-empires—who has not seen this?—and they lose sight of the human beings who get turned into capital for such imperial enterprises.[40] We also frequently see something less calculated: faculty who are unwilling or unable to understand graduate school as professional training and remain benignly indifferent to the job-seeking endgame. When we call them professionally irresponsible, we're using a lexicon that they themselves don't have (or won't use).

Teaching should free the imagination, not narrow it, yet the tragic spectacle of graduate students who can't get an academic job, but who can't imagine themselves doing anything else, is all too common a sight in Ph.D. programs throughout the country. As the Versatile Ph.D., a website dedicated to alternative careers for Ph.D.'s, pointed out in a comment to me, "Recognizing nonacademic placements as legit communicates a much more positive message about the skills and abilities that are nurtured by graduate education. It affirms the value of the entire enterprise."[41]

Professors, departments, and programs must do this in concert. It follows that we must also make employers more aware of the value of a Ph.D. in nonacademic workplaces. As enlightened commentators like Grafton and Grossman have suggested, we need above all to mainstream the alt-ac movement in our Ph.D. programs. First of all, this commitment should involve the office of career services. Career-services offices need to be able to outfit Ph.D.'s for the alt-ac world, and they also need to spread the word to the corporations that come to them that Ph.D.'s are undervalued fair game. Most important, they need to do these things in harmony with the "other" search for academic jobs, not separately.

Graduate programs have not sought alliances with career-services offices before this because they haven't seen it as any of their business. Professors in most graduate programs have generally assumed that they have no part to play in students' efforts to train for jobs outside the professoriate, or any responsibility to assume any. That has to change. The partnership that will result between graduate school and career services should be productive for both—but in order for it to be so, departments and programs need to welcome these partnerships in public ways that graduate students can see. The resulting alliances are bound to be more flexible—and they have to be. Given the array of possible jobs for students with the Ph.D., our training programs are rigid and insensible to the realities of the world in which they take place.[42]

Second, all of us (not just students) have to insist on the publication of detailed placement data—nonacademic and alt-ac as well as academic. This information will help to make professors into better-educated providers of graduate education and graduate students into better-educated consumers.

The key phrase in this context is "placement rate," again broadly conceived. Too many graduate students believe that the numbers don't apply to them. They must instead scrutinize the data on what a program's graduates are doing—which should be within easy reach. The figures should track graduates' employment and compensation at intervals: one, five, and ten years after getting the degree. Many departments do a careless job of capturing and maintaining this data. For example, Paula Stephan quotes a 2008 survey of electrical engineering, chemistry, and biomedical programs at fifteen top universities—that is, a total of forty-five graduate programs—which found that only *two* made full placement information available on their websites.[43] I'm sure that more departments publish more information than that now, but when it comes to delivering this information about outcomes, we're nowhere near where we need to be. Prospective graduate students ask for these numbers much more than they used to, and that's a welcome development. Greater demand for the numbers will create a more available, better-quality supply of them. Many law schools and business schools routinely supply salary and placement information to prospective students. It's past time for graduate programs to do the same.

Again, professors themselves should demand these numbers. Faculty need to know their own departments' placement rates and placement histories. At the very least, placement information—not just who got jobs but also who did not—should be announced at department meetings each semester, and placement should be understood as a department priority, every year, all the time.

A final keyword is "transparency." An increasing number of commentators are calling for departments and programs to make placement information readily available, no matter how embarrassing it may be.[44] Put it on websites, plaster it everywhere. It should be broken out by field and subfield, and (here's an idea I haven't seen) also by adviser. Students should know which advisers have the best chance to get them jobs, and where. (The savviest of them already do.) When an adviser gets overloaded with students (as can happen to the good ones), that may increase the attractiveness of the alternatives. Advisers have no business taking on students when they lack the prospects for placing them in the jobs those students want—whether academic or nonacademic. An adviser who takes on three students in the same subfield—with all three set to graduate at approximately the same time and seeking professorships—is, in this extravagant hypothetical, exercising poor pedagogical judgment. If prospective students know the situation, they too will be wary, because graduate school is professional school. So we have to track placement in a way that makes realistic sense. The best reason to do so is simply humanistic: these are the lives of humans we're tracking, not just professors, and they deserve to be taken seriously.

Finally, we should remember that educating graduate students about placement before they go on the market is only part of the job. Professors instead must open the minds of graduate students to the jobs that they can get, so they need to learn what to do in order to help students get those jobs. Dissertation advisers have to shoulder some of the responsibility for teaching their students about the range of professional options, as I've said. Before students choose an adviser, the department as a whole can meet this student need through professional development seminars, which I described in Chapter 4. Professional development seminars give graduate students the tools to think critically about their career choices. Every graduate program should offer one.

Jack, whose sad story I told at the beginning of this chapter, couldn't imagine himself as anything but an academic, but he might have seen his alternatives more clearly if he had been able to compare them to a wider set of thoughtful professional choices both inside and outside academia. There are many ways to show graduate students what their wider professional world looks like, but all of them start with their teachers: our jobs include showing them that world.

Finally, the students have a responsibility too. It's "absurd," declared one of my readers, "to expect our advisors—who are already overworked and underpaid—to continue to babysit us." Their job, the reader continued, is "not getting us a job. That is up to us to figure out."[45] I'm not sure I'd let the teachers off the hook so easily, but it's certainly true that graduate students as well as their professors have responsibility for the choices they make. Good graduate advising is one thing, but we also expect good graduate studenting—and that too means looking outward. It doesn't make much sense for graduate students to think of themselves only as professors-in-training when professors' jobs are so scarce on the ground. We all have to expand our view—professors owe it to their students, and students owe it to themselves.

School is a place where teachers tell students—grads as well as undergrads—what to do. At the same time, school is supposed to prepare students to make choices for themselves. In between the two poles of this paradox lies a lot of teaching and learning—and professional development. Both professors and students have to adapt to the rapidly changing conditions before us. We all need to keep our eyes open as we move forward together.

We're living and laboring together in a system that doesn't make much sense, ecologically speaking. An environment in which graduate students are encouraged to write books that presses don't want to acquire but that many departments nevertheless demand that junior faculty publish somehow is not a coherent system. But graduate students are not just organisms in an ecosystem, no more than they're just potential professors and nothing else. Graduate students are human beings with lives. Everyone involved in graduate education needs to take those lives seriously.

In Search of an Ethic

THE FORMER DEAN of the graduate school at my own university, Nancy Busch, likes to ask whether there should be a core curriculum for graduate students. Educators debate the undergraduate core curriculum a lot, of course, but graduate students study all different subjects, so a core curriculum seems an impossible notion. Still, Busch's answer to her own question is yes: the subject of the graduate core should be the history of higher education.

The more I think about it, the more I agree with her. Graduate school in the United States today faces many problems, and that's putting it mildly. I've addressed those problems throughout this book: old-fashioned and incoherent course offerings, bloated time to degree, high attrition, a distorted academic job market and a failure to prepare students for alternative employment, and outdated dissertation requirements, to name a few. Those problems all have roots in the history of the research university in the United States, and we can understand them better if we know where they—and we—are all coming from.

The problems with graduate school can't be cordoned off from the problems that face American higher education generally. Graduate school in the

United States is inseparable from undergraduate education. Indeed, each makes the other possible. The problems of one are, in that way, the problems of both—and those problems proliferate. There is, as the musician Warren Zevon wrote just before he died, "disorder in the house. The doors are coming off the hinges."[1] There's an incoherence in humanities education that has led critics of the academy (and not only those on the political right) to bemoan the intellectual integrity of the enterprise.[2] The cost of higher education has outpaced inflation for so long that its upward spiral is a normal part of the landscape—and we're reprehensibly complacent before the fact that millions of young Americans of college age simply can't afford to go.[3] (Compare to-day's forbidding situation to the postwar period, when the G.I. Bill opened higher education's doors to people of different classes and made college, once the province of the elite, into a visible part of the democratic ideal.) The cost of higher education has raised other warnings as well. Reputable publications regularly air dark suspicions that higher education is a scam.[4]

We see this change in public attitude also in the now-constant political pressures that are deforming American universities by compromising their educational mission. Attacks on tenure are succeeding, and their success is partly due to the failure of professors to thoughtfully integrate the work they do in their own disciplinary houses with that of the larger community to which they belong. Such disciplinary isolation—in which intellectuals hole up in what are now called "information silos"—points to another problem with our larger house. The whole university, not just graduate school, needs attention too, if both are to survive and prosper. There comes a point where we have to view them together.

That's why higher education needs a new ethic. Because the old one— if there was an old one—isn't serving very well right now. An ethic isn't just a personal strategy. It requires engagement at the departmental level, at the university level, and inside government, and it needs professors to work to change policy beginning in their own programs and classrooms. It can be difficult to know where to begin. But an ethic provides a way to rethink day-to-day actions and a basis for larger-scale engagement. Graduate school needs to fix its own house, and I've been suggesting that the classroom, broadly conceived, is the place to start. If we don't teach graduate school right, then it's hard to make a case for the rest of higher education.

To aim upward from this slough of despond, I'll begin by looking more closely at the last problem I mentioned, the loss of respect for what professors do. First, let's acknowledge a fact: the nonacademic population is angry at the university. There are plenty of people out there who accuse faculty of goldbricking—which would be laughable to anyone who knows the amount of work that professors do, if the charge weren't so serious. Critics also accuse professors, especially humanists, of teaching ideology rather than content or skills.[5] I'm not going to argue with those charges—many others have done so—but I do want to consider why they proliferate.

The general public feels cut off from the university right now. The cost of university education surely sparks their alienation. We've become used to reading articles with titles like "Does College Education Pay?" or "The Practical Value of a College Education." The suspicion behind them marks a movement toward seeing universities as businesses and higher education as a good on a shelf. Actually, consumers have seen American higher education as a business at least since the early twentieth century, if not longer. Here's some proof: the articles whose titles I just quoted were written in the 1890s.[6]

THE BUSINESS OF THE UNIVERSITY

There has been much gnashing of teeth in recent years about the commodification of higher education. (And humor: Jane Smiley, for one, has a good time with the idea in her 1995 campus novel *Moo*.) But there is no arguing that in these times, the relation between town and gown has turned increasingly into a market relation. There's an overbearing focus on the value of college and graduate education in the marketplace and of higher education as a commodity in and of itself.

Loss of public support arises first of all from the cost of higher education—which in turn results (circularly) from lack of public support, even for public universities, many of which aren't so public anymore.[7] Most Americans who go to college and graduate school attend public universities, and federal support for public institutions has been dropping since the Nixon administration, with tuition marching consequently upward.[8] The tendency to see education as a consumer good also arises partly from the sheer size of some universities and the bureaucratization that has attended their growth. As a result, the image of the university as a business has eclipsed the idea of higher education as a higher calling (as some see it) or as a necessary and valuable public service (which it surely is).

Though universities are corporations and behave as such, they aren't exactly commercial businesses—that idea is an uncomfortable fit. Funds flow toward the university but not from it, and the not-for-profit university is not exactly "selling" its product. Producers can shape the desires of consumers, of course, but it requires careful persuasion to do so. When you produce a product that is not easy to value, there's a constant need to persuade its consumers that it's worth having. Graduate school—and higher education generally—is an obvious case in point: if we ask society to pay for it, then we need to show why it's worthwhile. Indeed, graduate school, whose bottom line is not so flush as the average business school's, stands as a visible symbol of the non-pecuniary value of higher education. (This is especially true of graduate school in the humanities.) But graduate school, especially in the humanities, is the engine that drives the college and that supplies so many of its teachers.

"Save the humanities" books have proliferated in recent years.[9] In the aggregate, they suggest a town meeting in which the people in attendance argue soberly for the social value of water while noting that, by the way, their hair is on fire. Making the case for the scholarly enterprise ought to be an activity for fair weather as well as foul—a point I'll return to later. That imperative needs recuperation these days, especially with the broad American middle class. One reason that higher education has been taking a beating in the public square is that the university, in the view of many members of that middle class, has tried to arrogate to itself the responsibility for setting the terms of its relationship to the public. That's a particular problem because it amounts to the store telling the customer what to buy.

The middle class pays for higher education in the first place, either directly (in the case of public universities) or indirectly (in the case of government grant money and other public support such as nonprofit status that goes to private institutions—and we should not forget about tuition). Though both American and European national governments support higher education, the U.S. model describes a different relation than in Europe because payments go directly from the student's family to the university (as well as through transfer payments), whereas in Europe, public support of higher education is entirely mediated by the tax collector. The American model creates a sense of direct accountability to the students—and in a relation that close, there needs to be more exchange. Students and their families are in a financial collaboration with American universities, and they need to feel collaborated with.

If collaboration is the goal, then it's especially clear that the business metaphor that governs higher education is limited at best. Treating education like a business is worse than clunky—for this purpose, it's downright pernicious. Higher education doesn't produce products that can be identified, and even if one could identify them, they can't be valued (often because their value—whether of a scientific innovation or a grounding in art history—doesn't become clear until much later, if at all). This danger is not just old news; it's *very* old news, having been deplored at length by economist Thorstein Veblen in the early part of the century in a still-valuable 1918 book called *The Higher Learning in America*.[10]

There may be a problem with the whole idea of education as a product, but it's still hard to argue against the idea. In a country where the free market is essentially a religion, is it realistic to expect its citizens to refuse to regard education—which people have to pay for, after all—as a consumer good?

It's not unfair to say that there's a battle for control of the idea of the university going on in the early twenty-first century. This is perhaps the most significant legacy of the culture wars—or we could call it the latest crucial battle in that conflict. Perhaps the most important part of the battle within the war is over the governing metaphor. Metaphors win rhetorical wars, and the business/corporate model—acknowledged by both university administrators and their opponents—is currently winning one for the critics of American higher education.[11]

We might have to resign ourselves to this financial relationship if it weren't against the grain of American history and tradition—and American practice. For most of the age of the university (that is, since the 1880s or so), higher education has held itself up as a useful good, a higher calling, and a public service, all at the same time. It's not just a business but also something more. As a cultural good and a social benefit, it's been seen as something special, even something sacred (as the long history of church-college affiliations suggests). In a country that worships the market, education has until relatively recently been placed in a special category. For centuries, it's been accepted as a product without value, an understood collective good—as Veblen and others would have it. In a country that worships the market, higher education has never played a simple part or a single one. It's a peculiarly American paradox that university education can be a sacred commodity and a social good that is also for sale, all at the same time.

THE MISSION OF THE UNIVERSITY

With this tension in mind, let us ask, what is the purpose of higher education in America? In the early years of American higher education—before the 1870s—the answer was fairly clear. Modeled on the English college (which the oldest American institutions originally were), the American college had a clear purpose: to produce students. Those students, equipped with education, would go on to become citizens who would do useful and productive things.

Foremost among those productive pursuits were religious vocations. The first president of Harvard, Henry Dunster, exhorted his faculty charges thus: "You shall take care to advance in all learning, divine and humane, each and every student who is or will be entrusted to your tutelage."[12] Similarly, Princeton's early educators focused on the need to train men who would do virtuous good:

> A general desire of knowledge seems to be spreading among the people. Parents are inspired with emulation of cultivating the minds of their offspring; public stations are honorably filled by gentlemen who have received their education here; and, from hence, many Christian assemblies are furnished with men of distinguished talents for the discharge of the pastoral office.[13]

These assertions from the seventeenth and eighteenth centuries ought not to surprise us: early America was filled with religious exiles who held religious vocations in the highest esteem, and English colleges were closely intertwined with the English church.

But the purposes of college were not limited to religion by any means. Writing in the mid-eighteenth century, Ebenezer Pemberton, a founder of Princeton, was already looking beyond the walls of the seminary:

> Though our great Intention was to erect a seminary for educating Ministers of the Gospel, yet we hope it will be useful in other learned professions— Ornaments of the State as Well as the Church. Therefore we propose to make the plan of Education as extensive as our Circumstances will admit.[14]

From its earliest days, Princeton made room for nonreligious as well as religious professions. The design at the University of Pennsylvania, founded at about the same time, was fully secular, as these words from its first provost show: "It is hoped that the student may be led through a scale of easy ascent, till finally rendered capable of thinking, writing and acting well, which are the grand objects of a liberal education."[15] These values persisted well into the nineteenth century. In a widely quoted 1853 report, the trustees at Columbia declared, "The design of a college is to make perfect the human intellect in all its parts and functions." These were both "physical" and "moral," with the "high design of education" being "to form the mind."[16]

So what should a college produce? For a long time, the answer was unambiguous. During America's age of the college, before the arrival of the university, higher education was focused on producing educated students who were supposed to go on to become leading citizens, pillars of church and state. (Because early colleges were small in size and few in number, only a tiny percentage of young men attended; American higher education thus started out as an elite enterprise, so the expectation that it would produce educated leaders was reasonable enough.)[17] These educated students would have social value, along with the things they go on to do. But—and this holds true now, as then—the college itself is not, and is not supposed to be, in a position to take possession of that value. That's because it operates according to a different economy: the people give their children to the institution, and the institution educates them and gives them back to society. Society in turn gives the institution the financial means to exist.[18]

This is a fundamentally different metaphor from business—it's one of mutual caretaking. "You take care of our children," parents tell the university, "and we'll take care of you." There's nothing old-fashioned about this notion of mutual caretaking in today's United States. Lots of parents still believe something like this, and there's no better evidence of that fact than the continuing faith that most middle-class Americans have in the value of a college education.

The American university has a strong tradition of in loco parentis then. The early college looked after its charges more assiduously than any but the most protective parent would now desire today. Still, there remains a legacy of those expectations in evidence even now.

That student-centered collegiate tradition was both augmented and challenged beginning in the second half of the nineteenth century. Aided by the rise of science and the huge surge in capital soon after the Civil War (and its concentration in the hands of a relatively small number of captains of industry—or, as they were also called, robber barons), the first research universities were established on American soil.

One of the first was the University of Chicago, endowed by John D. Rockefeller and others. Its first president was William Rainey Harper, who described his own mission early on as the creation of an institution that would support research above teaching:

> It is proposed to establish, not a college, but a university. . . . It is only the man who has made investigations who can teach others to investigate. . . . Freedom from care, time for work, and liberty of thought are prime requisites in all such work. . . . In other words, it is proposed in this institution to make the work of investigation primary, the work of giving instruction secondary.[19]

Harper could not be clearer: research comes first, then teaching. Daniel Coit Gilman, when he was inaugurated in 1872 as president of the University of California, similarly stressed research over the education of students:

> It is a University, and not a high school, nor a college, nor an academy of science, nor an industrial school, which we are charged to build. . . . The University is the most comprehensive term which can be employed to indicate a foundation for the promotion and diffusion of knowledge—a group of agencies organized to advance the arts and sciences of every sort.[20]

Gilman's emphasis on knowledge (as opposed to students) is particularly notable because he was soon recruited as the first president of the Johns Hopkins University, the truest expression of those ideals in the United States and the leading research university in the country during the time when the research university was taking its form. That form was inspired in significant part by the German research university, which is based on an idealized model of pure research under which the scholar pursues the truth, unencumbered by practical concerns.

But the German-inspired model explicitly conflicts with the homegrown American idea that the purpose of higher education is to produce citizens. Instead, the research model asserts something different: the purpose of the university is to produce knowledge. It is, we might say, a knowledge factory—but it's a factory built in a country whose middle class has never parted with the original idea that educating students, not producing research, is the highest ideal and most important goal of higher education. The production of students and the creation of new knowledge are, in the words of Nicholas Lemann, the "two noncongruent ideals of higher education" that exist side by side in the United States.[21]

Harper and Gilman gave early articulation to what I've been calling research culture. Generally speaking, research culture promotes knowledge creation over student education. Graduate education bridges the gap: in the United States, research culture has always been linked to graduate school and to graduate students. As we've seen, American colleges gave out small numbers of graduate degrees before the founding of research universities and graduate schools. However, research culture grew not from such isolated instances of higher study but from institutions that concertedly promoted it. In fact, the purest vision of the research university in those early days was supposed to dispense with undergraduate students entirely. The design of the new Johns Hopkins University did not include any undergraduates, nor did Clark University, another early and ambitious expression of the ideal of research culture. Hopkins, it turned out, added an undergraduate college before it opened. Although Clark ran on a small scale for some years as a graduate-only institution, it added undergraduates soon after the death of its namesake benefactor.[22]

The graduate-only model proved unviable, both financially and socially. Americans, it turned out, cannot easily imagine—or support—a university without a college attached to it. So the college, modeled on English examples, and the graduate school, whose roots are German, have been yoked together in the history of U.S. higher education.[23] Their coupling occurred because colleges were already there when universities arrived and also because most Americans see universities as education centers as well as research centers. Even the most devout partisans of research culture realized early on that in the United States, research universities had to produce students as well as knowledge. They saw the expectation of social service that was built into American beliefs about higher education, and that expectation has never disappeared. I don't want to suggest that Americans oppose the research enterprise—of course they don't. But they don't necessarily privilege it above the student enterprise. That's clear from some of today's criticisms of U.S. higher education.[24]

Historically, universities have brought these potentially conflicting obligations together and balanced them in different proportions. Columbia

University president Nicholas Murray Butler declared in 1902, for example, that "the university is for both scholarship and service."[25] Rutgers president Robert C. Clothier described the purpose of the university similarly in 1936 but with different shadings: "First, it strives, through creative research, to add to the sum of human knowledge in all fields of thought. . . . Second, and even more important, a university exists to impart knowledge to youthful minds."[26] Clothier's rhetoric reflects his position at the head of a public university: research leads off, but teaching gets extra emphasis. "By supporting faculty research," observes historian Julie A. Reuben, "universities could claim that they served society in two ways: they graduated students capable of the highest form of mental reasoning, and they produced knowledge that contributed to social progress."[27] Thus were melded the objectives of the English college and the American interpretation of the German university ideal.

That mixture has persisted, for the research philosophy articulated by Harper and quite a few other university administrators during the late nineteenth century hardly flattened opposing views. Research culture gained sway over the academic land—which we can see through the primacy that research credentials have gained in the measure of faculty achievement and values. But other views of the purpose and value of higher education have remained in play, creating a tangle of ideas, as historians of higher education have shown.

The past interaction of opposing ideas of the university's purpose continues to inform our present. To trace the origins of today's debates, I offer a couple of triadic metaphors drawn from the work of astute historians. One describes the university's relation to U.S. society, while the other depicts opposing ideologies within the university. Together, they suggest the practical and instrumental origins of the American research university.

Figure 1 represents the overarching argument of Burton Bledstein's *The Culture of Professionalism*. It shows that the birth of the American university in the late nineteenth century can't be separated from the circumstances of the society that birthed it. The university was a recipient of increased national wealth (which also gave rise to the middle class), and it soon became a destination for that middle class—creating a mutually dependent relation that endures still.

Professionalism changed the United States after the Civil War: a service economy replaced an agricultural economy, and workplace hierarchies necessitated new forms of organization. Cultural historian Alan Trachtenberg

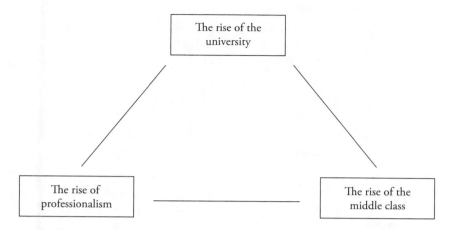

Figure 1. The birth of the American university, per Bledstein, *The Culture of Professionalism*

has described this transformation as "the incorporation of America."[28] These changes brought a new emphasis on credentials. The professional classes— doctors, dentists, lawyers, and others—now needed to acquire credentials, badges that soon became fundamental to their identities.[29] University presidents quickly recognized the role that their institutions could play in this new workplace, and the universities inserted themselves into the professional race to credentialize the workplace.

Middle-class students go to college and professional school in many countries, of course, but the United States is where the mission of higher education is inseparable from the identity and goals of middle-class people. Bledstein's findings show how the shape and form of the U.S. university results from its emergence at the same time that the country's professional middle class— and, as important, its middle-class identity—was forming. Born at the same time, the two grew up together. The alliance between the university and the middle class supported the belief (which became more entrenched as larger percentages of young people went to college) that higher education was a middle-class marker. So the university not only arose from the changes in social organization in the United States; it also contributed to them in symbiotic relation.[30]

Now let's look more closely at the university vertex of the triangle (Figure 2). This breakdown of conflicting views in the early American university reflects the argument of Laurence R. Veysey's *The Emergence of the*

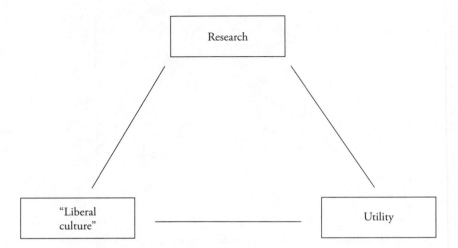

Figure 2. Tensions within the American university, per Veysey, *The Emergence of the American University*

American University, a magisterial history that is still fundamental nearly fifty years after its publication.[31] Veysey meticulously outlined a continuing tension between research, utility, and liberal culture, a tension that defined the modern university during its first decades.

Given Bledstein's observation that the growth of the university not only paralleled but also nourished and was nourished by the growth of the middle class, we should not be surprised to discover that today's higher-education business model planted its roots long ago. That business-oriented view is most closely represented in Veysey's rendering by "utility": the idea that the university should perform clearly useful functions in society. The belief in the utility of higher education was present from the beginning of the American university. American colleges rested on principles of utility, reflected in their stated purpose to produce educated leaders. But utility was important in America in a way that had nothing to do with colleges or universities: think of the rugged, resourceful, can-do frontier people who make up their own canon of American heroes.

Let me briefly address "liberal culture," since it has the smallest role in what I'm talking about. "Liberal culture" refers to the view that higher education should aim to create individuals with discerning powers of reasoning, judgment, and aesthetic appreciation: model citizens, in other words, who might lead society. Late nineteenth- and early twentieth-century Princeton is a good example of a university that was strongly guided by that philosophy, which helps to explain why it still has no professional schools.

I expect that most educators believe in the value of liberal culture. I know that I do. Though centered on the undergraduate experience, liberal culture should also encompass graduate school. Indeed, the idea that people with graduate degrees can become examples—even leaders—in the larger society is one of the themes of this book. Liberal culture plays an important continuing role in the history of American higher education, but I pay less attention to it here for two main reasons. One is that others have already argued eloquently for its value. Andrew Delbanco, for example, grounds his argument for higher education in liberal cultural values. He makes a deeply persuasive case that all Americans would benefit from going to a liberal arts college.[32] If only they could—but that's an expensive solution. Most Americans who get higher education go to public institutions: they're cheaper and have more available slots. Liberal culture, for all of its value, has a certain elitism to it that makes it impractical. Nor is elitism very popular in the United States, so liberal culture is perhaps not the best selling point to recuperate higher education in the United States today.

Instead, the conflict between research and utility informs my current purpose. The statement by William Rainey Harper at the founding of the University of Chicago ("It is proposed in this institution to make the work of investigation primary") exemplifies the values of research culture, which in the United States emphasized the scientific search for truth and the creation of knowledge from that search.

That cosmology contrasts with a utility-minded view that—during the same era—was well represented from Harvard to Stanford and at many midwestern campuses in between. Utility was present in the ideological DNA of the American university almost from the beginning. (It may be detected in decisions like Harvard president Charles Eliot's to start a business school, for example.)[33] If the research-minded view was enabled by German models, the utility-minded view was enabled by the Morrill Act, which was signed by President Lincoln in 1862. The Morrill Act created the land-grant schools—institutions that would be centered on students. The stated aim of the law was "to teach such branches of learning as are related to agriculture and the mechanic arts" and also "to promote the liberal and practical education of the industrial classes."[34] When, in the postbellum era, the land-grant institutions were finally brought into being, most of them entered the world as research universities.

The presidents of the land-grant universities predictably viewed the world somewhat differently than Harper of Chicago did. At about the same time that Harper was making his pronouncements about the primary of investigation, for example, James Canfield, chancellor of the University of Nebraska, was attacking what he called "mere erudition," which, he said, mistook "the scaffolding for the building." Canfield stressed the use value of learning. Those who love "scholarship and erudition for their own sake," he said, "hug themselves with joy." He holds them inferior to the "practical fellow, who always wishes to know what is to be done with what he is about to receive." Canfield saw a "divorce" between such elite colleges and "the activities of daily life."[35] Likewise, there was a split between institutional philosophies like Canfield's at Nebraska and Harper's at Chicago. But there is a continuity between worldviews like Canfield's and the statements of today's utility partisans, the ones who demand to know what they're getting for their tuition money.

The abundance of metaphors of tension and division that I've been sketching are suggestive—especially when we contrast them to the prospect of mutuality that I suggested earlier, in which the university enters into an unspoken bargain with society to exchange support of the institution for education of society's youth.

Veysey spotlights the period before 1910. What stood out as the twentieth century unfolded was growth—lots of it, exponential growth. The ever-increasing size of the university mitigated conflict and gave proponents of different visions of the university the opportunity to cultivate their own gardens. "Not talking about purposes," note the authors of the Carnegie-supported *The Formation of Scholars*, "helps maintain a precarious peace."[36] Bureaucracy, we might say, effected a détente by introducing a size and scale that allowed each camp to pursue its own interests apart from the others, with the university providing a giant umbrella for all.

That détente has very familiar contours: it looks like the research university of the present day. Looking at Bledstein's and Veysey's conclusions together, we can see that efforts to reform graduate school—then and now—drag partly because of the ingredients in the primordial soup of ideas that formed the university in the first place. The sacralization of research, which I have been examining throughout this book, prevents full recognition of what Bledstein made obvious: that professionalization (a value closely connected to utility, as is teaching) cannot be separated from the history of American higher education. But the need to be practical (and professional), though inextricable from the university's reality, ran counter to its founding ideals that exalted research. The tension emerged in a time of long-term growth and prosperity, when it could be managed. But that time is over, and the fault lines within the edifice are reemerging.

Today's university is organized along lines that support its large size (its growth being a twentieth-century development with many different causes). It houses different views of education, but its hierarchy is organized to privilege the production of knowledge through research. Faculty members, whether or not they teach in research universities, relate to each other according to the conventions that prevail in the research universities where they received their own training. That is, we professors, regardless of where we teach, tend to measure our own productivity primarily in terms of how much research we produce, not by how well we teach (which is a skill we've never figured out a good way to measure) or by the service we do.[37]

We pass this value system directly to our graduate students—usually to their detriment—and thus perpetuate it through the generations. For faculty and graduate students in their turn, research is the lingua franca, the coin of the realm, and it has given a crucial and long-lasting advantage to research culture over the years, against competing views of higher education. That means that even at small colleges where teaching matters most, research is what determines status, rank, and merit. That's not because we disrespect teaching, nor does it mean that researchers are necessarily bad teachers. German educator William von Humboldt, founder of the university that bears his name, argued that teaching and research are mutually self-sustaining. "At the highest level," said Humboldt (meaning, within the university), "the teacher does not exist for the sake of the student: both teacher and student have their justification in the common pursuit of knowledge."[38] Universities are filled with scholars and scientists who are also inspiring and committed teachers.[39] But research is the currency that circulates most readily among those of us at different campuses—partly because it's most easily quantified into values that can cross school borders. I believe that I'm a good teacher, but I gained the platform to write this book because of what I've previously written and published, and because of how often it's been quoted and cited.

Such one-sided devotion to research culture marks the problem that American higher education faces. Professors work in a system that runs as a bureaucratized knowledge factory and face a distressed public that is demanding renewed attention to our humanistic mission—and that increasingly views our enterprise as a business that has become inattentive to that humanistic mission. Viewed this way, college becomes the face of higher education, but graduate school forms the legs on which it stands. Graduate students occupy a middle space: they are apprentice researchers tasked with extending the values of research culture but also students who must be taught. As researchers, they learn our priorities and values. As students, they are badly treated in ways that protract their work to meet the research goals we set for them.

The modern American university supplanted the old caretaking metaphor soon after it imported its own idea of the German research university about a century ago. The change happened gradually, as part of a more complicated story than I have space to tell—but it was motivated by the paternalism of the old system, when autocratic presidents and department heads set themselves up as father figures to the rest of the faculty, who understandably resented it. This managerial caretaking took a sterner form than the caretaking of students did. At times it verged on malevolence. Without the protection of tenure, faculty worked at the will of the president. Disagreements could and occasionally did lead to professors getting fired. And as public executions will do, these dismissals had the larger effect of scaring others silent.[40] When the university expanded and tenure became widespread after World War I, professors threw off the presidential yoke and bureaucratized their research culture. Academic freedom surely improved their work lives, but it also resulted in a more diffuse institution that was guided by a single-minded emphasis on research and that turned away from the community.

In the early days, research culture had to be nurtured and protected by public-minded professors. "The professor," said Veysey, "had an important role as publicity agent for research." Hermann E. Van Holst, a historian at Chicago, was good at going beyond the university walls to defend the mission of research. In 1880, he described what he was doing as "scientific missionary work." Without the work of professors like Van Holst, said Veysey, "it is doubtful whether the ideal of research would have had the favorable publicity which enabled large graduate schools to come into being."[41]

In other words, public work originally sustained the research culture of the graduate school. Van Holst's "missionary work" brought the university to the community in a way that is seldom seen today. Such outreach is caretaking of a different sort, and I suggest that its neglect weakened the community's former sense of trust in higher education—and in response, they have turned it into an investment commodity. We have to bring that trust back.

THE ENVIRONMENT OF THE UNIVERSITY

The replacement of the caretaking metaphor of the nineteenth century by the business metaphor of the twentieth represents a terrible defeat that has to be reversed on the ground where it was lost. Yes, the caretaking in early American academia was antiquated to say the least, even in its own time. But to abandon the concept instead of adapting it has left U.S. higher education open to the kinds of attacks it regularly absorbs now.

Exactly what has happened? Most important, there has been a loss of trust. That loss of trust has many complicated and interlocking causes that are beyond my scope here (including the 1960s university unrest that politicized higher education as never before), but it has a clear bottom line.[42] The middle class no longer trusts the university to take good care of its children—and consequently now demands impossible concrete value in return for dollars. The financial equation has to be removed; the liberal arts will never be able to function under it except by inevitably converging on the profit-making paradigm of the University of Phoenix and its ilk. Trust has to be restored, and the only way to do that is to substitute a non-financial relationship for a financial one. Simply put, we have to bring back the idea of caretaking in a new form that's appropriate for the twenty-first century.

How can academia regain the public trust? Or to put it another way, how can "education" surpass "business" as the governing metaphor of the university? What would a new kind of caretaking look like?

I have suggested throughout this book that caretaking must begin with teaching. I've construed teaching broadly, because graduate education in particular does not take place only in classrooms or laboratories. Teaching graduate school more attentively and sensitively, with an eye to the graduate student's needs, would not just reform the institution. It would also publicly acknowledge that graduate school centers on education as well as knowledge creation. (This would be a big move, which is part of the problem.)

We can teach graduate students better, and I've stressed that point in these pages. But to put the idea into a larger frame, we can also take care of graduate students better. In the humanities, most of them teach too many courses for too little money, work that serves the university's needs before their own. (Graduate students in other fields have their own versions of the same problem.) They live in apprenticed poverty for too many years while they finish dissertations and amass professional qualifications to meet standards that keep rising. We collectively abet this credential inflation, because it's not just advisers who set those standards but also hiring committees. The system is out of control, but it's our system, and we're supposed to be in charge of it. Put simply, we don't take care of graduate students very well— and we have consequently lost the trust of many of them along with the general public. Everything I've said in this book may be understood as part of an attempt to regain that trust, and more important, to deserve it.

Nor do we take care of our own institution. That's my second point: the academy can start attending better to dialogue with the community. National town-and-gown relations may never have been in worse shape. Public outreach is both something we need to teach and a necessary form of teaching in itself.

As a way to formulate the problem, educators need to look at a new and different concept: environmentalism. Hard though it may be to believe, the environment was relatively recently seen mainly in financial terms. Thanks to changes during the past fifty years, most people today would agree that we are stewards of the land. Even the opponents of environmental measures are obliged to argue in terms of the dominant governing metaphor of caretaking. The environmental movement occupies the moral high ground, and in practical terms, this constitutes a huge advantage. In fact, environmentalism imposes a modern caretaking metaphor over a business one—which is exactly what academia needs.

Environmentalism, not business, describes the proper relationship between the stakeholders in the education debates. The key concept for environmentalists was ecology: the idea that organisms live together in an interlocking equilibrium. Clearly, higher education would benefit from the same sort of awareness. At earlier points in this book, I've called attention to the problems of graduate school (such as the job market) in ecological terms. Those analogies make sense because higher education exists in an ecosystem with the government, the tuition-paying middle class, and the entities that hire our credentialed graduates.

How might we impose an ecological consciousness on higher-education policy? The university cannot and should not become a parent to its faculty again, or to its students—that model was outdated in its own time. So caretaking must come from elsewhere. For an answer, we can look briefly to the history of the environmental movement. Though its intellectual origins lie in the nineteenth century in the work of thinkers like Henry David Thoreau, the issue didn't appear on the U.S. policy radar until the early twentieth century, during the Theodore Roosevelt administration.

Utilitarian thinking prevailed in American environmental policy at first. Gifford Pinchot, head of forestry under President Roosevelt, was one of the most important figures in early debates. "There are two things in the world: human beings and natural resources," Pinchot famously declared. He believed in conservation for the purpose of use—for example, he favored damming a river in Yosemite National Park for the sake of electricity and water supply. That was what environmentalism looked like a hundred years ago.[43]

Pinchot couched caretaking in the language of the market. Today's "green conservatives" now reverse that equation and express market concerns in terms of caretaking—which shows how sweeping a change has taken place since. Out of the efforts of environmentalists and others, a Western philosophy of collective responsibility to the planet has evolved. It's an *ethic,* which is simply a community-based way of thinking. Aldo Leopold articulated the environmental ethic in 1949, in the now-classic *A Sand County Almanac.* "We abuse land because we regard it as a commodity belonging to us," wrote Leopold. "When we see land as a community to which we belong, we may begin to use it with love and respect."[44] These words, which guided generations of later environmentalists to a philosophy of stewardship, could hardly contrast more strongly with Pinchot's. The breakthrough of ecology into policy came in the 1970s, driven by the public debate catalyzed by Rachel Carson's *Silent Spring* (1962), but that debate was made possible by Leopold—who was in turn responding to the arguments of the generation before.[45]

Much of the landmark environmental legislation of the past two generations was passed and renewed during Republican administrations, with a great initial burst during the Nixon administration (the Wilderness Act,

Endangered Species Preservation Act, Clean Water Act, Clean Air Act, and National Environmental Preservation Act). The Environmental Protection Agency was also formed during the Nixon administration. Obviously this was a synergistic moment, but it was built on bricks earlier laid. These were victories for ecological consciousness, a sense that we live within a system that we need to take care of.

Forty years later, the environmental movement has borrowed some of its own language and tactics from the utilitarian business model that it surpassed. Today's environmental discourse relies on cost-benefit analyses and features policies like carbon taxes. But these moves do not alter the larger fact that the language of stewardship dominates the debate. When President George W. Bush declared in 2009, "While there's a lot more work to be done, we have done our part to leave behind a cleaner and healthier and better world for those who follow us on this Earth," he was giving voice to a prevailing shared consciousness, even if his policies didn't necessarily reflect his words.[46]

Higher-education reformers have to build the same kind of consciousness. The university is a social organization in itself, but it's also a participant in the larger organization of society. Like the environmental movement, the university will be a credible steward only if it acknowledges its own experience of the market—it cannot play the innocent. Though European universities grew from clerical pursuits, American higher education has never been a cloister. Nor is it a self-contained monolith. It's an organic entity that has evolved, and will continue to evolve, within a larger social environment.[47] I'm suggesting that higher education needs its own ethic if it is to thrive in its surroundings. The idea is simple: we need a set of principles to guide our group conduct, and those principles need to acknowledge the needs of other groups to which we belong.

A higher-education ethic would define a relation between the university and the community. There's no consensus on that in the United States now. The land ethic led to a triumph of the caretaking metaphor, followed by the assumption of collective responsibility for that caretaking. The higher-education ethic needs to do the same. Let me end this section by spotlighting the most important feature of an ethic: collective obligation. Leopold calls for "individual responsibility for the health of the land" rather than a purely economic relation.[48]

That keyword "responsibility" is worth pausing over. "Academic freedom" is a phrase we've all heard—and with reason. It's a defining feature of the higher-education enterprise (though I should add that it's a relatively new one: the idea of academic freedom caught on less than a century ago in the academic workplace). Academic freedom comes with academic responsibility. I would suggest, in fact, that no freedom worth having comes without responsibility. Academics have a responsibility to the larger social system that makes our enterprise possible. As I've begun to suggest, that responsibility has been complicated by the events of many years, but that does not mean it doesn't exist. We can't be at war with society—society feeds us. And we're part of society.

THE RESPONSIBILITY OF THE UNIVERSITY

Higher education must reforge its public ties, and the best and only place to do that is in the public square. Graduate students and professors alike have to work to keep the enterprise viable—and to remake the symbiotic, mutually supportive tie that once benefited the university and the community. This new ethic centers on teaching and graduate school together, and its goal is to restore the partnership that once existed between town and gown.

Humanists particularly need what the religious studies scholar Jacques Berlinerblau calls "engaged humanism." Berlinerblau argues that academic work is largely unwanted by the public because we are "fanatically and fatally turned inward," writing only "for one another" because we "equate professionalism with specialization" and specialization with the desire to speak only with fellow specialists. Speaking for himself and (not implausibly) for "state legislators, boards of trustees, and belt-tightening administrations" as well, Berlinerblau argues that "the humanities had better start serving people, people who are not professional humanists."[49]

"The public redemption of the humanities," he says, "begins in graduate school." That is why I've placed a widely scoped discussion of the history of the entire university at the end of a book about graduate education. We will redeem ourselves, Berlinerblau says, "when we persuade apprentice humanists to engage their audience and then equip them with the tools to do so." We must, he insists, "impart critical communication skills to our master's and doctoral students. That means teaching them how to teach, how to write, how to speak in public."[50] That mandate has gained traction as the public plight of the humanities worsens along with that of higher education. Marc Aronson, a lecturer at Rutgers University and a historian who writes books for young adults, similarly suggests that all Ph.D. candidates be required to take a course he calls "Communications." The goal, Aronson explains, would be to teach Ph.D.'s—both would-be academics and those who will pursue other work—how to talk about what they do to a variety of public audiences.[51]

"Public" is the keyword here. I earlier suggested that we think about the keyword "placement" as a way of understanding a large chunk of the graduate-school-industrial complex. "Public" has the same resonance. If higher education is to get out of the trouble that it's in with legislators, with the general public, and—let's face it—with many present and former graduate students, we need to conceive of graduate school in a more public way. Because the work of humanists may be more easily communicated to nonspecialist audiences, they bear a special responsibility in this plan.

Going public requires a more outward-looking orientation. That need is consistent with the emphasis I have placed throughout this book on conceiving the mission of graduate school in terms that go beyond the university. The point is not that particle physicists should blog or that every anthropologist needs to be trained to write for the op-ed page of the *New York Times*.[52] That's actually a very narrow definition of "public" that just reassigns the need to publish. Instead, Aronson argues that graduate students need to learn to think about—and talk about—their work outside their narrow audience of specialists. They need to get out of the habit of imagining the intellectual universe as limited to the specialists working right next to them in the archives.

Lots of graduate students evidently want to go public—just look at how many of them blog, for example—but one reason they don't reach out more is that they are taught that public work does not "count." Indeed it does not, for research culture generally gives full rewards only to peer-reviewed publication for specialist audiences. Julie Ellison and Timothy K. Eatman, in their valuable study *Scholarship in Public*, argue for the need for institutional policies that encourage public scholarship. Public engagement, they note, is widely viewed as an unorthodox and risky early career option. To overturn that view, they suggest that community-based scholarship be evaluated in tenure reviews and suggest documentation and portfolios of public projects as the basis for evaluation of faculty. To help students and junior faculty choose academic public engagement, they advocate building in flexibility at the point of hire and maintaining it through the arc of a professor's career.[53]

That arc, as Berliner and Aronson stress, ought to begin in graduate school. Ellison and Eatman agree: a subdivision of their project is PAGE: Publicly Active Graduate Education. A Ph.D. "communications" course in the mold that Aronson suggests might bring together students from across a university. Together, they would explore disciplinary and interdisciplinary literacy in their different fields. The instructor might bring in such speakers as a documentary producer, a museum curator, or a book publisher. Those professionals would talk about the needs of their diverse audiences and how a specialist might respond to them.

The case of a publisher who focuses on books for younger readers is worth dwelling on for a moment because it points to the elementary and secondary school audience that academics mostly don't acknowledge. Professors have to spend a lot more time thinking about the K–12 curriculum than we do. What other industry shows so little concern for its main supplier? Our neglect of precollegiate teaching and learning symbolizes our inward turn—and something more.

The gap between K–12 and the barricaded divisions marking off college and graduate school arose as the university began to expand in size in the 1920s. History is a disciplinary case in point, lucidly documented by Robert B. Townsend. The problem, says Townsend, may be traced from "the assumption that academics are the normative definition of history professionals." When the university began to grow during the 1920s, says Townsend, history evolved into a top-down relation that separated the familiar academic castes of "teachers" and "researchers" but also—and as significantly—elevated the professors to a level distinct from other teachers. The American Historical Association began as an enthusiastic purveyor of "'modern' and 'scientific' research practices" to takers at all levels of the historical enterprise. When history coalesced as a discipline in the United States during the research university's first decades surrounding the turn of the twentieth century, the field came into being as open, inclusive, and outward looking. But specialization (which Townsend views in terms of what he calls "microprofessionalization") fractured this early unity. Specialized journals came into being to publish the new specialized scholarship, making it "harder to rely on a common language and tools" for assessment. The growth of the university, together with the demand for faculty under this newly fragmented regime, balkanized the field. The explosive expansion of graduate school after World War II cemented this fragmentation, as the large postwar generation of historians was trained into a culture with no "common vision": a divided land was their "normal." Thus did members of the profession "forget their common history" and with it any obligation to reach outside their increasingly fortified subdivisions.[54]

Relations in the field between the university and the K–12 grades followed a parallel and related trajectory. Scholars taught and credentialed the K–12 cohort, but their "attention began to drift," observes Townsend, so that as early as the 1910s, as K–12 education was professionalizing, the AHA was seen as "distant and disengaged from the realities of the precollegiate classroom." Primary and secondary school teachers not surprisingly broke away from the scholars and formed their own credentialing organizations. The AHA, bunkered in its self-created ivory tower, "did little to win them back."[55] The result was a familiar fragmentation—familiar because it's on display in other fields to this day.[56] K–12 and 13–16 (plus graduate school) have little to say to each other.

Such disunity in history and elsewhere has more than symbolic consequences. The state-by-state debate over the Common Core Standards in U.S. primary and secondary schools, for example, affects nearly all Americans. (These standards are law in forty-five states at this writing and mandate that elementary and secondary school teachers teach specific content and skills to tomorrow's college students.) National town-gown relations could only improve if academics—including graduate students—got more practice talking with the schoolteachers who have to meet those requirements.

Our failure in this area (and I say "our" because the fault lies mainly with the colleges and universities, not the precollegiate teaching establishment) betrays the vision of exchange associated most prominently with the philosopher John Dewey. Dewey advocated for wide scholarly communication. He believed that communication led to community, and conscious community forms the basis for democracy, the "ethical ideal of humanity."[57] Dewey is one of the founding fathers of academic freedom in the United States, but he saw academic freedom as the foundation for lively and substantive connection with the wider public, not the rationale for retreat from it.[58]

The legendary historian Charles A. Beard once said that to earn a master's degree you study one coal mine, and to earn a Ph.D. you study two. As a metaphor for the dangers of scholarly specialization, Beard's phrase resonates even more profoundly today: coal mines are narrow, dark, and deep. Ph.D.'s have to dig deep to advance knowledge, particularly if they're following veins that many miners have ventured down before. But the value of what they find will be limited if it stays in the mine. No matter how specialized their work, Ph.D.'s need to get out of the tunnel sometimes.[59]

Though it may not sound like it, I support specialization. Not just in science but also in humanities, specialization helps to create new knowledge. Most Ph.D.'s have to do specialized work, and they should. But specialization carries risks of the sort that Beard described. A Ph.D. communications course—or any policy that would serve similar goals—could ameliorate these risks. Aronson suggested to me that graduate students might be asked to develop a proposal for "a presentation to any nonspecialized audience that takes your work outside of itself." I see two immediate values to such an exercise. First, it teaches teaching. Graduate students who go on to professorships would hone the ability to present their work to audiences not unlike the undergraduate classes they will teach. A glance at the job postings in any academic discipline makes clear that most college teaching takes place at the general level, with specialized upper-division courses more the exception than the rule.

But would-be professors are not the only Ph.D.'s who should learn to teach in that way. Those who work outside the academy would get valuable practice dealing with nonspecialized groups of the sort they will encounter regularly in the workplace.

Second and more important, learning how to reach multiple audiences is not just a skill. It's a way of looking at the world that enables you to see complementary alternatives to specialization—and a need to forge ties outside the small world of specialists. It's a habit of thinking that provides a necessary counterweight to the default tendency of losing yourself in a narrow field of knowledge. "Public Ph.D.'s" are simply scholars who see the work that they do in terms of its propagation as well as its contribution to a specialty or subspecialty. By thinking about how to communicate knowledge at the same time they create it, they turn their creative powers outward.

What that outward turn might look like will depend on the scholar and the nature of his or her work. Duke University's Forum for Scholars & Publics is a good example; in this case, the university facilitates the exchange using various media.[60] Another admirable example may be found in the program at the University of Wisconsin–Madison called the Public Humanities Exchange (or HEX). The HEX program sponsors local projects—often involving graduate students—that take the university outside its own walls. In one project, two graduate students, Colleen Lucey (in Slavic languages and literature) and Janelle Pulczinski (comparative literature), sought to create a "literary environment" for recently released prisoners through reading and creative-writing groups.[61]

Such work does not amount simply to community service. Tracy Lemaster, a graduate student in English at the University of Wisconsin–Madison, extended her dissertation work in the interdisciplinary field of "girls' studies" (which focuses on girlhood as distinct from childhood and womanhood) by working with actual girls under the HEX aegis. "While researching this field throughout my graduate career, I began to feel removed from the subjects within it," Lemaster says, and she questioned the "practical applications" of the theoretical work she was doing. To answer her own questions, she created a media-literacy program for girls that she tested with some thirteen- and fourteen-year-olds at a local organization. "It was fascinating," says Lemaster, "to observe how real girls' feedback could support, nuance, or even contradict adults' theories of girlhood subjectivity in the field."[62]

The HEX program is a living legacy of the Progressive-era idea that the university should serve the whole state. In Wisconsin, that outreach mission was called simply the "Wisconsin Idea."[63] A cross between Populist idealism and the Deweyan public sphere, the Wisconsin Idea embodied the notion that, in the words of journalist Lincoln Steffens, the university should "teach anybody—anything—anywhere."[64] At the center of this public-service mission was "the concept of partnership."[65] That partnership expressed itself chiefly through a dedication to extension teaching. "State government's support of and interest in the University"—along with the support of citizens and the public advocacy of the university's early presidents—enabled that partnership to flourish. State lawmakers celebrating the Wisconsin Idea in 1958 called it "a munificent donation to the people of Wisconsin" by the government, "a sacred and inalienable trust, bequeathed to them for their own benefit and that of future generations" for "popular needs."[66]

But the idea faded in the 1970s. "Over time," noted the state's Legislative Reference Bureau, "the importance of research, especially publishable research, has increased and the emphasis on public service has decreased."[67] This decline follows the history of the university that I've elaborated in this chapter. Sociologist Craig Calhoun suggests that the dramatic growth of universities after World War II nourished "an ideology that opposed academic professionalism to public engagement" and that contained scholars inside the academy.[68] That is, research culture, coupled with bureaucracy, allowed professors to turn away from the public. So the Wisconsin Idea was marginalized. This most expansive ideal of higher education as a public service, in which the university reaches out into the community at large, now survives as an extracurricular activity.[69]

Such work needs to be curricular, not extracurricular. Ernest Boyer, in his last essay, published posthumously in 1996, argues for such "scholarship of engagement" as part of "a larger sense of mission" for the university in the life of the nation. Tracing some of the same history I've sketched in this chapter (such as the preparation of students at American colonial colleges for community engagement) and building on his monumental *Scholarship Reconsidered* (which I've referred to elsewhere in this book), Boyer lamented the decline of the university's role as public conscience and social critic. "I'm convinced," he wrote, "that ultimately, the scholarship of engagement also means creating a special climate in which the academic and civic cultures communicate more continuously and more creatively with each other."[70]

What might that look like? There are lots of possibilities. A physicist might take special pride—as Nobel Prize winner Richard Feynman once did—in teaching the introductory undergraduate course in the field. Or an academic historian might write a young-adult version of a scholarly monograph, as Scott Reynolds Nelson did about his hunt for the real "John Henry" who was memorialized in the old labor song.[71] An English professor might offer her expertise to her local "Big Read," a government project in which members of a community come together as one big book group.

In essence, we need to revive Hermann Van Holst's nineteenth-century missionary zeal to defend the university in our own time. But we should do more than defend ourselves. Edmund J. James, president of the University of Illinois, said in 1906 that the state university should mount "an ethical crusade" to educate the people of the state.[72] His idea was that the university should take care of society, not just be taken care of by it. Here's a relevant current example from the field of philosophy. Adam Briggle and Robert Frodeman, philosophers at the University of North Texas, have called on the field to embrace the public role it once had, when philosophers were figures in the agora. They've started the Public Philosophy Network to promote applied public ethics (the creation of what they call "philosopher bureaucrats") and "field philosophy," in which they seek alliances with applied fields like engineering. "Anything that takes philosophy out of the study and into the world," says Frodeman, "is good news."[73]

Academic ethics finally boil down to the actions of individual scholars. The Wisconsin Idea expresses the duty of the university, and as I have said many times in this book, universities need to change their orientation to encompass duty. Our institutions—and our institutional expectations, including the ones that attach to the academic job market—still reflect the practices we invented during the golden generation of postwar abundance, and it's way past time that we adapted them to the present. But we don't have to wait for the universities. Our institutions are made up of people, and each of us has a job we can do. Writing in 1947, Jacques Barzun saw the scholar as someone whose primary duty is to teach others—and not just in universities. More important, scholars are "transmitters of what they know."[74]

Much scholarship is bound to be specialized, and an outward orientation for Ph.D.'s does not change that fact. Looking outward does bid to change our view of our specialized work. The compartmentalization of inquiry surely makes our scholarship more efficient, but we shouldn't overlook the effects of our bureaucracies on how we view and act in the world. The growing group that resents the cost of graduate education surely does not. It's worth something in itself to reach out to nonspecialized audiences, but it also doesn't hurt to be friendlier to the public that feeds us. Let's train graduate students to advance knowledge and to talk about what they're doing at the same time. There's plenty at stake. We imperil our whole intellectual industry if we allow a life of the mind to become a life in the mine.

CODA

The university needs to articulate a new ethic, or it will be done for us. That is already happening, actually. Examples abound. Some are small scale, such as the assessment movement, advancing against faculty opposition instead of with faculty input. Large-scale developments are much more alarming. "Major universities are larger and more important than ever" to their states, says Hunter R. Rawlings III, president of the Association of American Universities, and "too many politicians and their board appointees want, therefore, to shape them as their ideology sees fit." Trustees at the Universities of Virginia and Texas have sought to oust their presidents, each of whom narrowly escaped. Trustees treat universities, says Rawlings, "as businesses in which productivity and efficiency are the primary goals."[75] A quick listen to a speech by Bill Gates led Governor Rick Perry of Texas to do a back-of-the-envelope calculation that a bachelor's degree should cost $10,000 altogether. Then he tried to implement the idea. A similar proposal has been floated in Florida, which has also introduced a series of performance-based funding guidelines that end up penalizing schools when their graduates leave the state, even to take prestigious fellowships.[76]

Such a list of absurdities could go on—but my point is that they result from a breakdown in communication. Higher education has the most to lose from this. To have the conversation we want to have, we need to re-create certain assumptions about what we do, so that they may take root. I'm not suggesting subterfuge. Instead, academia needs to invite collaboration, the creation of an ethic centered on the idea of higher education as a collective social good, not an individual investment—and not just to save the liberal arts, either. Higher education and society nourish each other when they're in healthy relation to each other.

Our credibility to join such a conversation begins with our care of our own house—and what goes on in that house is teaching. We have to think about our students. Doctoral students "who want to study the humanities," the MLA says, "will make contributions to academic and public life in their work." That argument presumes there's an inherent value in having more Ph.D.'s in public life because an educated population leads to a healthier democracy.

But that position makes sense only if those Ph.D.'s are contented in their work. The question shouldn't be how many Ph.D.'s we produce but whether they're happy or unhappy. When we teach Ph.D.'s to be satisfied only with professors' jobs, we are, quite simply, teaching them to be unhappy. That's more than just an ethical failure. It's a moral one and one of the worst that teachers can be guilty of. Across the humanities (and also other disciplines), we have been collectively guilty of it for years. Legions of embittered adjuncts are the living evidence.

On the other hand, if we make graduate students' prospects clear to them when they enter (i.e., that professorships are thin on the ground, and here are the numbers), and treat them decently during their studies, we help them choose. And if we emphasize their diverse career options from early on (not just let them know that other choices are out there somewhere), then we are teaching graduate students how to make a good life in the world they actually live in. The data on career outcomes—which are finally being collected—show that lots of people who get Ph.D.'s and work outside the university are happy in their jobs. And learning how to be happy in your work is maybe the most important—and most neglected—part of graduate education.

The academic profession forgot its own past during the years that it forged its postwar future. For one shining generation, anyone who wanted to be a professor could become one. More people became professors than ever had before, and that was their "normal." Their experience supplanted the memory of uneven supply and demand during previous generations. When prosperity gave way to uncertain economic times, the vast majority of those in academia harked back to their prelapsarian past, their own time of plenty. They taught their students to wait for it, and their students taught it to their students in turn.

We can advocate better for our vocation if humanists work throughout society, not just in universities. Then they can contribute to the common cause while also making an argument for their own training, just by doing their jobs. But we have to teach them how to do that. The need for a new higher-education ethic is greater than it has been in years—and we're all part of it. It's time for us to own our own academic responsibility and teach our way out of the mess we're in.

NOTES

ACKNOWLEDGMENTS

INDEX

Notes

INTRODUCTION

1. One blogger describes graduate school as "a cotillion for eggheads." To the question of whether to go, he responds: "Short answer: no." These views prevail in many circles these days, but it's perhaps worth noting where this one comes from: no less than a professor at the elite and very academic Swarthmore College—ordinarily someone you would expect to support graduate school. Timothy Burke, "Should You Go to Graduate School?," *Easily Distracted* (blog), n.d., http://blogs.swarthmore.edu/burke/permanent-features-advice-on-academia/features/.

2. The conversation took place on the public-access television show *Higher Education Today,* hosted by Steven Roy Goodman. The program is archived at http://youtu.be/mxs2NZdfkDY.

3. Michael Bérubé, speaking as president of the Modern Language Association in 2012, made this point nicely in a talk to the Council of Graduate Schools when he described the problems with graduate evaluation as "a seamless garment." See Michael Bérubé, "The Humanities, Unraveled," *Chronicle of Higher Education,* 18 February 2013, http://chronicle.com/article/Humanities-Unraveled/137291/; and Coleen Flaherty, "Fixing Humanities Grad Programs," *Inside Higher Ed,* 7 December 2012, https://www.insidehighered.com/news/2012/12/07/mla-president-says-reforming-graduate-education-humanities-requires-hard-decisions.

4. As Derek Bok puts it, "The traditional design of PhD programs, at least in the humanities and social sciences, has come to be woefully out of alignment with the career opportunities available to graduates. The requirements for such programs are constructed primarily to prepare graduate students to serve on the faculties of research universities." This is all the more important because, as Bok notes, only "one-quarter of new PhDs who take an academic position obtain a job at a research university of any kind." Bok, *Higher Education in America* (Princeton, N.J.: Princeton University Press, 2013), 232, 240.

5. The time-to-degree statistics come from the National Science Foundation's Survey of Earned Doctorates. See National Science Foundation, *Doctorate Recipients from U.S. Universities, 2012* (Arlington, Va.: National Center for Science and Engineering Statistics, 2014), 7, http:// www.nsf.gov/statistics/sed/digest/2012/Recent research by the American Academy of Arts and Sciences suggests that time to completion may be lower (though still high); see *Humanities Indicators,* November 2014, http://www.humanitiesindicators.org/content/indicatordoc.aspx?i=49. The discrepancies between the two results—which differ by about two years—are traceable to different data-collection procedures: it's not easy to separate time spent on doctoral study from time spent doing other things since getting the BA, nor is it simple to distinguish between time spent on a master's degree at one's doctoral institution from time getting a master's degree elsewhere.Debt levels for graduate students vary by field. Humanities students take on an average of $25,000, and the average time to degree in the humanities is around nine years. See Colleen Flaherty, "Fixing Humanities Grad Programs," *Insider Higher Ed,* 7 December 2012, https://www.insidehighered.com/news/2012/12/07/mla-president-says-reforming-graduate-education-humanities-requires-hard-decisions. Completion rates in the humanities are around 50 percent. See Robert Sowell, "Ph.D. Completion and Attrition: Analysis of Baseline Data," Council of Graduate Schools, 2008, http://www.phdcompletion.org/information/book2.asp.

6. Bok, *Higher Education in America,* 230–231.

7. Robert C. Clothier, "The Report of the President of Rutgers University, 1932," *Rutgers University Bulletin* 9, no. 4 (1932): 6.

8. Helen De Cruz, "Philosophers Who Work Outside of Academia—Part 1: How and Why Do They End Up There?," *New APPS* (blog), 23 June 2014, http://www.newappsblog.com/2014/06/philosophers-who-work-outside-of-academia-part-1-how-and-why-do-they-end-up-there.html.

9. Thomas Bender, Philip M. Katz, Colin Palmer, and the AHA Committee on Graduate Education, *The Education of Historians for the Twenty-First Century* (Urbana: University of Illinois Press, 2004), 6, 7, 20.

10. MLA Task Force on Doctoral Study in Modern Language and Literature, *Report of the MLA Task Force on Doctoral Study in Modern Language and Literature* (New York: Modern Language Association, May 2014), 1, http://www.mla.org/pdf/taskforcedocstudy2014.pdf.

11. Katina Rogers, "A Few Thoughts on #alt-ac," Katina Rogers's blog, 6 July 2012, http://katinarogers.com/2012/07/06/a-few-thoughts-on-alt-ac/.

12. Rebecca Tuhus-Dubrow, "The Repurposed Ph.D.," *New York Times,* 1 November 2013, http://www.nytimes.com/2013/11/03/education/edlife/finding-life-after-academia-and-not-feeling-bad-about-it.html?pagewanted=all.

13. Richard Wolff, interview with the author, 22 March 2012. Subsequent quotations from Wolff are also from this interview.

14. See, for example, Marc Bousquet, *How the University Works: Higher Education and the Low-Wage Nation* (New York: New York University Press, 2008); Christopher Newfield, *Unmaking the Public University: The Forty-Year Assault on the Middle Class* (Cambridge, MA: Harvard University Press, 2011).

15. MLA Task Force, *Report of the MLA Task Force,* 1. It obviously helps graduate students in the humanities to gain technological literacy, and for that reason, I fully support the recommendation by the MLA's task force on doctoral education to incorporate technological training into today's graduate programs.

16. Walter A. Jessup, introduction to *Studies in American Graduate Education: A Report to the Carnegie Foundation,* by Marcia Edwards (New York: Carnegie Foundation for the Advancement of Teaching, 1944), xi.

17. James Baxter, "Student Selection for Work in the Social Sciences," *Journal of AAU* 35 (1933): 45. Baxter laments that grad schools have been flooded "with large numbers of students neither capable of nor interested in creative scholarship or scientific research," due to the requirement of the Ph.D. for college teaching and the use of the M.A. as a prerequisite for secondary teaching. One problem this causes, he says, is a very high attrition rate: "A substantial majority fail to carry their graduate studies much beyond one year. The proportion of the total first-year group who ultimately attain the Ph.D. degree seldom exceeds a third" (45).

18. Bernard Berelson, *Graduate Education in the United States* (New York: McGraw-Hill, 1960), 181.

19. Jim Grossman, the executive director of the American Historical Association, described that hierarchy in honest and generous fashion at a Teagle Foundation meeting in 2014: "We train graduate students to be producers of new knowledge and to be research scholars in general. In addition, in the best of possible worlds, we are also preparing them to be teachers."

20. See Burton J. Bledstein, *The Culture of Professionalism: The Middle Class and the Development of Higher Education in America* (New York: Norton, 1976). I have more to say about these developments in the Conclusion.

21. Catherine Chaput, *Inside the Teaching Machine: Rhetoric and the Globalization of the U.S. Public Research University* (Tuscaloosa: University of Alabama Press, 2008), 50, 56. Rutgers president Robert Clothier's 1938 statement on graduate education is a good example of the usefulness idea: "The University's philosophy can be briefly stated. In the field of *research*, it is our obligation to provide men highly

competent in their areas of specialization to pursue truth and to expand our fund of knowledge, especially with reference to the problems which confront New Jersey agriculture and industry; to give them adequate laboratories in which to work and adequate supplies and assistance." Clothier, "The Report of the President of Rutgers University, 1937–38," *Rutgers University Bulletin* 15, no. 6 (November 1938): 6.

22. Isaiah Bowman, "The Graduate School in American Democracy," *Department of the Interior Bulletin* 10 (Washington, D.C.: U.S. Government Printing Office, 1939), 12. Bowman points out that graduate school serves different ends for different kinds of students—there is the researcher, the teacher in training, the student who will work in industry. "What is not so clear is the manner in which the provision shall be made for the interconnections of knowledge. This is the most important, as it is the most difficult, of graduate school problems," he says (13). That problem—how graduate school in the United States can unite its teaching and research missions—runs through this book, though I elaborate on it most globally in the Conclusion.

23. Henry Pritchett, "Shall the University Become a Business Corporation?," *Atlantic Monthly* 96 (September 1905): 298–299. Pritchett served as president of MIT before becoming the first president of the Carnegie Foundation for the Advancement of Teaching in 1905.

24. Kerr's book went through five editions in his long lifetime, the last in 2001. See Clark Kerr, *The Uses of the University* (Cambridge, Mass.: Harvard University Press, 2001).

25. Bruce M. Shore's very useful *The Graduate Advisor Handbook: A Student-Centered Approach* (Chicago: University of Chicago Press, 2014) appeared between the time I wrote these lines and the appearance of this book; also noteworthy is Margaret King's excellent pamphlet *On the Right Track: A Manual for Research Mentors* (2003; repr., Washington, D.C.: Council of Graduate Schools, 2010). But the larger point still holds: as important as advising is, it's only one part of graduate teaching, a subject that never gets the spotlight.

1. ADMISSIONS

1. This socialization process is discussed in Patricia Hinchey and Isabel Kimmel, *The Graduate Grind* (New York: Routledge, 2000), especially chapter 2. The role of the graduate admissions process in maintaining a prestige-based caste system is noted in Robert L. Oprisko, Kirstie L. Dobbs, and Joseph DiGrazia, "Placement Efficiency: An Alternative Ranking Metric for Graduate Schools," *Georgetown Public Policy Review*, 15 September 2013, http://gppreview.com/2013/09/15/placement-efficiency-an-alternative-ranking-metric-for-graduate-schools/. The importance of prestige to academic culture is treated by Shin-Kap Han, "Tribal Regimes in Academia: A Comparative Analysis of Market Structure across Disciplines," *Social Networks* 25,

no. 3 (2003): 251–280; Arthur L. Stinchcombe, "A Structural Analysis of Sociology," *American Sociologist* 10, no. 2 (1975): 57–64; and Robert A. Ellis and Thomas C. Keedy Jr., "Three Dimensions of Status: A Study of Academic Prestige," *Sociological Perspectives* 3 (1960): 29–34. The graduate student as a form of social capital in a prestige-based economy is examined by Val Burris, "The Academic Caste System: Prestige Hierarchies in PhD Exchange Networks," *Sociology* 69, no. 2 (2004): 239–264.

2. On undergraduate admissions, see, for example, Marcia G. Synnott, *The Half-Opened Door: Discrimination and Admissions at Harvard, Yale and Princeton, 1900–1970* (Westport, CT: Greenwood Press, 1979); and Jerome Karabel's highly influential *The Chosen: The Hidden History of Admission and Exclusion at Harvard, Yale, and Princeton* (New York: Houghton Mifflin, 2005).

3. It is worth mentioning, though, that histories of graduate school lag far behind comparable histories of undergraduate education.

4. Stanley N. Katz, email to the author, 2014.

5. Details about the University of Wisconsin's graduate admissions office may be found on its website, http://grad.wisc.edu/admissions/.

6. Leonard Cassuto, "The Part-Time Ph.D. Student," *Chronicle of Higher Education,* 7 October 2013, http://chronicle.com/article/The-Part-Time-PhD-Student /142105/.

7. J. Douglas Toma, "Institutional Strategy: Positioning for Prestige," in *The Organization of Higher Education: Managing Colleges for a New Era,* ed. Michael N. Bastedo (Baltimore: Johns Hopkins University Press, 2012), 118–159. I have more to say about the pernicious effects of institutional conformity in Chapter 7.

8. The records from Harvard attest to an overwhelming number of humanities students: "For more than half a dozen years, then, three-fourths of the members of the School have been students of the languages, modern and ancient, and of the historical and philosophical sciences, as against one-fourth who have been students of the mathematical, physical, and natural sciences." Harvard College, *Annual Reports of the President and the Treasurer of Harvard College, 1899–1900* (Cambridge, Mass.: Harvard College, 1901), 138. This data would suggest that humanists predominate.

9. American universities did not exactly reproduce European values, in part because the American situation—colleges already present where universities being built—was nothing like Europe. American values were also different. Laurence R. Veysey's discussion of the American misreading of the German ideal of *Wissenschaft*—which American educators translated as "investigation" and gave a scientific connotation—is a particularly revealing example. The "larger, almost contemplative implications" of the German term, says Veysey, were "missed by the Americans." Veysey, *The Emergence of the American University* (Chicago: University of Chicago Press, 1965), 127.

10. Ibid., 315. For example, Harvard's Graduate Department was granting, along with the A.M. and the Ph.D., the LL.B. and the S.D. See "The Graduate Department," in Harvard University, *Annual Reports of the President and Treasurer of Harvard College, 1885–1886* (Cambridge, Mass.: Harvard University, 1886), 74–80, 78.

11. John Henry Wright was professor of Greek at Harvard and dean of the graduate school from 1895 to 1908. He discusses the blurred definition of degrees in Harvard College, *Annual Reports of the President and the Treasurer of Harvard College, 1898–99* (Cambridge, Mass.: Harvard College, 1900), 158. The graduate school regularly accepted students without the bachelor's, and until 1903, such students could actually receive a B.A. from Harvard Graduate School as part of their studies in that school, as related in Harvard College, *Annual Reports of the President and the Treasurer of Harvard College, 1902–03* (Cambridge, Mass.: Harvard College, 1904), 151. Harvard annual reports hereafter cited by year.

12. Yale University, *Reports of the President, Acting Provost and Secretary of Yale University, and of the Deans and Directors of Its Several Schools and Departments for the Academic Year 1912–1920* (New Haven, Conn.: Yale University, 1919), 302. Certain master's degrees in science belonged to the professional schools at Yale until 1919, when the Yale Corporation transferred to the graduate school all of the university's master's degrees. Doctoral degrees in public health and an M.A. in fine arts, since established, are under jurisdiction of the grad school (302). Jurisdiction was tangled, since Yale's science schools also at certain points controlled these degrees. Which institution controlled what degrees was a perplexing and complicated issue.

13. University of California, Berkeley, *Biennial Report of the President of the University on Behalf of the Regents to His Excellency the Governor of the State of California, 1896–1898* (Berkeley: University of California Press, 1898), 19.

14. University of California, Berkeley, *Annual Report of the President of the University on Behalf of the Regents to His Excellency the Governor of the State of California, 1889–1890* (Berkeley: University of California Press, 1898), 17–18. Berkeley annual reports hereafter cited by year.

15. University of Michigan, *The President's Report to the Board of Regents for the Year Ending September 30, 1892* (Ann Arbor: University of Michigan, 1892), 13.

16. University of Michigan, *The President's Report to the Board of Regents for the Year Ending September 30, 1891* (Ann Arbor: University of Michigan, 1891), 16. Said Angell, "It must be admitted, however, that the instruction of these graduates, if properly done, is costly to us. One or two such students may require as much of the time and energy of a professor as a whole class of undergraduates. And if some of our professors, as is the case, are asked to care for several of these advanced graduates, then they must have help in caring for the undergraduates. I propose to ask the Faculty of the Literary Department to give consideration to the subject of organization of the graduate work, and to report to you at some future time" (ibid.).

17. University of Michigan, *The President's Report to the Board of Regents for the Year Ending September 30, 1888* (Ann Arbor: University of Michigan, 1888), 7; University of Michigan, *The President's Report to the Board of Regents for the Year Ending September 30, 1890* (Ann Arbor: University of Michigan, 1890), 11, 13; University of Michigan, *President's Report . . . 1891,* 7–8, 15, 28.

18. University of Michigan, *The President's Report to the Board of Regents for the Year Ending September 30, 1896* (Ann Arbor: University of Michigan, 1896), 11, 12.

19. University of Michigan, *The President's Report to the Board of Regents for the Year Ending September 30, 1892* (Ann Arbor: University of Michigan, 1892), 15.

20. University of Michigan, *The President's Report to the Board of Regents for the Year Ending September 30, 1893* (Ann Arbor: University of Michigan, 1893), 14.

21. Angell lamented in 1902, for example, that "Harvard annually expends just about double [Michigan's] income" (University of Michigan, *The President's Report to the Board of Regents for the Year Ending September 30, 1902* [Ann Arbor: University of Michigan, 1902], 12).

22. "The question," declared Angell, "with which this University and the other large State Universities is confronted is this; are the States willing to furnish the means for providing this kind of instruction? Just now, there is no more important questions [*sic*] concerning higher education to be passed on by our western States. Upon the answer to be given to this question it depends whether the State Universities are to have their development arrested at their present stage, and so are to fall behind the universities, which depend for their support on private endowments" (University of Michigan, *The President's Report . . . 1896,* 12).

23. University of Michigan, *The President's Report . . . 1892,* 14–15; University of Michigan, *The President's Report . . . 1893,* 15; University of Michigan, *The President's Report to the Board of Regents for the Year Ending September 30, 1894* (Ann Arbor: University of Michigan, 1894), 14.

24. University of Michigan, *The President's Report . . . 1894,* 14.

25. University of Michigan, *The President's Report to the Board of Regents for the Academic Year 1920–1921* (Ann Arbor: University of Michigan, 1922), 48–49.

26. Yale University, *Reports of the President . . . 1912–1920,* 311.

27. Harvard University, *Annual Reports of the President and Treasurer of Harvard College, 1891–1892* (Cambridge, Mass.: Harvard University, 1892), 116.

28. Harvard University, *Annual Reports of the President and Treasurer of Harvard College, 1892–1893* (Cambridge, Mass.: Harvard University, 1893), 115.

29. Harvard University, *Annual Reports of the President and Treasurer of Harvard College, 1889–1890* (Cambridge, Mass.: Harvard University, 1890), 44. According to William J. Brink, even into the early twentieth century, admissions procedures seem to have involved the graduate school administration rather than specific departments. Brink, "Selecting Graduate Students," *Journal of Higher Education,* 10, no. 8 (1939): 425.

30. W. C. Ryan, *Studies in Early Graduate Education: The Johns Hopkins, Clark University, the University of Chicago* (New York: Carnegie Foundation for the Advancement of Teaching, 1939), 24.

31. There were twenty such scholarships awarded when the university opened in 1876, along with five additional scholarships for students from any part of the country ("University Scholarships"), one for a student from Baltimore City College, and ten fellowships opened to advanced students; see Johns Hopkins University, *First Annual Report* (Baltimore: Johns Hopkins University, 1876), 22–23. The stipulated geographic distribution of these scholarships seems to have been designed to create some diversity, with funding lines created expressly for students from Baltimore, the South, and the whole United States.

32. Johns Hopkins University, *First Annual Report,* 30–32.

33. Ibid., 32.

34. Eighteen students had the B.A.; seven a bachelor's in philosophy, science, or letters; four were credentialed civil engineers; eighteen were doctors of medicine; and seven held the Ph.D.

35. Harvard University, "Report of the President of Harvard College and Reports of Departments for 1946–1947," *Official Register of Harvard University* 46, no. 30 (1949): 185.

36. As Wright notes, "many of the annual appointments to these positions are made from among applicants for fellowships and scholarships in the Graduate School" (Harvard annual report, 1897, 147). In other words, there was a strong overlap between those who were attending the graduate school as students and those who were receiving fellowships and scholarships. But there were marked ways in which these various roles diverged. Teaching assistants were charged a tuition fee in proportion to the amount of instruction that they received (ibid.). This means that, while we might classify them as "students," they were, from a financial point of view, regarded more as teachers.While the faculty appointed scholarships, the Harvard Corporation appointed instructors and assistants (ibid.). The faculty seem to have wished that teaching assistantships would serve as "aids" to the student, rather than as "salaries" to the teacher: when a new set of Teaching Fellowships was created in 1900, the faculty officially requested that the board limit the amount of teaching required of the fellow, in order that it not interfere with his or her research (Harvard annual report, 1900, 159–160).

37. Harvard University, *Annual Reports . . . , 1889–1900,* 160.

38. Henry Pritchett, an official in the Carnegie Corporation, speaking in 1922; quoted in Roger L. Geiger, *To Advance Knowledge: The Growth of the American Research Universities, 1900–1940* (New York: Oxford University Press, 1986), 141.

39. Ibid., 108.

40. At Harvard in 1917–1918, for example, "the effect of the first year of war has been to cut the [Graduate] School in half." See Harvard University, "Reports of the

President and Treasurer of Harvard College, 1917–1918," *Official Register of Harvard University* 16, no. 10 (1919): 71.

41. Geiger, *To Advance Knowledge,* 113. James L. Axtell remarks that the graduate population was not large in the 1920s: only fifteen thousand in 1920 and under fifty thousand in 1930. But there was a major surge during the Great Depression. The majority of doctoral degrees at the time were awarded by the large universities. Selectivity, then, was not an issue. Princeton in the 1920s accepted over half its applicants but awarded fellowships to only six. Axtell, *The Making of Princeton University: From Woodrow Wilson to the Present* (Princeton, N.J.: Princeton University Press, 2006), 412.

42. See Brink, "Selecting Graduate Students," 425.

43. See Charles M. Grigg, *Graduate Education* (New York: Center for Applied Research in Education, 1965), 7. Other sources suggest that between 1910 and 1919, approximately 546 Ph.D.'s were awarded per year. In the period 1920–1929, 1,081 were awarded annually. Ph.D. population doubled again in the 1930s, with roughly 2,697 produced annually. The 1940s were a period of relative stagnation, with only 3,349 produced annually (growth being noticeably smaller), followed by the huge postwar boom in the 1950s, when 8,376 Ph.D.'s were produced annually. The number doubled again in the 1960s, to approximately17,000 a year. See Barry R. Chiswick, Nicholas Larsen, and Paul Pieper *Production of PhDs in the United States and Canada* (Bonn: IZA, 2010). 3.

44. Geiger, *To Advance Knowledge*, 18.

45. Harvard University, *Annual Reports of the President and Treasurer of Harvard College, 1910–1911* (Cambridge, Mass.: Harvard University, 1911), 102.

46. Grigg, *Graduate Education,* 8. Furthermore, during this period, the Bureau of Education classified 344 colleges in terms of their fitness to prepare students for graduate work. This wholesale intrusion of the federal government brought forth violent protest, which quickly led to the withdrawal of this list at the direction of the president of the United States. This action did not deter the trend toward accreditation and in fact prompted some members of the AAU to compile their own lists of acceptable undergraduate institutions (ibid., 8–9). It should also be stated that the AAU never saw its primary mission as being an accrediting organization (ibid., 9).

47. Geiger, *To Advance Knowledge*, 19.

48. The classification system introduced in 1906 by the Carnegie Association for the Advancement of Teaching (Research I, Doctoral, Liberal Arts College, etc.) also served as a de facto accrediting system for institutions, as their entry into this texonomy granted them access to Carnegie-donated pension funds. Such was the power of Henry W. Pritchett, the first president of the foundation, that he was compared to the Prussian minister of education. Clyde Barrow, *Universities and the Capitalist State: Corporate Liberalism and the Reconstruction of American Higher Education, 1894–1928* (Madison: University of Wisconsin Press, 1990), 89.

49. Harvard University, *Annual Reports of the President and Treasurer of Harvard College, 1906–1907* (Cambridge, Mass.: Harvard University, 1907), 139–140. For more on the Carnegie Association for the Advancement of Teaching, see Hans-Jeorg Tiede, " 'To Make Collective Action Possible': The Founding of the AAUP," *AAUP Journal of Academic Freedom* 5 (2014): 12–13, http://www.aaup.org/file/Tiede.pdf; and Barrow, *Universities and the Capitalist State.*

50. Willard Thorp, Minor Myers, and Jeremiah Stanton Finch, *The Princeton Graduate School: A History* (Princeton, N.J.: Association of Princeton Graduate Alumni, 2000), 100–101.

51. Since the graduate school was liberally designed for "the enlargement and advancement of learning and science," there were "many different types of men in a Graduate School, men of different aims and schemes of work, men who are able to devote their entire time and men who can give but a portion of it to their studies." See Harvard University, *Annual Reports of the President and Treasurer of Harvard College, 1900–1901* (Cambridge, Mass.: Harvard University, 1902, 117). At this time, about one-fourth of the student body at Harvard Graduate School was made up of part-time students working as teachers and assistants at Harvard, teachers in neighboring schools, clergymen, students at other institutions, and students supplementing their coursework from elsewhere (ibid.). But such part-time students were stigmatized by the new rule of 1907 that teaching fellows not be allowed to devote more than half their time to advanced study, and one's time at Harvard could be "credited with only half a year towards his doctorate for each year in which he holds his fellowship" (Harvard University, *Annual Reports . . . , 1906–1907,* 141).

52. For a historicized account of recent practices, see Cassuto, "The Part-Time Ph.D. Student."

53. Harvard University, *Annual Reports of the President and Treasurer of Harvard College, 1909–1910* (Cambridge, MA: Harvard University, 1910, 94–95.

54. University of California, *Annual Report of the President of the University on Behalf of the Regents to His Excellency the Governor of the State of California, 1908–1912* (Berkeley: University of California Press, 1912), 6.

55. University of California, *Annual Report of the President of the University on Behalf of the Regents to His Excellency the Governor of the State of California, 1912–1914* (Berkeley: University of California Press, 1914), 7.

56. Similarly, when Harvard noticed a slight increase in the number of men who completed M.A. work (from 67 percent to 71 percent), the dean called it an "improvement" and attributed it to the raising of standards of admission. See Harvard College, *Report of the President of Harvard College and Reports of the Departments, 1931–32* (Cambridge, Mass.: Harvard College, 1933), 127.

57. Geiger, *To Advance Knowledge,* 130.

58. Harvard University, "Reports of the President and the Treasurer of Harvard College, 1923–1924," *Official Register of Harvard University* 22, no. 5 (1925): 70.

59. At Berkeley, for example, attrition in humanities and social sciences departments ranged from 70 to 85 percent during the two postwar decades. Roger L. Geiger, *Research and Relevant Knowledge: American Research Universities since World War II* (New York: Oxford University Press, 1993), 224, 225.

60. Harvard University, "Reports of the President and the Treasurer of Harvard College, 1924–1925," *Official Register of Harvard University* 23, no. 2 (1926): 109.

61. Yale University, *Report of the President for the Academic Year 1925–1926* (New Haven, Conn.: Yale University, 1927), 1, 3.

62. Harvard University, "Reports of the President and Treasurer of Harvard College, 1928–1929," *Official Register of Harvard University* 27, no. 8 (1930): 116–117; Harvard University, "Report of the President of Harvard College and Reports of Departments, 1930–1931," *Official Register of Harvard University* 29, no. 2 (1932): 128; James Baxter, "Student Selection for Work in the Social Sciences," *Journal of AAU* 35 (1933): 45–49.

63. University of Michigan, *The President's Report to the Board of Regents for the Academic Year 1923–1924* (Ann Arbor: University of Michigan, 1924), 238, 239. This report contains critiques of the M.A. as well (238–240).

64. University of Michigan, *The President's Report to the Board of Regents for the Academic Year 1921–1922* (Ann Arbor: University of Michigan, 1922), 233–234.

65. University of Michigan, *The President's Report to the Board of Regents for the Academic Year 1924–1925* (Ann Arbor: University of Michigan, 1925), 234.

66. University of Michigan, *The President's Report to the Board of Regents for the Academic Year 1929–1930* (Ann Arbor: University of Michigan, 1930), 108. Hubert says in his report of 1931 that this group of aspiring teachers "creates obligations" for the graduate school; University of Michigan, *The President's Report to the Board of Regents for the Academic Year 1930–1931* (Ann Arbor: University of Michigan, 1931), 220), and he repeats that training them "is an obligation which graduate schools must recognize" (ibid., 221).

67. University of Michigan, *The President's Report to the Board of Regents for the Academic Year 1931–1932* (Ann Arbor: University of Michigan, 1932), 110, 111.

68. University of Michigan, *The President's Report . . . 1929–1930,* 109.

69. University of Michigan, *The President's Report . . . 1930–1931,* 220–221.

70. Yale University, *Report of the President of Yale University, 1926–1927* (New Haven, Conn.: Yale University, 1928), 13.

71. Yale University, *Report of the President of Yale University, 1928–1929* (New Haven, Conn.: Yale University, 1929), 15.

72. Yale University, *Report of the President of Yale University, 1930–1931* (New Haven, Conn.: Yale University, 1931), 5.

73. Yale University, *Report of the President . . . , 1926–1927,* 6. See also Malcolm M. Willey, *Depression, Recovery, and Higher Education: A Report by Committee Y of the American Association of University Professors* (New York: McGraw-Hill, 1937).

Willey reported that faculty size remained unchanged during the first years of Depression but then began to decrease around 1934 (23). In other areas, too, there was a "two-year lag": salary reductions (35) and promotions and tenure (64). Regarding how faculties reacted to the Depression, Willey notes that decisions were made by administration, requiring a considerable degree of mutual trust and understanding between faculty and administrators. Data show that faculty were not consulted about funding cuts or about later funding restorations (90).

74. Yale University, "Report of the President for the Academic Year 1931–1932," *Bulletin of Yale University* 29, no. 11 (1933): 15.

75. University of California, *Report of the President of the University of California, 1930–1932* (Berkeley: University of California Press, 1932), 7.

76. Yale University, "Report of the President for the Academic Year 1932–1933," *Bulletin of Yale University* 30, no. 11 (1934): 26.

77. Harvard University, "Report of the President of Harvard College and Reports of Departments, 1931–1932," *Official Register of Harvard University* 30, no. 1 (1933): 125; University of California, *Report of the President . . . , 1930–1932,* 7, 8; Yale University, "Report of the President . . . 1931–1932," 14; Yale University, "Report of the President . . . 1932–1933," 3, 5, 19, 20, 26; Harvard University, "The Report of the President of Harvard College and Reports of the Departments, 1934–1935," *Official Register of Harvard University* 33, no. 4 (1936): 140; Yale University, "Report of the President for the Academic Year 1935–1936," *Bulletin of Yale University* 33, no. 8 (1937): 17.

78. Brink, "Selecting Graduate Students," 425, 426.

79. George H. Chase, Algernon Coleman, W. B. Fite, Helen S. Hughes, R. A. Law, W. F. Loehwing, H. W. Odum, Julian Park, and Tucker Brooke, "Requirements for the Master's Degree: Report of Committee M," *Bulletin of the American Association of University Professors* 18, no. 3 (1932): 173.

80. Brink, "Selecting Graduate Students," 427, 430. Later observers have also suggested that graduate admissions procedures should find students disposed toward teaching. See James L. Bess, "Anticipatory Socialization of Graduate Students," *Research in Higher Education* 8, no. 4 (1978): 289–317. That prediction proved errant, for reasons that will become clear.

81. Thorp, Myers, and Finch, *The Princeton Graduate School,* 214.

82. Yale University, *Report of the President of Yale University to the Alumni, 1941–1942* (New Haven, Conn.: Yale University, 1942), 24. Matriculation declined by half at Yale, for example.

83. Harvard University, "The Report of the President of Harvard College and Reports of the Departments for 1944–1945," *Official Register of Harvard University* 45, no. 40 (1948): 124; University of Michigan, *The President's Report for 1945–1946* (Ann Arbor: University of Michigan, 1946), 153; University of Michigan, *The President's Report for 1941–1942* (Ann Arbor: University of Michigan, 1942), 166, 167.

84. Yale Unversity, *Report of the President of Yale University to the Alumni, 1944–1945* (New Haven, Conn.: Yale University, 1945), 10.

85. University of Michigan, *The President's Report for 1945–1946*, 154; Harvard University, "Report of the President of Harvard College and Reports of Departments for 1947–1948," *Official Register of Harvard University* 47, no. 12 (1950): 164; Yale University, *Report of the President . . . , 1944–1945*, 11; Yale University, *Report of the President of Yale University to the Alumni, 1949–1950* (New Haven, Conn.: Yale University, 1950), 19.

86. Grigg, *Graduate Education*, 2.

87. James A. Davis, *Great Aspirations: The Graduate School Plans of America's College Seniors* (Chicago: Aldine, 1964), 59.

88. For example, Charles Grigg wrote in 1965 that there was "considerable room for improvement in the recruitment to graduate school of high performers from social groups whose motivation and location work against them" (*Graduate Education*, 140).

89. See Kathleen Anderson Steeves, Philip Evan Bernhardt, James P. Burns, and Michele K. Lombard, "Transforming American Educational Identity after Sputnik," *American Educational History Journal* 36, no. 1 (2009): 71–87. The National Defense Education Act (NDEA) of 1958 radically increased the federal education budget (ibid., 75). NDEA allocated $300 million to fund the purchase of equipment for science classrooms, training for teachers, and the establishment of National Defense Fellowships for graduate students; see Paul Dickson, *Sputnik: The Shock of the Century* (New York: Walkerbooks, 2007), 227; quoted in Steeves et al., "Transforming American Educational Identity," 75. For a thoughtful account of the meanings of this expansion, see also Christopher P. Loss, *Between Citizens and the State: The Politics of American Higher Education in the Twentieth Century* (Princeton, N.J.: Princeton University Press, 2012), 156–161.

90. I have drawn in this paragraph on R. C. Lewontin's "The Cold War and the Transformation of the Academy," in *The Cold War and the University: Toward an Intellectual History of the Postwar Years*, ed. Noam Chomsky (New York: New Press, 1997), 1–34.

91. "After the rise in federal support for research and graduate education dating approximately from World War II through 1968, a substantial change occurred in the composition and amount of federal support for these activities. Federal support for fellowships and traineeships declined by 57 percent between 1968 and 1972, with further substantial reductions scheduled for 1973 and 1974. These reductions were offset by the rapid, though temporary, increase in G.I. Bill benefits, with the result that federal support for graduate students fell by approximately 10 percent in real terms from 1968 to 1972. . . . In addition, institutional support declined by 52 percent and research support by 5 percent in real terms over those years." These reductions seem to have been caused by changes in the job market, as well as a new philosophy in the Congress and administration. National Board on Graduate Education, *Federal Policy Alternatives toward Graduate Education* (Washington, D.C.: National Academy of Sciences, 1974), 23.

92. David W. Breneman, *The Ph.D. Production Function: The Case at Berkeley* (Berkeley: University of California Press, 1970), 11. Breneman's numbers, collected in 1975, are based on data from the National Board on Graduate Education.

93. University of Michigan, *The President's Report for 1945–1946,* 155.

94. University of Michigan, *The President's Report for 1946–1947* (Ann Arbor: University of Michigan, 1947), 166.

95. Harvard University, "Report of the President of Harvard College and Reports of Departments for 1945–1946," *Official Register of Harvard University* 45, no. 30 (1948): 150.

96. Harvard University, "Report of the President . . . 1946–1947," 183.

97. Harvard University, "Report of the President . . . 1947–1948," 164.

98. Harvard University, *The President's Report, 1993–1995* (Cambridge, Mass: Harvard University, 1995), 27.

99. Thorp, Myers, and Finch, *The Princeton Graduate School,* 150. Still, administrators were working out the meaning of the GRE, as at Princeton, where it was found to be unsatisfactory as an admissions factor due to its inappropriateness to assess the qualifications of former soldiers (ibid.).

100. Harvard University, "Report of the President . . . 1945–1946," 150.

101. Harvard University, "Report of the President . . . 1946–1947," 183.

102. Harvard University, "Report of the President . . . 1945–1946," 150.

103. Harvard University, "Report of the President . . . 1946–1947," 164.

104. For a contemporary account of this problem, see Marc Bousquet, *How the University Works: Higher Education and the Low-Wage Nation* (New York: New York University Press, 2008).

105. Harvard University, "Report of the President . . . 1946–1947," 167.

106. Harvard University's "Report of the President . . . 1946–1947" notes the usefulness of the G.I. Bill but raises concerns about what would happen after G.I. aid was exhausted. The end of government assistance, worried administrators, would mean that many students could not go into grad school, meaning sterner competition for students (186). Dean Seymour at Yale in 1946 was concerned that the government hadn't made enough provisions for funding the humanities; see Yale University, *Report of the President of Yale University to the Alumni, 1945–1946* (New Haven, Conn.: Yale University, 1946), 13. He repeated this concern again in 1948; see Yale University, *Report of the President of Yale University to the Alumni, 1947–1948* (New Haven, Conn.: Yale University, 1948), 25.

107. Harvard University, "Report of the President . . . 1946–1947," 185.

108. Ibid., 166.

109. See John R. Thelin, *A History of American Higher Education* (Baltimore: Johns Hopkins University Press, 2004), 268–271.

110. Harvard University, "Report of the President . . . 1946–1947," 166.

111. University of Michigan, *The President's Report for 1945–1946,* 155.

112. Harvard University, "Report of the President . . . 1945–1946," 30; Harvard University, "Report of the President . . . 1946–1947," 151, 169.

113. University of Michigan, *The President's Report for 1946–1947,* 168.

114. University of Michigan, *The President's Report to the Board of Regents for the Academic Year 1951–1952* (Ann Arbor: University of Michigan, 1952), 179.

115. University of Michigan, *The President's Report to the Board of Regents for the Academic Year 1952–1953* (Ann Arbor: University of Michigan, 1953), 157, 158.

116. University of Michigan, *The President's Report to the Board of Regents for the Academic Year 1960–1961* (Ann Arbor: University of Michigan, 1961), 49.

117. Bernard R. Berelson, *Graduate School in the United States* (New York: McGraw-Hill, 1960), 144, 145.

118. Lewis B. Mayhew and Patrick Joseph Ford, *Reform in Graduate Education* (Atlanta: Southern Regional Education Board, 1972), 117.

119. David W. MacKinnon, "Selecting Students with Creative Potential," in *The Creative College Student: An Unmet Challenge*, ed. Paul Heist (San Francisco: Jossey-Bass, 1968), 484–495.

120. James Harvey, "Graduate School Admissions," *College and University Bulletin,* November 1971, 4; Mayhew and Ford, *Reform in Graduate Education,* 266.

121. Mayhew and Ford, *Reform in Graduate Education,* 118, 119.

122. See James A. Hedrick and Chester S. Williams, "Negroes in Southern Graduate Education," *Phi Delta Kappan* 36, no. 2 (1954): 103. In the 1950s, administrators developed certain devices in order to overcome the "background deficiencies" of black students (ibid.).

123. Loss, *Between Citizens and the State*, 221. Loss argues that due to a combination of political and economic factors, "educating students in the name of diversity has been what American colleges and universities do." Since the 1960s, it has become the "core value" of higher education (233).

124. Breneman, *Ph.D. Production*, 1.

125. This background is drawn from the website of the University of Michigan's Rackham Graduate School: see Mary M. Easthope, "A Chronicle of Graduate Education 1845 to 1982," https://www.rackham.umich.edu/about/what-is-rackham/chronicle; and "1990s," https://www.rackham.umich.edu/about/what-is-rackham/timeline/1990s.

126. See Breneman, *Ph.D. Production*, 1. Although federal funding for graduate education declined in the late 1960s, the number of students enrolled in graduate programs continued to increase. From 1969 to 1979, for example, the total U.S. graduate student population increased from 1,120,175 to 1,571,922, or 40 percent. Data are from the National Center for Education Statistics, which in turn gathered its data from the U.S. Department of Education, National Center for Education Statistics, Higher Education General Information Survey (HEGIS), "Fall Enrollment in Colleges and Universities" surveys, 1967 through 1985; Integrated Postsecondary Education

Data System (IPEDS), "Fall Enrollment Survey" (IPEDS-EF:86–99); and IPEDS Spring 2001 through Spring 2011, Enrollment component.

127. William G. Bowen and Julie Ann Sosa predicated the boom in the academic labor market to continue indefinitely in *Prospects for Faculty in the Arts and Sciences: A Study of Factors Affecting Demand and Supply, 1987 to 2012* (Princeton, N.J.: Princeton University Press, 1989). Marc Bousquet discusses the report and its failures in "The Rhetoric of 'Job Market' and the Reality of the Academic Labor System," *College English* 66, no. 2 (2003): 207–208.

128. Geiger, *Research and Relevant Knowledge*, 225.

129. Julie Renee Posselt, *Faculty Gatekeeping in Graduate Admissions* (Cambridge, Mass.: Harvard University Press, 2015). Posselt observed graduate admissions practices at three universities, two private and one public, in departments of classics, linguistics, and philosophy in the humanities; economics, political science, and sociology in the social sciences; and astrophysics, biology, and physics in the sciences. All quotations are drawn from a copy of the manuscript that Professor Posselt generously shared with me while the book was in press.

130. For more on such "useful fictions" and their role in graduate student self-presentation, see Leonard Cassuto, "What's Your Teaching Philosophy?," *Chronicle of Higher Education*, 2 December 2013, http://www.chroniclecareers.com/article /Whats-Your-Teaching/143315/.

131. John Guillory, "How Scholars Read," *ADE Bulletin* 146 (2008): 8–17.

132. The National Center for Education Statistics (NCES) provides the raw data showing that the graduate population has continued to increase since 1967, though at changing rates of increase. From 1969 to 1979, the number increased from 1.12 million to 1.57 million, or about 40 percent. The 1980s saw a more modest increase: from 1979 to 1989, the study population grew from 1.57 million to 1.79 million, or 14 percent. From 1989 to 1999, the number of students increased by 17.5 percent, from 1.79 million to 2.1 million. The first decade of this century saw a huge increase, by 35.6 percent, from 2.1 million in 1999 to 2.86 million in 2009. In the humanities, according to the Council of Graduate Schools, graduate enrollment grew by 0.7 percent between 2002 and 2012; see Council of Graduate Schools, *Graduate Enrollment and Degrees: 2002–2012* (Washington, D.C.: Council of Graduate Schools), viii.

133. Robin Wilson, "Cutbacks in Enrollment Redefine Graduate Education and Faculty Jobs," *Chronicle of Higher Education,* 11 March 2012, http://chronicle.com /article/Graduate-Programs-in/131123.

134. The connection also conferred disproportionate help afterward. "There really was something of an old-boys network," Paul Lauter noted recently. Lauter, a Yale Ph.D. who is now a professor of English at Trinity College in Connecticut, recalled that in his job search, in the late 1950s, "I always introduced myself as 'Paul Lauter from Yale.'" Lauter, email to the author, November 2012.

135. Thomas Bender, Philip M. Katz, Colin Palmer, and the AHA Committee on Graduate Education, *The Education of Historians for the Twenty-First Century* (Urbana: University of Illinois Press, 2004).

136. The problem is both similar and related to the one with "need-blind" undergraduate admissions identified by Andrew Delbanco, who points out that "as a matter of practice, 'need-blind' is a slogan that does not mean much except in relation to the needs of the applicant pool. If most applicants come from places like Greenwich or Grosse Point, a college can be 'need-blind' without having to dispense much aid." Delbanco, "Scandals of Higher Education," *New York Review of Books,* 29 March 2007, http://www.nybooks.com/articles/archives/2007/mar/29/scandals-of-higher-education/. Also see Delbanco's *College: What It Was, Is, and Should Be* (Princeton, N.J.: Princeton University Press, 2012), 112. It's one thing for graduate schools to say that they welcome applications from members of underrepresented groups and another for them to show that they welcome those students by actually seeking them out.

2. CLASSWORK

1. See Laurence R. Veysey, *The Emergence of the American University* (Chicago: University of Chicago Press, 1965), 153–156.

2. Roger L. Geiger, *To Advance Knowledge: The Growth of the American Research Universities, 1900–1940* (New York: Oxford University Press, 1986), 219.

3. Derek Bok, *Higher Education in America* (Princeton, N.J.: Princeton University Press, 2013), 245.

4. Ed Neal describes this tendency more charitably, perhaps, when he points out that professors may underprepare out of the conviction that students will "find their own way." Neal, "Leading the Seminar: Graduate and Undergraduate," *Essays on Teaching Excellence* 8, no. 1 (1996–1997), http://podnetwork.org/content/uploads/V8-N1-Neal.pdf.

5. David A. Gerber, "Rethinking the Graduate Research Seminar in American History: The Search for a New Model," *Teaching History* 13, no. 1 (1988): 9.

6. Frank J. Donoghue, "Can the Seminar's Death Bring Life to the Ph.D.?," *Chronicle of Higher Education,* 6 December 2013, http://chronicle.com/article/Can-the-Death-of-the-Seminar/143609/.

7. Gerald Graff, "Presidential Address 2008: Courseocentrism," *PMLA* 124, no. 3 (2009): 736, 728; Joseph Tussman, *Experiment at Berkeley* (New York: Oxford University Press, 1969), 115. Graff quotes Tussman to support his argument.

8. A third, related assumption is the sense of entitlement that professors feel to teach the graduate courses that they want to teach, irrespective of the students' needs.

9. R. C. Lewontin notes in his remarkable analysis of how American academia was shaped by the Cold War that "it has been obvious to all makers of national policy

in Europe, North America, and Asia since the end of World War II, and even to most economists, that the prosperity of modern capitalism is critically dependent on massive state intervention in the economy." Lewontin, "The Cold War and the Transformation of the Academy," in *The Cold War and the University: Toward an Intellectual History of the Postwar Years,* ed. Noam Chomsky (New York: New Press, 1997), 2.

10. Josiah Ober, telephone interview with the author, June 2012.

11. Russell Berman, interview with the author, June 2012. Subsequent quotations from Berman are also from this interview.

12. Gerald Graff, *Clueless in Academe: How Schooling Obscures the Life of the Mind* (New Haven, Conn.: Yale University Press, 2004), 9–11.

13. Andrew Delbanco, *College: What It Was, Is, and Should Be* (Princeton, N.J.: Princeton University Press, 2012), 94–95.

14. Gerald Graff addresses the inadequacies of the coverage model in his important *Professing Literature: An Institutional History* (Chicago: University of Chicago Press, 1987). Composition scholar E. Shelley Reid worries that "coverage-based pedagogy" limits learning possibilities. She proposes an "uncoverage" model that casts graduate training "as practice in a way of encountering the world rather than mastery of skills or facts." Reid, "Uncoverage in Composition Pedagogy," *Composition Studies* 32, no. 1 (2004): 16.

15. Jim Grossman, address to Teagle Foundation convening, "Community of Scholars, Community of Teachers: An Introduction," New York, April 10, 2014.

16. Peter Khost, Debie Lohe, and Chuck Sweetman, "Rethinking and Unthinking the Graduate Seminar," *Pedagogy* 15, no. 1 (2015): 21.

17. Ames proposed a joint initiative with Hopkins's department of education to seek this goal. Joseph S. Ames, "Annual Report of the President," *Johns Hopkins University Circular* 419, no. 11 (1930): 6.

18. Gilbert Ryle, "Knowing How and Knowing That," presidential address, *Papers Read before the Aristotelian Society at the University of London Club,* 1946, 16; Robert Frost, "At Woodward's Gardens" (1936), in *The Poetry of Robert Frost: The Collected Poems, Complete and Unabridged* ed. Edward Connery Lathem (New York: Henry Holt, 1969), 293–94, l. 37.

19. Barbara E. Lovitts, "The Transition to Independent Research: Who Makes It, Who Doesn't, and Why," *Journal of Higher Education* 79, no. 3 (2008): 306.

20. Diane F. Halpern and Milton D. Hakel, "Applying the Science of Learning to the University and Beyond," *Change,* July–August 2003, 38.

21. Ibid., 39.

22. Committee on Developments in the Science of Learning, with additional material from the Committee on Learning Research and Educational Practice, *How People Learn: Brain, Mind, Experience, and School* (Washington, D.C.: National Academies Press, 2004), 14–19.

23. For more on backward design, see Grant Wiggins and Jay McTighe, *Understanding by Design* (Alexandria, Va.: Association for Supervision and Curriculum Development, 2005).

24. George E. Walker, Chris M. Golde, Laura Jones, Andrea Conklin Bueschel, and Pat Hutchings, *The Formation of Scholars: Rethinking Doctoral Education for the Twenty-First Century* (San Francisco: Carnegie Foundation for the Advancement of Teaching / Jossey-Bass, 2008), 76.

25. Maureen E. Kelleher, "Teaching a Graduate Proseminar: An Experiential Approach," *Teaching Sociology* 19 (1991): 363.

26. Psychologist Paul Taylor, for example, writes of a training program to improve graduate students' seminar presentations, and as far back as 1971, chemist Keith Laidler called for chemistry Ph.D. programs to add a requirement that graduate students give public seminars—and that they learn principles of public speaking in order to do so. Taylor, "Improving Graduate Student Seminar Presentations through Training," *Teaching of Psychology* 19, no. 4 (1992): 236–238; Laidler, "The Graduate Student Seminar," *Journal of Chemical Education* 48, no. 10 (1971): 671–674.

27. Neal, "Leading the Seminar."

28. Gerber, "Rethinking the Graduate Research Seminar," 12.

29. Ibid., 14.

30. John Dewey, "The School and the Life of the Child," in *The School and Society* (Chicago: University of Chicago Press, 1907), 56–57.

31. Steven M. Cahn offers an example from philosophy in the form of his professor and eventual dissertation adviser Richard Taylor. When Taylor taught graduate courses, Cahn recalls, he put almost no philosophical texts on the syllabus. Instead, he asked students to write: "We would not study the writings of famous philosophers of the past or pore over learned commentaries about them. Rather, we would *do* philosophy. We would not read about philosophers; we would ourselves *be* philosophers." Taylor's course "content" included only a few articles; students wrote three papers in which they themselves had to try to solve philosophical issues. Taylor told Cahn that his writing in the course should become a chapter of his dissertation, advice that Cahn took. Cahn, *From Student to Scholar: A Candid Guide to Becoming a Professor* (New York: Columbia University Press, 2008), 76.

32. Khost, Lohe, and Sweetman, "Rethinking and Unthinking the Graduate Seminar," 21; Laura R. Micciche and Allison D. Carr, "Toward Graduate Level Writing Instruction," *College Composition and Communication* 62, no. 3 (2011): 478.

33. Khost, Lohe, and Sweetman, "Rethinking and Unthinking the Graduate Seminar," 24, 28, 26. Mary Louise Pratt introduced the humanities to the genre of autoethnography in 1991, though it remains largely obscure outside of sociology. See Pratt, "Arts of the Contact Zone," *Profession 91* (1991): 2; and Carolyn Ellis, Tony E. Adams, and Arthur P. Bochner, "Autoethnography: An Overview," *Forum: Qualitative*

Social Research 12, no. 1 (2011), http://www.qualitative-research.net/index.php/fqs/article/view/1589/3095.

34. Neal, "Leading the Seminar."

35. Walker et al., *The Formation of Scholars,* 129. For more on the teaching commons idea, see Mary Taylor Huber and Pat Hutchings, *The Advancement of Learning: Building the Teaching Commons* (San Francisco: Jossey-Bass, 2005).

36. Anthony T. Grafton and Jim Grossman, "No More Plan B: A Very Modest Proposal for Graduate Programs in History," *Perspectives on History,* October 2011, http://www.historians.org/publications-and-directories/perspectives-on-history/october-2011/no-more-plan-b. Subsequent quotations from Grafton and Grossman are also from this article.

37. The document was quickly reprinted in the *Chronicle of Higher Education* as well, on 9 October 2011, http://chronicle.com/article/No-More-Plan-B/129293.

38. Leora Auslander, interview with the author, December 2011. Subsequent quotations from Auslander are also from this interview.

39. The four programs are Columbia, Chicago, the University of New Mexico, and UCLA, as well as the American Historical Society. The grant is designed to give doctoral students room to explore work outside of academia. See Vimal Patel, "$1.6-Million Grant Will Better Prepare History Ph.D.'s for Range of Careers," *Chronicle of Higher Education,* 20 March 2014, http://chronicle.com/article/16-Million-Grant-Will-Better/145399/.

40. Edward Balleisen, interview with the author, December, 2011. Subsequent quotations are from the same interview.

41. Michael Elliott, email to the author, March 2011.

42. Julian Zelizer, interview with the author, November 2011. Subsequent quotations from Zelizer are also from this interview.

43. Peter Struck, interview with the author, February 2012.

44. Zachary First, presentation at a meeting of the National Forum for the Future of Liberal Education, February 2012.

45. Robert B. Townsend traces the origins of that reputation in *History's Babel: Scholarship, Professionalization, and the Historical Enterprise in the United States, 1880–1940* (Chicago: University of Chicago Press, 2013).

46. Among many examples I could cite, I want to single out the University of Iowa's Obermann Graduate Institute on Engagement and the Academy, which trains fifteen graduate students a year for six years in the methods and practices of publicly engaged research and teaching. See the program's website at http://obermann.uiowa.edu/programs/graduate-institute-engagement-and-academy. Iowa has a related book series, Humanities and Public Life (see the series website: http://www.uiowapress.org/authors/humanities-and-public-life.htm). I am grateful to Teresa Mangum, one of the coeditors of the series, for calling my attention to these worthy initiatives.

47. Lauren Tilton, interview with the author, November 2011.

48. Matthew Jacobson, email to the author, November 2011.

49. Laura Wexler, interview with the author, November 2011.

50. David Blight, interview with the author, November 2011.

51. Dana Schaffer, interview with the author, November 2011.

3. THE COMPREHENSIVE EXAM

1. The exams have also been called "prelims," but I don't hear that term much anymore.

2. See Heidi Estrem and Brad E. Lucas, "Embedded Traditions, Uneven Reform: The Place of the Comprehensive Exam in Composition and Rhetoric Ph.D. Programs," *Rhetorical Review* 22, no. 4 (2003): 396–416.

3. John Gravois, "In Humanities, 10 Years May Not Be Enough to Get a Ph.D.," *Chronicle of Higher Education,* 27 July 2007, http://www.csun.edu/pubrels/clips /July07/07-23-07C1.pdf. I have more to say about attrition later on, in Chapter 5.

4. Barbara E. Lovitts, *Leaving the Ivory Tower: The Causes and Consequences of Departure from Doctoral Study* (Burlington, Mass.: Elsevier, 2006), 6. I consider student debt in more detail in Chapter 4.

5. Grant Wiggins and Jay McTighe, *Understanding by Design* (Alexandria, Va.: Association for Supervision and Curriculum Development, 2005), 3.

6. Committee on Developments in the Science of Learning, with additional material from the Committee on Learning Research and Educational Practice, *How People Learn: Brain, Mind, Experience, and School* (Washington, D.C.: National Academies Press, 2004), 25.

7. Diane F. Halpern and Milton D. Hakel, "Applying the Science of Learning to the University and Beyond," *Change,* July–August 2003, 37, 38.

8. David Jaffee, "Stop Telling Students to Study for Exams," *Chronicle of Higher Education,* 22 April 2012, http://chronicle.com/article/Stop-Telling-Students-to -Study/131622/; Halpern and Hakel, "Applying the Science of Learning," 38.

9. Cary Nelson and Stephen Watt, *Academic Keywords: A Devil's Dictionary for Higher Education* (New York: Routledge, 1999), 74. Nelson's separate call to abandon comprehensive exams remains one of the few references to the subject in *PMLA,* the flagship journal of the literature and language fields. Cary Nelson, "Graduate Studies and the Job Market," *PMLA* 115, no. 5 (2000): 1202.

10. John H. Williams and William J. Berg, "Preliminary Exams and Graduate Education," *SubStance* 1, no. 2 (1971–1972): 136. The authors claim that the exams gain inordinate importance due to faculty irresponsibility in other areas. Some of their complaints are specific to the time that they were writing, when graduate programs could be quite large, such as their complaint that programs accept too many students and then use the exams to winnow them out. But it's remarkable how applicable their broadside remains.

11. *The University of Tennessee/ORNL Graduate School of Genome Science and Technology Graduate Student Handbook,* 7th ed., 22, http://gst.tennessee.edu/GST%20Handbook%207th%20edition.doc.

12. Daniel Simons, interview with the author, February 2012.

13. For example, the director of professional development in my own department compared exams in about twenty English departments in 2013 and found no real pattern or through line.

14. Jaffee, "Stop Telling Students to Study for Exams."

15. Robert E. Bargar and Jane Mayo-Chamberlain, "Adviser and Advisee Issues in Doctoral Education," *Journal of Higher Education* 54, no. 4 (1983): 413, 414.

16. See Paula Wasley, "Portfolios Are Replacing Qualifying Exams as a Step on the Road to Dissertations," *Chronicle of Higher Education,* 11 July 2008, A8, http://chronicle.com/article/Portfolios-Are-Replacing/9141/.

17. Matthew Mancini, email correspondence with the author, February 2012.

18. See Ellen MacKay's report on Indiana, Corrinne Harol's on Alberta, Anthony L. Geist's on Washington, and Don Bialystocky's on Pittsburgh, all in the appendix to the *Report of the MLA Task Force on Doctoral Study in Modern Language and Literature* (New York: Modern Language Association, May 2014), 24, 28, 36, 34, http://www.mla.org/pdf/taskforcedocstudy2014.pdf.

19. John Thompson, email correspondence with the author, February 2012.

4. ADVISING

1. "The overwhelming evidence," according to Michael T. Nettles and Catherine M. Millett, "is that advisers play an important role for students and that the quality of their relationship has consequences." Nettles and Millett, *Three Magic Letters: Getting to Ph.D.* (Baltimore: Johns Hopkins University Press, 2006), 95.

2. John Grote, in the 1856 essay that marks the first known use of the word "professionalism," actually describes his students as "sons." Laurence R. Veysey reports that the students of the legendary historian Frederick Jackson Turner used to refer to him as "my professional father" and that they would do so "in direct address." Grote, "Old Studies and New," in *Cambridge Essays, Contributed by Members of the University* (London: Parker, 1856), 75; Veysey, *The Emergence of the American University* (Chicago: University of Chicago Press, 1965), 157n113.

3. Some veteran professors even become the trunk nodes of their own family tree diagrams. A site called PsychTree even builds an adviser-student family tree in the field of psychology. PsychTree may be found at http://academictree.org/psych/index.php.

4. On the German origins of academic charisma, see William Clark, *Charisma and the Origins of the Research University* (Chicago: University of Chicago Press, 2006). Veysey provides a short and pungent account of the role of charisma in the early American research university (*Emergence of the American University,* 156–157).

5. Rebecca Schuman, "My Academic Metamorphosis," *Chronicle of Higher Education*, 17 May 2013, B20. Unless otherwise noted, all quotations from Schuman are drawn from this article.

6. Rebecca Schuman, "Thesis Hatement," *Slate*, 5 April 2013, http://www.slate.com/articles/life/culturebox/2013/04/there_are_no_academic_jobs_and_getting_a_ph_d_will_make_you_into_a_horrible.html. Schuman, who has gone on to a job as a columnist for *Slate*, has also noted that the "Don't Go" genre has lately been complemented by an "I Quit" category. Schuman, "'I Quit Academia,' An Important, Growing Subgenre of Essays," *Browbeat* (blog), *Slate*, 24 October 2013, http://www.slate.com/blogs/browbeat/2013/10/24/quitting_academic_jobs_professor_zachary_ernst_and_other_leaving_tenure.html.

7. William Pannapacker, writing as Thomas H. Benton, "Is Graduate School a Cult?," *Chronicle of Higher Education*, 30 June 2004, http://chronicle.com/article/Is-Graduate-School-a-Cult-/44676/.

8. For an insightful reading of Schuman and her less-well-known epigone, see A. W. Strouse, "Academe's Firing Squads," *The Conversation* (blog), *Chronicle of Higher Education*, 23 July 2014, http://chronicle.com/blogs/conversation/2014/07/23/academes-firing-squads/.

9. Robert E. Bargar and Jane Mayo-Chamberlain, "Adviser and Advisee Issues in Doctoral Education," *Journal of Higher Education* 54, no. 4 (1983): 410.

10. Michael Rosenberg, "His Time, His Place," *Sports Illustrated*, 26 November 2012, http://www.si.com/vault/2012/11/26/106258862/his-time-his-place.

11. Elizabeth Leake, interview with the author, December 2011.

12. See Sigmund Freud, "The Technique of Psycho-Analysis," in *An Outline of Psycho-Analysis: The Standard Edition* (New York: Norton, 1969), 49–62, especially 52–56.

13. My thanks to Elizabeth Knoll for pointing this out to me.

14. *The King's Speech*, dir. Tom Hooper, screenplay by David Seidler, The Weinstein Company and Anchor Bay Entertainment, 2010.

15. James A. Hedrick and Chester S. Williams. "Negroes in Southern Graduate Education," *Phi Delta Kappan* 36, no. 2 (1954): 103.

16. Lewis B. Mayhew, *Reform in Graduate Education* (Atlanta: Southern Regional Education Board, 1972), 120.

17. Martin Davidson, "Mentoring in the Preparation of Graduate Researchers of Color,"*Review of Educational Research* 7, no. 4 (2001): 549.

18. See, for example, W. G. Tierney and R. A. Rhoads, *Faculty Socialization as a Cultural Process: A Mirror of Institutional Commitment* (1994), and J. S. Antony, "Reexamining Doctoral Student Socialization and Professional Development" (2002), both cited in Ferlin G. McGaskey, "The Potential Benefits of Attending Historically Black Colleges and Universities for Black Doctoral Students," in *Black Graduate Education at Historically Black Colleges and Universities: Trends, Experiences, and Outcomes,*

ed. Robert T. Palmer, Adriel A. Hilton, and Tiffany P. Fountaine (Charlotte, N.C.: Information Age, 2012), 85.

19. McGaskey, "The Potential Benefits," 86–87.

20. Davidson, "Mentoring," 549, 550. Davidson also laments the lack of opportunities for students of color to experience same-race mentoring (550); indeed, there is a separate literature that considers the races of adviser and advisee; see Scott Jaschik, "White Male Advantage," *Inside Higher Ed,* 1 March 2011, http://www.insidehigh ered.com/news/2011/03/01/study_explores_impact_of_white_male_dissertation _advisers_on_minority_doctoral_candidates_in_sociology#sthash.2ZEwhcuV .AzdAf2xK.dpbs.

21. Davidson, "Mentoring," 561. Nor does the problem lie entirely with advisers; Davidson observes that protégés often "collude in avoiding discussion of race" (562).

22. Marissa K. López and Daniel Heath Justice, "On Mentoring Graduate Students of Color." MLA Commons, 25 April 2014, http://clpc.commons.mla.org /2014/04/25/mentoring-graduate-students-of-color/. Full disclosure: I am a part of the story that the authors tell about their efforts to publish their essay. I originally solicited it for a 2015 special issue on graduate education that I guest edited for the journal *Pedagogy.*

23. Derek Bok, *Higher Education in America* (Princeton, N.J.: Princeton University Press, 2013), 226.

24. Leonard Cassuto, "To Apply or Not to Apply," *Chronicle of Higher Education,* 3 June 2013, http://chronicle.com/article/To-Apply-or-Not-to-Apply/139539.

25. See, for example, Elizabeth Keenan, "The No Baby Penalty," *Chronicle of Higher Education,* 19 June 2014, https://chroniclevitae.com/news/570-the-no-baby -penalty.

26. Mary Ann Mason, Nicholas H. Wolfinger, and Marc Goulden, *Do Babies Matter? Gender and Family in the Ivory Tower* (New Brunswick, N.J.: Rutgers University Press, 2013), 24. At the very least, the Family and Medical Leave Act (FMLA) guarantees faculty at American colleges and universities a minimum of twelve weeks of unpaid leave. Department chairs, the ones who should be promoting these provisions, are often ignorant themselves (111). Somewhat surprisingly, there is also a notable gender disparity in available campus policies: 58 percent of colleges and universities offer at least six weeks' paid leave for faculty mothers, but only 16 percent offer one week's paid gender-neutral "parental" leave (110). Yet even when such leave exists, fathers often pass on the chance to take time off out of fear that they'll be seen as not rigorous or serious enough. Faculty mothers are more likely to take leave, but the numbers suggest that many are also reluctant to briefly step away from the workforce; many don't take advantage of leave options available to them.If academia wants to gain a reputation as supportive of families, the authors suggest, administrators and department chairs need to strip bias from their family-related policies, com-

municate their existence, and go out of their way to encourage faculty to take advantage of them. The authors add that this family friendliness needs to be nurtured in the graduate school years. Many people make decisions about family during their doctoral programs. The research shows that women (far more than men) often delay or forgo having children because, from the graduate student's vantage point, the academy doesn't seem a viable place to mix family and career. If female graduate students have children during or shortly after their doctoral degree programs, many will wind up with adjunct or other contingent employment. Universities can counter these trends by making on-campus child care, family leave, and other basic entitlements available to working graduate students. Only 13 percent of universities offer graduate students six weeks of paid maternity leave, and only 23 percent offer six weeks' leave to postdocs (108). Such provisions, note the authors of *Do Babies Matter?*, would signal to emerging scholars that it is possible to integrate the roles of parent and professor in academia.

27. The emergence of this second tier of full-time off-tenure ladder faculty is a change that professors, departments, and administrations must reckon with openly. Michael Bérubé and Jennifer Ruth open the conversation in their lucid and forcefully argued book, *The Humanities, Higher Education, and Academic Freedom: Three Necessary Arguments* (New York: Palgrave Macmillan, 2015).

28. Mason, Wolfinger, and Goulden, *Do Babies Matter?*

29. Bruce M. Shore, *The Graduate Advisor Handbook: A Student-Centered Approach* (Chicago: University of Chicago Press, 2014), 46, 21.

30. Sidonie Smith, "From the President: An Agenda for the New Dissertation," *MLA Newsletter,* Summer 2010, http://www.mla.org/blog&topic=134. For an interesting and cautionary personal narrative of a graduate student's efforts to submit a digital dissertation, see Melanie Lee, "The Melancholy Odyssey of a Dissertation with Pictures," *Pedagogy* 15, no. 1 (2015): 93–101.

31. MLA Task Force on Doctoral Study in Modern Language and Literature, *Report of the MLA Task Force on Doctoral Study in Modern Language and Literature* (New York: Modern Language Association, May 2014), 1, http://www.mla.org/pdf/taskforcedocstudy2014.pdf.

32. Daniel Denecke, email to the author, June 2012.

33. Patricia Hinchey and Isabel Kimmel, *The Graduate Grind: A Critical Look at Graduate Education* (New York: Falmer, 2000), 104.

34. For example, the University of Missouri requires graduate students to file annual reports through its Graduate Student Progress System, and advisers are required to review these reports. See the system's website at http://gradstudies.missouri.edu/academics/progress/graduate-student-progress-system.php. The biomedical group within Brown University's Ph.D. program in engineering requires written and oral progress reports each year (see the program's website at http://www.brown.edu/academics/biomedical-engineering/graduate-program/phd-program-overview). The botany and plant sciences department at the University of California, Riverside,

requires that an annual "Student Progress Report" be submitted following a meeting between the student and "all members of his/her Guidance, Thesis, or Dissertation Committee" (see the department's website at http://plantbiology.ucr.edu/graduate _programs/current_students.html.

35. I first made this suggestion in 2012 ("The Adviser and the Committee," *Chronicle of Higher Education,* 15 July 2012, http://chronicle.com/article/The -Adviserthe-Committee/132841/). Since then, I've noticed that more doctoral programs in the humanities have adopted progress reports, mostly as a way of monitoring time to degree. The MLA endorses the practice in the 2014 *Report of the MLA Task Force on Doctoral Study in Modern Language and Literature.*

36. Barbara E. Lovitts, "Being a Good Course-Taker Is Not Enough: A Theoretical Perspective on the Transition to Independent Research," *Studies in Higher Education* 30, no. 2 (2005): 144.

37. Barbara E. Lovitts, "The Transition to Independent Research: Who Makes It, Who Doesn't, and Why," *Journal of Higher Education* 79, no. 3 (2008): 313, 316.

38. For more on the dissertation proposal, see Leonard Cassuto, "Demystifying the Dissertation Proposal," *Chronicle of Higher Education*, 11 September 2011, http://chronicle.com/article/Demystifying-the-Dissertation/128916/.

39. A person with stigma, says Goffman, "is disqualified from full social acceptance." Erving Goffman, *Stigma: Notes on the Management of Spoiled Identity* (New York: Simon and Schuster, 1986), 7.

40. I am drawing in this short paragraph on the ideas of Derek Bok (*Higher Education in America,* 234) and Barbara Lovitts (*Leaving the Ivory Tower: The Causes and Consequences of Departure from Doctoral Study* [Burlington, Mass.: Elsevier, 2006], 28). Bok observes that professional schools have a graduation rate of over 90 percent, making a sorry comparison with the arts and sciences. Lovitts suggests that departing students often blame themselves; I've seen nothing in my own decades teaching graduate school that would lead me to disagree with her.

41. Completion and attrition rates vary by field and discipline as well as by race and gender, but in the humanities, attrition levels are at about 50 percent; see Council of Graduate Schools, *Ph.D. Completion and Attrition: Analysis of Baseline Demographic Data from the Ph.D. Completion Project: Executive Summary,* 2008, http://www.phd completion.org/information/Executive_Summary_Demographics_Book_II.pdf. On attrition as a historical problem, see William G. Bowen and Neil L. Rudenstein, *In Pursuit of the PhD* (Princeton, N.J.: Princeton University Press, 1992), 107.

42. Roger L. Geiger, *To Advance Knowledge: The Growth of the American Research Universities, 1900–1940* (New York: Oxford University Press, 1986), 219.

43. Bernard R. Berelson, *Graduate Education in the United States* (New York: McGraw-Hill, 1960), 144.

44. Roger L. Geiger, *Research and Relevant Knowledge: American Research Universities since World War II* (New York: Oxford University Press, 1993), 224, 225.

45. David W. Breneman, "Ph.D. Production Process" (1970), as cited in Geiger, *Research and Relevant Knowledge,* 224–225. Breneman's research centered on UC Berkeley, which had some of the highest attrition rates in the country. On national attrition rates, see Geiger, *Research and Relevant Knowledge,* 226.

46. Lovitts, *Leaving the Ivory Tower,* 30.

47. Council of Graduate Schools, *Ph.D. Completion and Attrition: Executive Summary,* 2.

48. Lovitts, *Leaving the Ivory Tower,* 6.

49. Bok, *Higher Education in America,* 237. Some programs, Bok notes, allot money to departments according to size, creating an incentive to enroll more students but not to retain them (237). Of course, this funding practice, which rewards the wrong things, is disturbing in itself.

50. For example, Bok says that "in theory, . . . departments can get tough with laggards," but "in practice," they rarely do (*Higher Education in America,* 232).

51. Susan Bassow, Dana Campbell, and Liz Stockwell, "Nontraditional Academics," in *Mama, Ph.D. Women Write about Motherhood and Academic Life,* ed. Elrena Evans and Caroline Grant (New Brunswick, N.J.: Rutgers University Press, 2008), 180.

52. Leo Braudy, "Doing Public Pedagogy: Speaking Outside the Walls," *Profession,* 1999, 30–31. Braudy's essay is adapted from remarks he made at a 1998 MLA Presidential Forum sponsored by then-president Elaine Showalter, called "Creative Collaborations: Alternatives to the Adversarial Academy." Showalter's endorsement of alternative career possibilities was, in retrospect, too far ahead of its time, as it generated more controversy than change.

53. Jacqueline Jones, talk at the meeting of the American Historical Association, January 2015. Jones, a professor and former chair of the history department of the University of Texas at Austin, told of how she organized one such panel each semester for graduate students. That looks like good practice to me.

54. Braudy, "Doing Public Pedagogy," 27, 28.

55. John S. Adams describes the course and lesson plans in "Reality Therapy for Geography Ph.D. Programs," in "Rethinking the Ph.D. in Geography," special issue, *GeoJournal,* 2014, http://link.springer.com/search?query=Reality+Therapy+for+Geography+Ph.D.+Programs&search-within=Journal&facet-journal-id=10708#page-1.

56. See Maura Ives, "Teaching the Market: Graduate Placement in the Classroom," *ADE Bulletin* 119 (1998): 14–18; Heather Dubrow, "Workshop on Placement Services." *PMLA* 115, no. 5 (2000): 1263–1265.

57. The PREP program may be found online at http://grad.msu.edu/prep/.

58. Matt Helm, interview with the author, February 2014. Subsequent quotations from Helm are also from this interview.

59. I first reported on this in "More Than One Possible Future," *Chronicle of Higher Education,* 17 March 2014, http://chronicle.com/article/More-Than-One-Pos

sible-Future/145317?cid=megamenu. L. Maren Wood, "What Doors Does a Ph.D. in History Open?," *Chronicle of Higher Education,* 30 October 2012, http://chronicle .com/article/What-Doors-Does-a-PhD-in/135448/. Wood discussed paranoid students in a talk at the American Historical Association's annual meeting in January 2014.

60. Matt Helm, Henry Campa III, and Kristin Moretto, "Professional Socialization for the Ph.D.: An Exploration of Career and Professional Development Preparedness and Readiness for Ph.D. Candidates," *Journal of Faculty Development* 26, no. 2 (2012): 5–23.

61. PREP has a strong online component, which works well for a university with a large population. Its website is thick with information and video tutorials—what Helm calls "knowledge networks." The office tries "to hit graduate students in large numbers," says Helm. Indeed, the live workshops are popular: "We fill everything, all the time." This success comes partly from ongoing assessment. "We need," says Helm, "to show what works."

62. For the names of these graduates and a good group interview with them, see Helen De Cruz, "Philosophers Who Work Outside of Academia—Part 1: How and Why Do They End Up There?," *New APPS* (blog), 23 June 2014, http://www.newapps blog.com/2014/06/philosophers-who-work-outside-of-academia-part-1-how-and -why-do-they-end-up-there.html.

63. Edward Mendelson calls the wish for a mentor "a fantasy" whose essence is located in the word itself: "In *The Odyssey,* the Ithacan elder Mentor is not a mentor at all; the protective guide who takes Telemakhos in hand is Athena disguised as Mentor, a divinity filling a role that no ordinary mortal could manage." Mendelson, "Old Saul and Young Saul," *New York Review of Books,* 26 September 2013, http://www .nybooks.com/articles/archives/2013/sep/26/old-saul-and-young-saul-bellow/. The point brooks no dispute, but I would add that if mentorship is an idealistic fantasy, it's still one worth chasing.

5. DEGREES

1. See William Clark, *Academic Charisma and the Origins of the Research University* (Chicago: University of Chicago Press, 2006, chap. 4.

2. See Roger L. Geiger, *To Advance Knowledge: The Growth of American Research Universities, 1900–1940* (New York: Oxford University Press, 1986), 8.

3. See Laurence R. Veysey, *The Emergence of the American University* (Chicago: University of Chicago Press, 1965), 175–176.

4. See Burton J. Bledstein, *The Culture of Professionalism: The Middle Class and the Development of Higher Education in America* (New York: Norton, 1976), especially 95–96.

5. MLA Task Force on Doctoral Study in Modern Language and Literature, *Report of the MLA Task Force on Doctoral Study in Modern Language and Literature*

(New York: Modern Language Association, May 2014), 8, http://www.mla.org/pdf /taskforcedocstudy2014.pdf.

6. Proponents of this argument claim that too many professors spend too much time pursuing highly specialized research with their graduate students and not enough time in the undergraduate classroom. For a recent example of this argument, see Jacques Berlinerblau, "Survival Strategy for Humanists: Engage, Engage," *Chronicle of Higher Education*, 5 August 2012, http://www.chronicle.com/article/Sur vival-Strategy-for/133309/.

7. If I think that a graduate student's dissertation may have book potential, I recommend William Germano's excellent *Getting It Published,* 2nd ed. (Chicago: University of Chicago Press, 2008), as postdoctoral reading. Germano's *From Dissertation to Book,* 2nd ed. (Chicago: University of Chicago Press, 2013), is another good choice.

8. See Karen Kelsky, "When to Publish Your Book and When to Hold Off," *Chronicle Vitae,* 9 June 2014, https://chroniclevitae.com/news/537–the-professor-is-in -when-to-publish-your-book-and-when-to-hold-off.

9. Lindsay Waters, *Enemies of Promise* (Chicago: Prickly Paradigm, 2004), 25.

10. The task force's report, available on the MLA website, is worth reading: MLA Task Force on Evaluating Scholarship for Tenure and Promotion, *Report of the MLA Task Force on Evaluating Scholarship for Tenure and Promotion* (New York: Modern Language Association, December 2006), http://www.mla.org/tenure_pro motion. Full disclosure: I served on that task force.

11. Anthony T. Grafton, "Humanities and Inhumanities," *New Republic*, 17 February 2010, http://www.newrepublic.com/article/politics/humanities-and -inhumanities#. For a different perspective, William James counseled similar caution a century earlier: "We ought to look to the future carefully, for it takes generations for a national custom, once rooted, to be grown away from." James, "The Ph.D. Octopus," in 1903 in *Writings 1902–1910*, ed. Bruce Kuklick (New York: Literary Classics of the United States, 1987), 1111–1118, 1117.

12. Louis Menand, *The Marketplace of Ideas: Reform and Resistance in the American University* (New York: Norton, 2011), 152.

13. A description of the program may be found at its website: http://gsll.colo rado.edu/node/52.

14. Mitch Smith, "Humanities Ph.D. in 4 Years," *Inside Higher Education,* 2 May 2012, http://www.insidehighered.com/news/2012/05/02/proposed-Ph.D.-german-colo rado-aims-halve-time-degree#ixzz35DNeIdZ2.

15. Ideas like the one implemented at Colorado have been out there for some few years, but they almost never gain traction, perhaps because of the risks that attend early completion (in which potential replaces publication), which I explore in more detail in Chapter 6. For example, Steven M. Cahn says of the dissertation-writing phase, "In my judgment, any time beyond two years is excessive. Indeed, I would expect the task to be completed in twelve to eighteen months." Cahn, *From Student to Scholar* (New York:

Columbia University Press, 2008), 10. We might therefore say that the most notable aspect of the Colorado program is that it was implemented at all.

16. Derek Bok, *Higher Education in America* (Princeton, N.J.: Princeton University Press, 2013), 232.

17. MLA Task Force on Doctoral Study in Modern Language and Literature, *Report,* 2.

18. The long list of luminaries who wrote three-chapter dissertations in my own field includes luminaries like Eve Kosofsky Sedgwick and David Bromwich.

19. In the literary fields, a critical edition might be an appropriate dissertation for a student committed to going into publishing or library work. A single-author dissertation—currently out of fashion among those who aim for the professoriate— would be a good subject for someone committed to secondary-school teaching. But the larger point is that for more years than not, these various kinds of dissertations were considered just fine—and should be again. *The Report of the MLA Task Force for the Evaluation of Scholarship for Promotion and Tenure* (on which I served) advocated in 2006 for a more expansive vision of what "counts" for faculty—including critical editions, translations, and other forms of intellectual work. Graduate students deserve no less.

20. Bernard R. Berelson, *Graduate Education in the United States* (New York: McGraw-Hill, 1960), 177, 180.

21. MLA Task Force on Doctoral Study in Modern Language and Literature, *Report,* 23.

22. Witness the rise of popular websites like The Versatile Ph.D. and Beyond Academe. See Alexandra Lord, "Don't Reform Graduate Education in a Vacuum," *Chronicle of Higher Education,* 1 February 2013, http://chronicle.com/article/Dont -Reform-Graduate/136825/.

23. The paper is available online as a Microsoft Word document:http:// humwork.uchri.org/wp-content/uploads/2014/09/Future_of_the_humanities _ph.d.docx. Subsequent quotations from the document are also from this source.

24. Russell Berman, quoted in Leonard Cassuto, "The Multi-Track Ph.D.," *Chronicle of Higher Education,* 30 September 2012, http://chronicle.com/article/The -Multi-Track-Ph.D./134738/.

25. Jennifer Summit, quoted in ibid.

26. See Sidonie Smith, "An Agenda for the New Dissertation," *MLA Newsletter,* Summer 2010, http://www.mla.org/blog&topic=134 (her forthcoming book is titled *The Humanities Manifesto*); David Damrosch, *We Scholars: Changing the Culture of the University* (Cambridge, Mass.: Harvard University press, 1995); MLA Task Force on Doctoral Study in Modern Language and Literature, *Report,* 14.

27. Ernest L. Boyer, *Scholarship Reconsidered: Priorities of the Professoriate* (Princeton, N.J.: Carnegie Foundation for the Advancement of Teaching, 1990).

28. The Stanford plan has received some criticism from those who have argued that Berman and his coauthors need to pay more attention to issues of contingent labor within the academy—that is, the way that many graduate programs exploit their students as a source of cheap, fungible labor for undergraduate courses. In response, Berman has pointed out that the white paper is a Stanford document, not a blueprint for the whole country. Stanford graduate students, he notes, have modest teaching obligations and thus don't qualify as "labor." At Stanford, he says, "it's not a labor problem but an education problem." If universities need staff, he says, they should hire people in permanent positions. Stanford's wealth enables it to sidestep a problem that most other graduate programs will have to reckon with. (Berman, interview with the author, May, 2012.)

29. For example, Michael Bérubé, "The Humanities, Unraveled," *Chronicle of Higher Education*, 18 February 2013, http://chronicle.com/article/Humanities -Unraveled/137291/.

30. One such book is Michael Bérubé and Jennifer Ruth, *The Humanities, Higher Education, and Academic Freedom: Three Necessary Arguments* (New York: Palgrave Macmillan, 2015).

31. This change would bring humanities graduate education into line with what is generally done in the sciences. See Chapter 4.

32. Fredson Bowers, "Doctor of Arts: A New Graduate Degree," *College English* 27, no. 2 (1965): 127, 128.

33. "College age" is widely considered to mean ages eighteen to twenty-one. In 1900, there were 237,592 students enrolled in American institutions of higher education, or about 0.3 percent of the total population. See Center for Education Studies, *120 Years of American Education: A Statistical Portrait*, ed. Thomas D. Snyder (Washington, D.C.: National Center for Education Studies, U.S. Department of Education, 1993), 75, http://nces.ed.gov/pubs93/93442.pdf. Thomas D. Snyder, of the Center for Education Statistics, further reports that in 1900 there were about 238,000 college students, or about 2 percent of all eighteen- to twenty-four-year-olds (ibid., 64). In 1910, for example, Columbia enrolled 6,232 students, Harvard 5,558, and Princeton 1,400 (Veysey, *Emergence of the American University*, 339). Berkeley enrolled 4,071 the same year (University of California, *2011 Accountability Report, Part III: Data Tables*, http://accountability.universityofcalifornia.edu/documents /accountabilityreport11_tables.pdf), while Wisconsin enrolled 5,539 (Hermon C. Bumpus, "The University of Wisconsin: A Study of the Enrollment of Students for the Decennium 1903–04–1912–13," *Bulletin of the University of Wisconsin*, May 1914, 5.

34. McBain was addressing the AAU. His remarks are quoted in Richard J. Storr, *The Beginning of the Future* (New York: McGraw-Hill, 1973), 59–60.

35. Berelson, *Graduate Education in the United States*, 24–25.

36. Such doctorates began in the United States in the eighteenth century, when Columbia University first introduced the M.D. in 1767 (Columbia University, "About Columbia: A Brief History of Columbia," http://www.columbia.edu/content/history .html). The J.D., or juris doctor, first introduced in 1870, is also a professional doctorate. One telling sign that most Americans no longer view these professional degrees as doctorates is the interesting recent move by Yale to grant a Ph.D. in law. See Kevin Jon Heller, "Yale Creates the First American Ph.D. in Law," *Opinio Juris,* 12 July 2012, http://opiniojuris.org/2012/07/11/yale-creates-the-first-american-phd-in-law/.

37. Lee S. Shulman, Chris M. Golde, Andrea Conklin Bueschel, and Kristen J. Garabedian, "Reclaiming Education's Doctorates: A Critique and a Proposal," *Educational Researcher* 35, no. 3 (2006): 25–32, especially 26.

38. Ibid., 26, 27 (quotation on 25). The authors note that only a quarter of Ed.D.'s enter into professorate, suggesting a mismatch between career preparation and actual career path (26).

39. Elizabeth Redden, "Envisioning a New Ed.D.," *Inside Higher Education,* 10 April 2007, http://www.insidehighered.com/news/2007/04/10/education#sthash .TXsawcig.dpbs.

40. F. N. Freeman, *Practices of American Universities in Granting Higher Degrees in Education: A Series of Official Statements,* vol. 19 (Chicago: University of Chicago Press, 1931).

41. Shulman et al., "Reclaiming Education's Doctorates," 26.

42. Bowers, "Doctor of Arts," 127.

43. H. M. Rabura, "New and Neglected Programs: The D.A. Program," *Teaching German* 5, no. 1 (1972): 127.

44. See Paul L. Dressel and Mary Magdala, *A Degree for College Teacher: The Doctor of Arts* (San Francisco: Jossey-Bass, 1978).

45. Stephen R. White and Mark K. McBeth, "A History of the Doctor of Arts Tradition in American Higher Education," *Education* 123, no. 4 (2003): 771.

46. Their confusion has a long paper trail. For arguments on eliminating one of the two degrees or creating an increased distinction between them, see Dale G. Anderson, "Differentiation of the Ed.D. and Ph.D. in Education," *Journal of Teacher Education* 34, no. 3 (1983): 55–58; Laurence D. Brown and Marlowe J. Slater, *The Doctorate in Education* (Washington, D.C.: American Association of Colleges for Teacher Education, 1960); Geraldine Joncich Clifford and James W. Guthrie, *Ed School* (Chicago: University of Chicago Press, 1988); Thomas E. Deering, "Eliminating the Doctor of Education Degree: It's the Right Thing to Do," *Educational Forum* 62, no. 3 (1998): 243–248; David D. Dill and James L. Morrison, "Ed.D. and Ph.D. Research Training in the Field of Higher Education," *Review of Higher Education* 8, no. 2 (1985): 169–186; Arthur Levine, *Educating School Leaders* (New York: Education Schools Project, 2005); Russell T. Osguthorpe and Mei J. Wong, "The Ph.D. versus the Ed.D.: Time for a Decision," *Innovative Higher Education* 18, no. 1 (1993): 47–63.

47. Redden, "Envisioning a New Ed.D."

48. Kaustuv Basu, "The Country's Oldest Ed.D. Program Will Close Down," *Inside Higher Education,* 29 March 2012, http://www.insidehighered.com/news/2012 /03/29/country%E2%80%99s-oldest-edd-program-will-close-down#sthash.arSxjqck .dpbs.

49. University Senate, University at Albany, State University of New York, "Proposal to Discontinue the Doctor of Arts Program in Humanistic Studies," 21 January 2004, http://www.albany.edu/senate/images/senate_bill_0304-18.htm.

50. National Board on Graduate Education, *Outlook and Opportunities for Graduate Education: The Final Report, with Recommendations* (Washington, D.C.: National Board on Graduate Education, 1975). Not quite everyone has given up on the D.A., however. Kinta Serve, Nathan Clements, Kaleb K. Heinrich, and Rosemary J. Smith argue that the few remaining D.A. graduates occupy "a niche unfilled by graduates of most Ph.D. programs." Serve, Clements, Heinrich, and Smith, "The Tale of Two Degrees: The Need and Power of the Doctor of Arts," *College Teaching* 61 (2013): 115.

51. Bowers, "Doctor of Arts," 123, 124, 125.

52. Rabura, "New and Neglected Programs," 127.

53. Idaho State is the poster child of the D.A.: the university created D.A.'s in English, math, biology, and political science in 1971, and its website proudly points to eighty-five graduated D.A.'s in its forty-year history. "DA graduates," the site declares, "are deans, chairpersons, and many (who graduated in the 1970s and early 1980s) are now retired or retiring. Other graduates have ended up working in state and local government administration, non-profit organizations, or even private enterprise." Department of Political Science, Idaho State University, "Doctor of Arts Graduate Stories," http://www.isu.edu/polsci/arts_successStories.shtml.

54. Storr, *Beginning of the Future,* 89, 90.

55. Philip L. Harriman, "The Master's Degree," *Journal of Higher Education* 9, no. 1 (1938): 27–28.

56. Jean-Pierre V. M. Hérubel, "Contextual Culture of the Master's Degree and the Decline of the M.L.S. Thesis: An Exploratory Review Essay," *Libraries & Culture* 40 (2005): 65.

57. Carol Lynch, interview with the author, 6 June 2014. Subsequent quotations from Lynch are also from this interview.

58. Philip M. Katz, *Retrieving the Master's Degree from the Dustbin of History: A Report to the Members of the American Historical Association* (Washington, D.C.: American Historical Association, 2005), 1.

59. Ira Remsen, *Report of the President of the Johns Hopkins University, 1908* (Baltimore: Johns Hopkins University Press, 1909), 18–19, http://babel.hathitrust .org/cgi/pt?id=nyp.33433076015449;view=1up;seq=496.

60. Frank J. Goodnow, "Annual Report of the President," *Johns Hopkins University Circular* 348, no. 7 (1923): 4. Goodnow actually directs his criticism at master's

students elsewhere. He defends the two-year M.A. that Hopkins had instituted, which he claimed resulted in better students than at other institutions that awarded the degree after only one year. Hopkins students, he said, were consequently more capable of joining Ph.D. students in small-group instruction.

61. Ephraim Emerton, "The Requirements for the Historical Doctorate in America," *American Historical Association Annual Report 1893,* http://www.historians.org//about-aha-and-membership/aha-history-and-archives/archives/the-requirements-for-the-historical-doctorate-in-america.

62. U.S. schools granted 1,744 master's degrees in 1900. By 1932, the number was 19,339 (Harriman, "Master's Degree," 23).

63. See O. Heller, "The Teaching Degree," *School and Society* 35 (1932): 135–140.

64. See Laura Pappano, "The Master's as the New Bachelor's," *New York Times,* 22 July 2011, ED16.

65. Harriman, "Master's Degree," 25.

66. Hérubel, "Contextual Culture," 66.

67. J. P. Elder, "The Master's Degree for the Prospective College Teacher," *Journal of Higher Education* 30, no. 3 (1959): 133.

68. Erika Wright, "Graduate Degree on the Margins: Education and Professional Concerns of the MA Student," *Journal of the Midwest Modern Language Association* 37, no. 2 (2004): 31.

69. See Anne Clark Bartlett, "Is It Terminal? Re-evaluating the Master's Degree," *Journal of the Midwest Modern Language Association* 37, no. 2 (2004): 26.

70. I owe this insight to Michael Teitelbaum, who cited it in a 2012 interview.

71. Maria Theodosiou, Jean-Philippe Rennard, and Arsia Amiri-Aslani, "The Rise of the Professional Master's Degree: The Answer to the Postdoc/Ph.D. Bubble," *Nature Biotechnology* 30, no. 4 (2012): 367.

72. Michael Teitelbaum, interview with the author, July 2012. Subsequent quotations from Teitelbaum are also from this interview.

73. Books like *Rethinking Science as a Career* (Tucson: Research Corp., 1995), by Sheila Tobias, Daryl E. Chubin, and Kevin Aylesworth, spotlighted this gap.

74. For a magisterial recounting of the development of—and frequent opposition to—the arguments for utility and pure inquiry (i.e., research), see Veysey, *Emergence of the American University.*

75. The three-year plans, recalls Teitelbaum, compared actual to projected enrollments. Faculty were also asked to assess "the quality of their applicant pools." The Sloan Foundation also "tracked the number of graduates and their initial job experience."

76. At the same time that Sloan was identifying gaps in graduate science education and developing the PSM, another education-policy-oriented foundation, the W. M. Keck Foundation, was separately noticing the same problem. Its approach to the disconnect between graduate science education and market demands was more

centralized: it supported the creation of a new institution, focused on the biosciences. The Keck Graduate Institute (KGI) was founded in 1997 and is housed at the Claremont Colleges in Southern California. Keck has been successful in developing and providing PSMs in bioscience and more recently has begun a post-Ph.D. master's degree that is meant to make Ph.D.'s more T-shaped. Today the Keck Institute is also the base of a national PSM Office that reviews and assesses PSM programs to make sure that they meet the specified guidelines for the degree. (The Council of Graduate Schools previously handled this job, with funding by the Sloan Foundation, until July 2012.)

77. By 2008, says Teitelbaum, "energetic faculty and administrators on some of the system campuses were taking leadership and demonstrating real commitment." A couple of extra years of funding would, the foundation reasoned, help them at a time when they could add more new programs.

78. See the website celebrating the three hundredth PSM program: http://psmmilestone.com/.

79. Though federal agencies claim to care about the scientific workforce, the only federal money that has been spent on the PSM was essentially involuntary, a $15 million grant that was handed to the National Science Foundation specifically for PSM programs as part of the stimulus bill (that is, the American Recovery and Reinvestment Act) of 2009.

80. These assessments were based on surveys. CGS conducted one initially (2002) and then another five years later (2007). A third survey was planned but was never conducted as the program wound down. Council of Graduate Schools, *Professional Science Master's: A CGS Guide to Establishing Programs* (Washington, D.C.: Council of Graduate Schools, January 2011), 121.

81. In 2003, the CGS, with Ford support, awarded planning grants to thirty-eight institutions to determine the feasibility of creating new PMA programs (or adding to existing programs). On the basis of these efforts, in 2005, Ford (through the CGS) awarded grants to eighteen universities to implement twenty-six PMA programs. Programs ranged from professional sociology to nonprofit administration to economic forecasting. Information from Council of Graduate Schools, "PMA Initiative," 2014, https://www.cgsnet.org/pma-initiative. For more on the M.A. in applied public history at Appalachian State University, see http://history.appstate.edu/academics/graduate-programs/ma-public-history-0; for the M.A. in applied philosophy at Charlotte, see http://catalog.uncc.edu/graduate-catalogs/current/MA-ethics-applied-philosophy.

82. Carol Lynch's comments are drawn from interviews conducted in July 2012 and June 2014.

83. "A survey would be really useful," says Lynch, to determine which institutions have made such goals part of their mission. But, she adds, so would development money to start more PMAs to see what they can accomplish.

84. The University of Colorado Boulder offers the concurrent B.A./M.A. in twenty-eight different majors (from art history to French to aerospace engineering). Some (like French) cap off with exams, while others (like art history) require a thesis and oral defense. See http://www.colorado.edu/admissions/graduate/programs /bama. Boston University offers similar programs, e.g., a B.A./M.A. in economics. See http://www.bu.edu/academics/cas/programs/economics/ba-ma/. The University of Chicago has a B.A./M.A. in the humanities. See http://collegecatalog.uchicago .edu/thecollege/jointdegreehumanities/.

6. PROFESSIONALIZATION

1. Cary Nelson argues that students should remain focused on their dissertations rather than on building their résumés in "No Wine before Its Time: The Panic over Early Professionalization," *Profession,* 2000, 157–163. Gerald Graff takes an opposing view, arguing that students are expected to be professionalized without being taught how. Graff, "Two Cheers for Professionalizing Graduate Students," *PMLA* 115, no. 5 (2000): 1192–1193. Andrew Hoberek looks at this debate from a different angle: he argues that students are prepared for the market but not for the profession. Hoberek, "Professionalism: What Graduate Students Need," *Symplokē: A Journal for the Intermingling of Literary, Cultural and Theoretical Scholarship* 10, nos. 1–2 (2002): 52–70. The quote appeared in Leonard Cassuto, "Pressures to Publish Fuel the Professionalization of Today's Graduate Students," *Chronicle of Higher Education,* 23 November 1998, B4–B5, http://chronicle.com/article/Pressures-to-Publish-Fuel-the/5317.

2. Barbara Lovitts describes how graduate students are forced to conform in "Being a Good Course-Taker Is Not Enough: A Theoretical Perspective on the Transition to Independent Research," *Studies in Higher Education* 30, no. 2 (2005): 137–154.

3. The academic profession, as Christopher Newfield explains in *Ivy and Industry* (Durham, N.C.: Duke University Press, 2003), is a mash-up of craft-labor ideals and corporate modes of management (215).

4. Robbins describes how literary specialization developed historically as a kind of Romantic antiprofessionalism in *Secular Vocations: Intellectuals, Professionalism, Culture* (New York: Verso, 1993), 73–77. Robbins calls for distinguishing between different kinds of intellectual legitimacy (95). For more on Boyer, see Chapter 5.

5. John Grote, "Old Studies and New," in *Cambridge Essays, Contributed by Members of the University* (London: Parker, 1856), 75. Thanks to A. W. Strouse for his insightful reading of Grote's essay, which informs my own.

6. For a thorough account of the link between professionalism and the rise of the middle class, see Burton J. Bledstein, *The Culture of Professionalism: The Middle Class and the Development of Higher Education in America* (New York: Norton, 1976). I take up this connection in more detail in the Conclusion.

7. Michel Foucault has quite a lot to say about this process in *Discipline and Punish: The Birth of the Prison*, trans. Alan Sheridan (New York: Pantheon Books, 1977).

8. Chris M. Golde, and Timothy M. Dore, *At Cross Purposes: What Do the Experiences of Doctoral Students Reveal about Doctoral Education?* (Philadelphia: Pew Charitable Trusts, 2001).

9. Janet Malenchek Egan, "Graduate School and the Self: A Theoretical View of Some Negative Effects of Professional Socialization," *Teaching Sociology* 17 (1989): 204.

10. Ibid. Hoberek ("Professionalism") makes a different argument: he says that graduate students develop hyperindividualism, while Egan and others point to an oppressive collectivism. It may be that both are correct, a living contradiction that is expressed through the frequent references to professors as a herd of cats. On hyperindividualism in the academy, see also David Damrosch, *We Scholars: Changing the Culture of the University* (Cambridge, Mass.: Harvard University Press, 1995), 7.

11. Jody D. Nyquist, Laura Manning, Donald H. Wulff, Ann E. Austin, Jo Sprague, Patricia K. Fraser, Claire Calcagno, and Bettina Woodford, "On the Road to Becoming a Professor: The Graduate Student Experience," *Change* 31 (1999): 20.

12. E. W. Tayler, "Self-Help Sheet" (privately distributed).

13. When professors scorn "professionalism," their sense of rarefication and refinement points to the medieval origins of their pursuit, when professors were cloistered and their vocations were closely tied to the religious ones. See Robbins, *Secular Vocations*.

14. Beth A. Boehm and Ghanashyam Sharma, "The Importance of Professional Development in Graduate Education," manuscript under consideration.

15. Full details may be found on the PLAN website: http://louisville.edu/graduate/plan.

16. Beth Boehm, interview with the author, October 2013. Subsequent quotations from PLAN staff are drawn from personal interviews conducted at Louisville during my visit to observe PLAN in October 2013.

17. Roger L. Geiger, Research and Relevant Knowledge: *American Research Universities since World War II* (New York: Oxford University Press, 1993), 227–228. As Geiger reports, the grants were implemented without really changing existing structures, and officers of the Ford Foundation later complained that universities had acted in bad faith, taking Ford money without really intending to reform their graduate programs.

18. According to Geiger, Ford invested mostly in elite, prestigious universities, thus increasing the advantage of those leading schools (*Research and Relevant Knowledge,* 228).

19. Geiger cites several scholars who suggest that additional funding for graduate study does not lessen time to degree (*Research and Relevant Knowledge,* 384n36), including David W. Breneman, *The Ph.D. Production Function: The Case at Berkeley* (Berkeley: Office of the Vice President–Planning and Analysis, University of California,

1970), 38, as well as Kenneth Wilson, *Of Time and the Doctorate* (Atlanta: Southern Regional Education Board, 1965).

20. Geiger, *Research and Relevant Knowledge,* 227.

21. Michael T. Nettle and Catherine M. Millett, *Three Magic Letters: Getting to Ph.D.* (Baltimore: Johns Hopkins University Press, 2006), xxi; Ronald G. Ehrenberg, Harriet Zuckerman, Jeffrey A. Groen, and Sharon M. Brucker, *Education Scholars: Doctoral Education in the Humanities* (Princeton, N.J.: Princeton University Press, 2010). Ehrenberg et al. argue that guaranteed financial aid packages may reduce productive competition and increase time to degree (252–253). As well, "the practice of awarding guaranteed multiyear packages raises the cost of selection errors and is likely to discourage risks in making awards" (253). They cite William G. Bowen and Neil L. Rudenstine, who argued that cohort size, not funding, is linked to time to degree. Bowen and Rudenstine, *In Pursuit of the PhD* (Princeton, N.J.: Princeton University Press, 2014), 6.

22. See National Science Foundation, *Doctorate Recipients from U.S. Universities, 2012* (Arlington, Va.: National Center for Science and Engineering Statistics, 2014), 7. http://nsf.gov/statistics/sed/digest/2012/ As of 2012, average time to degree in the social sciences was nine years; in the life sciences, eight years; and in the physical sciences, seven years. In the nonsciences, education took twelve years, humanities took ten, and other nonscience fields average ten years as well. Time to degree in fields other than science and engineering has declined over past twenty years, but it still takes longer to complete doctorates in these fields than it does to complete doctoral training in science and engineering fields (ibid., 6).

23. Derek Bok notes that those who take longer have diminishing success in finding tenure-track jobs. Bok, *Higher Education in America* (Princeton, N.J.: Princeton University Press, 2013), 231–232. He cites *Educating Scholars,* by Ehrenberg, Zuckerman, and Groen (194–196), a study of students receiving the Ph.D. between 1985 and 2000—though according to this study, the relationship between time to degree and success in the academic job market varies by field.

24. For a vivid case study that illustrates the points I'm making here, see Audrey Williams June, "The Long Odds of the Faculty Job Search," *Chronicle of Higher Education,* 24 May 2013, A22–26, http://chronicle.com/article/The-Long-Odds -of-the/139361/. June breaks down two job searches in the humanities by the numbers, including descriptions of the experience and qualifications of leading candidates. The results support the position that one should stay longer in graduate school in order to bespangle one's résumé.

25. Paula Stephan, *How Economics Shapes Science* (Cambridge, Mass.: Harvard University Press, 2012), 169.

26. See Marc Bousquet, *How the University Works: Higher Education and the Low-Wage Nation* (New York: New York University Press, 2008), and also his "The Waste Product of Graduate Education: Toward a Dictatorship of the Flexible," *Works and*

Days 41/42, vol. 21, nos. 1 and 2 (2003): 129–152. Bousquet suggests that professionalism functions as a ruse to obfuscate the true nature of labor relations and to enable the exploitation of graduate students.

27. Stacey Patton, "Brandeis Tries a New Tactic to Speed Students to the Ph.D.," *Chronicle of Higher Education,* 8 July 2013, http://chronicle.com/article/Brandeis -Tries-a-New-Tactic-to/140139/.

28. Jason M. Gaines, interview with the author, August 2013. Subsequent quotations from Gaines are also from this interview.

29. Bob Meister, "Debt and Taxes: Can the Financial Industry Save Public Universities?," *Representations* 116, no. 1 (2011): 128.

30. Ibid.; Andrew Ross, "Is Student Debt a Form of Indenture?," https://www .youtube.com/watch?v=MwDKZYMbZDc.

31. According to the Institute for College Access & Success's Project on Student Debt, "Nationally, 68 percent of 2012 graduates of public and nonprofit four-year colleges combined had student debt, with an average of $27,850 per borrower." Institute for College Access & Success, *Student Debt and the Class of 2012,* December 2013, http://projectonstudentdebt.org/files/pub/classof2012.pdf.

32. Jason Delisle, *The Graduate Student Debt Review: The State of Graduate Student Borrowing* (Washington, D.C.: New America Education Policy Program, 2014), 1, http://newamerica.net/sites/newamerica.net/files/policydocs/GradStudentDebt Review-Delisle-Final.pdf.

33. The Council of Graduate Schools reports that "about half of all doctorate recipients now graduate with debt. According to the National Science Foundation (NSF), individuals earning research doctorates in academic year 2009–10 did so owing over $20,400 on average in education-related debt, of which about $14,100 on average was graduate debt and about $6,400 on average was undergraduate debt (National Science Foundation, 2011). While 52% of all research doctorate recipients graduated with no debt, 16% did so owing more than $50,000 in combined undergraduate and graduate debt." See Council of Graduate Schools, "Data Sources: Graduate Student Loans and Debt," 4 June 2012, https://www.cgsnet.org/data-sources-graduate -student-loans-and-debt-0; and National Science Foundation, *Doctorate Recipients from U.S. Universities: 2010,* 2012, http://www.cgsnet.org/data-sources-graduate-stu dent-loans-and-debt-0.

34. It follows that certain majors will be seen as better investments than others, leading to a whole host of invidious comparisons. In 2012, for example, a Florida task force suggested charging lower tuition for college degrees in fields considered to be in demand. See Lizette Alvarez, "Florida May Reduce Tuition for Select Majors," *New York Times,* 9 December 2012, http://www.nytimes.com/2012/12/10/educa tion/florida-may-reduce-tuition-for-select-majors.html?pagewanted=all&_r=0. Also in 2012, a partnership called College Measures prepared a study of undergraduate salaries broken down by major, "The Earning Power of Graduates from Tennessee's

Colleges and Universities." The *Chronicle of Higher Education* calls it "the arrival of a new way of evaluating higher education that brings conversations about college productivity and performance to the program level." See Dan Berrett, "All About the Money," *Chronicle of Higher Education*, 21 September 2012, http://chronicle.com /article/All-About-the-Money/134422/.

35. Paul Krugman, "The Debt-Peonage Society," *New York Times*, 8 March 2005, http://www.nytimes.com/2005/03/08/opinion/08krugman.html?_r=0.

36. Leonard Cassuto, "The Time to Degree Conundrum," *Chronicle of Higher Education,* 16 October 2011, http://chronicle.com/article/The-Time-to-Degree-Co nundrum/129360/.

37. Ross elaborates this proposal in *Creditocracy and the Case for Debt Refusal* (New York: OR Books, 2015).

38. A. W. Strouse, "Getting Medieval on Graduate Education: Queering Academic Professionalism," *Pedagogy* 15, no. 1 (2015): 125.

39. Golde and Dore, *At Cross Purposes,* 9n29, quoted in Bok, *Higher Education in America,* 238.

40. B. A. Pescosolido argues that academic work necessitates facing ethical issues as professional rather than personal matters. This provides a way for academics to think about ethics in teaching and research. Professionalism needs to be considered in this way. Pescosolido, "The Sociology of the Professions and the Profession of Sociology: Professional Responsibility, Teaching, and Graduate Training," *Teaching Sociology* 19 (1991): 351–361.

7. THE JOB MARKET RECONCEIVED

1. Marc Bousquet, *How the University Works: Higher Education and the Low-Wage Nation* (New York: New York University Press, 2008), especially chapter 6, "The Rhetoric of the 'Job Market' and the Reality of the Academic Labor System."

2. See the comments to Leonard Cassuto, "Changing the Way We Socialize Doctoral Students," *Chronicle of Higher Education,* 10 January 2011, http://chronicle .com/article/Changing-the-Way-We-Socialize/125892.

3. These figures come from Frank Donoghue's article "An Open Letter from a Director of Graduate Admissions," *Chronicle of Higher Education*, 4 April 2010, http:// chronicle.com/article/An-Open-Letter-From-a-Director/64882/.

4. See Robin Wilson, "The New Faculty Minority," *Chronicle of Higher Education*, 22 March 2013, http://chronicle.com/article/The-New-Faculty-Minority /137945/. A study by the American Federation of Teachers reports that today about 70 percent of college teachers hold temporary, contingent jobs; see JBL Associates, *Reversing Course: The Troubled State of Academic Staffing and a Path Forward* (Washington, D.C.: American Federation of Teachers, 2009), i.

5. See David Laurence, "Opportunity Costs of the PhD: The Problem of Time to Degree" (14 May 2014) and "Our PhD Employment Problem" (26 February

and 11 March 2014), *The Trend: Blog of the MLA Office of Research,* http://mlaresearch
.commons.mla.org/author/dlaurence/. Laurence writes that "the shrinking share of
the faculty workforce with tenure or eligibility to earn tenure is well known and,
among those in the academic community at least, widely deplored. Even in four-year
colleges and universities, the percentage of faculty members holding full-time tenured or tenure-track appointments has dropped from 51.3% in 1995 to just 33.4% in
2011," and for potential hires, this means that "the sense that the bar for earning tenure
was getting higher likewise worked to raise the bar for entry to a tenure-track
position."

6. Paula Stephan, *How Economics Shapes Science* (Cambridge, Mass.: Harvard
University Press, 2012), 169. Stephan discusses the role of the postdoc as an indicator
of job market conditions (160–162).

7. Anthony Grafton and Robert B. Townsend, "Historians' Rocky Job Market,"
Chronicle of Higher Education, 11 July 2008, B10, http://chronicle.com/article/His
torians-Rocky-Job-Market/35469.

8. Robert B. Townsend, "The PhD Gap: Worrisome Trends in the Hiring of Junior Faculty," *AHA Today* (blog), American Historical Association, 19 September
2012, http://blog.historians.org/2012/09/the-phd-gap-worrisome-trends-in-the-hiring
-of-junior-faculty/.

9. See Sydni Dunn, "A Brief History of the Humanities Postdoc," *Chronicle of
Higher Education,* 7 July 2014, https://chroniclevitae.com/news/593–a-brief-history
-of-the-humanities-postdoc?cid=VTEVPMSED1. Dunn's main source is Harriet
Zuckerman, formerly of the Mellon Foundation.

10. Prestige also perpetuates itself. Sociologist Val Burriss looks at data on the
exchange of Ph.D.'s among sociology departments in order to show that prestige is
rooted not in scholarly productivity (though this is generally believed and would be
bad enough if it were true, as this chapter goes on to suggest) but rather in a network
of association and social exchange—that is, social capital. In other words, it only
seems like what you know, but it's really who you know. See Burriss, "The Academic
Caste System: Prestige Hierarchies in Ph.D. Exchange Networks," *American Sociological Review* 69, no. 2 (2004): 239–264. Also see Robert L. Oprisko, Kirstie L.
Dobbs, and Joseph DiGrazia, "Pushing Up Ivies: Institutional Prestige and the
Academic Caste System," *Georgetown Public Policy Review,* 21 August 2013, http://
gppreview.com/2013/08/21/pushing-up-ivies-institutional-prestige-and-the-academic
-caste-system/; and Shin-Kap Han, "Tribal Regimes in Academia: A Comparative
Analysis of Market Structure Across Disciplines," *Social Networks* 25, no. 3 (2003):
251–280.

11. J. Douglas Toma, "Institutional Strategy: Positioning for Prestige," in *The
Organization of Higher Education: Managing Colleges for a New Era,* ed. Michael N.
Bastedo (Baltimore: Johns Hopkins University Press, 2012), 118.

12. Ibid., 119, 120.

13. Ibid., 119.

14. Audrey Williams June, "Ph.D.'s from Top Political Science Programs Dominate Hiring," *Chronicle of Higher Education,* 5 December 2012, http://chronicle.com /article/Ph.D.'s-From-Top/136113. Oprisko's own account may be found in "Superpowers: The American Academic Elite," *Georgetown Public Policy Review,* 3 December 2012, http://gppreview.com/2012/12/03/superpowers-the-american-academic-elite/. Oprisko, together with Kirstie Lynn Dobbs and Joseph DiGrazia, wrote up further findings in "Pushing Up Ivies: Institutional Prestige and the Academic Caste System." Philosophy departments exhibit much the same hiring bias toward top-rated research programs that political science does. See Robert Frodeman, Adam Briggle, and J. Britt Holbrook, "Philosophy in the Age of Neoliberalism," *Social Epistemology* 26, nos. 3–4 (2012): 311–330.

15. The exception is the field of history, which has compiled its own data, analyzed the data persuasively, and graphed it. The pictures tell the story I described in the last paragraph: the reach of top-ranked programs diminishes as their job-seekers extend their search down the rankings, while their lower-ranked peers tend to do better. See Robert B. Townsend, "Key Differences between Programs," part of a larger section on career diversity for history Ph.D.'s: https://www.historians.org/jobs-and -professional-development/career-diversity-for-historians/the-many-careers-of-history -phds/key-differences-between-programs.

16. Geoffrey Layman, email to the author, November, 2013. Quotations from graduate directors and young faculty members in this chapter, both named and anonymous, are from interviews conducted in November and December 2013.

17. Thorstein Veblen, *The Theory of the Leisure Class: An Economic Study of Institutions* (New York: Modern Library, 1934 [1899]), chapter 5.

18. Donald E. Hall offers realism and optimism to those who may feel trapped in jobs with higher teaching loads. See Hall, "Professional Life (and Death) under a Four-Four Teaching Load," *Profession,* 1999, 193–203.

19. Ernest L. Boyer, *Scholarship Reconsidered: Priorities of the Professoriate* (Princeton, N.J.: Carnegie Foundation for the Advancement of Teaching, 1990), 17.

20. Toma, "Institutional Strategy," 120. Toma identifies the following considerations when developing a strategy: (1) positioning (what you do and how), (2) diversifying and/or expanding, (3) the current state of the industry, (4) increasing competitive advantage, and (5) developing a strong brand (129).

21. Susan Welch and Christopher P. Long, "Where They Are Now," *Chronicle of Higher Education,* 14 February 2014, A28, http://chronicle.com/article/Where -They-Are-Now/144627/.

22. Jonathan Auerbach, interview with the author, November 2013. Subsequent quotations from Auerbach are also from this interview.

23. Or they can receive the wrong kind of training. Stuart Brown argues that many graduate students receive inadequate teacher training because the student populations at the research universities where they are taught do not mirror the students

whom these future teachers will eventually encounter. See Brown, "Obscured Agendas and Hidden Failures: Teaching Assistants, Graduate Education, and First-Year Writing Courses," in *Reforming College Composition: Writing the Wrongs,* ed. Ray Wallace, Alan Jackson, and Susan Lewis Wallace (Westport, Conn.: Greenwood Press, 2000), 203–212.

24. All quotations in this paragraph and throughout this section are drawn from interviews conducted in November and December 2013.

25. Further explanation of the DEVOUT idea may be found on the Maryland English department's website: http://www.english.umd.edu/academics/graduate /placement/prepare.

26. For example, I praised Susan Welch and Christopher P. Long's Penn State Ph.D. placement study ("Where They Are Now") earlier in this chapter, and it is indeed excellent role modeling—in the academic job-search sector. But Welch and Long split the academic into four parts (research university, "other tenure track," postdocs, and fixed-term academic) according to the prevailing caste system, and all other employment is lumped into "nonacademic."

27. Nathan Tinker, interview with the author, February 2012.

28. Angela Brintlinger, "Advisers Should Ban the Word 'Placement,' " *Chronicle of Higher Education,* 11 January 2013, A21, http://chronicle.com/article/Advisers -Should-Ban-the-Word/136451/. By contrast, Robert L. Oprisko, Kirstie L. Dobbs, and Joseph DiGrazia suggest ranking schools according to placement efficiency, but they only consider professorships at research universities: "Placement Efficiency: An Alternative Ranking Metric for Graduate Schools," *Georgetown Public Policy Review,* 15 September 2013, http://gppreview.com/2013/09/15/placement-efficiency-an -alternative-ranking-metric-for-graduate-schools/.

29. The circular methodology of the study is described in Jeremiah P. Ostriker, Paul W. Holland, Charlotte V. Kuh, and James A. Voytuk, eds., *A Guide to the Methodology of the National Research Council Assessment of Doctorate Programs* (Washington, D.C.: National Academies Press, 2009). The whole calculation process is spelled out in "Appendix A: A Technical Discussion of the Process of Rating and Ranking Programs in a Field" (33–52). The weights given to each variable are listed in "Appendix F: Weights and Variables for the Dimensional Measures" (see 175–176).

30. Maresi Nerad and Joseph Cerny, "From Rumors to Facts: Career Outcomes of English Ph.D.s: Results from the Ph.D.'s Ten Years Later Study," *Communicator* 32, no. 7 (1999): 1–12.

31. Council of Graduate Schools and Educational Testing Service, *Pathways through Graduate School and into Careers: Report from the Commission on Pathways through Graduate School and into Careers* (Princeton, N.J.: Educational Testing Service, 2012), 20. The full report may be found online at http://pathwaysreport.org/.

32. Katina Rogers, *Humanities Unbound: Supporting Careers and Scholarship beyond the Tenure Track* (Charlottesville: University of Virginia, Scholarly Communications

Institute, 2013), http://katinarogers.com/wp-content/uploads/2013/08/Rogers_SCI
_Survey_Report_09AUG13.pdf.

33. Katina Rogers, interview with the author, July 2012. Subsequent quotations
from Rogers are also from this interview.

34. In an unusual move, an MLA officer presented at AHA, and vice versa. The
AHA has published some early findings at this writing. L. Maren Wood and Robert
Townsend's "The Many Careers of History Ph.D.'s" is now on the organization's
website (https://historians.org/Documents/Many_Careers_of_History_PhDs_Final
.pdf), along with other research and discussion about the range of career paths taken
by historians.

35. Maresi Nerad and Joseph Carny were already noticing this in their 1999
study "From Rumors to Facts: Career Outcomes of English PhDs, Council of
Graduate Schools," *Communicator* 32, no. 7 (1999): 1–11. For a more recent summary, see Elizabeth Segran, "What Can You Do with a Humanities Ph.D. Anyway?,"
Atlantic, 31 March 2014, http://www.theatlantic.com/business/archive/2014/03
/what-can-you-do-with-a-humanities-phd-anyway/359927/.

36. See, for example, L. Maren Wood, "The Ph.D.'s Guide to a Nonfaculty Job
Search," *Chronicle of Higher Education,* 6 January 2014, http://chronicle.com/article
/article-content/143715/. As I've said, university career services offices are becoming
increasingly savvy at advising such job searches.

37. Doherty was a member of the Public Fellows Program sponsored by the
American Council of Learned Societies (ACLS), https://www.acls.org/programs
/publicfellows/. For more on the program, see Leonard Cassuto, "Teaching in the
Postdoc Space," *Chronicle of Higher Education,* 17 April 2011, http://chronicle.com
/article/article-content/127150/.

38. Megan Doherty, "The Humanities Ph.D. at Work," *Chronicle of Higher Education,* 20 February 2013, http://chronicle.com/article/The-Humanities-PhD-at-Work
/137393/. An interesting thought piece on these issues is Peter Coclanis, "Wanted:
Dedicated Deep Thinkers," *Chronicle of Higher Education,* 18 March 2012, http://
chronicle.com/article/Wanted-Dedicated-Deep/131153/?sid=cr. Coclanis suggests
that because Ph.D.'s are good at asking good questions, corporations should consider
hiring them for that purpose.

39. Brintlinger, "Advisers Should Ban the Word 'Placement.'"

40. My colleague Heather Dubrow presents a thorough account of what this
practice can look like in "Dissertation Advisers and Their Motives," *Inside Higher
Ed,* 30 June 2014, https://www.insidehighered.com/views/2014/06/30/essay-motives
-faculty-members-seeking-dissertation-students-advise.

41. See comment from "versatilephd" to Leonard Cassuto, "Keyword: Placement," *Chronicle of Higher Education,* 9 April 2012, http://chroniclecareers.com
/article/Keyword-Placement/131437/.

42. Graduate career counseling has become much more responsive over the past
generation, but faculty can be slower. See Stacey Patton, "What Some Faculty Really

Think about Non-academic Careers," *Chronicle of Higher Education*, 8 July 2014, https://chroniclevitae.com/news/598–the-conferencegoer-what-some-faculty-really -think-about-nonacademic-careers. See also the examples of Michigan State (which I elaborated in Chapter 4) and the University of Louisville (in Chapter 6).

43. See Stephan, *How Economics Shapes Science,* 162. Her study has been published separately as "Tracking the Placement of Students as a Measure of Technology Transfer," in *Advances in the Study of Entrepreneurship, Innovation, and Economic Growth,* ed. Gary Libecap (London: Elsevier, 2009), 113–140.

44. For example, Derek Bok recently endorsed this position. Bok, *Higher Education in America* (Princeton, N.J.: Princeton University Press, 2013), 227. And it was likewise a welcome recommendation of the 2014 MLA Task Force on Doctoral Study in Languages and Literature's *Report of the MLA Task Force on Doctoral Study in Languages and Literature* (New York: Modern Language Association, 2014), 2, http://www.mla.org/pdf/taskforcedocstudy2014.pdf.

45. See the comments to Leonard Cassuto, "Changing the Way We Socialize Doctoral Students," *Chronicle of Higher Education,* 10 January 2011, http://chronicle .com/article/Changing-the-Way-We-Socialize/125892.

CONCLUSION

1. Warren Zevon, "Disorder in the House," *The Wind* (Artemis, 2003).

2. See, for example, William Chace, "The Decline of the English Department: How It Happened and What Could Be Done to Reverse It," *American Scholar,* Autumn 2009, http://theamericanscholar.org/the-decline-of-the-english-department /#.U-uDNU-reic.

3. It is true—and important—that the cost of higher education is misrepresented when the sticker price is reported without taking the discount rate (what students actually pay) into consideration; this is a grievous marketing failure by colleges and universities nationwide. See David Leonhardt, "How the Government Exaggerates the True Cost of College," *New York Times,* 29 July 2014, http://www.nytimes .com/2014/07/29/upshot/how-the-government-exaggerates-the-cost-of-college .html?_r=1. But even at its real price, higher education is still pricing out the poor. Andrew Delbanco has written particularly eloquently about how higher education is betraying its democratic ideals. Delbanco, "Scandals of Higher Education," *New York Review of Books,* 29 March 2007, http://www.nybooks.com/articles/archives/2007 /mar/29/scandals-of-higher-education/.

4. The headline of the September 2014 issue of the *Atlantic* is "Is College Doomed?" See also Daniel B. Smith, "The University Has No Clothes," *New York,* 1 May 2011, http://nymag.com/news/features/college-education-2011-5/.

5. Seminal to these critiques is William F. Buckley Jr., *God and Man at Yale: The Superstitions of "Academic Freedom"* (Chicago: Regnery, 1951). Allan Bloom argues that humanists teach a deadening kind of moral and cultural relativism, in *The Closing of*

the American Mind (New York: Simon and Schuster, 1987). Numerous critics have built on the ideas laid out in these books in succeeding decades.

6. See J. C. Jones, "Does College Education Pay?," *Forum* 26 (1898): 354–363; W. H. Johnson, "Does College Training Pay?," *Lippincott's Monthly Magazine* 45 (1890): 758–762; H. E. Kratz, "Does College Education Pay?," *Educational Review* 17 (1899): 297–299; S. N. Fellows, "Practical Value of a College Education," *National Education Association Journal of Proceedings and Addresses* (1885): 214–222. These sources are discussed in Laurence R. Veysey's doctoral dissertation, "The Emergence of the American Universities, 1865–1910: A Study in the Relations between Ideals and Institutions" (University of California, Berkeley, 1962), 1030n415. The cover story of the May 26, 1900, issue of the *Saturday Evening Post* was titled "Does a College Education Pay?" It was written by no less a personage than former president Grover Cleveland.

7. The *Chronicle of Higher Education* provides a state-by-state guide to the twenty-five-year-long decline in state support for public colleges. See "25 Years of Declining State Support for Public Colleges," *Chronicle of Higher Education,* 3 March 2014, http://chronicle.com/article/25-Years-of-Declining-State/144973/. Many public universities have seen state funding levels drop by over 50 percent. The University of Virginia, for example, receives 14.4 percent of its support from the state, down more than 60 percent since 1987.

8. For a good overview of the debate over what causes universities to raise the price tag (the "market power model," which holds that government aid simply allows universities to charge more, versus the "spending constraint model," which holds that tuition goes up because it must cover the loss of government support), see Gary Fethke, "Why Does Tuition Go Up? Because Taxpayer Support Goes Down," *Chronicle of Higher Education,* 6 April 2012, A28, http://chronicle.com/article/Why-Does-Tuition-Go-Up -/131372/. Fethke makes a brief but forceful case for the latter position. Christopher Newfield has done indispensable work on the ideological underpinnings of the defunding of the public university; see *Unmaking the Public University: The Forty-Year Assault on the Middle Class* (Cambridge, Mass.: Harvard University Press, 2008).

9. "Save the university" books have also arisen in quantity, including this one, perhaps. Stanley Fish does an idiosyncratic roundup in "The Woe-Is-Us Books," *Opinionator* (blog), *New York Times,* 8 November 2010, http://opinionator.blogs.nytimes .com/2010/11/08/the-woe-is-us-books.

10. Veblen describes how universities take up business principles in *The Higher Learning in America: A Memorandum on the Conduct of Universities by Business Men* (New York: B. W. Huebsch, 1918). He complains that, in trying to market academic learning as prestigious rather than useful, publicity overtakes the university. "This business of publicity necessarily, or at least commonly, accounts for a disproportionately large share of the business to be taken care of in conducting a university, as contrasted with such an enterprise, e.g., as a bank, a steel works, or a railway company, on a capital of about the same volume" (138).

11. Walter Mondale's 1984 evisceration of Gary Hart with the question, "Where's the beef?" (drawn from a then-popular commercial for the Wendy's hamburger chain) is a good example of the potency of metaphor in the rhetorical arena.

12. Quoted in Frederick Rudolph, *The American College and University: A History* (1962; repr., Athens: University of Georgia Press, 1990), 6.

13. "The Value of the College at Princeton," in *A General Account of the Rise and State of the College, Lately Established in the Province of New Jersey* (1754), by Samuel Davies and Gilbert Tennent, http://www.constitution.org/primarysources/princeton .html.

14. This quotation comes from a letter of 1748–1750 that is attributed to Ebenezer Pemberton, a founder of Princeton, by Alexander Leitch, *A Princeton Companion* (Princeton, N.J.: Princeton University Press, 1978), 199.

15. William Smith, *Life and Correspondence of the Rev. William Smith, D.D.*, vol. 1, ed. Horace Wemyss Smith (Philadelphia: S. A. George, 1879), 62.

16. "Report of a Committee of the Trustees of Columbia College," in *Documents of the Senate of the State of New York,* vol. 2 (Albany, N.Y.: C. van Benthuysen, 1855), 72.

17. Thomas D. Snyder reports, "During the latter part of the 1800s, enrollment grew rapidly in higher education institutions, but much of this growth was due to increases in the population. Enrollment grew by 278 percent between 1869–70 and 1899–1900, but students as a percent of 18- to 24-year-olds rose from 1 percent to 2 percent." Snyder, *120 Years of American Education: A Statistical Portrait* (Washington, D.C.: U.S. Department of Education, Office of Educational Research and Improvement, 1993), 64, http://nces.ed.gov/pubs93/93442.pdf.

18. For example, Marion Leroy Burton of the University of Michigan described fellowship monies as "investment," but they are more like a back-and-forth exchange, a social investment in which the university collects money from society, money that it spends on educating scholars, from whose contributions society at large collects the return. University of Michigan, *The President's Report for the Year 1923–1924* (Ann Arbor: University of Michigan, 1925), 233.

19. William Rainey Harper, the first president of the University of Chicago, "First Annual Report," 1888, quoted in "From the History of the University," *University of Chicago Magazine* 8 (1915): 257.

20. Quoted in Ansel Adams and Nancy Wynne Newhall, *Fiat lux: The University of California* (New York: McGraw-Hill, 1967), 12.

21. Nicholas Lemann, "The Soul of the Research University," *Chronicle of Higher Education,* 28 April 2014, http://chronicle.com/article/The-Soul-of-the-Research /146155?cid=megamenu. Charles W. Anderson frames the same conflict in different terms in *Prescribing the Life of the Mind: An Essay on the Purpose of the University, the Aims of Liberal Education, the Competence of Citizens, and the Cultivation of Practical Reason* (Madison: University of Wisconsin Press, 1993). Anderson sees a fundamental tension in the objectives of the university: education is the public purpose of the

university and inquiry its intrinsic function (42). For Anderson, the university's aim is to provide understanding; "we expect the university to tell us what it all means but we do not really believe that it knows" (56). This kind of skepticism reflects the ambivalent reception of the university in the United States.

22. For an account of the early days of Clark University, see Veysey, *The Emergence of the American University* (Chicago: University of Chicago Press, 1965), 165–171. Today, Clark is an undergraduate-centered institution, not a research university.

23. Esoteric graduate-only scientific institutions like Rockefeller University— which most observers don't think of as a university at all—constitute a rare exception.

24. Mitch Daniels, a former federal government official taking up his new position as president of Purdue, recently said, "Too many professors are spending too much time 'writing papers for each other,' researching abstruse topics of no real utility and no real incremental contribution to human knowledge or understanding." Scott Jaschik, "New Sheriff in Town," *Inside Higher Ed,* 21 January 2013, https://www.insidehighered.com/news/2013/01/21/new-purdue-president-outlines-critiques-higher-education.

25. Nicholas Murray Butler, "Scholarship and Service," in *Scholarship and Service: The Policies and Ideals of a National University in a Modern Democracy* (New York: Charles Scribner's Sons, 1921), 11.

26. Robert C. Clothier, "Report of the President of Rutgers University," *Rutgers University Bulletin* 13, no. 4 (1936): 5. Historian and administrator Page Smith argued in his grumpy book, *Killing the Spirit: Higher Education in America* (New York: Viking, 1990), that the university's "primary task" is "teaching undergraduate students," while its "secondary one" is "producing genuinely significant research" (17).

27. Julie A. Reuben, *The Making of the Modern University* (Chicago: University of Chicago Press, 1996), 68.

28. Alan Trachtenberg, *The Incorporation of America: Culture and Society in the Gilded Age* (New York: Hill and Wang, 1982).

29. A good literary example is the title character of Frank Norris, *McTeague: A Story of San Francisco* (San Francisco: Colt Press, 1941 [1899]), a dentist who learned his trade through apprenticeship. McTeague is expelled from the profession for want of a diploma by a newly created regulatory body.

30. During these more tranquil town-and-gown relations, the university was seen as so much a part of the public interest that it was even able to exercise eminent domain. When the University of Michigan sought private property for its own use, the state supreme court upheld it as "public necessity." See University of Michigan, *The President's Report for the Year 1922–1923* (Ann Arbor: University of Michigan, 1924), 11.

31. Veysey, *Emergence of the American University.* So persuasive was Veysey's monumental work that few have risen to challenge it. An exception is Julie A. Reuben's *The Making of the Modern University.* Reuben reasonably argues that Veysey particularly underrates the influence of religion in the ferment of university intellectual culture.

32. Andrew Delbanco, *College: What It Was, Is, and Should Be* (Princeton, N.J.: Princeton University Press, 2012).

33. For more on this decision and on Eliot's celebration of utility, see Veysey, *Emergence of the American University*, 81.

34. The Morrill Act of 1890, 7 U.S. Code §§301–309, 304.

35. J. H. Canfield, "Ethical Culture in Higher Education," *National Education Association* 92 (1892): 111, quoted in Veysey, *Emergence of the American University*, 78n50.

36. George E. Walker, Chris M. Golde, Laura Jones, Andrea Conklin Bueschel, and Pat Hutchings, *The Formation of Scholars: Rethinking Doctoral Education for the Twenty-First Century* (San Francisco: Carnegie Foundation for the Advancement of Teaching/Jossey-Bass, 2008), 44.

37. Derek Bok cites surveys that show that "over 70 percent of college professors claim to be oriented more toward teaching than research." Following from this, he rightly asks, "why have so many colleges and universities decided to require their faculties to publish in order to win promotions and tenure?" Bok, *Higher Education in America* (Princeton, N.J.: Princeton University Press, 2013), 336. That's a good question, but Bok might have asked it more loudly when he was president of Harvard.

38. Wilhelm von Humboldt, "On the Spirit and Organizational Framework of Intellectual Institutions in Berlin" (1810), trans. Edward Shils, *Minerva* 8, no. 2 (1970): 243. But not everyone saw—or sees—it exactly that way. When American colleges became universities, says Vanessa L. Ryan, "they grafted the Humboldtian model onto a tradition of liberal education that didn't at all see teaching and research as a unity." Ryan, "Redefining the Teaching-Research Nexus Today," paper presented at the Modern Language Association convention, 2015. For example, Cardinal John Henry Newman, in *The Idea of a University*, proposed an entirely different model, in which the university exists to teach—to extend knowledge rather than advance it. "To discover and teach are distinct functions," said Newman. For Newman, "research was left to the research societies, learned societies, and specialist academies outside the university." Newman, *The Idea of a University* (1852), ed. Martin J. Svaglic (Notre Dame, IN: University of Notre Dame Press, 1982), xxxvii, xl. Today, there are those who argue that teaching and research are not united or even complementary anymore. Ronald Barnett, for example, says that in the twentieth century, teaching and research have become "mutually antagonistic" functions with different orientations and aims, drawing on different skills. Barnett, *Beyond All Reason: Living with Ideology in the University* (Philadelphia: Open University Press, 2003), 157.

39. Bok notes "the effect that graduate (PhD) training and a pronounced research orientation have on curriculum" and on professors' time to reform teaching—researchers are too busy, in other words, to consider how their institutions might teach better (*Higher Education in America*, 341). He observes that research specialization (which I address later in this chapter) thus leads to conservatism in curricular

and teaching matters, with the result that "the public is indeed being disserved" (335). Bok diagnoses an important problem here but without addressing the value system that created it.

40. On the history and development of academic freedom in American higher education, see Richard Hofstadter and Walter P. Metzger, *The Development of Academic Freedom in the United States* (New York: Columbia University Press, 1955). In part 1 of that volume, Hofstadter discusses the precariousness of university faculty before the invention of tenure (261–274).

41. Veysey, *Emergence of the American University,* 171, 172.

42. For one account of the roiling politics on U.S. campuses during the Vietnam era, see Kenneth J. Heineman, *Campus Wars: The Peace Movement at American State Universities in the Vietnam Era* (New York: New York University Press, 1994). Many years later, we can see the resultant lack of trust everywhere. In "Contract with Academia," Andrew Delbanco gives one pungent example in the form of the controversy that erupted when Lee M. Bass attempted to withdraw his $20 million gift to Yale on the grounds that the university had not founded a Western civilization program according to his wishes. Delbanco, "Contract with Academia," *New Yorker,* 71, no. 5 (1995): 7. Today, many foundations demand a hand on the steering wheel in exchange for their gifts to higher education. See Stanley N. Katz, "Beware Big Donors," *Chronicle of Higher Education,* 25 March 2012, http://chronicle.com/article/Big-Philanthropys-Role-in/131275/.

43. Pinchot was voicing the rationale behind the reclamation era. Organizations like the Sierra Club and the Wilderness Society (est. 1935) formed during this period to combat this utilitarian philosophy. On the environmentalism of Pinchot and Roosevelt, see David N. Cassuto, *Dripping Dry: Literature, Politics, and Water in the Desert Southwest* (Ann Arbor: University of Michigan Press, 2001), 35.

44. Aldo Leopold, "A Sand County Almanac," in *A Sand County Almanac & Other Writings on Ecology and Conservation* (New York: Library of America, 2013), 4.

45. Rachel Carson, *Silent Spring* (Boston: Houghton Mifflin, 1962). Leopold speaks of the importance of measures besides economic ones, including the idea that the animals (in this case, predators) that we exterminate are also "members of the community" (ibid., 247).

46. George W. Bush, remarks on conservation and the environment, 6 January 2009, http://georgewbush-whitehouse.archives.gov/infocus/environment/.

47. Clark Kerr's still-essential account in *The Uses of the University* (Cambridge, Mass.: Harvard University Press, 1963) of the formation of the "multiversity" is particularly relevant in this regard. The authors of *The Formation of Scholars* speak of the scholar as "a steward of the discipline, or the larger field, not simply the manager of her own career" (George E. Walker et al., *The Formation of Scholars: Rethinking Doctoral Education for the Twenty-first Century* [San Francisco: Jossey-Bass, 2008], 12). This emphasis on a view "larger than the individual" (12) is welcome, but the focus

is intramural, with the assumption that disciplines live only within universities and no attention given to individuals who seek an intellectual life outside it. I propose a much wider frame for this kind of environmental thinking.

48. Leopold, "Sand County Almanac," 258.

49. Jacques Berlinerblau, "Survival Strategy for Humanists: Engage, Engage," *Chronicle of Higher Education,* 5 August 2012, http://chronicle.com/article/Survival-Strategy-for/133309/.

50. Ibid. Berlinerblau says that most academic research is boring and useless, a point that deserves brief rebuttal. I don't contest Berlinerblau's description as such, but his assessment is not fair because it's not the whole story. In fact, most research in all fields at all times is bound to be useless, because you have to dig more than one hole if you're looking for treasure. Instead of bemoaning the proliferation of bad work—an inevitable symptom of the effort to produce something that will survive the test of time—we should instead celebrate the amount of good work that is done.

51. Aronson discusses his proposal in "Dating Service for Grad Students and Society" on his blog, *Nonfiction Matters,* 14 March 2012, http://blogs.slj.com/nonfictionmatters/2012/03/14/dating-service-for-grad-students-and-society/. I gained further information from an interview with Aronson in January 2012. Salutary initiatives along these lines include one at Duke University, where graduate students would be required to film thirty- to sixty-second videos describing their dissertations in which they speak "in plain English" for nonacademic audiences. See Colleen Flaherty, "Snapshot Dissertations," *Inside Higher Ed,* 22 February 2013, http://www.insidehighered.com/news/2013/02/22/duke-proposes-mandatory-short-video-pitch-accompany-dissertations.

52. John Dewey, whose vision of public engagement I consider shortly, understood that some intellectuals will be better suited to communicate outside the group than others—perhaps due to temperament or because of what they study. Dewey discusses the difference between "knowing" and "communicating" in *The Public and Its Problems: An Essay in Political Inquiry,* ed. Melvin L. Rogers (University Park: Pennsylvania State University Press, 2012), 136. Similarly, and in keeping with the environmental theme of this chapter, Jacques Barzun imagined a diverse array of scholars, part of a kind of intellectual ecosystem. This is a lovely long sentence: "If scholars with a knack for organizing materials will freely turn to writing textbooks; if those having the gift of accurate rhetoric will deliver the classroom lectures and radio broadcasts; if the minute philosophers will edit documents and write monographs; if the generalizing minds will produce the broader syntheses; if the ready pens will enlighten the public with vivid restatements of important truth; if bibliophiles and antiquaries will staff libraries and museums and facilitate, as they already do, every branch of study and research; and if the versatile will combine two or more of these activities at choice; then we shall not only be sure that the institution of American scholarship is a flourishing concern: we shall also be sure that the culture which it serves lives mentally

upon something better than superstitions, catch-words, and the fashionable ideas of thirty years ago; we shall be in a fair way to fulfill the destiny which every scholar takes as his privilege and his justification." Barzun, "The Scholar Is an Institution," *Journal of Higher Education* 18, no. 8 (1947): 445.

53. Julie Ellison and Timothy K. Eatman, *Scholarship in Public: Knowledge Creation and Tenure Policy in the Engaged University, a Resource on Promotion and Tenure in the Arts, Humanities, and Design* (Syracuse, N.Y.: Imagining America: Artists and Scholars in Public Life, 2008); see iv, iii, 1–4. Ellison and Eatman seek ways to create environments that attract scholars who are committed to the public good. For some interesting examples of public engagement projects, see vi–vii. They argue that the work of publicly engaged faculty ought to allow them to be promoted all the way to full professor (17, 20). See also Timothy K. Eatman, "The Arc of the Academic Career Bends toward Publicly Engaged Scholarship," in *Collaborative Futures: Critical Reflections on Publicly Active Graduate Education,* ed. Amanda Gilvin, Georgia M. Roberts, and Craig Martin (Syracuse, N.Y.: Graduate School Press, Syracuse University, 2012), 25–48.

54. Robert B. Townsend, *History's Babel: Scholarship, Professionalization, and the Historical Enterprise in the United States, 1880–1940* (Chicago: University of Chicago Press, 2013), 2, 135, 133, 13, 87, 181, 9. Townsend makes an important distinction between the discipline and the profession of history; to avoid "hairsplitting," he uses the broad term "historical enterprise" (3).

55. Ibid., 115, 116, 179.

56. As MLA president in 2012, Russell A. Berman urged, "We should be standing with our teacher colleagues in K–12." He urges "strategic collaborations and coalitions" with the professional associations that we foolishly parted ways with long ago. Berman, "Presidential Address 2012—Teaching as Vocation," *PMLA* 127, no. 3 (2012): 451–459, 457. But Robert Orrill shows that K–12 and 13–16 were not rent asunder; rather, they were never really joined. Orrill, "Grades 11–14: The Heartland or Wasteland of American Education?," in *A Faithful Mirror: Reflections on the College Board and Education in America,* ed. Michael C. Johanek (New York: College Board, 2001), 81–99. Orrill writes that there is no "strong record of school-college cooperation" and that "more often than not, direct relations between schools and colleges have been problematic and short-lived rather than purposeful and productive" (81). Orrill shows how the modern college is a broken link between the research university and the high school system (90–93).

57. John Dewey, *The Ethics of Democracy* (Ann Arbor, Mich.: Andrews, 1888), 248.

58. One reason that Dewey found himself needing to make the argument for public intellectual engagement is the historical barrier between academia and the public. As Leo Braudy points out, this is a particularly American problem compared to Europe, where academics are accepted members of the public, and exchange between them occurs much more readily. Braudy, "Doing Public Pedagogy: Speaking Outside the Walls," *Profession,* 1999, 29.

59. Fun fact: in 1882, during a lecture tour of the United States, Oscar Wilde famously delivered a talk on aesthetics inside a Colorado silver mine to a group of silver miners. Wilde was not just a famous poet and playwright but also a serious scholar who had once been expected to take a chair at Oxford. See Joseph Pearce, *The Unmasking of Oscar Wilde* (San Francisco: Ignatius, 2004), 150.

60. Duke's own description of the forum is online at https://fsp.trinity.duke.edu/.

61. See Hex Center for the Humanities, University of Wisconsin–Madison, "Past Projects," http://humanities.wisc.edu/public-humanities/exchange-program /past-projects/2011-2012-projects/.

62. Tracy Lemaster, email to the author, April 2012.

63. This mission also resounded outside Wisconsin at the time. Edmund J. James, president of the University of Illinois, wrote in 1906 that the state university should be "a great civil service academy, preparing the young men and women of the state for the civil service of the state, the country, the municipality, and the township" (quoted in Veysey, *Emergence of the American University,* 73).

64. Steffens coined the phrase in 1909 (quoted in Veysey, *Emergence of the American University,* 107).

65. Alan B. Knox and Joe Corry, "Wisconsin Idea for the 21st Century," *1995– 1996 Wisconsin Blue Book* (comp. Legislative Reference Bureau), 81, http://legis.wis consin.gov/lrb/pubs/feature/wisidea.pdf.

66. Jack Stark, "The Wisconsin Idea: The University's Service to the State," *1995–1996 Wisconsin Blue Book* (comp. Legislative Reference Bureau), 10, 12, 14; legislation quoted at 49.

67. Ibid., 64, 69.

68. Craig Calhoun, "Social Science for Public Knowledge," Academia & the Public Sphere essay series, Social Science Research Council, http://publicsphere .ssrc.org/calhoun-social-science-for-public-knowledge/.

69. The Wisconsin Idea came under prominent siege from the state's governor, Scott Walker, in February 2015, while this book was in press. Walker submitted a budget that would cut into the university's public funding but received more attention for his simultaneous attempt to amend the university's charter. Walker proposed to delete language that calls on the university to "search for truth" and replace it with the mandate that the university "meet the state's workforce needs." In terms of the history I've been recounting in this chapter, Walker's proposal may be easily identified as a push for utility against the values of research culture. The bluntness of Walker's attempt shows the confidence that utility partisans enjoy in these times, and the tattered state of relations between public research universities and the state governments that fund them. A firestorm of opposition came hot and fast against Walker's proposal, and the governor retreated just as quickly; he called the suggestion "a drafting error." But largely obscured by all of this is the likely passage of his budget cuts.

70. Ernest L. Boyer, "The Scholarship of Engagement," *Journal of Public Service & Outreach* 1, no. 1 (1996): 13, 19.

71. See Scott Reynolds Nelson, *Steel Drivin' Man: John Henry, the Untold Story of an American Legend* (Oxford: Oxford University Press, 2006); and Scott Reynolds Nelson and Marc Aronson, *Ain't Nothing but a Man: My Quest to Find the Real John Henry* (Washington, D.C.: National Geographic Books, 2008).

72. Quoted in Veysey, *Emergence of the American University,* 79.

73. The Public Philosophy Network may be found at http://publicphilosophynet work.ning.com/.Robert Frodeman, "Experiments in Field Philosophy," *Opinionator* (blog), *New York Times,* 23 November 2010, http://opinionator.blogs.nytimes.com /2010/11/23/experiments-in-field-philosophy/?_r=0. See also Adam Briggle and Robert Frodeman, "A New Philosophy for the 21st Century," *Chronicle of Higher Education,* 11 December 2011, http://chronicle.com/article/A-New-Philosophy-for-the-21st /130025/.

74. Barzun, "The Scholar Is an Institution," 397.

75. Hunter R. Rawlings III, "Texas Makes an Appalling Mess of Education 'Reform,' " *Chronicle of Higher Education,* 9 July 2014, http://chronicle.com/article /Texas-Makes-an-Appalling-Mess/147561/.

76. See Eric Kelderman, "Getting to the Bottom of the $10,000 Bachelor's Degree," *Chronicle of Higher Education,* 4 March 2013, http://chronicle.com/article /Getting-Down-to-the-Reality-of/137637/; Ry Rivard, "Punished for Its Mission?," *Inside Higher Ed,* 7 August 2014, https://www.insidehighered.com/news/2014/08/07 /one-liberal-arts-college-loses-money-after-its-state-adopts-performance-funding.

Acknowledgments

I decided to go to graduate school for its own sake, not necessarily to get a tenure-track job. A professor's job certainly looked attractive to me when I enrolled in the early 1980s, but the academic job market wasn't very good then, either. Moreover, I wasn't sure that I would be willing to relocate to wherever a job was, so I concluded before I began that I might well wind up taking my degree, whether M.A. or Ph.D., in search of some other kind of employment. But before all that, I thought that graduate study might be fun. For me, it was.

Like so many graduate students, I didn't start thinking carefully about the job market until I was about to land in it. When I got a good academic job, it felt less like an achievement than an improbable success in the lottery. (I recall my father saying years later that if he had known how horrendous my chances were, he would have tried even harder to talk me out of going to graduate school in the first place.) My early professional life lacks the arc of heroic narrative, but as I look back at it, I see that I was at least thinking outside the library carrel—and I remember how it helped. I've tried to bring that awareness to this book.

Writing *The Graduate School Mess* has been an unexpected and welcome journey outside an English professor's usual precincts. It's one thing to write about old books, and quite another about issues that are being debated every day in the academic public square. I've been part of that public conversation for awhile, and I'm glad to see that we're finally starting to look more closely and critically at graduate school. Of course the overdue attention has meant that current events and headlines kept affecting (and even overtaking) what I was writing about, right up to when this book entered production.

With those shifting sands in mind, I've tried in this book to bring a sense of history to the problems at hand. Even if we solve the problems of graduate school in the next few years—yes, that's a joke, but I'm trying to be hopeful—you can still read this book for some good stories of how they came about.

Another interesting challenge has been to write about a community from within its ranks. I've made many of the mistakes that I describe here, and I've tried to stay aware of that fact. So I've sought to limit the "you must do this" rhetoric—because we have to change graduate school together, so it can make sense for students to come.

My first thanks go to A. W. Strouse, who started working as my research assistant several years ago. He burst out of that job description almost right away, and has become a valued colleague and friend. Not just his research but also (and more important!) his advice and comments have been indispensable to shaping this book. He is publishing books of his own; I'm grateful that he has had time to help with this one. My Fordham colleague John Bugg, whose own work with graduate students sets the bar somewhere in the upper atmosphere, also read large portions of the manuscript with acuity and exceptional care. His fingerprints are all over this book.

The Graduate School Mess would never have occurred to anyone, least of all me, without the energy and insight of my wonderful editors at the *Chronicle of Higher Education*. Denise Magner gracefully edits my columns every month and has helped me shape many of the stories woven into this book. Karen Winkler, my editor at the *Chronicle Review,* first started editing me in the 1990s, when I began writing about academia. I often hear her voice in my head, and I'm a better writer for it. And Liz McMillen, now the editor of the whole paper, has been unfailingly supportive of my ideas for years. My *Chronicle* readers have been my constructive critics for many years—I'm honored by their attention and grateful for their feedback.

Two editors at Harvard helped to bring this book into the world. Elizabeth Knoll originally acquired it, and our collaboration on the proposal helped bring the shape of the book into focus for me. I'm grateful for her smarts and judgment, and also for her patient understanding of life beyond books. Elizabeth departed the press for provostal pastures while I was writing, leaving me concerned that my book might become a Dickensian orphan when it was done. But Andrew Kinney banished that worry. He adopted this book as his own, and read it deeply and carefully. Andrew has shown a sympathetic understanding of what I was trying to do from the start of our work together, and his wisdom has advised my course.

I complain a lot in this book about how so many of us educators limit our views and allow our problems to fester. But there are some clear-eyed people out there, and I've been lucky that some of them have been willing to help me. Andrew Delbanco, Tony Grafton, Jim Grossman, and Stan Katz are my higher-ed rabbis. They've inspired my course even as they've advised it. Russell Berman and Jeff Williams have been fountains of advice and ideas. Judith Shapiro has not only offered her good counsel and friendship, but has also brought me into the creative conversations about teaching and learning that take place at the Teagle Foundation.

I've also profited from talking to good administrators and watching them do their work. My gratitude begins at home, with thanks to Fordham graduate school deans Eva Badowska and Nancy Busch; my exemplary department chair, Glenn Hendler; and Fordham's provost, Stephen Freedman. Their respect and support has made my work both easier and better. I've also learned a lot from deans at other schools, especially Beth Boehm (Louisville), Michael Elliott (Emory), George Justice (Arizona State), and Vanessa Ryan (Brown). Thanks also to Jennifer Cason, Jonathan Levin, Brian Norman, and David Shumway, for friendship, good conversation, and insight into how universities work—and sometimes don't work. Sidonie Smith's writing was helping me before I met her. Heather Dubrow and Bob Weisbuch offered the same—and read portions of the manuscript. David Hollinger read a skeletal version of the final chapter more than a decade ago, and generously provided comments to an admiring colleague he still has never met. Thanks to Daniel Denecke, Julia Kent, and Michael Teitelbaum for their help with the research.

The Graduate School Mess is the kind of book I could only have written after being out in the professional world for awhile. Academia can be a harsh environment—just ask a graduate student—but I've been fortunate to have good friends to bank my own course through it. Without the support of Frank Boyle, Clare Eby, Robert Levine, Ben Reiss, and Bruce Robbins, I would know less, do less, and have much less fun.

I tested parts of *The Graduate School Mess* before audiences at Arizona State, Carnegie Mellon, Columbia, Emory, Fordham, Lindsey Wilson College, Louisville, Loyola University of Maryland, Missouri, Stanford, Syracuse, UCLA, and the University of Maryland. The give-and-take from administrators, professors, and students helped me sharpen my thinking, and expand it.

I want especially to thank Julie R. Posselt, who generously shared the manuscript of her excellent forthcoming book on graduate admissions with me. Her research was just what I needed to conclude my own chapter on admissions. The Introduction and Chapter 5 are informed by findings developed in "Graduate School, Graduate Students, Graduate Teaching" and "The PhD Dissertation: In Search of a Usable Future," *Pedagogy* 15, no. 1: 13–18 and 81–92. Paul Jay and I wrote the latter essay together, a partnership from which I've learned a lot.

Two citations I save for last. First, I thank my own graduate students. Our collaboration has enriched my life both intellectually and personally, and your successes give meaning to my work.

The final word to my family of educators. My parents were my first teachers and have always been my implied readers (as we in the lit biz call them), meaning that they're the ones in my head reading what I write. They've also been among my actual readers, as has my brother David, a fellow professor. My partner, Debra Osofsky, added teaching to her professional portfolio during the time that I was writing this book; our journey together has been one of teaching and learning for me—and of love and support. My daughter, KC Osofsky, is a high school student without much concern for graduate school messes, which is as it should be. But there is a way that she helped me think about my work and its purpose. This book, and the hope that resides in it, are for her.

Index

Note: Page numbers in *italics* indicate figures.

ABD (all-but-dissertation) students, 111, 114, 120–121, 201–202

Academia. *See* Higher education

Academic career. *See* Alt-ac (alternative academic) careers; Professorships

Academic job market. *See* Job market; Professorships

Academic professionalism. *See* Professionalism, academic

Adjunct faculty positions, 3, 8, 11, 105, 143, 187–188, 203, 237. *See also* Part-time faculty positions

Administrators, 1, 4–5, 9–10, 15–16; admissions and, 21, 41–43, 45–46; history of graduate schools and, 22–28, 31–38, 41–43, 45–46; affirmative action and, 45–46, 101–103; graduate students

as teachers and, 53, 73; student differences and, 106; dissertations and, 107; time to degree and, 107, 143, 179; attrition from Ph.D.'s and, 115–117; D.A.'s and, 148

Admissions, 17–22, 47–57; diversity and, 6, 36, 39, 43, 46, 49, 55, 63–64; class size and, 6–7, 10–11, 31, 45–47, 52–53, 52–56; GRE and, 17, 38–39, 41–43, 49; institutional identities and, 17–18, 20, 23–24, 50; prestige culture and, 17–18, 20–21, 24–25, 30–31, 34–38, 40–41; gatekeeping and, 18, 48; student identity and, 18, 51; undergraduate schools and, 18, 21, 24, 32, 34, 41–42, 45, 54; history of graduate schools and, 18–19, 22–48, 53; early years and, 19, 22–30, 47–49;

Admissions *(continued)*
　middle years and, 19, 30–38; postwar
　years and, 19, 38–47; administrators and,
　21, 41–43, 45–46; procedures and,
　22–23, 27–29, 34, 37–43, 45, 48–49;
　research universities and, 22–35, 38–40,
　43–44, 47, 49–51, 55; scholar-researchers-
　in-training and, 24–26, 28–32, 34–35,
　42–44, 47, 50–52, 55; teachers-in-
　training and, 25–26, 29–32, 35, 39–40,
　42–44, 47, 50–52, 55; funds and, 26–30,
　35–36, 38–40, 42–44, 46–47, 49;
　committee members and, 28, 34, 37, 39,
　48, 117–118; golden age and, 38–39,
　44–47; math programs and, 40, 53;
　affirmative action and, 45–46, 55;
　conservatism and, 48–49, 51; issues and
　solutions and, 49–56; teaching career
　status and, 51–52; job market and,
　51–53; teaching graduate school and,
　52–53, 55
Advisors, 14–16, 91–95; terms for, 14;
　mentorships and, 16, 91, 102, 129;
　committee members and, 60, 84, 86–87,
　107–110, 133; job market and, 93, 122;
　undergraduate schools and, 93; tenure-
　track positions and, 94; student-adviser
　relation and, 95–101; collaborations and,
　99, 110–111; student differences and,
　101–106; diversity and, 106; student
　progress rates and, 106–121; math
　programs and, 108; postdoctoral degrees
　and, 121–122; nonacademic careers and,
　121–129; professional development
　seminars and, 124–125, 207; career-
　services offices and, 125–128. *See also*
　Dissertations, doctoral
Affirmative action, 45–46, 55, 101–103.
　See also Diversity
Alt-ac (alternative academic) careers:
　humanities and, 6–7, 32, 77–78, 117, 123,
　137, 169, 184, 200–203; teaching career
　status and, 22, 24–25, 29, 51–52, 193;

　research universities and, 121, 126.
　See also Nonacademic careers
American Historical Association (AHA), 3,
　6, 67, 74, 127, 136, 187, 203, 231–232
Ames, Joseph S., 68
Andrew W. Mellon Foundation (Mellon
　Foundation), 76, 174, 203
Angell, James Burrill, 25–27, 33–34.
　See also University of Michigan
Angell, James Rowland, 33–34, 36. *See also*
　Yale University
Aronson, Marc, 230–231, 233
Association of American Universities
　(AAU), 31–33, 131, 146, 153, 236
Attrition from Ph.D.'s, 4, 14, 33, 83–84,
　115–119
Auerbach, Jonathan, 195, 197
Auslander, Leora, 75–76, 81

B.A. (bachelor of arts), 22, 24–25, 31–32,
　43–44, 153, 160, 237. *See also* Degrees
Balleisen, Edward, 76–78
Bargar, Robert E., 89, 97
Barzun, Jacques, 236
Baxter, James, 10–11, 34
Beard, Charles A., 232–233
Berelson, Bernard R., 11, 45, 115, 145, 171
Berg, William J., 86–87
Berlinerblau, Jacques, 229–231
Berman, Russell A., 65–66, 73, 139–140
Bledstein, Burton J., 132, 218–220, *219,*
　222–223
Blight, David, 80
Boehm, Beth A., 168–169
Bok, Derek, 4, 58, 119, 138
Bousquet, Marc, 8, 53, 183–184
Bowers, Fredson, 144, 146–149
Boyer, Ernest L., 141, 164, 194–196, 235
Brandeis University, 174–175
Breneman, David W., 40, 116, 171
Briggle, Adam, 235–236
Brink, William J., 37
Bundy, McGeorge, 170–171

Busch, Nancy, 209
Bush, George W., 228
Business of universities, 211–213
Butler, Nicholas Murray, 217–218

Calhoun, Craig, 235
Campbell, Dana, 121–122
Canfield, James H., 222
Career-services offices, 125–128, 205. *See also* Alt-ac (alternative academic) careers
Caretaking ideal, 180, 215
Carnegie Foundation for the Advancement of Teaching, 10, 37–38, 69, 94, 146–147, 171, 222
Carnegie Mellon University, 146, 178
Carr, Allison D., 71
Carson, Rachel, 227
Children and families issues, 103–106
Civil War, post–, 215, 218
Clark University, 217
Clothier, Robert C., 4, 218
Cold War, 40, 146
Collaborations: humanities and, 2, 140–141; coursework and, 62–63, 65, 69–70, 72–73, 76–77, 81; teacher-student collaboration and, 65, 73, 88–89
Collaborations, 69–70; social sciences graduate programs and, 77; comprehensive exams and, 88–89; advisors and, 99, 110–111; funds and, 212; ethic for higher education and, 212–213, 237
Columbia University: admissions and, 37–38, 189; advisors and, 99, 109; models of higher education and, 131; teacher-in, 144; degrees, 146; ethics of higher education and, 215, 217–218
Communications: job market issues and, 184–188; with public, 229–237
Comprehensive exams, 82–83, 82–83, 88–90; student fitness and, 82, 84, 90; attrition of students and, 83–84; time to degree and, 83–84, 89–90; oral exams and, 84–85, 87–90; conservatism and,

85; teaching careers and, 85; "retention and transfer" and, 86–88; professionalism and, 87; science programs and, 87; professionalization and, 87–88; research universities and, 87–88; authentic assessment and, 88; teacher-student collaboration and, 88–89; issues and solutions and, 88–90; portfolio-based systems and, 89–90. *See also* Dissertations, doctoral
Comprehensive professionalization programs, 168–169
Conservatism: graduate schools and, 2, 9–11, 58, 189; admissions and, 48–49, 51; comprehensive exams and, 85; dissertations and, 136
Core curriculum, 209
Council of Graduate Schools (CGS), 118–119, 147, 158–160, 202
Coursework, 5, 11, 57–61; undergraduate schools and, 15, 60, 63–67, 75; liberal culture and, 30; seminars and, 57–61, 67–68, 70–73, 76–77, 79, 88; tutorial system and, 60–61; collaborations and, 62–63, 65, 69–70, 72–73, 76–77, 81; offerings versus curriculum and, 62–66; content of, 66–72; graduate students as teachers and, 72–73; nonacademic careers and, 73–81; K–12 curriculum and, 231–232. *See also* Teaching graduate school
Cultism, and higher education, 94

D.A. (doctor of arts), 145–150. *See also* Degrees
Damrosch, David, 140
Davidson, Martin, 102
Debts, student, 4, 15, 176–180, 210
De Cruz, Helen, 128
Degrees, 130–131, 160–161; admissions and, 24–26, 31–32, 34, 43–44; tenure-track positions and, 134–135, 148; multitrack models and, 137–150; scholar/scholarship defined and, 141–142;

Degrees *(continued)*
Psy.D.'s and, 142; Ed.D.'s and,
145–149; D.A.'s and, 145–150; funds
and, 146, 155–159, 170–171, 174,
210; M.B.A.'s and, 151, 156–157; M.A.'s
and, 153; PSMs and, 155, 156–160;
utility-driven argument and, 155, 157.
See also B.A. (bachelor of arts); Dissertations, doctoral; M.A. (master of arts);
Ph.D.'s
Delbanco, Andrew, 65, 66, 221, 257n136,
286n3, 290n42
Denecke, Daniel, 108
DEVOUT (Diversity, Experience,
Versatility, Outcomes, Usefulness, and
Technology), 197. *See also* University of
Maryland
Dewey, John, 67, 71, 232, 234
Digital technologies, 2, 9–10, 197
Dissertations, doctoral: issues and
solutions and, 2–4, 8, 10–11, 13–15,
136–137; publication of, 31, 133–135,
167; dissertation proposal and, 89–90,
110–111; dissertation prospectus and,
90; administrators and, 107; math
programs and, 108; undergraduate
school as preparation for, 110, 115,
117, 133; ABD students and, 111,
114, 120–121, 201–202; history of,
132–133; conservatism and, 136;
multitrack models and, 138–141.
See also Comprehensive exams; Time
to degree
Diversity: admissions and, 36, 39, 43, 46,
49, 55, 63–64; advisors and, 106;
teaching graduate school and, 197. *See
also* Affirmative action; Minority-group
members
Doherty, Megan, 203
Donoghue, Frank J., 60
Dore, Timothy M., 166–167
Duke University, 76–78, 90, 233
Dunster, Henry, 214

Eatman, Timothy K., 230
Ed.D. (doctor of education), 145–149.
See also Degrees
Educators, 4–5, 9, 13–16
Egan, Janet Malenchek, 166
Eisenhower, Dwight D., 43
Elder, J. P., 153
Elementary school education, 231–232.
See also K–12 curriculum
Eliot, Charles, 64, 221
Elliot, Michael A., 77
Ellison, Julie, 230
English college model as early basis for
American higher education, 214, 217
Environmentalism, 226–229
Ethic for higher education, 210–211,
236–238; public service and, 5–7,
224–225, 230, 233–237; caretaking ideal
and, 180, 215; core curriculum, 209;
business of universities and, 211–213;
collaborations and, 212–213, 237;
mission of universities and, 214–225, *219,
220;* research culture and, 217–218, 221,
223–225, 230, 235; research universities
and, 218, *220,* 220–225; liberal culture
and, *220,* 220–221; utility in higher
education and, *220,* 220–223; teaching
graduate school and, 225–226; trust by
community and, 225–226; environmentalism and, 226–229; communication
with public and, 229–237; politics and,
236–237
Europe, and higher education: German
model and, 12, 26, 64, 92, 131, 216–218,
221, 224; funds in, 212; clergy and, 214;
English model and, 214, 217

Federal government funds, 38–40, 42, 44,
46, 146, 155, 158, 177, 210. *See also*
Morrill Act of 1862
Feynman, Richard, 235
First, Zachary, 79
Ford, Patrick J., 45

Ford Foundation, 158–159, 170–171, 174

Frodeman, Robert, 235–236

Frost, Robert, 68

Funds: science programs and, 8; admissions and, 26–28, 30, 35–36, 38–40, 42–44, 46–47, 49; private philanthropy and, 27; undergraduate schools and, 28, 30; teachers-in-training and, 29–30; teaching graduate school and, 36, 39–40; federal government and, 38–40, 42, 44, 46, 146, 155, 158, 177, 210; graduate students as teachers and, 72–73, 108; degrees and, 146, 155–159, 170–171, 174, 210; professionalization and, 174–175; collaborations and, 212; politics and, 237

Gaines, Jason M., 175

Geiger, Roger L., 33, 57, 115, 131, 171

General exams. *See* Comprehensive exams

Geographical location, and job market, 173, 191

Gerber, David A., 58–59, 70–71

German model of higher education, 12, 26, 64, 92, 131, 216–218, 221, 224

G.I. Bill of 1944, 38–39, 42, 155, 210

Gilman, Daniel Coit, 216–217

Golde, Chris M., 166–167

Golden age, 2, 6, 12–13, 38–39, 44–47, 83, 144, 154, 162, 167

Goodnow, Frank J., 152

Graduate Center of the City University of New York (CUNY), 20, 50, 153–154

Graduate Record Exam (GRE), 17, 37–39, 41–43, 49. *See also* Admissions

Graduate schools: issues and solutions and, 1–14, 49–56, 209; conservatism and, 2, 9–11, 58, 189; system of, 5, 8; German model for, 12, 26, 64, 92, 131, 216–218, 221, 224; history of, 18–19, 22–48, 53

Graduate students. *See* Students

Graduate students as teachers, 42, 46, 53, 72–73, 108, 113–114, 147–148

Graff, Gerald, 63, 65, 276n1

Grafton, Anthony T., 74–75, 136, 187, 205

Great Depression, 30, 33, 36, 64

Grossman, Jim, 67, 74–75, 205

Grote, John, 165

Hakel Milton D., 68–69, 86

Halpern, Diane F., 68–69, 86

Harper, William Rainey, 216–218, 221–222

Harvard University: administration at, 4, 41; admissions and, 19, 24–25, 27–29, 32–39, 41–42; institutional identities and, 23–24; degrees and, 24, 43–44, 140–141, 146, 148, 153; history of graduate school and, 24, 28; fellowships and, 27–28; funds and, 27–29, 35–36, 42–43; scholar-researchers-in-training and, 29, 43; teachers-in-training and, 29, 31, 43; fellowships, 29–30; research universities and, 29–31, 33; humanities history and, 31–38; diversity and, 32; models for higher education and, 64, 131; publication of scholarship and, 134–135; multitrack models for dissertations and, 140–141; ethics of higher education and, 214, 221; utility-driven argument and, 221

Haskins, Charles H., 32

Hawn, Heather, 193

Helm, Matt, 126–128

Hérubel, Jean- Pierre V. M., 151

HEX (Public Humanities Exchange), 233–234. *See also* University of Wisconsin

Higher education: utility-driven argument and, 3, 12–13, 18, 157, *220,* 220–223; issues and solutions and, 8, 14, 16, 79, 209–210, 225–226, 237; caretaking ideal and, 9, 16, 180, 215; conservatism and, 11, 58, 189; Morrill Act and, 12, 221; liberal culture and, 30, *220,* 220–221; cultism and, 94. *See also* Undergraduate schools; Universities

Homophily, 48, 50, 56

Huber, G. Carl, 34–35. *See also* University of Michigan

Humanities: collaborations and, 2, 140–141; issues/solutions and, 2–3; utility-driven argument and, 3, 13, 155, 220, *221;* history of, 4, 12–13, 22–28, 31–38, 41–43, 45–46, 218–221, *219, 220;* public service and, 6; academic careers and, 6–7, 32, 77–78, 137; alt-ac careers and, 6–7, 32, 77–78, 117, 123, 137, 169, 184, 200–203; funds and, 8, 46; digital technologies and, 10; nonacademic careers and, 13; private philanthropy and, 46; two-track Ph.D. model and, 135–136. *See also* Admissions; Advisors; Comprehensive exams; Coursework; Degrees; Ethic for higher education; Job market; Professionalization; Social sciences graduate programs; Time to degree

Idaho State University, 139, 141, 150
Identity/ies: professorships and, 3, 40, 163–164; institutional, 17–18, 20, 23–24, 50, 189–190; student, 18, 51, 162–166, 189, 193; professional, 162–166
Institutional identities, 17–18, 20, 23–24, 50, 189. *See also* Prestige culture; Research culture
Irving, Washington, 152

Jacobson, Matthew, 80
Jakubiak, Katarzyna, 196
James, Edmund J., 235
Jessup, Walter, 10–11
Job market, 2, 4–9, 183–184, 204–208; golden age and, 2, 6, 12–13, 38–39, 44–47, 83, 144, 154, 162, 167; part-time faculty and, 3, 8, 11, 105–106, 143, 186–188, 203, 237; nonacademic careers and, 5–7, 9, 13, 121–128, 139; tenure-track positions and, 8, 11–12, 47, 54–55, 74, 171, 184–188, 190, 202; prestige culture and, 50, 189–194; rankings of universities and departments and, 50, 190–200; admissions and, 51–53;

advisors and, 93, 122; postdoctoral degrees and, 94, 156, 173, 180, 187–188, 200; two-track Ph.D.'s and, 142–150; science programs and, 157–158; scholar-researchers and, 163, 194; geographical location and, 173, 191; time to degree and, 173–176, 179, 202; communications issue and, 184–188; adjunct faculty and, 187–188, 203, 237; political science and, 190–195; teachers-in-training and, 191–198; teaching graduate school and, 192–193; teaching career status and, 193; comparative advantage viewpoint and, 194–198; placement in jobs and, 198–204. *See also* Professorships
Johns Hopkins University: job market and, 12; history of graduate schools and, 19, 23; models for higher education and, 28, 131; funds and, 28–29; admissions and, 29; research universities and, 29; coursework and, 68; degrees and, 152; ethics of higher education and, 216–217
Johnson, Lyndon Baines, 43
Justice, Daniel Heath, 103

K–12 curriculum, 231–232. *See also* Elementary school education
Katz, Stanley N., 19
Keck Graduate Institute, 158
Kelleher, M. E., 69–70
Kennedy, John F., 43
Khost, Peter, 67, 71–72
Krugman, Paul, 179

Land-grant universities, 12, 218, 221–222
Layman, Geoffrey, 191
Leake, Elizabeth, 99
Lemaster, Tracy, 234
Leopold, Aldo, 227
Liberal culture, 30, *220,* 220–221
Lincoln, Abraham, 12, 221
Lloyd, Alfred H., 34

Lohe, Debie, 67, 71–72
Long, Christopher P., 195
López, Marissa K., 103
Lovitts, Barbara E., 68, 110, 116, 119
Lucey, Colleen, 234
Lynch, Carol, 152, 158–160

M.A. (master of arts), 150, 160–161; admissions and, 21, 24–26, 34, 43–44, 60; teachers-in-training and, 25–27, 35, 145, 153–154; history of, 132, 151–155; science programs and, 155; utility-driven argument and, 155, 157; professionalization and, 155–161; debts of students and, 178. *See also* Degrees
Mancini, Matthew, 90
Massive online open enrollment courses (MOOCs), 10–11
Mayhew, Lewis B., 45
Mayo-Chamberlain, Jane, 89, 97
M.B.A. (Master of Business Administration), 151, 156–157. *See also* Degrees
McBain, Howard Lee, 144–146
Meister, Bob, 177
Mellon Foundation (Andrew W. Mellon Foundation), 76, 174, 203
Mentoring. *See* Advising
Mentorships, 16, 91, 102, 129
Micciche, Laura R., 71
Michigan State University (MSU), 126, 128, 158
Millett, Catherine M., 171
Minority-group members, 45–46, 55, 101–103. *See also* Diversity
Mission of universities, 214–225, *219, 220*
Modern Language Association (MLA), 3, 6, 63, 65, 107, 135, 138–141, 203, 237
Morrill Act of 1862, 12, 221
Muller-Sievers, Helmut, 137

National Board on Graduate Education, 148–149
National Institutes of Health, 44

National Research Council (NRC), 191, 194, 200
National Science Foundation, 44
Neal, Ed, 67, 70, 72
Nelson, Cary, 86
Nelson, Scott Reynolds, 235
Nettles, Michael T., 171
Nixon, Richard M., 40, 211, 227–228
Nonacademic careers, 5–7, 9, 13, 121–128, 139. *See also* Alt-ac (alternative academic) careers

Ober, Josiah, 64
Okkelberg, Peter, 39, 44
Oprisko, Robert L., 190
Oral exams, 84–85, 87–90. *See also* Comprehensive exams

Part-time faculty positions, 3, 8, 11, 105–106, 143, 186–188, 203, 237. *See also* Adjunct faculty positions
Part-time students, 32
Pedagogy. *See* Coursework; Teaching graduate school
Pemberton, Ebenezer, 214
Perry, Rick, 237
Ph.D.'s: school issues and solutions and, 3–9, 11, 16; attrition from, 4, 14, 33, 83–84, 115–119; admissions and, 21, 24–28, 31, 53–55, 60; specialization and, 62, 77, 164, 180, 192, 229, 231–233, 236; portfolio-based systems and, 89–90, 122; women and, 103; history of, 131–137; two-track model and, 135–136, 142–150
Pinchot, Gifford, 227
Placement, job, 198–204. *See also* Job market
PLAN (Professional development, Life skills, Academic development, and Networking), 168–169. *See also* University of Louisville
Political science, 190–195
Politics, and ethic for higher education, 236–237

Portfolio-based systems, and comprehensive
exams, 89–90, 122
Posselt, Julie R., 47–49
Postdoctoral degrees: fellowships and, 29,
93, 173, 188, 203; job market and, 94,
156, 173, 180, 187–188, 200; advisors
and, 121–122
PREP (Planning, Resilience, Engagement,
Professionalism), 126–127. *See also*
Michigan State University
Prestige culture, 20–22; admissions and,
17–18, 20–21, 24–25, 30–31, 34–38,
40–41; institutional identities and, 17–18,
20, 23–24, 50; student identity and, 18,
189; rankings and, 21, 50, 72–73, 141,
190–200, 223; job market and, 50,
189–194; teachers-in-training and,
196–199. *See also* Research culture
Princeton University: admissions and,
32, 37–38; coursework and, 78, 81;
dissertations and, 136; professorships
and, 187, 190; ethics of higher education
and, 214, 221
Private philanthropy, 27, 30, 46. *See also*
specific foundations
Professional development seminars,
124–125, 207
Professionalism, academic: comprehensive
exams and, 87; history of, 132, 164–166,
180–182, 218–219, *219;* graduate school
and, 169; debts and, 179; time to degree
and, 179; specialization and, 229; public
engagement versus, 235
Professionalization, 4–6, 13–14, 180–182;
nonacademic careers and, 5–7, 9, 13,
121–128; comprehensive exams and,
87–88; PSMs and, 155–161; student
identity and, 162–166; publication of
scholarship and, 163–167, 172, 174–176;
tenure-track positions and, 165, 171;
professorships and, 167–168; comprehensive programs for, 168–169; time to
degree and, 170–176, 179; funds and,
174–175; debts of students and, 176–180.
See also Professionalism, academic
Professional master of arts degree (PMA),
158–160
Professional science master's degree (PSM),
155–161
Professorships, 3–4, 184; golden age and, 2,
6, 12–13, 38–39, 44–47, 83, 144, 154,
162, 167; teachers-in-training and, 2–3,
13, 24–25, 40, 42–44, 47, 50–52, 55, 233;
adjunct faculty and, 3, 8, 11, 105, 143,
187–188, 203, 237; identity and, 3, 40,
163–164; scholar-researchers-in-training
and, 28–32, 34–35, 42–44, 47, 50–52,
55; assistantships and, 41, 50, 73, 163,
173, 184–185, 188, 193–194, 204;
children or families and, 105–106; women
and, 105–106; professionalization and,
167–168. *See also* Tenure-track positions
Psy.D. (three-year degree), 142. *See also*
Degrees
Publication of scholarship, 9–10, 167;
dissertations and, 31, 133–135, 167;
professorships and, 40, 51; undergraduate
students and, 54; tenure-track positions
and, 134–135, 163, 175; professionalization and, 163–167, 172, 174–176;
assistant professorships and, 173; graduate
school and, 174
Publicly Active Graduate Education
(PAGE), 231
Public Philosophy Network, 235–236
Public service, 5–7, 224–225, 230,
233–237
Pulczinski, Janelle, 234

Rankings, university and department, 21,
50, 72–73, 141, 190–200, 223
Rawlings, Hunter R., III, 236–237
Remsen, Ira, 152
Research 1 (R1) classification, 94, 192
Research culture: history of, 20, 24–26,
29–30, 34, 38, 40, 44, 47, 49–51; Ph.D.'s

and, 133; ethic for higher education and, 217–218, 221, 223–225, 230, 235. *See also* Institutional identities; Prestige culture

Research universities, 3–5, 10–13; collaborations and, 10; teaching career status and, 22, 24–25, 29; funds and, 30, 131; private philanthropy and, 30; publication of scholarship and, 40, 175; admissions and, 57, 144; coursework and, 62, 64; German model and, 64, 216, 224; comprehensive exams and, 87–88; advisors and, 95, 121; academic careers and, 121, 126; alt-ac careers and, 121, 126; nonacademic careers and, 125, 135; Ph.D.'s and, 131, 135, 142; two-track Ph.D. model and, 135, 142; utility-driven argument and, 155, 157, *220,* 220–223; prestige culture and, 189, 191; job market and, 194, 196; history of, 209, 215–218, 221–223, 231; ethic for higher education and, 218, *220,* 220–225

"Retention and transfer," 68–69, 77, 86

Robbins, Bruce, 164, 277n13

Rogers, Katina, 7

Roosevelt, Theodore, 227

Ross, Andrew, 177, 180

Rutgers University, 4, 218, 230

Ryle, Gilbert, 68

Saint Louis University, 89–90

Schaffer, Dana, 80

Scholar defined: scholarship of application and, 141, 194–195; scholarship of discovery and, 141, 148, 194–195; scholarship of integration and, 141, 194–195; scholarship of teaching and, 141, 164, 194–196

Scholar-researchers-in-training: student identity and, 3, 24–25, 40; admissions and, 21, 28–32, 34–35, 42–44, 47, 50–52, 55; job market and, 163, 194

Schuman, Rebecca, 93–95

Science programs: funds and, 8; STEM and, 40; attrition from Ph.D.'s and, 83–84, 118; comprehensive exams and, 87;

advisors and, 101; M.A.'s and, 155; PSMs and, 155–161; job market and, 157–158

Secondary school education, 231–232

Sharma, Ghanashyam "Shyam," 168–169

Simons, Daniel, 87

Sloan Foundation, 156–159

Smiley, Jane, 211

Smith, Sidonie, 107, 140

Social sciences graduate programs, 2, 13; coursework and, 60, 64, 69, 77; collaborations and, 77; comprehensive exams and, 87–88; professorships and, 93; advisors and, 108; dissertations and, 108; professionalization and, 155–156; time to degree and, 170; job market and, 185, 195. *See also* Humanities

Specialization, and Ph.D.'s, 62, 77, 164, 180, 192, 229, 231–233, 236

Spencer, Stephen, 197

Stanford University, 64–65, 72–73, 76, 139–143, 221

Steffens, Lincoln, 234

STEM (science, technology, engineering, and mathematics), 40, 53, 83–84, 108, 118, 146

Stephan, Paula, 173

Storr, Richard J., 150

Strouse, A. W., 180

Struck, Peter T., 79

Students: identity and, 3, 18, 24–25, 40, 51, 162–166, 189, 193; attrition rate and, 4, 14, 33, 83–84, 115–119; debts of, 4, 15, 176–180, 210; student-centered graduate education and, 13, 66–71, 87, 101, 106, 197, 215, 221; part-time, 32; women as, 33, 103–106, 234; graduate students as teachers and, 42, 46, 53, 72–73, 108, 113–114, 147–148; undergraduate students and, 54; teachers' collaboration with, 65, 73, 88–89; fitness for dissertations and, 82, 84, 90; adviser's relation with, 88–89, 95–101; differences among, 101–106; with children and families,

Students *(continued)*
103–105; progress rates for, 106–121;
ABD, 111, 114, 120–121, 201–202
Sweetman, Chuck, 67, 71–72

Teachers-in-training, 1–3, 6–7, 9–11;
admissions and, 25–26, 29–32, 35,
39–40, 42–44, 47, 50–52, 55; M.A.'s
and, 25–27, 35, 145, 153–154; funds and,
29–30; women and, 33; scholarship of
teaching and, 141, 164, 194–196; prestige
culture and, 196–199; professorships and,
233. *See also* Professorships
Teaching career status, 22, 24–25, 29,
51–52, 193
Teaching graduate school, 4–5, 8–9, 13–16;
student-centered graduate education and,
13, 66–71, 87, 101, 106, 197, 215, 221;
teacher-centered approach and, 13, 65,
70–71, 87, 116, 148; funds and, 36,
39–40; admissions and, 52–53;
teacher-student collaboration and, 65, 73,
88–89; collaboration on comprehensive
exams and, 88–89; communications issue
and, 184–188; diversity and, 197; ethic
for higher education and, 225–226.
See also Coursework
Teagle Foundation, 72–73
Teitelbaum, Michael, 156–158
Tenure-track positions: job market and, 8,
11–12, 47, 54–55, 74, 171, 184–188, 190,
202; women and, 93, 105; advisors and,
94; degrees and, 134–135, 148; publication of scholarship and, 134–135, 163,
175; professionalization and, 165, 171;
issues and solutions and, 210. *See also*
Professorships
Thompson, John, 90
Thoreau, Henry David, 227
Tilton, Lauren, 80
Time to degree, 2, 132, 138; comprehensive
exams and, 83–84, 89–90; advisors and,
103, 107, 116–117, 121; administrators

and, 107, 143, 179; multitrack models
and, 137–138, 140, 142–144, 146–147;
professionalization and, 170–176, 179;
job market and, 173–176, 179, 202; debts
and, 179
Tinker, Nathan, 198–199
Toma, J. Douglas, 20, 189, 195
Townsend, Robert B., 187, 231–232
Trachtenberg, Alan, 218–219
Truman, Harry S., 43
Trust, by community, 225–226
Tutorial system, 60–61
Two-track Ph.D. model, 135–136, 142–150

Undergraduate schools: coursework and, 15,
60, 63–67, 75; admissions and, 18, 21,
24, 32, 34, 41–42, 45, 54; history of,
23–26, 30, 39; funds and, 28, 30;
graduate students as teachers in, 42, 46,
53, 57–58, 72–73, 108, 113–114,
147–148, 184; faculty publication of
scholarship by faculty in, 54; graduate
advisors and, 93; affirmative action and,
101; dissertation requirements and, 110,
115, 117, 133; debts and, 176–178, 210
Universities: history of, 4, 12–13, 218–221,
219, 220; German model and, 12, 26,
64, 92, 131, 216–218, 221, 224;
land-grant universities and, 12, 218,
221–222; English model and, 214, 217.
See also Undergraduate schools;
specific universities
University of Alberta, 90
University of California at Berkeley, 19, 25,
29, 33, 35–36, 202
University of Chicago, 27, 75, 131, 216,
221–222, 224
University of Colorado, 137–139, 160
University of Louisville, 168–169
University of Maryland, 52–53, 89,
195–197
University of Michigan: history of graduate
schools and, 19, 23, 25–27; administration

at, 25, 34–35; models for higher
education and, 25–26; professorships and,
26; scholar-researchers-in-training
and, 26, 29, 34, 44; research universities
and, 26–27; teachers-in-training and,
26–27; admissions, 27, 34–35; funds and,
27, 34, 35; degrees and, 34, 44; prestige
culture and, 34; admissions and, 38–41,
43–44, 46; professional development
and, 125; dissertations and, 140
University of Minnesota, 125, 190
University of North Texas, 235
University of Notre Dame, 191
University of Pennsylvania, 214–215
University of Tennessee, 87
University of Texas, 237
University of Virginia, 144, 149, 237
University of Washington, 90
University of West Virginia, 89
University of Wisconsin, 19–20, 83, 115,
190, 233–234
Utility-driven argument: higher education,
3, 12–13, 18, 157, *220,* 220–223;
humanities, 3, 13, 155, 220, *221;* degrees,
155, 157; research universities, 155, 157,
220, 220–223; ethic for higher education,
220, 220–223

Van Holst, Hermann E., 224–225, 235
Veblen, Thorstein, 194, 213
Veysey, Laurence R., 131–132, 219–220,
220, 222, 224, 245n9, 274n74, 286n6
Von Humboldt, William, 223

Watt, Stephen, 86
Welch, Susan, 195
Wexler, Laura, 80
Wheeler, Benjamin, 25
Williams, Jeffrey J., 178
Williams, John H., 86–87
Wisconsin Idea, 234–236. *See also*
University of Wisconsin
Wolff, Richard, 7–8
Women: as graduate students, 33, 103–106,
234; teachers-in-training and, 33;
tenure-track positions and, 93, 105;
Ph.D.'s and, 103; part-time faculty and,
105; with children or families, 105–106;
professorships and, 105–106; girlhood
studies and, 234. *See also* Children
and family issues
Wood, L. Maren, 127
World War I, post–, 30, 224
World War II, post–, 30, 38, 40–41, 54–55,
83, 232, 235
Wright, John Henry, 24

Yale University: history of graduate schools
and, 19; institutional identities and, 23;
degrees and, 24, 131, 190; fellowships
and, 27, 28; funds and, 27–28, 33, 35;
admissions and, 28–29, 33–39; diversity
and, 35–36; collaborations and, 80–81;
coursework and, 80–81
Yoakum, Clarence S., 38

Zelizer, Julian E., 78–79, 81